DOWN
TO THE
BONE

*The Mud Brick Press acknowledges the traditional owners of the unceded country on which we write and work, the Wunundjeri people of the Kulin nation, who have held rich stories of country for many thousands of years, and pays respects to their elders, past and present.*

Published in Australia by Mud Brick Press
PO Box 256 Doreen,VIC 3754 Australia
3902 E. Montecito Ave PHX AZ 85018
info@clemenceoverall.com

www.clemenceoverall.com
First published in Australia 2024
Copyright © Clemence Overall 2022



National Library of Australia Cataloguing Publication entry

 A catalogue record for this book is available from the National Library of Australia

Application for Library of Congress Catalogue Number in progress

ISBN 978-0-6456684-07 (paperback)
ISBN 978-0-6456684-1-4 (hardback)
ISBN 978-0-6456684-2-1 (epub)

Cover design and typesetting Sophie White
Printed by Ingram Spark

Disclaimer: This book is a memoir based on meticulous field notes. The conversations in the book are based on the field notes and remain as true to actual conversations as possible. In all instances the essence of the dialogue is accurate. All the stories in this book are true, although some events have been compressed and some names and identifying details have been changed to protect the privacy of the people involved. The author and publisher shall not be responsible for any person with regard to any loss or damage caused directly or indirectly by the information contained herein.

# DOWN TO THE BONE

## A JAIL, A JOURNEY, FOUR WOMEN

Clémence Overall

*All the women in this book are a testament
to the power of family. And I would be
nothing without mine. Endless gratitude
to my parents, along with my sisters and
brothers, Mary Jane, Rollins, Phoebe, and
Curtis, my first intrepid fellow adventurers.
And to Mark, always beside me, and to
Thomas and Clemmie who make
all things possible.*

*Only when it is dark enough*
*can you see the stars.*


MARTIN LUTHER KING JR

# CONTENTS

# FOREWORD BY
# JULIA AJMAC CUXIL

This is a story of four women, with four very different lives and histories. Clémence traveled far into mountains and across the sea to listen to these women, to understand their lives. She went to dangerous places and lonely places, but she is a woman like that. She has always had adventure in her blood. And when you read this story, you will go with her walking through mountains or sitting on logs, listening or even traveling to the holy places where women seek peace. You will also learn some secrets of our greatest traditions: our love of Dios and each other.

I met Clémence many years ago, working together in a Guatemalan political group in Washington DC. People were always kind to me, but because Clémence had lived with the women in this book, she could understand me in a deeper way. She accepted me even though I am very different from her.

You see, I am Mayan. I am Julia Ajmac Cuxil. I will tell you about my life because in this book Clémence looks at the lives of women. One of the women is like me—with her *traje*, traditional dress, and with her traditions. The other women are also like me with their love of their families, their struggles to keep on going no matter what, and with their love of Dios. It is important to look at these lives because women, from the time they are born, are treated as second-class citizens. When a boy is born, we say: *"Se ganó la gallina!"* The chicken won! But when a girl is born, we are disappointed and say: *"Se perdío la gallina."* The chicken lost.

This is an attitude that we must change and one of the ways we will change it is by knowing the truth; the truth about our own lives and other women's lives so we can accept each other. In the ancient book of the Popul Vuh it says, "Todos se levantan y que nadie quede atras." Everyone stands up and leaves no one behind. You are a Haitian woman or a Black American woman. It's the same. We have to step forward.

I know this from my own life. I was born in a village called Pasolot, in the Department of Chimaltenango in 1941. I am 82 years old and consider myself to be Dios's blessed daughter. From what I remember I had a lovely childhood with lots of fields and flowers around me. Most of what we ate came from our land and the animals that we had. We had cows, chickens, a horse, sheep, and other animals.

As children we didn't have store-bought things; we played with dolls made of corncob or straw, made by our grandfather Juan who would make the dolls at night. There was no school nearby and both my parents didn't know how to read or write. Yet my father had a great interest in us studying and valued education very much. In the day we worked. My job was to watch the cows, but I was always afraid because there was a big bull in the field.

We didn't have water in the house. About a kilometer from our home there were rivers where we would bathe and wash clothes. Near to the river was a well of crystalline waters and from there, every morning, we took water and carried it to the house. And for this reason, we learned to be careful with water. Every day we wore our traje, which was sacred to us. I never cut my hair and I would braid it with a soft silk cloth in the traditional way. At night we would recite the rosary. And this is how we passed the years.

In October, 1947 we suffered the fury of a wintery storm. It rained for one week. The river grew. The river took away the best land we had

to grow crops on. It took the horses, cows and the other animals and we were left with almost nothing. So later I went to the capital to live with my brother. We lived in a wooden shack with a tin roof and a dirt floor. There I washed my brother's clothes and cooked his food by starting a wood fire. After that I had many jobs until my sister made arrangements for me to go to the United States.

I was lucky and went by airplane. When I got to the airport to go on January 8, I was one person and when I left the airport, I was a different person. My new bosses and my sister were waiting for me at the American airport. Isabel, my sister, took me to the bathroom. "Take those clothes off," she told me, "and put these clothes on." I was wearing my *traje*. My mother always told me: "My *traje*, I will always keep it. Kill me if I can't have my *traje*. It's a sin." But like every generation there is something different that happens, something new that you learn. My sister gave me a shirt and a pair of pants. She gave me socks and boots and told me, your traje won't serve here. It's no good for the cold. When I went outside, it was true. It was very cold. I had those new clothes on. Now I was a different person.

I faced that new world. I didn't know English. I cut off my braid. I worked hard as a nanny, a housekeeper, a teacher, and a social worker to my own people. I faced storms and sometimes a fierce loneliness. But I also had a sense of caring. It was our tradition. If people didn't care for me, then I was caring for them and that was my healing as it was theirs. Things have changed since that time. My daughter doesn't wear a *traje* and instead of cleaning houses or taking care of children, she works at Stanford University. But she continues our tradition of caring just like the women in this book. They show us through the simple things: a cup of coffee, a tortilla, a walk together that our lives become meaningful. The women keep the rituals. In this book there are special rituals for vodou; there is the ritual of marriage even in a prison. There are rituals for birth and death and always the women make sure they happen. And their faith, which seems so childish to some, carries them through genocides, prison, and squalor. We are all in different worlds but are one.

We Mayans say: *No hay peor que no hacer nada*, there's nothing worse than doing nothing. We always have to take a step. And in these stories you see women taking steps no matter what is in front of them. There's the hope of having a little house, of getting your child an education, of even escaping to the United States. We ask ourselves: What shall we do to survive? We hope and we pray and we take action.

I am Catholic but I am also Mayan. Our beliefs tell us that we are one with this sacred world. And it is our duty to care for the life around us. These women live far apart but they are of one world connected through the simple acts they do—the simple acts of love that carry us through this tumultuous sea of life.

Read these stories and you will find that same love repeated far in the mountains of Guatemala and through the streets of the United States. Clémence has been able to capture the soul of these women and that is who you will meet in these pages.

*Julia Ajmac Cuxil*
*Indigenous Mayan Advocate*
February 2024
Santo Domingo Xenacoj, Guatemala

# PROLOGUE

I wasn't scared the night I was thrown in jail.

I was an archaeology student on a break. The night was moonless, and I was drunk. Singing at the top of my lungs, I staggered between my two Guatemalan friends, Pedro and Mateo. We were walking home from the little dusty town of San Benito where we had danced the Merengue all night.

"Amor, amor, amor," I crooned into the night while six police officers crept behind us, then surrounded us. Two of them shouted orders as they grabbed my friends and shoved them to the dark roadside.

A cop, the one with two badges sewn on his shirt, stepped forward. He was about three inches shorter than me but something about the way he stood, and the way his left eyelid drooped, told me he could hurt me. He looked me straight in the face, nodding his head slightly. "You can go free if you give me a blow job."

I laughed.

His scowl changed into a taunting smile revealing sharp, tight teeth. And he added, "Not just me!" He cocked his head toward the other cops who were standing like a pack of half-starved dogs.

"Fuck you," I yelled and turned to leave.

He grabbed my arm and shoved me back toward the town center. The police pushed Pedro and Mateo as they marched ahead of me, silent. I was certain they wouldn't hurt us. No, for me, Guatemala, the Land of Eternal Spring where I had been working on an archaeological site, was magical, with its Mayan Indians and ancient ruins set in emerald jungles. This police encounter was just another dream that would soon fade.

Inside the building's crumbling walls, the police shoved Mateo and Pedro into a large cell among stocky Indian men who stared at us. They were silent, leaning against the bars, their eyes as steady and unfeeling as dead fish.

The cop marched me by them and through empty, dimly lit lime-green rooms with corners darkened by mold. His hand slipped across my back and my waist, up my hip then into my bag.

"*Para!* Stop it, don't rob me!" I slurred. I could feel his hand digging into my purse. He looked away and led me to a room where a gaunt man sat waiting for me. He declared himself to be *el juez*, the judge. His dark-colored clothes hung on him like rags when he leaned forward over a pine table that sagged in the middle. A folding screen behind him barely concealed an unmade bed.

"Empty your bag on my table," the judge ordered. Among my pens, comb, and wallet was a little red bag I'd never seen.

"*Bueno*," he said jabbing at my bag and scooping out some marijuana with a gnarled finger. "*Que es esto?*"

I stared, incredulous. Was I being framed?

He leaned forward, stinking of booze, his mouth twitching as he offered me an alternative to jail. Pointing to the screen, the judge now spoke in English: "Fucky fucky and you go free." He restated his offer, and I gave the same answer repeatedly until a cop hauled me off to the women's jail.

※

The cell was so dark I could barely make out the cluster of bodies sleeping on the floor. I smelled something tangy and moist, but I couldn't name it. I was sure I'd get out, but grim scenarios kept playing in my mind. When the morning sun finally slid across the floor, I could see Indian women huddling together on the floor. Squinting, I could nearly decipher words scrawled on the dull walls and a cross that someone had tried to carve over the cell door.

When the door finally opened, I could see barbed wire and broken glass on top of high walls that formed a courtyard. A tiny shed with a rusty barrel in one corner served as a fireplace where we could warm up food. Beside the courtyard was the female warden's apartment.

A young Mayan man brought in three buckets: one was filled with sweet, watery coffee; another with thin porridge; and the third with stale tamale. Our food for the day. That first morning, when I was allowed one phone call to my family, the young man was silent and serious as he led me to the local phone center.

After that he was always friendly to me. "Good morning, Señorita," he would say in that quiet Spanish that Indians use, stumbling, like me, over a second language. He wouldn't look at my face, only at the ground, a trait I had noticed with other Indians. But because he was a guard, it made me feel uneasy. I couldn't help but be suspicious. Everyone I had seen in jail was an Indian. So why was he, an Indian, working as a guard, while my cellmates, who seemed harmless, were locked up?

During the day I sat with the women along the edges of the courtyard, hiding from the hot white sun. They all dressed identically, their long black hair braided with bright ribbons. Their feet, calloused yellow like old plastic, peeked out from under colorful skirts, vivid splashes across the concrete. Kneeling on *petates*, thin straw mats, they'd speak softly as they embroidered or wove their traditional garments. One carried an infant on her back. She'd nestle in a shaded corner, tenderly clicking her tongue and murmuring to the baby.

Every evening we'd watch through an apartment window as the warden danced drunkenly with the cops. Then, sometimes still humming the dance melody, the warden would round us up and lock us in the jail room. We threw *petates* on the cement floor. The Indians would curl up like snails, wrapped in their *rebozos* shawls, inching together for warmth, while I, lying there on my own, listened as their soft lilting sounds drifted toward me and soothed me to sleep.

In the early morning the women sat in the courtyard, busy with their weaving. It passed the eternal hours and deflected the question of what might happen next. It was their escape and their way of telling the story of their lives. Each design, every thread, told the tale of the language they spoke, the village and family they cared for, and the faith they nurtured. The weaving techniques and designs had been handed to them from woman to woman, grandmother to granddaughter for hundreds of years. It was their story and their escape.

Mine was writing. The Mayan guard bought a notebook, a pen, and cigarettes for me. Through writing I traveled away from the impenetrable walls, the Mayan women and the baby who grew sicker each day. I would daydream or write about the past when my family traveled and lived in many countries. Our father took us on trips to teach us about the world and to bring us together as a family. We stayed in fine hotels, but as we drove around or sat on trains, I always looked out the window at the shanties or the Bedouins riding camels and fantasized about going off into the desert with them or sitting in the shanties listening to stories. Something about these scenes spoke to my soul.

But it was the Egyptian temples that first gave me permission to harbor fantasies about being an archaeologist. The hieroglyphics told a story, a story thousands of years old. I was only twelve and I wondered: was it like my story? Did some words resound between us? I had a sense that there was a common thread between the stories that made us; that our stories mirrored each other in different languages. As did our gods: Ra, Allah, Jesus.

These experiences eventually brought me to this Mayan culture. Not to the ancient past when Mayan kings and queens built sprawling cities deep in the jungle but today, here, sitting between the jail walls. I wondered exactly what these particular Mayan women's designs meant and perhaps the women wondered where my scrawling took me. Was there any connection between us outside of these walls? Their stories. My story.

My other escape was getting to know the women a little. They only spoke Kaqchiquel with each other, reserving their little bit of Spanish for the warden and me. An older Mayan woman made friends with me first. She dressed identically to the others but wore gaudy red plastic dangling earrings. She may have been somewhat wealthy because her two front teeth were outlined in gold.

"Adios," she said, her hand grazing my arm. Neither one of us was going anywhere but I had learned Indians sometimes use that, adios, to say hello.

"Adios," I answered.

"What do you call yourself?" she asked in Spanish.

"Clémence," I told her.

"Eh?"

"Clemencia."

"Ah, Clemencia," she responded, then shook her head. "No, Mincha," she renamed me and quickly added, "La Mincha," my name in Kaqchiquel.

She started to caress my arm, murmuring, "*Pobrecita, pobrecita*, poor thing," her eyebrows locked together, her mouth turned down like she was overwhelmed by deep pity for me. I felt a flush of shame. I was the one who should feel sorry for her; I was the one with power and money to get out of this godforsaken place.

After she spoke with me, others did too. At first when I asked why they were locked up, they answered in wretched voices: "*Aye Dios*, I couldn't feed my family. There was no corn to make tortillas. No salt. So, I made *kusha*, moonshine, to sell. That's why I am here."

Even the woman with the baby chanted the same refrain: "Yes, I couldn't feed my family, so I made kusha." She had bags under her eyes and was the only one whose voice sounded husky, as if she smoked.

"Do you smoke?" I asked, offering her one of my cigarettes.

"No," she answered timidly, tilting her head to kiss her wheezing baby.

But it was when I finally had a laugh with the old lady that I started to feel close to her. We started talking about our brothers and sisters. For some reason I told her about the time I played a trick on my sister and put toothpaste in her shoes. She laughed but I was sure she was like the rest of them and probably had never even worn shoes or been able to buy toothpaste. Then she told me how when she was little, she had long eyelashes, very long eyelashes. Her sister had said, "Here, I will help so you can see better." And she cut off her eyelashes. Then her mother came home and said, "Oh, no, what happened to your eyelashes?"

I loved that story because I pictured it happening in a home, a regular home like the one I came from, even though I knew that wasn't true. Her life was in a hut. My life was in what she would see as a mansion: running water, electricity, separate bedrooms. But for a moment our stories replaced our loneliness with a laugh.

✕

We had our laugh but over the next two weeks I heard bits and pieces of stories revealing a pain that had been buried. In school, I had learned about settlers conquering the New World and wars with Indians, but I had never thought much about it. Until now. The old lady explained to me how five of the Mayan women were from a village that soldiers entered. They burned it to the ground and shot all the men. The women were brought here.

The story sounded unbelievable, like an old tale from the Wild West, but this was today. Instead of cowboys killing Indians, it was Ladinos. When I asked why this was happening, the old lady whispered her responses as if it were some secret code, "It happens because we are Indiginas, Naturales, the Natural Ones."

And with those words she planted a seed in me. I wondered how these gentle women really got here. Who were they? What did they think about? What did they care about? Most of all, I sat there feeling a connection with these women—but what kind of connection? Was it just our immediate circumstances? These questions would haunt and finally drive me to investigate. But at that moment, I wanted to say something, to explain something about myself, yet I was confused about what to tell her.

She'd look at me, poised, her gaudy earrings bobbing beside her crusty brown skin. Her conviction overshadowed rancor, yet she was powerless. The matron stomped around us every day and proved the Mayan's powerlessness when she refused the mother's pleas to bring her baby to the hospital. Finally, I was able to bribe her, and the baby saw a doctor, but it was too late.

It was even almost too late for these growing friendships. I was getting restless. I had heard about people forgotten in jails. But I was innocent. My government would help me. I had contacts and some money. When, I wondered, would they get me out of this place? I planned. I surveyed the courtyard wall. I could stand on the trashcan by the little tin shed, shimmy up the wall, leap somehow over the barbed wire and broken glass at the top, and then, I guessed, jump. It was a good ten feet, but I could make it. I never made plans beyond those. What I would do on the other side. Run? Keep running?

Each day I waited for lunch. Not for the food, since almost every day we had tamales wrapped in soggy cornhusks, but for the way we stood together around the barrel warming the tamales, me towering over the women as they prayed. They would whisper to God, then click their tongues making what sounded to me like bird trills. Then they'd turn to me to say, "Gracias, Nan. Thank you, Mother," as if I had husked the corn and made the tamales. And it was the gentle way they always spoke to me in that tiny tin shed that finally made me break down and cry.

As if my weeping was a divine request, on that same day two men dressed in black followed the warden into our courtyard. They were somehow related to the US Embassy. Outreach workers. Volunteers. I didn't know. One was a Ladino, the other, a man with a square body, short-cropped hair, wire-rimmed glasses and a demeanor that announced official business. It had been a month.

"What happened that night?" the man started to grill me. I looked at his well-shaven face, his kind, intelligent eyes and soft skin, and wondered what he was thinking. It was hot, noontime hot. The women were standing by the kitchen, very still, watching us. So still, eyes unmoving, as if they weren't breathing.

I told him every detail of that night and when I finished my story, he paused, crouched beside me. I knew he didn't believe me, so I told him, "Go visit the judge and you'll see."

I sat alone, uneasy under the women's gaze, uneasy with my relief. Such relief! I knew I would walk out of that place. Here was my government. My protectors. Yet I felt cowardly. I leaned against the wall until the old lady came over, sat next to me, took my hand.

"God will protect you," she assured me as if, once again, I was the one who needed comforting. "We are all praying for you." She stroked my head and sat holding my hand as if in a vigil. The sun burned down on us. I felt dizzy.

The men returned two hours later, laden with Cokes and cakes. When they had walked into the drunken judge's office, he had shouted, "You smoke marijuana!" They saw the screen and bed and smelled the *guaro* on his breath. He was the best evidence that my story was true. But the truth didn't matter.

The embassy men demanded, "Give us five hundred dollars so we can bribe the pharmacy to say it wasn't marijuana."

"No," I said. I looked around, somehow imagining I still had leverage even in jail. "I won't do it!" I added, "I am innocent."

Like hens clutched together in a corner, the women watched. A tightness in my throat grew so intense, I wasn't sure I could speak. It was still hot. Squatting in the courtyard beside me, the consul leaned over and touched my shoulder, "You don't understand. Someone has to be guilty. If you don't do this, you won't get out."

When I packed my few belongings, the women clicked their tongues and took turns praying over me and patting my head. I cried. For them there would be no lawyers, no money. They couldn't even fuck their way out of that hole because they were Indians, *Naturales*. After all that time locked up, it was when I was leaving that I finally got scared—of what I had learned about life and where that might take me.

※

Months later, back in my family home outside of Washington DC, even though they knew I had been in jail, no one spoke with me about jail, and I didn't mention it either. Yet it hovered in the recesses of my mind, emerging to sabotage my dreams. I got some work but even the life I imagined for myself in archaeology no longer had luster. I felt something pulling me in another direction, but I couldn't make sense of it.

After the Guatemalan jail, my eye was critical of everything around me. Every time I opened the refrigerator, the wealth and opulence of American people repelled me. Yet I couldn't drown out or condemn anything or anyone totally. This was my world. And the reason I was free, out of jail, was because I belonged to this world.

But just because you belong, doesn't mean you feel you belong.

After my time in jail, I was filled with a rage about the condition of the incarcerated women. I wanted to understand more about their lives. I stalked bookstores and libraries for information, any kind of information. I read ethnic studies, archaeological reports and international surveys. Soon I fell under the spell of the great Guatemalan writer, Miguel Angel Asturias, who began to unravel the mystery of their culture and the brutal forces surrounding it. He brought me into huts and then into the high courtrooms where decisions that were made by the few affected many. He led me to other Latin writers who also fleshed out worlds often hidden from our eyes yet struggling to survive.

I went to the Library of Congress, in and out of the Smithsonian. There, I was in the center of world knowledge, and I was discovering facts about women, about Guatemala. Yet it wasn't tangible. It didn't bring me to the meaning or allow me to really understand the people. The image of the women in jail followed me everywhere. The prayers they whispered at my departure urged me along. I could almost feel the way each one touched my head, then my shoulders, whispering a prayer that was pushing me toward something I couldn't quite discern. Then I got a sign.

I walked into my favorite café clutching Miguel Angel Asturias's *Hombres de Maiz* and sat down next to a table of three young men in an animated conversation. Normally, even in the midst of chaos, I can concentrate on a good book, but as I sat down, I heard the words "secret police," so the urge to eavesdrop was irresistible and soon I was sitting at the table with them. The words "Haiti," "Duvalier," and "vodou" were tossed back and forth. I had heard of Baby Doc, Duvalier, but I hardly knew where Haiti was and it seemed to be an enigma to these men too, who I, now, knew were journalists. "The boat people" seemed to be arousing their interest. The Haitians, half-starved, they all agreed, arriving on US shores on rickety boats, seeking amnesty. The men were discussing who were these people really were. What were they really fleeing? Or was it just money they wanted? Part of the American Pie, one inserted as he sucked with relish on his cigarette so ashes floated between his words. Part of the American Pie. Heads nodded in agreement. The American Pie. The conversation went in circles, confusing, disruptive, contentious. It was filled with emotion.

I felt a bitterness rise up in me. After jail I was pretty sure it wasn't just American Pie pulling people to these shores. The journalist sitting beside me had a similar view. In a month he would go to Haiti, to see for himself the truth behind the boat stories.

He befriended me, and listening to him as he planned for his journey and spoke about Haiti, something unexpected settled in me. I wanted to understand more about the Mayan women in jail, but it wasn't just them. What about the other women of the Earth whom we never hear about in news or see on television except when there is a major calamity, an earthquake, or civil war? What about the Haitian women on those boats?

I decided that somehow I, too, would go to Haiti and learn the backstory, the life stories of women, the connections between our worlds. Then I would go to Guatemala. But I would start in Haiti. It was only seventy miles from the United States; it was cheap, mysterious and controversial. My family tried to talk me out of it. It's dangerous, my father pleaded, go back to college.

I didn't listen, although there were moments I doubted myself. I was being pulled toward something. I didn't have a background as a journalist like my friend, nor was I a sociologist, an activist, or even a feminist. But I did know how to speak French and, by then, Spanish. And I loved to read and hoped that would count for something. My only real preparation, as far as I could see, and later I was proven right, was my life experience. My father was a career man in the navy, and later I was to find out he was also a CIA agent. He worked like he lived, with a sharp and feverish intelligence, but also with enough humor to drag the seven of us around the world. Even this he did in his own original style.

Unlike other fathers, despite the availability of international schools for diplomats or navy families, my father always chose for us to attend local Catholic schools. It didn't matter what food they ate, what language they spoke, or if the playground was only a dirt courtyard. He wanted us to learn about the cultures where we lived in Africa, the Caribbean, and Europe.

I got a bit of grant money and made plans to immerse myself in a world unlike my own. I knew little about Haiti and it was a deviation from my course. But like many deviations, it forced me into a truth.

So, as unprepared as I was, the love of adventure and the women in jail finally gave me the gumption to board that plane to Haiti and land at the Port-au-Prince airport: Mayi Gaté Airport, Rotten Corn Airport. People said it was named after the area where it was located, but I doubted it. The name was my first taste of that Haitian wry humor—disdainful, ironic, and always brutally honest.

# ONE

# Larian, Haiti

*Yon sel dwet pa kapab mange gumbo*

(One finger alone can't eat gumbo)

# Into the Northwest

Route Nationale No. 1 is the only highway leading to Northwest Haiti, but not many people take it. It winds past the waters of Port-au-Prince Bay, then past the lush tropical vistas near the capital. When you leave the city on Route Nationale No. 1, you assume it will be paved the entire way. Instead, you are soon greeted by a dirt road that ushers you off into a very different world. A world where only footpaths connect villages to the outside world. A wrong turn and you would be lost in miles of barren hills ruled by vodou drums, griots storytellers, and fear.

I had been warned not to go to Haiti, that Haiti would change my life. But as we jostled along the highway through village after village, the heat bearing down intensely, I felt I was in the right place. Alongside the road, slender barefoot Haitian women walked erect, carrying huge bundles on their heads which were wrapped with colorful *mouchoirs*. Sometimes hand-carved pipes dangled from their mouths. Their bodies were pure sculpted muscle and their poise alone seemed to defy the world around them.

These were the people I was looking for. Women who, I thought, had connection to the Earth, to each other and to life itself. They were the change I needed.

In the US I had daydreamed about the tropics, a place I imagined to be slightly damaged by poverty, but where detailed primitive art in Gauguinesque colors flourished in the villages along with intricate dance and music from the vodou heritage, made so famous by Katherine Dunham, "matriarch and queen of Black dance." The thought of this adventure overshadowed any fears I had about Haiti. I wanted to comb the hillsides and speak to women, discover their dreams and their innate power. And I knew Haitian power could be formidable.

Haiti was once so formidable that even Napoleon couldn't stand up against it. The French once had called Haiti its wealthiest colony, Perle des Antilles, and Napoleon wanted to hold onto that pearl. The Taino people had been victims of an attempted genocide with an imprint of a racially-based class system, with *grand blans* on top and *noirs* at the bottom, left behind. He planned to beat the rebellious Haitian slaves, then hightail it to New Orleans where he could conquer all of North

America. Unable to defeat the Haitians, he changed his plans, sold Louisiana to the US and moved on to other conquests. By then Haiti was the first Black republic in the Western Hemisphere. Yet the French wouldn't recognize Haiti as a country and the US was afraid of the freed slaves. For a hundred years, no White man tried to conquer Haiti. Nowadays the Tonton Makoute, secret police, ruled over every inch of the island, ghostly and horrifying in their dark garb and sunglasses worn day and night. I had been warned about the repressive regime and the poverty, but I was a veteran traveler and was certain I could navigate almost anything.

Creole, not French, was the language I heard when I arrived in Port-au-Prince.

Everything around me moved in waves of constant motion with no beginning or end. People spoke at the top of their voices that I, with my limited Creole, interpreted as anger. A continuous noise of people shouting, jabbering, singing, fighting surrounded me. Beggars and merchants grabbed my arms. It was like walking through an inferno, a huge pulsating circle of hell.

I left the city and stayed in a rural area where I practiced my Creole. Even there, street sounds, singing, and loud voices filled the air. I liked the camaraderie I sensed behind all the noise and felt welcomed everywhere I went. Most of all, I felt at ease walking the streets in a way that as a young woman I hadn't felt in other countries. The men greeted me politely, and I could walk the streets without being hounded by catcalls or whistles. Perhaps there was history and repression behind this politeness, but it served to affirm, that despite how different Haiti appeared, I would find my way through it.

After a few months in that rural town, I took a truck back to Port-au-Prince, unsure of where to go or even why I was going back to the capital, until a remarkable turn of events occurred.

Heading to the capital, the bumpy truck ride was exhausting, the sun blistering hot, and I had no water. After several hours, the truck veered into a village of dilapidated huts, a squat white building sitting amid them. The truck braked and I scrambled out, then darted toward that building, certain it could be a refuge from the sun and a source of clean water. As I walked up to it, I thought I heard my name called out. Clémence. It must be the sun, my imagination, I thought glumly. Then suddenly again: Clémence! and this life I was living—the desolation, the beggars, the children sitting staring off to nowhere—started to disappear and be replaced by the vague outline of someone sitting on the steps, smoking.

A *blan*.

A *blan* like me. A foreigner, White.

But this blan knew my name.

I walked closer and the image became clearer until I could see her hand poised in mid-air still holding the cigarette. Slowly details emerged: her thick long brown hair, her green glasses, her short strong body as she stood, as astounded as I was, to meet in a place one could easily call the ends of the earth.

Movement never stops in Haiti, and as soon as we hugged, a group of women beckoned us to follow them. They gave us mangoes and showed us how to suck on them to quench our thirst. We walked behind them, talking about a world far beyond their reach—our lives since we left boarding school in Switzerland, when Rebecca's family was living in Laos and mine in Paris.

What were the chances we would meet again and in a remote part of Haiti? How could I not feel that forces beyond me were at work here? This wasn't just a casual meeting of a past friend. This was a meeting with someone who understood much of who I was, who had the key to much of what I would do in Haiti and later in my life.

Later, when I joined her about a month later in Port-au-Prince, Rebecca had made connections for me in a small village Mare Rouge, where I would work in exchange for room and board. Her work in a development organization was satisfying, but besides visits to the Northwest, she had no need to immerse herself in rural culture; yet she was one of the few who understood my curiosity and my need for change.

※

The night before I left the capital on the National Highway I could barely sleep. I was about to embark on an odyssey to the depths of an unknown land. I was finally on my way to Northwest Haiti, where few Westerners went and certainly not tourists. Transport to the Northwest was scarce. There were tap taps, the hand-painted trucks that serve as buses, and old trucks weighed down with cargo, animals, and people that joggled down the highway.

The day I left, Rebecca loaded me down with maps, books, chewing gum, cigarettes, and four Toblerone bars like we used to share in high school. She negotiated travel for me so I could go directly to the village rather than making a stopover. In the early morning darkness, she led me through the market and directed me to an old truck with two Haitian men hauling a cargo of sacks of flour. Her green glasses fell to the tip of her nose as she said goodbye, promising to visit in a month or two "if you aren't out," as if I would be released from jail.

She had done a lot for me since my arrival in Haiti, but as I watched her walk away from the truck, for some reason, I didn't feel particularly grateful for her efforts. A half-eaten Toblerone bar jiggled on my lap when the driver started the engine, without keys, by simply joining two wires together. Sparks shot across our compartment and exhaust fumes saturated the air. The searing heat and the sticky sweat soon glued us together in the small cab. As we inched our way across the plains marked by thorny woods of *bayahonda*, those thorny mesquites, cacti, and acacias until we reached mountain ranges. The driver stopped in villages. They were noisy, raw places, people calling back and forth past clumps of huts and sometimes a little church. I wasn't sure if the stops were planned or if the driver just wanted to converse and bicker with people. In one village, a noseless woman hung on the open window begging, crying, blan, blan, the word that would be called out to me everywhere in Haiti.

For hours, the truck clattered past barren hills and huts that looked more and more like compost piles. After a few hours, I wondered if this trip would never end, this inferno, the driver stopping everywhere, the village children, the *ti moun*, little people, all staring at the blan. They didn't run or play. They just sat in the shade, cracked lips and bulging eyes, leaning on their bloated stomachs. Things were quickly becoming very different from what I had imagined. Everything about this country demanded my heart and soul.

※

The truck eventually left me on the plateau at Mare Rouge. The earth was a soothing red color and a spring of water was flowing nearby. Banana, orange, and coffee trees lined the road.

As the truck pulled away in a cloud of red dust, I was left standing infront of a yellow shack. I didn't know it yet, but I would live here with Anite, a Haitian woman and community leader, hired to start a weaving workshop. I would help her. Rebecca figured that this arrangement would satisfy my desire to know rural Haiti. Then I would come to my senses, return to Port-au-Prince where I would take a job as a non-profit administrator. It was a tentative plan. But it was her plan. I was ready for this adventure, this change of life, and the trees lining the roadside, the spring not far from town, encouraged me.

Anite was waiting for me. Her hair was cropped back tightly in two braids pinned to her head. Her high cheekbones were mottled by freckles. She was wearing a soft lilac print cotton dress with ruffles. The dress draped gently round her body that looked strong, powerful, and so defiant that when she smiled, I wondered how she really felt. Here I was, a Blan, invading her life.

"Come on, Blan," she ordered. "Let me show you the house. You will stay here with me. You will bring much movement to our town and that's what we need."

I was so dazed and exhausted by the trip that I stared back. I must have looked dumbfounded and it seemed that Anite was sizing me up.

"Heh, don't worry about anything, Blan," she said, putting her hand on my shoulder like she had known me forever. "Even if you don't know how to do anything, your white skin will bring movement. And that's what we need, Blan."

We were standing at the front of the house on a wooden balcony covered in moss and chips of blue paint. Just as Anite pushed open the front door, a young girl arrived, breathless and loaded down with wet clothes. She stood at attention between us.

"This is Marie," Anite explained, a hand now resting on Marie's shoulder. "She will stay here with us and help you with anything you need. She's one of my students and she loves me, Blan, and when she works, she works well." Then, as if to end her thought, Anite whirled around and spat on the ground.

We both followed Anite into a bright yellow room with a wooden table covered with pink plastic. There was another little table with pink plastic flowers on it and four chairs dispersed around the room. The smell of kerosene lingered in the air. There was a back door and a small foyer with a brown wooden cupboard filled to the brim with plastic glasses, pots, and a mirror. I looked out the door to a dirt courtyard with one lone tree and a cornfield on one side that was to serve as our outhouse. A basin and bucket sitting in the corner of the foyer, I soon learned, was the luxury Northwest version of a bath or shower.

After all the heat and dust, the cool of the house felt refreshing. It was the only house in the village that had actual windows with wooden shutters. I peered into the small adjoining room crammed with a large master bed and a wardrobe. Anite and I were to sleep in the bed and Marie on a mat on the floor.

"Sit down," Anite commanded, and I flopped onto one of the chairs, exhausted and tired of communicating in Creole.

Anite lit a kerosene lamp made from a tin can and proceeded to stuff me with a mixture of flour, bananas, and watery milk. She poured glass after glass of sugary sweet orange juice. Marie sat close by, silently shelling peanuts, listening.

By that dim light Anite leaned over the table and explained some of her mission. She sat with her cotton dress tucked between her spread thighs, occasionally leaning out the window to spit. "I teach girls here anything that I can. They come to me knowing nothing, not even how to thread a needle, and they end up with some skills. There's hope for these people, but not much. They plant their crops, but nothing grows, so what can they do?" She glanced out of the corner of her eye as if she suspected me of something. "Haitians work hard!" she barked at me. "I know, Blan, because I was once just like these people. My mother was a merchant. She sold soap, combs, and candy in the markets, and we lived deep in the country. It was only because my brothers and sisters died that my parents could afford to send me to school. I learned to read and write and work with my hands and eventually help my people. I'm glad you are here, Blan."

She stood up, gave some orders to Marie, then turned to me. "I am going next door. You can come there if you need me." She paused by the door. She looked so strong and seemed like the sort of person who could overcome situations that others might find impossible. She stood there with the night hanging all around her.

"I guess I'll go next door now. You want to come?" She was part way out the door and I could hear her spit again.

"No thanks, I'm fine here with Marie." I smiled at Marie who finally lifted her head, a pleased look on her face.

"Sure, I'll be back later." As I watched her leave, the pit of my stomach felt cold. Spitting was a common sign of tuberculosis, endemic to Haiti.

Marie sat next to me, sharing the flickering lights of the lantern. My red backpack, covered with stains from past trips, sat in the corner. I opened the top and dug out my toiletries. Then I reached further in and grabbed some books, wrapped in plastic. I wandered around the house, putting things on the tables, trying to transform the shack into a home and dispel my loneliness with the sight of something familiar. I put books on the table by Marie and toiletries in the cupboard out back. I really didn't know what to do with myself. I sat at the table, hoping perhaps writing in my notebooks would be calming.

"Blan," Marie looked up. I felt annoyed. I had already heard the term Blan over and over again. Would that always be my label here? Marie picked up the little lantern and brought it closer to me. She was squinting. "Blan," she asked. "Does everyone in your family have hair like that?"

"No, Marie, we all have different hair colors. One sister has black hair, and my other sister has brown hair."

"It's nice," she said and stroked my head lightly, then ran her hand through my fair strands of hair. She stood there beside me, stroking my head as if she were my mother. I closed my eyes as she wove her hands through my tangled hair. Slowly, calm descended upon me. Then I watched as Marie sealed the windows tight with the wooden shutters. The hut was already stuffy, but when I protested, Marie prevailed, "No Blan, we must keep out the spirits, the *loa*."

I sat there alone, slowly taking it in: I was now in the far reaches of Haiti, miles away from telephones, electricity, and, most of all, I was finally on an adventure.

Yet an uneasy fear welled up in me—that I might not be accepted, that something could happen. And what about Anite's spitting? The hut felt suffocating so I stepped outside to the back courtyard. It was a dark night; the only lights were the stars and candles flickering like tongues in the neighboring huts. A muffled sound of vodou drums echoed like a pulse in the distance. The night air was cooler and even the small courtyard felt expansive, spacious, as I stood there.

Behind me I heard a noise, as if someone was dragging something across the ground. Then I heard a voice in the distance. Again, the dragging sound. What was it? My imagination went to work. Branches—or maybe it could be a body! My exhaustion overcame me as I stood there, frozen in place. I concentrated on the sound. Slowly, the shape of a lone man, stooped over and limping, balancing on a gnarled wooden walking stick, came into sight. He was pulling something roughly behind him up the road toward me. He was singing and as he came closer, I heard his chant:

*What man can be a happy man*
*When he stands alone?*
*What man can be a happy man*
*When he stands alone?*
*Me, my Lord, me*
*Standing with you.*

The evening mist took his song and sailed it into the darkness. The air felt heavier in the ensuing silence of this deep, dark night.

※

How strange it was to wake up in this little house with Anite snoring soundly beside me. It was a cold night. Since I didn't have a blanket, I wrapped myself in a towel as best I could. The sun was barely up. I got out of bed, stumbling over Marie as I made my way outside to pee in the cornfield. I went to sit under a tree but right there on the ground was a man snoring, his hands outstretched like claws. A pile of dirty clothes was planted beside him like a nest that he had abandoned. On the other side, a gnarled wooden stick.

Marie finally emerged and started making us coffee over a fire.

I sat on the ground beside her. "Who's that?" I asked, pointing to the bundle under the tree.

"Oh, that's St Jerome."

"St Jerome?" I lit a cigarette.

"Yes, St Jerome, he's a Malheureux."

An Unhappy One, I thought. Most people on the island should fit into this category but they didn't. Instead, they seemed vivacious and even a bit sassy.

Marie took a second look at me and said sharply, "You are sitting in the dirt."

"It's okay, I'm fine." I could already see that between Anite and Marie, I had two bosses here.

Marie seemed offended. She rushed away to find me a roughly carved stool.

When she returned, she pulled the boiling water off the fire, pouring it over the coffee through the *passoire*. The bundle of St Jerome began to squirm, but he was less interesting to me than the intoxicating smell of coffee. It was thick, sweet black coffee. Soon Marie handed me a bowl of warm milk with bananas.

# The Big Taste

The morning sun was already harsh as Anite and I sat in front of a little limestone hut painted a colorful blue. A cardboard box sagged under our weight as we sat waiting for students to appear at the weaving workshop. Anite was armed with a notebook but sadly, even after an hour, no one materialized. Chickens darted in and out around our feet, but Anite gruffly shooed them away as if, somehow, they were to blame. Finally, exasperated, she grabbed my hand, "Come on, Blan, I'll show you the nutrition center."

An equatorial sun blazed overhead as we marched through the dusty town—scattered huts, a Catholic church, a marketplace, and a hut that served as a little store. Small beads of sweat collected across our foreheads and Anite's yellow bandana darkened. She was still clasping my sweaty hand when she cut away to a deserted path toward a thatched hut that looked like it's roof had been chewed by rats.

Squatting in the shade was a group of women, all with bandanas covering their heads, pipes dangling from their mouths, their skinny arms wrapped around their knees. Their dresses hung loosely over their lean bodies, making them look like a ragged flock of scarecrows. They were gaping at an instructor who was telling them about the benefits of eggs, milk, and meat, precious items they seldom saw.

Close by, in another small hut, a gruel of wheat and beans simmered in a huge cauldron. Infants sat in the dirt staring listlessly off into space. Their arms resembled thin black twigs and their ankles were swollen like the aged. A tiny girl began crawling toward Anite and me. One of her eyes was gone and she wore a black cap to fend off evil. For an awful instant her face looked like a death mask, the cap's black material blending with her premature wrinkles. Tears and snot glazed her little face. I yearned to hold her and cradle her as she whimpered.

Suddenly a howl replaced her whimper, a howl so piercing it felt like splintered glass shooting into my gut. Anite jerked away from me and dashed over to the baby in one quick, effortless motion. One of her hands, black and strong as iron, reached around the toddler's bloated belly while her other hand lifted high and fell with a great slap across the girl's naked bottom. She put the girl back on the ground, picked up a stick and started shaking it at the girl. Anite's jaw clenched while the child sobbed, frightened and helpless. Repulsed by the entire scene, I struggled against the urge to belt Anite in her mouth.

"Come on, Blan," she said, casting the stick on the ground as she tried to grab my resisting hand.

"Anite, why did you ...?"

"Don't look at me like that," she interrupted me. "That scream was from hunger, and I just wanted to get her to cry about something else. They start wailing that way when hunger grabs them, and you must hit them, hit them hard, so that hunger won't. My mother used to do that to me. That's what you must do, Blan. If you want to stay around here, you must learn that." Her hand tightened around mine.

"Does the child have some kind of disease, her eye ...?"

"Yes, a sickness, Blan, the one sickness that ravages all of Haiti. It's called death." She spat ahead of us, her phlegm seeping into the red earth. "But I see the nutrition center is helping us. That child will eat today. I used to watch twenty people carried to the cemetery every day."

"Twenty people!" I echoed, shocked.

Tossing her head back, she laughed at me. "Well, more like fifteen. Now there are only ten a day so that's progress. What we are doing is trying to persuade the women to use birth control but it's hard. IUDs don't work because many work in the fields, wear the same underpants and get infections. Women forget to take the birth control pills. They are so tired by the time they get home, they just fall down and sleep. Men don't want them to use it because they think it will spoil the women.

"Though the women have problems with so many little people, the children are their only joy. Of course," she confided slowly, "these women have their own methods. There are *chichi* leaves that will make the baby come out, but usually cause a lot of bleeding, so much that they sometimes die. Then there's an herb that stops menstruation and another one that prevents pregnancy. The people have their ways and are proud of them."

Anite spat as we re-entered the lonely workshop hut. More people were passing back and forth, headed to the marketplace, but no one came into her workshop hut.

"Birth control is the great independence, though." She picked up the notebook and began drawing circles and jagged lines across the paper.

"What do you use, Anite?"

"I don't use anything."

"And the great independence?"

She laughed, leaning her arm on my shoulder. "I just take my chances." She tucked her dress between her spread legs. "So far, I have been lucky. I can't take the pill because I had hepatitis when I was little."

As noon approached, the village filled with market vendors, mostly women, *les marchandes*, carrying bundles of vegetables, grains, salt, and tobacco. Men occasionally strode by with roosters on their shoulders, ready to gamble at the cockfights. Spotting an acquaintance, Anite jumped up and spoke in a low voice to a tall man, then called me over. "This is the town president," she announced.

A gaunt figure stood before me with impenetrable sunglasses, a deep-green shirt, black trousers with a gun conspicuously by his side. Isolated tufts of whiskers patched his skinny face. We shook hands ceremoniously while Anite explained my presence in his town. Two assistants waited behind him, Tonton Makoute, also wearing sunglasses, their dark lenses eliciting the right amount of mystery and coldness.

"We are enchanted to have you here," he said in a near whisper that could easily be mistaken for a threat. He bowed elegantly, then faded into the steadily mounting crowd.

"Come on, Blan, I'll tell people about the workshop." Anite grabbed my hand to steer me through the market. A cacophony of sights and sounds immediately assailed my senses. People bickered good naturedly, bargaining over goods they'd carted in desperation over so many miles. The place was swarming with beggars, some crawling, some limping, plus a contingent of children playing or carrying loads. Anite pushed through the crowd, skirting around mounds of raw tobacco, fruit, and bags of charcoal. She roughly elbowed her way past a myriad of faces, faces etched with wrinkles, scars, whiskers, smooth young faces, sick faces. Women stood straight and still with great loads balanced on their heads.

Anite surveyed the crowd, keeping an eye on the president as he roamed, smiling like a celebrity. We finally reached a small clearing where she confided to me under her breath, "You see, the main reason Haitians never advance is because we can't speak freely. We are all too afraid. As slaves we always had masters watching over us and many of us still carry the heart of slavery inside. We never really learned to work together because we were kidnapped from so many different tribes, speaking separate languages. Even now there are masters watching over us."

The officials wearing sunglasses strolled away from the market and down the road toward the church. "But I am Anite, Blan! I don't care what anyone says because I know in my heart, I am doing good work." Her feet shuffled restlessly on the dry earth. "I learned a lot of things from a priest who came here to teach my people. He took in orphan girls and taught them. He treated TB patients and pulled teeth. He was finally deported, poor devil, for political reasons. He preached against injustice, so he was kicked out!" She arranged her yellow bandana. "But it's hard, it's so hard." Her voice trailed off. There was a small mound beside us. She leaped atop it, waving her hands through the air. She pulled the bandana off her head and began to slide it through her fingers as she summoned the people around her.

A curious throng soon gathered while beggars inched along the edges of the market. Black-clad women squatting over heaps of charcoal strained their necks like scrawny chickens, but somehow looked bold and fierce staring straight at us. The men also assembled, sleeveless rags whipping their strong shoulders. Anite's speech, inviting them to her workshop, was simple, but she riveted the crowd with her fiery gestures and dramatic pauses. She periodically leaned over to spit, cementing her identity with the other women who spit because of tuberculosis or the wooden pipes they smoke continuously.

✳

In the evening I retreated to our hut to a small table made of plain wood; the legs were painted lime green. The table leaned against the adobe wall between two windows that were sealed tight from sunset to sunrise, so the room became dark as soon as the sun went down. I lit my lantern made from the small Kern's fruit juice can. It gave me a flickering light with lots of black, sour-smelling smoke from the kerosene. In my notebook were notes scrawled out that day: *grangou*, the big taste; baby; brutality or love.

I wrote and smoked my raunchy cigarettes, though mine were the expensive ones: Comme Il Faut, How It Should Be. Little bits of dried-out tobacco fell onto my journal. Not fresh stringy tobacco, but little speckles like freckles growing across the page as I wrote. But why was I smoking? I was already inhaling that thick black smoke from the lantern that left a very fine residue around my nostrils. I didn't care. Cigarettes were my luxury and what set me apart from the only other White people in this area: the nuns and priests. As I smoked, the cigarette smoke curled round me and collected my thoughts for me. Now that I was here, my purpose seemed vague. I couldn't believe I had decided to come out here alone into this no man's land and I wasn't even sure, if I did want to escape, how I would do it. How far would I have to walk to find a tap tap or truck? I kept scratching out these thoughts in my notebook. The writing eased my loneliness, my self-doubt, as I settled into this new life.

"Look at these peanuts," Anite complained bitterly to me one day as we were sitting outside the hut. "So many of them are still green. Marie bought them before they were ripe. Here I rescue her from a place where she lived like an animal, and she won't even do her work properly! It's discouraging. And what can I say to her? 'Go back home?' She would die of the big taste."

"How did you meet Marie?"

"She comes from a family of beggars in Anse Rouge. She walked for days to come here as my student. Her parents finally gave her to me."

"They gave her to you?"

"Well, I paid two gourdes, coins."

"Two gourdes?" I ask, a sense of horror caught in my throat. "You bought Marie?"

"Yes, so that she could have a better chance in this world. You must do that for humanity."

"For humanity?" I objected, stunned. "That's slavery!"

"Oh no, it's not slavery. If Marie stayed at home, she would have met a worse slavery called death. Any child you buy is treated as a family member: she works in your home, she attends school, you give her clothes. Last year the children were sold for one gourd. I bought one for my mother so she could have some help keeping house. My mother takes good care of that girl. That's how you help humanity. You can't stand by and watch people die. And you can't just hand them something for free and turn them into beggars. You see how many beggars there are in Haiti? Marie will work for me and stay alive."

The peanut shells crunched between our fingers, disturbing the calm of the village. I looked at the great empty clearing in front of us, the gnarled tree with St Jerome curled beneath its shade. Anite spat.

"Unlike Marie," she continued, "my bad fortune—of having everyone die in my family—was also my big advantage. I had enough to eat, so my mother never had to sell me. Being sold is one way Haitians like Marie lift themselves out of misery. Besides that, there aren't many alternatives. The wealthy pay their maids ten gourdes a month. Factory workers earn a gourd or two a day. Who can feed a family on such wages? Even the churches steal from the people. And with no rain, where can people turn?"

"What about a change of government?" I asked.

"What you suggest I would never even talk about," she answered.

"And what is the hope for your people, Anite? To learn to weave so they sell their labor for a gourd a day? It just goes on and on, Anite."

"You finally appreciate our situation, Blan! That's why we choose to escape to foreign soil. I wouldn't want to live in your country though, because they say it's dangerous, that people attack you on the street. Plus, I love my Haiti. Some people must leave, however, or die. There's just no chance for improvement here."

# The DeVrai Family and Special Leaves

One by one, people started arriving at the workshop. Suddenly shy outside their familiar world, they stood gaping, their arms hanging limply by their sides: a girl, a woman, and two young boys. The girl had an enormous TB abscess on her neck. All of them were barefoot and dressed in rags. They were ready to work but the hut was bare except for a pile of small looms, yarn, and cord piled in one corner. Anite instructed them to collect wood to make shuttles while we marched up a small hill to the carpenter. The organization Anite worked for would pay for him to make tables. There was one carpenter in town who was known for his skillful work. He worked outside under the palm trees, planks of wood balanced on sawhorses, shavings spilling across the ground.

He was a handsome, lean man, tall and muscular with green eyes set against his brown skin. He had a quick laugh and was easy to talk to. I was a young woman alone and although I knew better than to go beyond flirting with the local men, I couldn't help but feel the pull of attraction to this man.

For weeks in the village, Anite and I tried to organize the workshop. We had more rough wooden tables made, visited huts to talk about the project. Anite went to markets, stood on mounds, and expounded like a preacher trying to interest people. Slowly, a few more people drifted into the little hut where four small looms sat waiting for them. A daily routine evolved but I knew, sitting in that workshop, that I would never know about rural Haitian life, and I didn't know where to begin. Then, Anite heard that Larian was sick and unable to feed her newborn. She went to see how she could assist.

It was midday when I followed Anite to Larian's hut. When I first walked in, the transition from the blazing midday sun to the dark room left me temporarily blind. Like the other shanties strewn across this Haitian village, the hut leaned precariously on bare earth. It was constructed of mud, coated by a dingy whitewash with a roof of withered palms that rustled in the wind like scampering rats. Once inside, the air felt dank and cool; I could sense other human beings lingering in the shadows. When I regained my sight, I could see Larian stretched across the dirt floor on a straw mat, her newborn, Adele, lying beside her.

Larian smiled as her mother, Madame DeVrai, approached from behind and offered us a rickety wooden bench to sit on. But I stood, holding a packet of cotton swabs for Anite while she leaned over to inspect Larian's nipple, clogged by an abscess. Grumbling about no doctors or medicine, Anite cleaned it with alcohol. It wasn't until I handed her a clean cotton swab that she remembered to introduce me, and I finally sat down.

The room was still and silent. I could feel my shirt clinging to my damp back as I discerned the outline of Candid, Larian's father, and his handsome son Renaud, leaning against the wall. Larian's other daughter, Vivien, was standing by the doorway, peculiarly silent for a four-year-old. It wasn't until much later that Madame DeVrai explained to me that the *grangou*, the big taste, Creole's ironic word for hunger, had stolen her ability to speak. That day she just stood there and stared at us. Anite and I left quickly.

✳

A few days went by before Anite checked on Larian to make sure the infection was clean. The infection had cleared up a bit and Madame DeVrai claimed her remedies could heal Larian, so Anite soon stopped her visits.

But it was easy for me to continue dropping by the DeVrais' home. Though Anite and I were like an old couple already, knowing each other's habits, it was a relief to be with a gentle soul like Larian. Every time I stopped by the hut, Larian would tenderly hold my hand, then squeeze it, asking me to sit beside her on that rough wooden bench. She would begin with a litany of courteous questions about my family as if they were right around the corner, "And your mother, Blan, how is she? And your sister, is she well?" And then she would add a little lie to please me. "Oh, you look so beautiful today, Blan," she would tell me, touching my cheek. She'd speak softly to me about common everyday things like the weather, the people walking by the market. For many hours we would just sit in silence, watching the baby sleep. Sometimes Larian would hand me the baby to hold. These were tender moments I cherished in this hardened, dry landscape.

Yet one thing almost held me back from getting to know Larian:

Madame DeVrai, a lean, tight woman who always positioned herself at the hut's doorway, scowling, watchful, her manlike arms tensing as if primed for action. Sometimes she would snicker at my broken Creole. In any case, when she saw me pull out a cigarette, she finally smiled, although she must have thought it odd, that I, a woman, didn't smoke a pipe.

She smiled, but she was unsettling and so were the circumstances. Our relationship was limited to the confines of that small, dilapidated hut and the monotony of everyday tasks: hauling water, starting a fire, sitting, and watching the day go by. Hunger was another presence in the hut, draining the family's energy, focusing all their thoughts on survival. Plus, Larian was a timid, quiet person. I started to think that Larian was unusual. Her family was so impoverished, truly scraping out their lives each day. I felt I needed to stop seeing her and meet other women who were more representative of how Haitian women were living.

But I was wrong. Larian's neighbors were fighting the same battle and so were the people in the next town, all the way to the capital.

Soon I recognized these thoughts as my way of rejecting Larian's desperation. I was haunted by dreams of lifeless babies floating down a river; of myself trying to feed children with cloth. Those reasons for stopping to see her were mere excuses—my own survival kicking in and screeching: Run for it! But slowly, Larian and I began to find our common ground.

It was finally my interest in "the special leaves" that launched our relationship.

※

Larian was holding her breast stiff with coagulated milk and pus. Her mother had just finished trying to soften it by massaging it with Vaseline that Anite had given her. Larian inspected her lopsided nipple and purple veins that ran like mysterious messages across her dark skin. Finally resigned, she stuffed it back inside her dress and stood, her foot knocking clumsily against a large wooden bowl.

"What's that?" I asked. I hadn't noticed it before in this hut, furnished only with a wooden table, a bench, and a small chair.

"That's what I bathed in after giving birth," Larian replied. "I soaked my body in special leaves."

"Special leaves?"

"Yes," Madame answered for her daughter. "This land is filled with plants that cure illness." She stood by the doorway. Her strong face with a thin aquiline nose, her sturdy frame sheathed inside tight, black skin made a formidable presence. She watched with large, slightly jaundiced eyes. A ragged blue dress with faded flowers hung sloppily around her. Her ungainly bare feet stuck out from under its frayed hem. She constantly scanned the room, stirring the air with a mixture of power and frustration.

"Really? And are you familiar with those plants?" I knew that there weren't any doctors close by so maybe these plants were how the Malheureux survived in rural Haiti. Plus, this was an easy escape from our monotony of the silent staring and sitting in the hut.

"Yes, I know many remedies. But my sister knows them all."

"Do they grow far from here?" Maybe this would bring us out of the hut, take us on walks through the Haitian countryside.

"Oh no, Blan," Madame corrected me. "Just wait a minute." She headed out the door and a moment later returned with a fistful of wild herbs and weeds. She placed a stem of leaves in my hand.

"You wash with this plant and it will protect you. People can't harm you. Sickness can't grab you." I dimly recognized the sweet scent of basil. Protection. Fragrance rose as I rubbed the leaves between my fingers, remembering this aroma mixed with garlic. But she took my hand, then extracted an intricate white flower from her bundle and pressed it into my palm.

"This is a milk flower for women like Larian. We brew it into tea for her to drink, so she will give milk."

I twirled the dainty flower in my hand. It survived in this dry land.

"But," Madame added thoughtfully, "it doesn't work right now. *Bondye*, God, just doesn't want it to work right now." She reached for another weed. "And this is *zeb rouge* and *zeb*. Both are for stomach pains and diarrhea. The land is full of remedies."

Putting down the herbs, I rummaged in my backpack, fished out my notebook and started recording each herb, one page for each. Larian and Madame watched, studying my scribbling, then Madame tromped back outside. She returned holding healthy sprigs of mint mixed in with other plants. I rubbed the red dust off the leaves as if to clean them for tea. Madame jammed another spray in my hand. St Joseph, an herb to help people sing. But there was an even stranger plant.

"Now these pink flowers," she instructed me, "are *alai-kiki*, used to cure madness."

"Madness?" Perhaps my Creole was too limited for this conversation.

"Yes, you hit the person's head and rub it over and over with this plant. It helps you if you become so sad because someone has left your village. Like your mother must feel now. This herb could help her sadness."

I stared at her, wary, suspecting some kind of joke.

Larian's father, Candid, shuffled into the room, lugging some grass to feed their pig. Monsieur DeVrai, shorter than his wife, shaded his face with a straw hat, gnawed by wind and sun. Fuzzy tufts of white hair poked out of his chin and upper lip. He quickly noted the plants in my hand, my writing in the notebook, and ordered his son to help Madame DeVrai. None of them could read or write, but just this act of writing their information down in a notebook overcame an awkwardness between us. Larian knew I was helping with the workshop in town but that didn't explain my presence in her home. She couldn't imagine why anyone would be interested in her life. But she was kind and perhaps always hoping that the Blan would help advance her life. I had come for adventure but also to understand women's lives. It was confusing to both of us. The special plants and my notebook finally connected us.

Larian's role as my teacher was clarified and I became more comprehensible to the entire family. We all relaxed, admiring the plants as Madame DeVrai and her son ran in and out of the hut with handfuls of obscure-looking roots, flowers, and berries, excitedly explaining their names and uses. There were so many, I could barely keep up.

"And where are the special plants for women having babies?" I broke the rhythm.

"Oh, those plants grow far away from here," Madame answered. "I will get you some. They help a mother sleep and rest after giving birth."

"And are there any that help her with labor?" I smiled but was confused by Madame's answer, a bellowing laugh. She shock her head, still laughing at me, and reached along the folds of her bandana for her pipe. "No, Blan," she told me as if I was a child.

"Only *Bondye*, only God, can help you with that. Only God." She smirked, then lit her pipe.

"And do you have leaves to stop women from having babies?"

"We don't know about that here." Madame became very serious.

"Do other people ever use leaves to stop children or even to lose a baby? Sometimes a woman may not want to have the baby."

She stared at me hard for a moment. "Here, when mothers lose their little people, you can hear them cry all night for weeks and weeks. That is how we are in Haiti. We don't want to lose our little ones." Crisp, disparaging words. But I persisted, ignoring her reproachful tone. I wanted to know about birth control, about abortions.

"Well, what about leaves to stop the baby from growing inside the woman's belly in the first place?"

"And what do you think about that, Blan?" She looked at me as if I had just slapped her—arms folded under her breasts, stance sturdy. Indomitable. "We don't know about that in this house. We don't want little people to die. We love our little people." She locked her jaw, turned away, her bare feet thumping against the dirt as she left.

I felt relieved watching her back as she disappeared out the door; yet now I sat accused. It felt cramped and I had an urge to leave. I sat, feeling stuck between Larian and Madame DeVrai. I forced a grin, but my face felt tight.

"Don't worry," Larian uttered faintly. "Don't worry, I will take you to visit my aunt," she continued as if nothing had happened. "She knows all the remedies. You see, there is this relative of mine who lived to eighty years old. He's dead now, but still comes to my aunt in her dreams as an archangel. He enters her soul and helps her do many things. If someone has a broken leg, she can fix it. If someone has a bad heart, she can fix it too. An archangel helps her. She can do magic, too. My friend was so in love with a man and my aunt helped her with magic. Would you like to meet her, Blan?"

"Yes, Larian," I answered, stretching my legs out in front of me, repositioning myself on the hard bench. Maybe I was uncomfortable with Madame's character; but after all, I had come to this village to get to know women like Madame and Larian.

"Good, Blan. I'll take you to meet her, all right?"

Before I responded, Madame DeVrai returned carrying a large flat basket filled with beans. She squatted next to me and began sorting through them. Vivien, Larian's daughter, eyes filmy, stared from the doorway. Her frail arm gripped the hut while the other hung limply over her belly, bulging as though she were pregnant too.

"As you can see, Blan," Madame picked up as if in the middle of a conversation with me, "we don't have time for disorder here in this house. We have to work and work to live." She nodded toward the small pile of beans. Her mood had shifted rapidly. "I will take these beans and spread them outside. After the sun dries them up, I beat them, and they fall to the ground. But you see what happened? We planted three *mamits* of beans." She pointed to a rusty can, her *mamit* measurement, "and we harvested three *mamits*. Only three *mamits*. That's why we live in misery. But it's God's will. If our hearts are happy, they say we will profit in the next world. We keep our hearts happy and praise God even in our suffering." The beans rattled, sifting through her hand. I looked away, irked; either God or *loa*, a spirit, is always the answer to problems.

The beans sifted, Madame stared out to the horizon, and, as if reciting a poem, continued, "God's will is in all of this," she said, shifting from foot to foot, staring back at the horizon again. "He knows we are all here. We can't dig a well to irrigate our gardens because the water is too far down. The rain doesn't come. But God watches over us. He sees everyone in our family working hard, planting, harvesting. We harvest, then we replant and pray for a good crop. We pray every day."

Madame rattled on but Larian was scrutinizing her breast. She interrupted Madame, her voice louder than normal. "My milk won't come. I hardly have any milk left. My baby screams when there is no milk. I have to buy some. I just have to buy some milk."

Madame stopped talking, pulled out her pipe, jamming it into her mouth. Smoke soon spiraled round Madame DeVrai's head, obscuring her husband in a blue haze. The scent of raw tobacco permeated the air with a strong sweetness that overcame the stench of sweat. She sucked on her pipe.

Her shiny hands reached into the front of her dress where coins, kobs, were hidden safely away. She tossed a few kobs on the ground. Then she contributed her small bundle of tobacco to be sold at the market for a few more kobs for milk. Larian smiled at her mother, but she was already staring off at the horizon, surveying the gray, ungiving sky.

✳

I wondered that night about those herbs as I stood in the foyer in my underwear, trying to clean my back. Maybe they could help me. A sort of acne rash had grown across my back and along my sides. It was itchy, red, and beginning to ooze. How was it that Haitians kept so clean just washing in these small basins of water? When they weren't in the fields or markets, they were always so immaculate—not a sign of dust or dirt.

Water had sloshed all over the floor and I felt ashamed because every day it took Marie so long to carry basin after basin of water, balanced on her head, from the spring. But it couldn't be helped; I still hadn't learned how to wash in a teacup. After I dried off, I tried to dab on flea shampoo Anite gave me to cure the rash. But I had resisted her. I thought it a bit extreme. "This will help you," she assured me just like a nurse in a rural clinic.

I didn't just wonder about the herbs that night. When I sat to write at the wooden table, the image of Larian's pus-filled breast kept returning to mind. And the baby needing milk. I wrote and smoked. Writing was an escape from the uneasy feeling that followed me everywhere and a place that could quiet that question: should I just empty my pockets of all my money and give it to Larian's family? Or perhaps the next family? Or the next?

I thought I was going to contribute by helping Anite's workshop. But each day that seemed to be more and more of a joke, a pitiful dream. The problems seemed so complex and far reaching, stretching across the sea to the shores of my own country, the US, where my government helped prop up Duvalier's regime. But here and now, the situation was straightforward: Larian was struggling just to keep her baby alive.

※

It was almost the end of the day when Larian and I were sitting on the bench and Madame entered the hut, a tall woman striding in right behind her.

"This is my sister, Atilia." Madame nodded toward the lanky woman standing beside her. She held a large flat basket filled with beans.

They squatted in the doorway so the bright sunshine played across the beans, giving them enough light to work. Atilia smiled at me, politely muttering a pleasant greeting. Like Madame DeVrai, a barely suppressed ferocity crouched in her brawny physique. The women resembled identical twins in their bandanas, their spindly legs jutting out at the hips like black needles.

Atilia laughed and I noticed she had no front teeth  "Yes, it's true, I'm her sister. But you know, there are thirty-five children in our family."

"Thirty-five! *Mezanmi!*" I echoed the Haitian expression, wondering if she wasn't teasing me. But I knew that huge families existed in the Northwest, a result of the *plaçage* system, a sort of common law marriage that exists among several households. People in these unions live together with commitment and understanding, the man providing what he can for the households. It is seen as the result of a combination of polygamous heritage, the demands of slavery and a skewed sex ratio in the early slave years of Haiti. Whatever the roots of *plaçage*, it seems many families have survived intact because of its unwritten laws.

"Oh yes," she answered nonchalantly. "Our father had five different women and they had thirty-five children from him." The sisters snickered like a pair of crones. "Yes, he certainly knew how to treat women!"

"Of course, he could sing," Madame DeVrai observed, cradling a handful of beans while her other hand pecked out straw and gravel.

"He sang at every funeral," the sister added in a voice devoid of sentiment.

"You mean that singing at funerals attracts women?" I was intrigued by the idea.

Madame DeVrai nodded. "You see, women love music and our father had a beautiful voice. Women also love men who play the guitar. If a woman keeps herself clean and dances well, then the man will want to take her."

Atilia dumped the sorted beans into a small pot that Madame held. Together, they snatched another handful of beans.

Slouching in the shadows on a tiny bench, Candid lifted his tired head to smile at his wife's statements. His pants had gaping holes at the knees, his shirt tattered and filthy from work in the fields. Without a comment, his head slumped back down.

"Did you hear about Sislau?" Atilia asked like an old busybody. "He took his wife away from her dancing and locked her up in the house. He didn't let her out for days! Oh, she screamed and shouted but he refused to let her out. The little people finally got their cousin to come and set her free. She was crying and crying."

Atilia stomped her foot on the ground, roaring with laughter as though this story was the funniest thing she had ever heard in her life. "That's jealousy for you! Our father didn't have time for jealousy," she screeched, her voice getting louder as everyone gave her full attention, amused by her story. "He was too busy making all of us!" The sisters howled, bending over their beans, filling the hut with their happiness. Larian, cradling Adele, also rocked with laughter. Even Candid let out an audible chuckle.

From the doorway, Vivien, her little mouth hanging open, gazed at me. Her eyes were so glassy and yellow, I wondered if she could actually see.

Madame then lurched into one of her God speeches as her hands combed through the beans. "That's why we live in misery, but it's God's will," she proclaimed for the umpteenth time. "If we keep our hearts happy, they say we will profit in the next world. We keep our hearts happy and praise God in our suffering."

"Look at that child!" Atilia interrupted, slapping Madame DeVrai's knee. She pointed at Vivien, who seemed stone deaf to the woman's words. The child was breathing heavily like an asthmatic. "What's wrong with her? Look how she stares at the Blan." Dried snot was glued across Vivien's face; her little round bottom peeked through the holes of her threadbare dress.

"What's wrong with you?" Atilia yelled, forcing the frightened child to turn away.

"It's all right," I assured Atilia softly, fearing she might strike the child. "She'll get used to me." Vivien remained mute, poised by the doorway, her body inclined toward the outside.

"God's will is in all of this," Madame DeVrai cut in, her commanding voice overpowering the interruption, her hands burrowing into the vanishing pile of beans. "He knows we are here. He sees everyone in the family work hard all April and May, when we harvest the beans and replant them in hopes for a better crop."

"And exactly where is your land?" I asked, not wanting to hear another God speech but relieved to talk about anything but Vivien.

Madame looked toward her husband who pensively studied the

ground, formulating an answer. "Our fields are far away. There are high mountains and rocks you must pass over to reach our land. It's on the way to Môle."

"Môle? That's a long way from here," I agreed. "But I would like to see it someday. Can I go there with you?"

"You!" He looked up in a quick, sharp movement "You? But blans can't walk!"

"Oh no?" I objected, laughing at his certainty. "Blans can walk!"

He shook his head, skeptical, but Larian defended me. "Yes, my father, I have heard of some Blans who can walk."

"That's right," Madame DeVrai jumped in. "I know of a Blan who walks all over this countryside to bring mass to people." Atilia nodded, siding with her sister and Larian.

"You can visit our land," Madame decided for her husband as she returned to her beans.

Candid sat straight up, his calloused feet folding over each other. "Yes, you can, Blan," he relented. "And did you know that in Môle you can hear the roosters crowing from Cuba?"

"What?" I exclaimed.

He repeated his claim and immediately instigated another family feud.

"No, you can't hear roosters!" Madame asserted.

"My friend's cousin," he reasoned, "who's been to Nassau, told me they were roosters from Cuba." He leaned back, satisfied with his evidence.

"Those are just roosters from the hills," Larian muttered.

"There are no roosters in Cuba!" Madame then declared.

"*Cica riqui! Cica riqui!*" Atilia cawed, flapping her arms like a rooster.

"Men always believe their cawing can be heard!" Madame snickered.

Candid started laughing and the women joined in. Larian was laughing, kissing her baby's head. Their laughs were so open-hearted and loud, I couldn't help but join in and even make a cawing sound. It felt so freeing just watching them slap each other, overcome with joy at this short escape from reality. Laughing, their lively ridicule said, is reality too. Soon, like raucous drinkers in a bar, they calmed and settled down, pulled out their pipes until smoke spiraled in a blue haze around Madame DeVrai's head.

✳

As I walked back to my hut, I made sure to pass by the carpenter's outdoor workshop, waving to him, laughing flirtatiously at his greetings. I smiled to myself, pleased to have met Atilia and witnessed the love and joking between the sisters. Thinking about the entire conversation made me chuckle. Hearing roosters crow from Cuba! But maybe Candid wasn't so far off. Môle was close enough to Cuba that it was once part of the reason marines occupied Haiti.

Rebecca told me some of Môle's grisly story. She explained that, before World War I, Môle St Nicolas was once an important shipping route to Mexico and Latin America, and the US wanted to control the passage. The US also wanted a stable Haiti to protect business interests, especially those of the National City Bank, but it couldn't quite figure out how to get a hold of Haiti and particularly Môle.

Finally, one of the Haitian presidents in the early 1900s gave the US a good excuse. The president had two hundred political enemies rotting in the national penitentiary. All were slaughtered in a day, without trial. The Haitian outrage was so great, the next day the president was dragged out of his office and hacked to death by relatives of the victims, then torn apart by an angry mob. These outrageous acts were just the excuse the US needed to invade and occupy Haiti for the next twenty years. Môle, just a dusty village today, was the place where the US Marines focused their counterinsurgency, or "pacification" campaign, to suppress any uprisings led by the *cacos*, peasant guerillas. The campaign left thousands dead and countless others tortured or maimed. Yet the occupation was good for business, especially for the National City Bank that owned 66 percent of the Haitian Bank. All this occurred under the banner of human rights, while the US Marines left their own blazing trail of tears behind, probably close to Candid's field.

✳

I visited Larian and her family for weeks and looked forward to our conversations and being near her sweet disposition. But some days as I climbed the hill, past the carpenter and toward her hut, a tightness grew in my stomach, wondering what I would find: the baby always wheezing and Vivien's glassy stare. On those days, a heaviness would overcome my body as I walked.

What was this sense of trepidation I felt every time I went to visit Larian? This was the world I had traveled through as a child. In and out of huts, different languages, open fires in fields, dirt playgrounds. But I always saw it through the glaze of my secure home where a box of crayons and picture books and breakfast were a given.

My parents told us to respect all nationalities and customs but never said we had to "respect" our mother's friend when she got her PhD. This was the closest they ever got to telling us about the distances, the hierarchies, the sheer injustice of it all. But it was too subtle for a child to understand, especially one like me who only cared about playing, no matter with who or where. Out from under the cover of my family, now I was starting to see the truth.

I reached the hut, and it was so silent, I paused, unsure of what I might find.

The hut felt calm when I entered. Larian sat on the straw mat feeding her baby. Outside, Madame DeVrai stoked the fire with scraps of wood as if the scorching sun was only a mirage.

"How is Adele today?" I asked, squatting beside Larian.

"She's well. She almost drank the entire bottle of milk you brought us and my breasts are much softer."

"Yes, but you see," Madame DeVrai interrupted angrily, "you see, she hardly has any milk. Whenever she gets a few kob, Larian buys milk for the baby instead of eating herself."

As if in agreement with her, the baby sucked furiously, then expelled a bitter scream, pounding her miniature fists on her mother's chest.

"I eat when I can," Larian answered simply, absorbed by the infant.

Without a sound, Vivien staggered up to the doorway where she stood, pathetic and withdrawn. Her hair looked like it was falling out by the handfuls. Like a wizened old woman, she hobbled to her mother's side and leaned against her back to stare at me. Haitians were always so doting on their *ti moun*, little people, that the family's apparent disregard of Vivien was surprising. My gaze fixed on the fire as Madame DeVrai stirred her pot with a long wooden spoon.

"What are you cooking today, Madame?"

"Oh, nothing," she muttered. "Nothing at all."

And, to me, that was not far from the truth. It was the wateriest broth I had ever seen, though Madame claimed there was a smashed tomato in it. She stirred the soup and pointed to an ulcerated dog that wandered into the hut, tail tucked between his legs, mange corroding his back. He stood fearlessly before us, panting with hunger and heat.

"There's not enough traffic in this hut even for a dog," Madame mocked, scratching at the earth. "Poor devil."

Madame tossed some earth at him and Larian and I watched as he limped away, whimpering. She leaned over her pot to stir some more. The family was here in a cooking hut, stirring watery soup, but intact as a family. Then there were the beggars, like St Jerome, wandering the streets and markets, often alone and crazed.

"You know," I began, "there are more beggars in Haiti than I have ever seen in my life. There are hundreds. Where do they all come from?"

Madame DeVrai tilted her head, pulling the pipe from her bandana, tied tightly around her head like a cap. Without even a flinch she picked up a piece of smoldering wood and held it to the pipe until small puffs of smoke rose between us.

"They all have homes and some even have families. When a person can't earn enough, he begins to beg."

"But your family doesn't have much," I answered hesitantly for fear of insulting her, "and none of you beg."

"They were born for that," she replied tersely.

"Born for that?"

"Well, some were. Some had parents who were beggars, but most of them just had land that won't produce. They just stand in front of their fields with their arms crossed. When you plant a seed in the earth and no rain comes, nothing will grow. If no little plant grows," she waved her hands over the fire, "then you beg. The big taste makes you beg. If you had no harvest, you would beg too, Blan."

"Yes, you're right," I muttered. "I suppose I would."

Madame stared at me as she rose to her toes, crossing one foot over the other until she was squatting beside me. She offered me her pipe and began stroking my hair. I was softened by her concern. Still, I wanted to change the subject.

"Yes, you are right, Madame, and you always have family to help you. How did you meet your husband, Madame?"

"Well, he is much older than me. My parents decided; I never chose him. For me, there was no choice. He went to my parents' house and talked. Then we made lots of little people together and that's how it will stay until we are placed beneath the earth."

"Wasn't love important to you?"

"No, my parents decided, and I came to live in this hut. You see, nothing is important to me," she continued neutrally, still gently caressing my hair. "If you have nothing, what can be important to you? You see you have wood for your fire and beans to cock. If you have two sets of clothes, you give one to your little people. If there's some food, you give that to your little people too. God gave you your little people. You want them to eat and wear clothes, but when you have nothing, then nothing is important."

"For me," Larian interjected, leaning toward us, "everything is important. If you need wood, it's important. If you need food, that's important. Everything is important to me because my heart is filled with joy."

"It's in her heart," Madame said sourly, nodding her head. "That joy is her treasure."

"Yes, it is my treasure," Larian repeated. I gazed at her soft demeanor, her hands gently caressing her baby, and wondered about her happiness, her so-called joy. Madame DeVrai's bitterness made more sense to me. It seemed impossible for joy to exist amid this fight to survive. Maybe the *grangou* hurt Larian to the point that her brain suffered, that she was almost delusional? Yet there was something real about her joy; I, myself, was nourished by her calm when I entered this hut. But what could possibly be feeding it? At the same time, as I watched her that day, I felt there was something else buried under her resolve to be happy. But I didn't ask any questions.

Suddenly, Madame DeVrai leaped up, scattering dust at our feet.

"Look!" she shouted. "A mouse!" Madame lunged into a dark corner and rustled among the fallen thatch. Grinning, she held up an old soda bottle that she was plugging up with a rag. Inside, the rodent's pink feet clawed futilely at the glass. Larian and her mother gazed fixedly at it.

"It's easy!" Madame DeVrai exclaimed. "All you have to do is put some grease or a kernel of corn in the bottle and the mouse will climb in and eat it." She twirled round the fire and set the imprisoned mouse on a rock. Meticulously, she greased another bottle, and then tucked it underneath the thatch.

The homemade mousetrap now became our entertainment. We sat attentively, waiting for the next victim. Suddenly it dawned on me, sitting there beside Larian in her ragged, hemless dress, that this family couldn't possibly be that preoccupied with ridding their home of mice. I looked again at Larian, her mother, and Vivien, all crouching vigilant as cats round the bottle, and shook off an involuntary wave of nausea. A tiny mouse peeked out but fooled us by scampering across the wall and back into the maze of thatch.

# Peyi—Countryside

Anite's workshop was bustling with activity. The floor was covered with wood shavings, yarn, and string. Fourteen students bent over their small looms, humming as they worked. I walked around the workshop, stopping to show one how to warp the loom; another how to weave. I had learned a bit of weaving in Guatemala, and guiding the students helped ward off my sense of hopelessness and guilt amid the depravity surrounding us. And the students were teaching me something too as they swept up, laughing, teasing me about my Creole, as we closed shop and went home to eat.

The menu for our meals rotated between bulgur wheat and milk, bulgur wheat and beans—all food from the crisis relief agency, CARE. When that ran out there would be flour and water or flour with bananas and water. I knew Anite was doing her best to provide for me and that our lives in this village were luxurious. The food was basic but satisfying, and in an unpredictable way, it gave me another insight into the Haitian way of thinking.

Anite watched me as I ate, making certain I cleaned my plate. I ate slowly.

"Don't you want more?" she asked me.

"No, thank you. I am full." I had eaten a huge mound of wheat.

"You don't eat enough." She had told me this before.

"Oh, I eat much more than I do in my own house!" And it was true. At home I would have been picking at a salad.

"You don't like our food," she accused, so I tried to eat more, but it was impossible. I hated being forced by social pressure to eat and eat. Politeness seemed to be a national code. Haitians everywhere were generous with their time, their concern for me, and with their food no matter how scarce it was. I was grateful but I felt trapped.

"You have to eat more beans because you don't eat meat," she said, sliding a plate of beans toward me.

"Still," Anite said, leaning back in her chair, her eyes squinting as if she was appraising me. "Still, a lot of people in town have told me you have gotten fat."

"I've gotten fat?"

"Yes, immensely fat. I told them it must be the temperature because you hardly eat."

"Immensely fat?" Now I had to chuckle.

"Yes, you are fat," she said, deadpan.

There were no mirrors, but my clothes fit. Fat? How could it be with people starving all around me? I laughed, quickly deducing this was the greatest compliment you could give a person in Haiti. It was ironic when I thought of my world: of the diets, the slimming clothes, the angst women had concerning fat. I had no idea how I looked anymore and even in my regular life never gave it much importance as I was naturally lean. When friends dieted and complained about their "fat" I'd tease them, "Fat is good. Don't you know a skinny horse is a dead horse?" But the joke no longer seemed so funny.

I moved back from the table and we sat silently together for a while.

"Well, Anite, I am going for a walk and I'll meet you at the house for sunset."

"At sunset? Wait, you have to drink some juice."

"I'll have it when I return." I couldn't imagine another drop of anything since I was so filled with wheat.

"No, you have it now."

"Yes mother," I answered half-jokingly and half contemptuously.

※

I walked out the door hoping to find some quiet on a walk. I longed for solitude, an unheard-of state in Haiti. If I was in the hut, soon Marie or Anite would be there talking to me, taking care of me. Their company was cheerful and kind. There could never be any loneliness in this village. Nor could there be silence or calm. There were always people watching me. There was always noise outside. Animals braying, people gossiping, others shouting.

Out of kindness and concern, when Haitians saw me alone they would come to my rescue. A Haitian proverb explained this response: *Yon sel dwet pa kapab mange gumbo*; One finger can't eat gumbo—You can't achieve anything alone. There was protection in the company of others. Protection from *loa*, from the Tonton Makoute, from robbers. Plus, to them, a person alone would be someone suffering from tragedy, a death in the family, a loss of money, or a person gone crazy like St Jerome. But a sane healthy person doesn't go off walking alone.

Still, I walked off alone. I left the village following the dirt road in the direction of Môle. That road was flatter than in the other direction toward Jean Rabel where I'd have to endure steep climbs. Walking relieved me of tension, but I knew my solitude wouldn't last for long.

As I walked, I heard "Blan, Blan," in the distance, people calling out to me from their hovels. Most of the time it was just that unending Haitian politeness and friendliness mixed perhaps with the hope that this White person might have something to offer: some CARE food, a mass, extra money. I felt like plugging up my ears, sick of hearing those words. If only I could be invisible—but that's hard to do when you are the only White person for miles.

A young voice called out, "Blan!" behind me and soon three boys from Anite's workshop were loping along beside me. Marie had sent them to walk with me. I had explained many times I was fine walking alone, but Marie still sent these three boys and they decided to bring me to their home to meet their parents. The air was burning hot and the boys walked quickly. I was sweating as I tried to keep their pace. People passed us on the way to the market and every passerby was greeted loudly, "How are you?"

"Not worse."

"And the kids?"

"Not worse either."

This reply mirrored a way of thinking, a way of coping day after day, battling for survival. Not just now but also in the past: as slaves, as Maroons, as beggars, and businessmen in the Perle des Antilles. It was a sort of backhanded gratitude for just being alive. And it seemed to work.

We trotted along and I asked the three boys, "Are you brothers?"

"Yes," they answered almost in unison. Two minutes later we met their mother, who was rushing back to the Mare Rouge market. A strong, stout woman with a clean yellow *mouchoir* covering her head.

"She looks like the two of you," I said later," but not like him."

The three of them laughed. "Oh, we don't make a difference between who is our brother," the older one cried out. "We are all brothers!"

"Oh, I see, but are you blood brothers?"

"Yes, we two are, but he's our brother too." The boy took my hand

and repeated the statement slowly like I was a child who needed to learn the basics in life. "We are all brothers and sisters, Blan. Even you." And then he laughed, that full Haitian laugh so filled with abandon, cunning and knowledge. And like a grown man he started again down the path.

Men armed with machetes to work the fields passed us on the path. Women strode by carrying heavy burdens on their heads, their muscles taut and the look in their eyes unwavering. They walked as if they had been walking forever. Just like with Madame, no matter what happened, nothing interfered with the life rhythms: markets on Saturday, food cooked, and laundry washed; mass once a month; harvests and plantings. Nothing could throw these women off. Not even hunger or the Tonton Makoute.

We turned off a small path lined by stout bayonet trees. It went past rolling hills covered in green corn, beans, and millet. The path crossed into a settlement of homes with a main hut, a small hut, and then a very tiny cooking hut made of sticks. The main huts were white limestone. The walls were painted with brown stripes, circles and people's bodies in a womb form. Butterflies flew everywhere. We passed through it to reach an almost identical settlement. Finally, we had arrived at the boys' home.

Their father, his pants rolled up to his knees, immediately stopped hoeing to greet us. He darted into the hut and returned with a straw mat that he cast over a log making it a throne for his honored guest. He chatted, then jumped up to leave for a moment and returned with a green coconut, a miraculous treasure in this desolate zone. The children gathered round, staring as he chipped away the green skin.

They had rust-colored hair and their feet looked shredded from so much use. Their hair was cropped so close to the scalp, discouraging lice, that it looked like a cap of flattened, rusted wire.

*Why is their hair that color?* I remember wondering when I first arrived in Haiti. The answer should have been obvious to me because of the skinny legs, the extended bellies popping out from underneath raggedy clothes. But I couldn't read the clues. I wanted things to be different: for the hair to be a tradition, a message, maybe even an artistic expression. When I asked some local missionaries, they set me straight: rust is the color black hair turns when you starve.

The father split open the coconut, nodding at me as if to check that all was well.

"Is this where you were born?" I asked him.

"This is my land," he told me, handing me a piece of coconut. The kindness of his gesture moved me. The juicy sweetness dried on my lips and the rest flowed down my chin. He smiled and pointed to the fields with his machete.

"This is my land. This is where my parents lived and their parents lived and they gave it to me." He pointed to a hill covered with rocks; there was hardly any soil in sight. "That one over there, I bought it for 350 gourdes from my cousin."

The man literally bought a hill of rocks. How did he exist? And he was so proud! What machete can break through that brittle crust? Is there a seed so strong it grows through rock?

Yet this was his land inherited through his family. It was fought for and won long ago, during the revolution against the French. After the revolution, in reaction to the system of large plantations, land was parceled out to pay the soldiers, all former slaves. They worked on their little plots of land and set up local markets where they could sell their goods. An informal system of each family fending for itself grew. People barely scratched out a living, but they lived, and they were free.

But through the ages the land was divided and re-divided among sons. Small plots became smaller. Peasants like this man didn't have enough land to allow it to lay fallow. In desperation, peasants started clearing new land so they could cultivate larger areas. But slowly, these practices started draining the land. The government ignored the problem and instead welcomed foreign investors to harvest mahogany until soon the mahogany forests were destroyed, more land stripped. Peasants turned to charcoal for fuel and income, indiscriminately chopping down more trees until less than seven percent of the forest was left. The island, which in the time of Columbus had been covered in trees, rich soil and plentiful water, now lay barren. When it rains, dirt erodes from the highest mountains into the sea where it surrounds the island like a brown halo.

More and more young people like this man's sons were abandoning their land and heading to the crowded city for work. But right now, this family was somehow surviving on this pile of rocks and still had the generosity to share their one coconut.

The children were less timid once they shared food. The littlest one sat on her father's lap and the others took turns caressing my hair.

Afterwards, we walked down the path, the man chuckling, his laughter unnatural to me. Was it, like the rusted hair, another symptom of the big taste? We walked into the sun's dying glow. He left us at the dirt road and shook my hand as if it were made of blown glass.

# Dokté de Fey—The Herbal Doctor

The heat of the tropical afternoon was already weighing down on us when Larian decided to bring me to visit the *dokté de fey*, the herbal doctor, Madame Linet. Besides teaching me about medicine in her country, Larian was hoping to get some medicine for Atilia who had "fever," as every sickness in Haiti seemed to be called. Larian handed her sleeping baby to her mother. "Let's go visit my Aunt Linet now," she said and took my hand, guiding me through the doorway into the white-hot sun. Despite the heat, I was pleased to get out of the hut and walk through the countryside.

"My aunt will tell you about the remedies of the mountains. She knows them all and helps everyone." We branched off into a twisting footpath that headed toward the hills, speckled yellow with dying plants. Larian turned on her heel and her face went blank as she trotted down the path. She bounded over every obstacle. I stumbled. The country hike I imagined was quickly becoming a marathon for me. Much of the trail was no more than a dried riverbed, choked with granite boulders and thick roots wrapped like serpents over the banks. The scraggly shrubs, barren of wildlife, grew thicker and thornier as we went deeper into the mountains. Anonymous pathways, a veritable network of dirt paths serving as mini highways, crossed our route.

After a while, just as suddenly as we began, Larian jolted to a halt. Sweat curled across the bridge of her nose as she yelled toward a hut in front of us, but a continuous hum of insects was the only response. Two cooking huts instead of one flanked the tiny dwelling. The newly limestone-coated walls contrasted with the walls of Larian's home, which was muddied by time and pockmarked by branches jutting out. There was a cleared courtyard out front with banana, orange, and mango trees marking the perimeter.

We squatted in the shade, waiting for her aunt. Larian rose occasionally to retrieve whatever herb she happened to spot growing in the nearby bush. She plucked each one, then proceeded to instruct me on its use. She seemed at ease with her role as my teacher.

"This one is for flu ... this is for stomach cramps." She showed me all the familiar remedies as we waited for Madame Linet to return. Larian sat beside me, her bare shins jutting out from under her orange dress that hung on her skinny body for the sake of modesty rather than adornment. Then we sat quietly together.

"Clémence," Larian finally spoke up.

"Yes?"

"Bicare, my man, is coming soon to visit. He will walk from Eaubonne, the village where he cultivates his land. I'd like you to meet him."

"Yes, Larian, of course. What does he grow?"

"Manioc, potatoes, maize. You know—whatever he can. He doesn't have that much land, not even a hectare, but he will harvest plenty if it rains. We can't marry yet because we don't have any money. My mother still gets angry. 'What's this man for you?' she says. 'He doesn't build you a house or a table. He only gives you little people, then lives in another village.' But I say he's a good father who brings food and money for his child whenever he can."

"And you love him," I added, but I thought that maybe Madame had a point. This was perhaps just Larian's way of once again twisting an ugly reality into a romantic fantasy.

"Yes, but no more than anyone else. I love him because he loves me. I love everyone, Clémence, especially my little people."

She scrutinized my face then asked timidly, "Have you ever had little people?"

"No," I answered and could see she was disappointed. "Was it difficult for you?"

"Oh, no," she leaned over, laughing at me. "It hurt but I didn't scream or cry because my mother was there to help me. There was a lot of blood, but it only took an hour because I squatted against the wall, and she pushed my sides and helped me squeeze the baby out. Then I fell into a deep sleep like you do after you have a baby.

"All your friends and relatives, the living and the dead, come to speak with you in your dreams. Then, when you wake up, you take a bath in tea made from these." She separated some stumpy fingerlike leaves from the bundle. "These are trumpets that you bathe with after your little person comes out. It's very hot and warms you right up to your head. After that I bury the umbilical cord in the floor of the hut. That way my baby will never be harmed. I kill three chickens and pour their blood over the spot. Then, if my little people ever get sick, they come and stand right over that spot on the floor, and they'll be totally remade. Some people travel to other lands, to Miami, to Nassau. They come all the way back here when they are sick, to the spot where their cord is buried, and they are remade. They just stand over that spot and give three chickens. And that's what I am going to do, Blan," her voice lowered.

"You have chickens?" I repeated, trying to follow her thread.

"No Blan, I will come back once I go to Miami."

"Miami?" It was starting to get stranger than the archangel stories.

"Don't talk to anyone about this, not even my mother. It is dangerous. I want to leave with Bicare, the father of my baby."

"Leave? How can you do that?"

"You see, Bicare had a friend who left Haiti trying to reach Florida, but when he got to Cuba, the police stopped him and sent him back to Haiti. The Haitian officials met him at the dock. 'You're political,' they accused. 'You leave your country and don't want to return. You're political against Haiti!' And they began to beat him. 'No, no,' he screamed. 'I love my Haiti! Think about my situation, about my family. I need money and food and there's no work in Haiti!' 'No, you are political,' they said and beat him until he passed out. They shaved his head and put him in prison where he almost died of the big taste. Then, after four months, they let him go."

She looked around and continued, "Well, he is making another boat now and this time they plan to sail all the way to Miami with five women, one girl and ten men. He never tells me or Bicare any details because, in that life, you can't talk. There are *tueurs*, killers, here, and even you, Blan, who visit this country, should be careful. If a policeman, a chief or anyone hears you, he might say to himself, 'Well, if I inform on this person my rank will be elevated or I'll get money.' So, you are betrayed. No, in my country you look and listen, but you never talk." Dumbstruck, I listened. She knew some of the dangers but there were many more dangers. What was she thinking?

"I want to go. Bicare will help. Yes, Blan. The people in my dreams have told me about this. And every day I pray to God for help. And vodou. It will help me. The *loa* will help me. The only way for me is to leave."

It seemed impossible that the timid Larian was telling me about this dangerous and seemingly impossible plan. Her circumstances were so dire it hardly seemed possible even to conceive of such a notion as escape. I felt a headache stewing in the back of my head, thinking that it was hunger, not Larian, speaking to me. But maybe she had the same iron will within her as her mother. Her dreams were impossible, but here she was, reaching far beyond those thatched walls, ready to brave the worst. "And your children, the little people?"

"If I hold the baby on the boat, then I don't pay for her. Maybe Vivien stays with my mother. I don't want to leave her, but she loves my mother, Blan. I don't want to leave Vivien, so I say, 'No, Bicare, we must wait until Vivien can come.' 'No,' he tells me, 'she can't come.' I know now what I must do."

She stopped talking abruptly and waved her arms, then shouted into the bush. I looked over in time to see a petite woman emerging from the dense thicket. She was wearing a bright yellow dress and a lobster-red bandana that covered her graying hair. She strode over, calling out to Larian, then embraced her tightly. Her presence interrupted us but was a relief from Larian's far-fetched notions.

Madame Linet's mouth drew tightly shut while Larian explained the reason for our visit. Madame Linet squatted on the ground. Larian and I followed her example. Compared to Madame DeVrai, Madame Linet was short but strapping, perhaps she belonged to a different ancestral tribe. She murmured to Larian, her back slightly turned to me, as if she didn't want me to hear what was said. I could see Larian from where I sat. Her voice was low but animated, then silent. The three of us squatted there for a while in silence, our knees almost touching. Madame Linet twisted round to look at me. Instead of looking off toward the horizon when speaking, like Madame DeVrai, she held my gaze. I felt that I was being evaluated, and I was.

After a long silence, she confided her suspicions in me: "You know these remedies come to me in dreams. No one told me about them. I can cure any sickness that a doctor can by grinding my herbs and putting drops of them into people's eyes or mouths. But these are secrets of my heart that I shouldn't reveal to anyone. I don't want anyone stealing my secrets and I have ways to revenge them if they do."

Unsure if this was a threat, I stared back at her.

"My dreams will tell me if you steal from me. I have ways to revenge if you do."

Startled by this unexpected threat, I didn't know what to do but hold her gaze. "I'm just curious," I finally mumbled.

She tilted her head to one side and smiled. "Yes, I know," she nodded. "I dreamed all about you and I know you aren't here to steal my plants."

This was the same quick mood swing from cantankerous to warmhearted that I experienced with Madame DeVrai. It was hard to know what to believe in any of these conversations. Sometimes, they were just teasing me, a sign of friendship; or sometimes they were teaching me about their world. I felt like she had tricked me just to see the blan's reaction. I kept squatting though I wanted to get up and leave.

"Eh, Blan." She scrutinized me, then wrapped her arm around my shoulders as if no threat existed between us. "I will give you remedies, but do you believe they work?"

This felt like another test. "Well, I don't know," I stammered hesitantly.

She leaned over and patted my stomach gently. "Eh? Where's your stomach? It's so little. You haven't eaten right, and you sleep in a little place where bugs can bite you. So now you have a sickness on your back. But I have some plants for you."

Larian leaned over and yanked up my shirt. "Oh Blan! Oh Blan!" She laughed and slapped Madame Linet's knee.

I felt myself blushing. The fungus had only gotten worse. Marie scrubbed it with the flea killer for me each night, yet the fungus oozed and tormented me with its ugliness and pain. Threats or not, I was a willing convert to her methods. Foregoing any other explanations, she trotted off and returned quickly with a fresh bundle of herbs.

"You take these leaves and bathe with them every night. Use only a handful and scrub hard. In four days, your illness will be gone." That said, she sorted through the miscellaneous collection of leaves. A botanist in her lab, she spoke explicitly, rattling off the name of each herb, its use and preparation. She handed me a sample with a solemn air, waiting patiently while I recorded her explanations in my notebook.

After some time, she patted my shoulder and reminded me to bathe with the leaves each night. She clasped my hands together, bent her head over my hands and recited what sounded like a mixture of the Hail Mary and incantations. Making a sign of the cross over me, then over Larian, she departed as suddenly as she came, the bush swallowing up her nimble figure. The air was cooler and the sky pinkish as Larian and I headed homeward.

"And do you really believe these leaves will kill my sickness? I have already tried everything," I asked the back of Larian's head.

"They will."

# Malheureux—The Unhappy Ones

A week later, I strolled through the marketplace, the sun warmed my back that was slowly clearing of the fungus. Just a short distance from Larian's hut, voices hollered back and forth so I barely understood them as I walked through. I lumbered past large lumps of raw sugar, tiny bundles of salt and an occasional egg for sale. I stopped in front of a lady crouched before a pile of dried beans and relief food from the US.

This relief food was often stolen or given as part of a Food for Work Program, a program despised by Haitians because it reminded them of the days of slavery. After slavery, the Haitian government tried to form peasant work groups called *covées* that were paid in food and rum. But the peasants boycotted the system because they preferred working on their own land. Later, the marines tried to reinstate the *covées* to build roads to help the economy and to make it easier to control the peasants. Sometimes they dragged peasants out of their homes, tied their ankles together and beat them into service. They were hauled away from their plots of land, their sole income and sure sustenance. The marines were looking to build infrastructure but instead the *covée* system only created resentment. Now the US Food for Work system replaced the *covée*, but was also a system that was regularly abused.

Still, the relief food reached the homes and the market. Maybe it was keeping many of the Malheureux alive. This woman was selling US wheat. "Bonjour, Blan." She reached out to touch my hand like she already knew me, then patted my hair, all the while asking about my family. I knew she was doing this so the following week I would return and buy from her again. But her warmth and interest appealed to me. It filled a deeper loneliness that went unnoticed in the States. These little interactions with Haitians were like a balm, soothing a deeper isolation endemic to my world. I dawdled, chatting with her while she wrapped my wheat in a leaf.

A man with a huge bag over his shoulder trotted past me. He was followed by a woman with an enormous bag balanced on her head. They both unloaded their cargo next to other towering gray bags of charcoal lined up, on the far side of the market. I knew the woman was a charcoal vendor because all the charcoal vendors dressed in black so the charcoal dust wouldn't show. And they were all women. Sometimes if they were lucky, the charcoal vendors sold an entire bag. More often, in a small village like Mare Rouge, they sold charcoal by the handful or rusted can or in a basin. Yet creating the charcoal took time and effort.

Both men and women made the charcoal by digging a huge pit that they stuffed with wood, usually chopped-up small trees since there were barely any big ones left. They set the wood on fire, then covered it with earth, but left gaps so the smoke could escape. There was so much heat and smoke near these pits that you could hardly breathe. For all that work, each bag usually went for two or three dollars.

I watched as other people streamed into the market, desperate with wares of rags and charcoal. Normally I watched them from the outside, but now something was moving inward, and I felt myself stumbling under the weight of it all. Questions were moving to the very corners of my heart. Unanswerable questions. I was watching the truth of humanity, and I was complicit and confused. How would I live after this adventure? It almost made me feel ill. The two realities tugged at each other in my head. The marketplace and our brick home, shaded by hundred-year-old trees. I knew I had to submerge these thoughts. The only way I could continue was by being curious every moment, observing closely. And by distracting myself. I swallowed and looked around for a way to silence my thoughts.

A woman was squatting nearby selling shoelaces that no one would ever use and black plastic combs. I walked over to her and bought a comb. I would never use it, but it had already served its purpose. My mind was refocused on counting out gourdes and placing them in her calloused hand then moving on slowly through the crowd.

The women sold wares, but they also came here just to talk, screeching at each other, howling with laughter over nothing, somehow sustained by each other, freed from their dismal futures as they gathered, smoking their pipes, selling their pitiful goods.

I saw Madame DeVrai and Atilia squatting with a group of women. Madame gestured, probably entertaining them with a story, then impressed them by calling me over and demanding a cigarette. She hugged me, kissed my cheek, and bragged about me to the women. Atilia stood beside me, holding my hand like an old friend. I lingered, absorbing their intimacy. Then, as I started to weave my way through the young children milling around, a beggar grabbed at my leg, trying to latch onto me. He had one leg twisted to his shoulders while the other dragged uselessly behind him. His bowl jutted out in front of me and I dropped two kobs without looking. His scrawny leg left a trail through the dirt as he slithered away.

Back in my hut, it was cool and quiet. The thick mud walls muted the loud voices. I lit a cigarette and lay down on my bed, watching the smoke spiraling up. I tried to remember my own home: safely tucked in a neighborhood shaded by trees, lined with clean stone sidewalks and asphalt roads. I tried to remember what it was like walking in the house. The air always felt warm, almost body temperature. There would usually be noise in the kitchen: in the morning, quiet chatter and the smell of coffee; in the evening, the clinking of ice and boisterous laughter.

I saw myself walking into the den, a small, wood-paneled room. On the walls was the pastel portrait of my mother in her younger days. My father's portrait hung on the other wall, done when we lived in Paris—eyes looking out from under his tangled brows, the slight smile, his shoulders pulled back making his back erect, strong, imposing. The bookshelves were stocked with literary masterpieces, some handed down through the generations still bound in their leather covers with gold lettering. My grandfather was said to have had a library of 10,000 books.

I tried to remember the living room, but we hardly ever used it; I saw the huge, gilded mirror that looked like it belonged in a chateau, the elegant antique French furniture, and in an ideal spot, the love seat next to the large bay windows looking out to the garden.

What I remembered best was the outside, the yard with a pool filled with turquoise water, fresh, clean, surrounded by lounge chairs and little glass tables. I could practically hear my family joking, my mother's teasing leading the foray, glasses clinking, the scent of cigarette smoke. Happy hour.

Suddenly a head peered through the window. St Jerome. "Help me. Help me, Mother. I'm hungry!" A vast aching filled his voice as he repeated, "Help me!" I handed over two kobs, cursing him silently for invading my privacy, assaulting my reverie with the endlessness of this damned misery. I just wanted to cry alone in my hut. But there is no privacy in Haiti. A sense of despondency overcame me. "See," I could almost hear Marie saying to me, "you shouldn't be alone." This time I felt like she was right and left my reveries behind to head toward Larian's hut.

When I arrived, Madame DeVrai was sitting on the ground inside her cooking hut, crumbling tiny dirt clods with her fingers. Larian stood in the doorway watching Adele fall asleep. Her little head was wrapped in a ragged blouse. Larian hadn't changed out of her orange dress since we met, though I had seen her wash pitiful rags as though they were fine, spun lace. Vivien seemed uncomfortable, like she had an infection, when she stuck her index finger in her mouth, coating it with spittle, and then rubbed it absentmindedly between her legs. Her bare brown butt shifted in the dirt.

Madame DeVrai stood occasionally to stir a simmering brew that I referred to as "sweat soup." This salty gray broth with flour balls floating on top seemed to be consumed in the homes of the Malheureux throughout the Northwest. Madame gave Larian her share in a soap dish while my portion was served in a saucer that I couldn't refuse. Vivien flinched. She pulled her dress up over her head, her belly jutting out, showing a network of purple streaks as though the arteries themselves were teeming with worms. She whined as Madame DeVrai nonchalantly stirred her spoon through the gruel. Larian hissed at her to shut up, but Vivien persisted until the soup was safely in her tiny hands.

They slurped it down until Candid arrived, his face tired and worn. He took a large spoon and began to circle around the women, sampling their portions. The women acted like they barely noticed him, but their bodies stiffened whenever his spoon approached. Larian's brother walked up, laden with a huge sack of sawdust. He worked as an apprentice for the handsome carpenter, Marcel. Marcel paid Renaud with a few gourdes and sawdust, a paltry income that Larian told me the boy had to supplement with fishing. Madame DeVrai handed him an old tin can filled with the soup. He sat down with crossed legs and wolfed down the meal. Candid relaxed on a small bench in the courtyard where he could observe the people passing by.

A man ran up to the hut, waving his arms at Candid and yelling, shattering the moment of quiet. Candid leaped to his feet to shout back. Confused by their rapid exchange in Creole, I wasn't sure what was happening, but I saw Renaud's eyes brimming with tears. Madame

DeVrai ran to her husband's side, standing tall and fierce beside him. Her face froze as Renaud began to yell back at the top of his lungs.

"It's a lie! His dog came chasing after me. What am I supposed to do, let it run up and bite me? I tried to get away, but it kept coming after me. So, what could I do? I slapped it. I only slapped it." His adolescent chin trembled as tears trickled from his deep black eyes, his muscular body awkward with fear.

Candid whirled around. "You, you!" he screamed, shaking a clenched fist at his son.

The accusing neighbor was yelling at the same time, "You were walking through my courtyard. You had no right to do that. What were you doing there anyway? Trying to steal? Of course my dog came after you! He was protecting my house! You don't have to throw rocks to kill him."

"You, you!" Candid roared and slapped Renaud across the face.

Renaud kept pleading, undaunted by his father's fury. "What else could I do? I was just taking a short cut. I only threw rocks at him."

Madame DeVrai looked the other way. Larian bent over her baby as if protecting her from the angry onslaught. People began to line up on the path, staring at the family and offering their own insults or support. Several men explained the scene over and over to newcomers in the growing crowd. A buzz of voices stirred the air. That too was fractured by another loud slap across Renaud's face, abruptly terminating his alibi in mid-sentence. Candid lunged to grab him and they both ran into the hut screaming at each other, all the neighbors yelling, interpreting, commenting.

Madame DeVrai stood before the crowd, her face stiff as a cadaver's. Her eyes narrowed as she glared at them, her taut lips almost white. Her large hands swiped over her bandana, fumbling for her pipe. As if it would help her calm down, she jammed the pipe in her mouth, chewed on it a bit, then returned to the mat in the cooking hut to smoke away the pain, the shame of her son's public beating, the need for him to steal.

Screams and crashing noises from inside the DeVrais' hut seared through the growing dusk while bystanders gasped and cried like they were watching a horror show. Some of the older ones meandered off, satisfied. Candid yelled out, "I'm dreaming of a stick, a chain to beat him with!" More thuds, crashes and desperate words, the wind carrying Renaud's anguished cries, "I didn't do it! I didn't do it! I swear!"

Candid finally emerged from the hut and returned to his small bench by the path. His dark eyes stared unflinchingly at the remaining witnesses, demanding their immediate departure. The wind tugged at the walls while the drums began to rumble in the distance. Larian shifted from sitting to squatting, quiet and thoughtful. Offering me her pipe, Madame DeVrai crouched beside me, crackling her dry, brittle laugh until Larian finally broke the silence, "He's badly educated," she said, the Haitian version for "He has no shame," practically acknowledging that he stole something. "But food is difficult to come by. Finding food is my work, my family's work.

"But there's no work in Haiti. That is why my brother fishes and tries to work. We need to put our heads together and develop ourselves," she said as though quoting a community worker's speech. "Whenever there's work to be done in our village, people gather for a reunion, a meeting. The council asks for ten kob at the reunion or they come by with a white piece of paper and ask for whatever we can afford to give. If we have nothing I say 'I'm sorry' but will still try to pay next week because that way we can work together and build something for ourselves. Then no one must steal."

Madame DeVrai poked at the embers, grunting faintly when a small flame leaped up.

Larian's soft voice droned on, "Right now, we need a new cemetery."

"A cemetery?" I gasped. "But Larian, there's no water, no—"

"The old one is too far away," she interrupted. "And it's filled with rocks, so we never know if we can bury our people. Plus, we need roofing over the market so elders can keep the mud off and stay shaded from the sun."

Her mother grunted again, a web of shadows wavering across her face as Larian continued with her grandiose visions.

"When there's a reunion we go and sit on benches," she offered as proof her dreams were possible. "If you want to say something, you raise your hand, and the town president calls your name. You can say whatever you want to all the people."

"When did this last happen?"

Madame DeVrai listened and puffed again on her pipe, her parched lips scraping together like sandpaper.

Larian breathed in some of the smoky air and continued, "Once when I was a young girl, we built the road. We did it in two or three months without pay. That was another time of the big taste. We did it so food could come in from other countries. All day we carried the dirt and rocks on our heads. We carted water. Everyone worked together without pay. There had never been a road to this region, only paths. So, we ourselves built the road."

There was rustling outside of the hut. Renaud appeared at the doorway, his sharp chin jutting forward, his arms hanging limply by his sides. He looked at his mother and sister, then walked off and meekly slid onto Candid's bench, their adjacent shadows stretching across the rocky ground. The neighbors had disappeared into their huts before feeble fires, now murmuring among themselves, probably about Renaud's deviance.

"Our president Duvalier is good to his people," Larian resumed. "He gives us food and roads. He has built a school, but my little people can't go because I don't have any kob to buy them clothes or a little black book or pencils. You must buy these things if you want to send your little people to school. I pray that Vivien can go one day. She still can't talk but she can learn to write her name if God wills it. My brother Renaud went to school for three years and learned how to sign his name, even how to read a bit. The president gave us these schools. He wants to see us advance. When it's cold, he even gives us clothes."

I nodded. I walked by the school every day: a wall-less thatched hut where children recited history and numbers in French, a language unknown to them since Creole is the language they speak at home. There were no desks, no blackboards, no notebooks. The teacher had a book, the only school supply in sight.

Detached and bored, Madame DeVrai tapped her pipe gently against her palm.

"I don't see him giving you clothes or food or anything," I snapped cynically. Right beside me, tap, tap, tap, Madame DeVrai refilled her pipe and lit it.

"He doesn't give us anything," Larian's mother suddenly barked out, puffing out smoke. "The president of the town doesn't give us anything. They take our money and we never see any movement. If we don't give our money, they come and say, you didn't pay. They beat us or hurt us, and the people in the capital are the same. They don't want any movement here. They are afraid if we get water or roads, there will be too much progress. And the president, eh, he just forgets about us. But he has ears everywhere. That's why Larian lies to you. She is afraid because he has ears everywhere and he knows magic. He works with a great *houngan*, vodou priest, and he can kill you with magic, or sometimes they just put poison on the ground, and you walk on it. Then you die." Her jaw locked as she snorted through her nose. Larian was very quiet. "He has ears everywhere, but he forgets that we need to eat. An empty sack can't stand up," she said, an old Haitian expression about hunger. "But God," Madame raised her eyes, "never forgets us."

"And what about vodou?" I blurted. "Can't you use it to help the Malheureux?"

"If I use magic to help my people," Larian replied, "the town president would throw me in jail. Also, most of the *houngans* won't help the Malheureux because they can't afford to pay for magic. Strong magic costs money."

"That's an excuse," I mumbled under my breath.

Larian squatted nearer to me, "You see, the *mistès*, spirits, are in the air. They're everywhere. They talk to *Bondye*, God, for us. We have Papa Legba. He will help you with anything. We have Erzulie; and Damballa is always there to help people from this village."

Madame DeVrai nodded soberly in agreement, her burning pipe swaying like a great red eye in the dark room. The names were familiar to me. Since the time of slavery, Africans were killed or tortured, legs or hands cut off for practicing their religion. They shrewdly retained the African pantheon of the *mistès* or *loa* spirits by fusing them with the Catholic saints.

"Yes, always," she stated unequivocally. "We are still alive, but our crops don't grow. The *mistès* keep us alive. The big taste takes away so many people. When the big taste takes you, you get very sleepy. When our family doesn't eat, let's say for seven days, then we sleep every day. Sometimes I sit on the bench, but the rest of the village just sleeps. Even the market is silent. The big taste is forcing people now to sell their animals cheaply. Today I went to the market and sold Renaud's white chicken for two gourdes. Normally, it would be worth four." Larian shifted on her haunches, caressing her sleeping infant's face. "That's all the big taste."

"And has anyone from your family ever died from the big taste?"

"No, thank God, except my mother's little people who died before they had any personality. There's just no work and everything is so expensive. If you want some rice, a cup sells in the market for one gourd thirty. Now how are you going to feed your family with one cup of rice? Sometimes I grind it up and we eat it as flour, but it is the same thing, it just feels bigger in your stomach. So, everyone just stays inside when the big taste is grabbing people. We suck on rocks and don't feel it as much. Sometimes other countries send us food and we eat that, but you know the town council and the people in the capital eat most of that food."

Madame DeVrai picked up a burning ember and stood to relight her pipe, her prelude to speech. As she began to speak, her voice was louder and more determined than Larian's. "What Haitians do is walk all over this country looking for work. They search everywhere but there is no work. They cultivate their crops, but there is no harvest. Many Haitians sell their land, their corn, their millet and even a pig, and then go to Miami. That is the only way a Haitian can survive the big taste. They have to go to Miami. But Miami is dangerous. Sometimes they come back sick or with scars all over their bodies. Sometimes they get caught here before they leave and are locked up in prison where they are beaten every day. You know the house across the street from you?"

I nodded. It was the only cement house in the village.

"Well, that's Miami," she said. Miami, every time she uttered the word, I resisted looking at Larian. "That man went to Miami to earn money and came back to build his house. Before he left, he was a Malheureux. He lived in a hut like this and had to search all day for something to eat. Now he has a house."

"But we are afraid to go to Miami. If you are caught trying to go to Miami or Nassau, the police will beat you and put you in Fort Dimanche. I know a man who was put in there and he counted one person, two people, then up to a hundred people who died in his cell. Miami can be dangerous too. I know a woman who went to Miami looking for work. A man brought her to his house and said, 'Yes, I'll hire you for ten dollars a day.' She wanted to know what her job was, but he kept staring at her like a robber. She asked him again and he answered, 'Well, I promised my dog for his birthday that he could sleep with a Negress.' The woman cried, 'No! No!' but the man pulled out a gun and pointed it at her head, forcing her to do it right there. Bad things happen in Miami."

She shook her head sadly. "You know, the big taste can grab anyone, but we stay here in Haiti. *Depi tet ou pa koupe, ou espere mete chapo,*" she explained with another witty Haitian proverb; As long as your head isn't cut off, you can hope to wear a hat. "Yes, we aren't sick, and we aren't dead, so we are fine. That's how we the Malheureux think."

Mme De Vrais got up to go outside and talk to Candid.

Larian leaned over on the bench and said in a low indistinct voice, "My mother says bad things about Miami, but Miami is the only way Malheureux can have a life. I know it's dangerous, but I'm going. Miami is rich. I have to go. I am leaving Vivien here."

"Vivien..." I started, but Madame returned, smoking her pipe. We sat quietly, though my mind was churning. Was this a squabble between mother and daughter that would soon fade? Or was Larian serious? How could she be? Haitians were still leaving in the middle of the night on dilapidated boats to cross the seventy miles over to the States. But, as with any black market, the price was steep, and the danger even steeper. I could feel the hopelessness of her far-fetched dream.

We continued to sit silently until the night had fallen so, finally, I stepped out to leave. Madame stepped outside with me; her hand locked in mine.

"I'd better go," I began to offer in farewell.

"Aren't you afraid to walk alone at night?"

"No," I responded matter-of-factly. "When there's a full moon, it lights my path."

She stared, not saying anything but still holding my hand. She leaned forward and murmured in my ear, "You know what a full moon is?"

"Yes, a full moon," I repeated, unwilling to be warned again of spirits looming close by. "It will light my path."

"Yes, I'll see you tomorrow." We embraced.

I shuffled off toward the village, but soon Madame DeVrai was by my side, compelled to protect me from whatever a full moon brings, compelled to walk with me since my family wasn't nearby. "I'll walk our friend down," she said as we stumbled along the path arm in arm.

# Dreaming Miami

It was early afternoon when Anite and I walked toward the carpenter's workshop, dragging two chairs behind us for repairs. Anite was furious. Her boss, Samuel, the coordinator of the cottage industry workshops, had stopped to drop off a few supplies. This was a big moment in Mare Rouge: a vehicle entering the town, news from outside, and supplies. I thought she was angry because she had made a grandiose lunch for him and the driver—the regular wheat and beans but also potatoes, plus some kind of creamy dessert. But he didn't have time for a meal. No one wanted to get stuck out in Mare Rouge. But Anite, of course, thought they didn't like her food. But that wasn't why she stomped along beside me.

"Well," she huffed, indignant. "I'll tell you what happened. Remember a few weeks ago I went to the next town to catch a ride to Port-au-Prince? Well, the reason I didn't go to the capital is the man driving, Jean, was supposed to give me a ride. But his truck was full. But do you know what he did instead of stopping to inform me? He drove through town as fast as he could! That's no way to treat a friend. So, I asked him this morning, 'Why did you do that? Don't you have any manners?' 'Look,' he said, 'I'm not your servant.' 'Well,' I replied, 'I thought you were my friend and friends like to do small favors for each other. I thought you had more sense. You, my friend, are a man filled with complexes!' All he could do was repeat again that he wasn't my servant.

"I'm not like that with my friends, you know. I'm just the opposite—I'm servile with friends. It wouldn't bother me at all to wash someone's feet, I mean a friend's. I would wash his feet or walk kilometers to help him. I know I am Anite, and I'll never lose that. That's what's important, to give freely to others, but keep being yourself.

"You know, Blan, the same thing happens with administrators who oversee my work. They just refuse to treat me with respect. Samuel, the boss, was picked by Duvalier himself and what does he do all day? Nothing! Whenever I request something for a project he says, 'Oh, I don't know,' and leaves me stranded out here like an animal. It's not the people underneath who act that way, it's the bosses. They don't know what's going on, so they leave me running here and there to scavenge what I need. You can see the difference for yourself. If you asked for a vehicle, you would get one immediately. Have you worked here for five years? Of course not! But they would give you whatever you wanted, simply because of your white skin."

She probably thought I was scowling because of the injustice. But I had my own reasons to be mad. No one had bothered to get my mail. How could they forget? Didn't they understand where I was? No phone, no access to the world, to my world. I felt stranded and abandoned. Plus, Samuel made a comment I didn't like. I was wearing an old straw hat when he looked me over then declared sarcastically, "Now you really look like a missionary!" He laughed at me, then asked, "Anyway, what's a young woman like you doing here alone? What are you hiding from?" He was a White Haitian, a well-educated young man who spoke French to me. He stepped closer to me. And I resisted pushing him away. I didn't say anything and gave him some letters to mail.

I had heard that question before, and it was always asked by men. So, I had thought about it. Part of the insinuation was why wasn't I with a boyfriend or at least looking for one? I had already made that decision when I left the States. I was drawn to this adventure and wanted it to be me alone—a woman alone talking to other women—so I had said goodbye to my boyfriend, Mark.

Anite and I walked up the hill. She always held my hand when she walked with me and it comforted me. Our anger brought us together and soon started to subside under the trees near the carpenter's workbench. The four crooked chairs sat beside his workbench. When we pointed out that the backs of the chairs weren't sturdy enough to sit in, he teased me, "Well, in your land Blan, everything is already made, isn't it?" He set about fixing the chairs and entertained us with some folk stories. To my surprise, Miami had already entered the Haitian repertoire.

All the birds, he told us, were flying from Haiti to Miami. But Turtle could not go for he had no wings. Pigeon felt sorry for Turtle and said, "Turtle. I'll take you with me. This is what we'll do. I'll hold in my mouth one end of a piece of wood and you hold on to the other end. But you must not let go. No matter what happens, do not let go or you will fall into the water."

Pigeon took one end of a piece of wood and Turtle, the other end. Up into the air Pigeon flew and Turtle with him, across the land and toward the sea. As they came near the ocean, Turtle and Pigeon saw, on the shore, a group of animals that had gathered to wave goodbye to the birds who were leaving. They were waving steadily until they noticed Turtle and Pigeon. Turtle? They stopped waving and a great hubbub broke out.

"Look," they cried to each other, "the Turtle is going to Miami. Even Turtle is going to Miami!"

Turtle was so pleased to hear everyone talking about him that he called out the one English word he knew, Bye, bye! Oh, oh, Turtle opened his mouth and in opening his mouth to speak, he let go of the piece of wood and fell into the ocean.

Anite and I laughed at the story. It was filled with even more humor because it was told in Creole, a dynamic fusion of Spanish, English, and African languages. If the language itself isn't already vibrant enough, with a cacophony of Franco–African sounds, the Haitians imbued it with evocative proverbs like the carpenter's that often reflected his ironic humor, or the sharp perceptions of life and a daredevil, cocky sort of honesty about almost any subject. It was a kind of poetic defiance in the face of all the violence, corruption, and hunger in Haiti.

After all, as Madame DeVrai once told me, "With patience you'll see the ant's navel," meaning "Anything is possible!"

It was sayings like this that made me laugh and feel at home. I had felt it in the DeVrai family, with Anite and her students, and with Marie. The proverbs, the stories, the way Haitians laughed, the way they sauntered down the road, the way they were polite even if they were standing in front of you clad in the worst rags you had ever seen, the way they put body, mind, and soul into survival and whatever else they were doing ... well, despite all the poverty, sickness and general devastation, I was hooked from the get-go. To put it simply, I just liked being with these people. I am sure there's a Haitian proverb for that kind of connection.

※

In a dream I look up at the sky. It's the dead of night and as dark as can be. I panic. There I see in the dark night two moons. "That means I am going mad!" I scream.

A disembodied voice whispers, "Don't be afraid because there are two moons. Just take the beauty from each."

Then I see the *houngan* dressed in costumes from different eras and the voice says, "This is the *houngan* you knew during the French revolution. This is the *houngan* you knew during Egyptian times ..."

※

The dream rattled me all day until Larian and I went to the market. We sat in the marketplace, cross-legged, talking as people strolled by. A sweet melody of a flute floated out of a nearby hut. Larian told me the dream was the *lao* talking to me, but I felt it was all the destitution I had seen, seeping into me. I looked back on my life and knew I had seen destitution, but I was always sheltered by my family and our wealth. It was imaginary to me just as Miami and my life was almost a fantasy to the DeVrai family. I felt unnerved by the thought. I looked at Larian. She seemed tired but also seemed powerful, strengthened by this inner world she cultivated through vodou. Surrounded by her community and her rituals, Larian had a spiritual world she believed in and that she had earned.

Without the *loa*, Larian and her family had no control over their lives. There were no doctors or clinics to turn to, no way to avoid the endless exploitation. Vodou was community, faith and love for Larian; but it was also power.

Larian gazed at the woman squatting in front of a small pile of potatoes, then took a good look at me and made her final announcement, "Blan, I am leaving. I don't want to leave my Vivien, but I am leaving. I have to leave her with my mother. That is what I must do."

This was a different Larian speaking to me. A confident, assertive Larian—perhaps a young Madame DeVrai. I gazed at her, my head dense from all the market racket around me. I didn't respond this time, but my mouth felt dry just thinking of Vivien left behind, her life no more than endless days warding off the big taste. Larian believed this was how she would be able to finally buy Vivien clothes, notebooks, and schooling. I realized that Larian would leave, or at least attempt to. Or perhaps this was yet another story. There were so many stories I had heard about magic, departures, police, *houngans*.

Either way, I turned her decision over in my head. Did she really understand that if and and when she decided to leave, it was a permanent decision? There was almost no turning back. If she made it to the US, she would be obligated to work long hours to send money back to support her family and the extended family, probably about twenty-five people in all. If she left it meant that Vivien was vulnerable, without protection. And perhaps Larian wouldn't make it because she'd die if the boat capsized. Or if she were caught by immigration, sent back to Haiti, she would be raped, beaten, thrown in jail, an insufferable place where her family would be too far away in the mountains to visit or bring her fresh food. If she survived jail, perhaps she would return to her family, to the timelessness of her village. On the other hand, if she made it, the family would eat. It was as simple as that.

Larian must have read the worry in my face. As if to console me, she bent over, kissed my cheek, and took my hand. She wanted to bring me to a nearby cooking hut where her friends were preparing meals.

As we walked toward it, we came to a crowd gathered around a dilapidated hut. Madame DeVrai walked into the hut where a woman on a handmade stretcher was writhing in pain. It was Atilia, Madame's sister. I barely recognized her. A huge TB abscess gnawed at her cheek. Her toothpick legs were folded up to her hips as if she were giving birth, as though the blood flowing out of her vagina were life-giving instead of the opposite.

I didn't take a step closer. I wanted to feel compassion, but instead was overwhelmed by an intense hatred of Haiti and the brutal realities she thrust upon me. The dying woman jabbered unintelligibly toward the open door. Larian mumbled a prayer over her then turned back to me. "Her body is soft; that means she is going to die. People will cry for miles around."

"What's wrong with her, Larian?" I asked though I was fairly certain it was TB.

"She is dying."

"But from what? What disease is it?"

"She is going to die, that's all."

There was a finality in her words that stopped me from saying anything else about Atilia.

This was reality and this reality—the starvation, the *misère* as the Malheureux called it—was forcing me to see something and to make a decision. Do I stay here and devote myself to doing what I can to shift the world a bit from here, amid the flesh and bones left behind by those haunting ships loaded down with slaves crying out, still fueled by our aggressive capitalism? It baffled me and overwhelmed me. What could be done? The thought of it frightened me for it seemed to say: *abandon all you know and love for this, for something real.* A cruel thought emerged: wouldn't any outside assistance merely be moving the deck chairs around the Titanic? I shook off these thoughts.

Larian took my hand and guided me away from the crowd. She sensed my distress, but her gesture remolded my hostility toward this country and all its corruption into compassion for Atilia and her family. Haiti, such an incredible synthesis of extremes.

She led me to the cooking hut where the women were still sorting beans. Little girls, young women, old women, all crowded round the fires encircled by rocks. They squatted, helping to peel and cut vegetables, preparing for a *coumbite*, a work party, with more food available than I had ever seen in Haiti. One group of women peeled bananas in the shade of a huge avocado tree, surrounded by clusters of little people who dashed off periodically on mysterious missions. Immense cauldrons containing corn mush, kidney beans, squash, and rice simmered over the fires. Other pots were prepared for coffee and goat stew. Everyone, both young and old, smiled—for today they would eat.

The women chattered, weeping continuously from the acidic smoke. Their bare feet were stained red from the earth and their hands were so calloused they could smother fires, pick up burning charcoal, or move steaming cauldrons without a wince. Stirring the hot gruel with great wooden spoons, they laughed, spat, smoked their pipes. They bantered back and forth, teasing and bickering, sharing food, and serving each other coffee. Order and calm prevailed. Most of the faces I vaguely recognized.

Camille, a decrepit old lady, squatted down beside me, an unlit pipe dangling from her mouth. We had never met but something about her felt like I had always known her. She looked like the oldest person in the world.

"How old are you?" I asked, leaning toward her.

"I am fifty," she proudly declared.

The other women laughed as Larian slapped her knee. "You can't be fifty! You have grandchildren who are fifty!"

The ancient woman cackled. "Well, I guess I'm a hundred then."

The others shook their heads, amused.

✖

Walking past the fields to reach Larian's house, I could see people resting under the trees, their hoes deserted beside them, their voices mingling in that languid way people get when they are on break. Every now and then there was a burst of laughter. It reminded me of Guatemala, the reason I came here. But on one level there seemed to be nothing connecting these worlds. In Haiti there were no *traje*, no ancient ruins. There was only the solidarity of survival, of the commitment to remain human, to rise above it all. But even this I could barely understand.

When I entered the hut, Larian moaned, folding down the top of her dress. Her abscess had returned, a festering wound, a splotch of pus across her breast. The wound pulsated with each breath. Vivien hung on her knee.

"My baby," she murmured, looking down at the infant on her lap. Like Vivien, the baby was wheezing. "My baby is so skinny and weak. The milk comes but it is no good."

Vivien wailed. Larian wiped her baby's forehead, then leaned over to gently wipe Vivien's chin. "Bicare will be here soon to see his baby again. He will bring some milk."

"Vivien will be happy to see her father again!"

"No," she chuckled softly. "Bicare isn't Vivien's father."

"He isn't? Who is the father?"

"Marcel," was her curt reply.

"Marcel?"

"Yes."

"Which Marcel?"

"The carpenter," she told me.

"You mean the carpenter your brother works for?"

Larian nodded, brushing back Vivien's hair that was stuck to her cheek.

"He's much older than you." It felt like my voice had gone to a higher pitch, "And I have never seen him here with Vivien."

"No, he won't come here," she paused, "even though he's my uncle."

"Your uncle! Oh ..." I repeated, feeling myself becoming flushed. But the story only got worse.

"You see, I was alone one day while the rest of the family went to Libeau where our land is. Marcel walked right into this hut and put his hand over my mouth so I couldn't scream. He threw me on the ground and took me right there. I cried and cried after he left, but there was no one to hear. When my parents returned, I told them.

"My father said, 'Women are always looking for disorder!' I kept weeping until my mother took me aside. 'What do men know about these things?' she said. 'Nothing! Don't cry. God will care for you.'

"Marcel only spoke with me one time after that. I would have left my parents and gone to live with him, but he didn't love me. He just took me. Plus, he never gives me any food or clothes for Vivien. In fact, he has never even come to see her."

"Larian!" I exclaimed in horror as she stared off into space. "Larian, can't you report him to the police?"

"No," she sighed. "You see, lots of women report problems like this, but the police only say: 'Women always cause disorder.' Plus, Marcel is wealthy. He can pay the police, the Tonton Makoute. He can pay for magic against me. He can poison me with vodou."

"You must hate him or just hate men!" Now I hated every moment I had spent with him, flirted with him. Plus, we had actually paid him to repair the chairs, to build tables.

"No, I don't think about him, I just think about Bicare," she gently explained.

Nothing she was saying made sense to me anymore. I just couldn't imagine it. Couldn't know how she was really feeling or coping.

"Anyway, he's my uncle and I don't hate anyone. I just don't like him." Her tone and stature told me this subject was closed for now.

Suddenly I felt exhausted, as if her complacency had drained my energy. So many simple acts, so many acts that I took for granted, were impossible for her. Reporting a rape, taking a shower, having a steady income, reading a novel. I sat on the bench with Larian. I didn't say anything to her. I felt my body becoming more rigid. I wanted to do something. To call the police. To go beat up Marcel. To scream. But instead, I just sat there, watching her, her strong arms holding her baby.

"I don't think about the past," Larian continued. "What we Haitians say is, *Fe tan kite tan*, Leave time to time. Now I am alive, yesterday is gone and now I have Bicare. I met him at the market in Eaubonne, his village. I was sitting there when he came up and started talking with me. We talked every day for a few months and then he asked me to *placée* with him. We went over to his parents' house. They were gone but all the little people were there, so we had to scare them away. We took sticks and yelled at them. The little people always know what's going on and will try to steal from you whenever you lay with a man.

"Well, because of them it didn't take us long. I kept most of my clothes on. He kissed me on my head and my breasts and caressed my whole body until it gave me great pleasure. I have great pleasure with Bicare because most women are like me and want that pleasure. If a woman doesn't want pleasure, then she won't have it. But I have great pleasure. That's why I cry every time Bicare has to leave me. He is good to his child and I began to love him."

Vivien staggered past the doorway like a drunk and collapsed on a mound of dirt. She sat up and stared at her mother. "Just look at her, Clémence," Larian sighed. "It's so nice to be a little person."

"Nice?" I stammered, looking at Vivien.

"Yes, when I was a little person, I played games in the dirt too, just like these little people do. When you're a little person, you just want to sit in the dirt all day and play. When I was little, I loved water. We used to walk miles and miles just to take a bath. I really loved it, but when I would come home carrying my calabashes of water, my father would hit me. He hates laziness, you see. 'Look at you,' he would scream. 'You're sent for water, not to play around. You have work to do. I don't like lazy people.' But I always still took my bath when I went to carry water. I always took a bath because I loved water so much."

Vivien stared up at her mother.

"Everyone's your friend when you are little. You don't think evil of people. You just want to play with everyone. Then you start to grow up. I look at her now and think one day she will be a mademoiselle. Everything changed for me when that happened. I was here in my parents' house and saw blood in my pants. I didn't know what that sickness was, so I put some rags down there. My mother never told me about these things. But now I know when I am pregnant my blood stops until a month or two after the baby.

"I was scared when I first saw that blood and I am still afraid every month. That was around the time I started growing closer to girls. I saw that I could trust them more. They were more like me. I could have ten or fifteen girlfriends and we'd walk down the road together, laughing, holding hands.

"I can't do that with a man unless he's my brother or cousin. It's just different with men. They have their own lives. All my activities are now with other women. I don't know, maybe it's a custom of my country, but I'm closer to women like you. You're from another land, but I can talk to you and hold your hand. I can't do that with any man unless he's from my family."

But I hadn't seen her with any women friends. "Who are your close friends?" I asked.

Madame DeVrai walked in and squatted next to me. "Don't you have a cigarette, Blan?" she interrupted. I reached in my backpack and she laughed, ruffling my hair. "You Blan, always carrying things on your back!" They both chuckled at this peculiar habit.

"Deveronica is my friend," Larian resumed, "and so is another woman named Sissause, but she lives in Port-au-Prince now, working as a maid. I haven't seen her for a year, but I dream of her all the time."

"Just like we will dream about you when you leave," Madame DeVrai promised, leaning on my knee, staring at me with her wild eyes. "You have such pretty eyes and such a pretty nose."

"And so do you both," I answered sincerely. "Both of you are very beautiful."

"Ah no, Blan," Madame tells me. "You have such pretty eyes. I used to have dreams about a person like you. I would see her by the sea walking along the coast. Did you know there are people like you under the water?"

"Under the water?"

"Yes," she nodded gravely. "Especially under the sea. If they like you, they take you with them and you never have to worry again."

I laughed, then growled, grabbing at Madame DeVrai. "Just like I'm going to take you away with me!"

"But it's true," she said, laughing at me, leaning back on her haunches. "You have to go as far as Cuba or Nassau to see them. Sometimes fishermen catch them in their nets and bring them to the market to sell.

They have heads like people and bodies like fish. The fishermen cut off their heads and sell the bodies in the market."

"Oh, that's just fantasy we tell children," I answered, barely able to contain my smirk. Madame looked disappointed. "Have you seen these creatures?"

"No," she answered slowly. "I haven't. I have just heard about them at the market in Gonaives."

"Have you been to Gonaives?" Larian asked, then continued, "I went to Gonaives once and my mother has been there three times. You walk the whole way, with all your merchandise on your head, but it takes a very long time. You bring along potatoes, *mantioc* and a bottle of water. Then if you have an animal, you take that too. For three days and three nights you walk without sleeping. You feel very tired and want to sleep, but you can't unless you have an animal. Then you sleep on its back. When you finally arrive, your whole body feels stiff and sore. But I don't like to go to Gonaives because of the Mapou tree."

"The Mapou tree?" I had heard of these trees because Mapous or Ceiba trees are the largest species of tree that grows in Haiti; their roots and branches are considered homes for the spirits. People stuff offerings into *makouts*—straw bags—and hang them on the Mapous. The offerings are to Legba, Papa Legba as he is often called, the keeper of the crossroads who allows humans to communicate with other spirits. He is the first called down in the vodou ceremonies.

Larian continued, "The Mapou tree is a huge tree that fills up with water whenever it rains. It has a secret door and, if you fall through, you will drown. Or maybe you wouldn't, Blan, because you know the water, right?" I agree, telling her that yes, I do know how to swim.

She explained her own version of the Mapou tree. "The tree fills with water because one of its roots goes all the way down to the sea. That's why we're always so afraid when we walk to Gonaives. There is an evil spirit who lives in that tree, and he will grab you. So, if you walk to Gonaives, you should never rest or tire. Just walk straight into the town. It's a nice town. Have you ever been there?"

Gonaives was the ugliest town I had seen in Haiti—dusty, dilapidated buildings, skinny dogs sniffing the streets, open sewers covered in scum. Fortunately, my personal opinion wasn't pursued, because a young man entered the hut and quietly sat beside Larian. His freshly scrubbed slacks, white flowered shirt and new straw hat glowed next to her rags. He was followed by Candid, back from scraping the ground, gathering weeds for their pig.

"Clémence," Larian announced, "this is the father of my baby, Bicare."

We exchanged smiles, handshakes and idle chatter. "I work in our fields. Sometimes I help Larian with her family's field," he explained to me. "We go to Cadesse. It's a long way from here. I work hard for Larian," he continued, "and I miss her when I go back to my village, but we can't marry yet because I don't have my own house. I want to build a house alongside of my parents. But who knows, maybe next year? It takes money to get married."

Everyone chatted while he sat staring at me, scrutinizing me, evaluating me. Finally, he asked, "Would you take a baby from Larian if she gave it to you?" He was seriously studying my face.

"I can make one of my own," I told him frivolously.

"*Mezanmi*," Madame screeched, "you hear the Blan! She can make her own!" Even Larian joined in the fun teasing me. I had never seen Candid laugh so much. But Bicare remained watchful.

"You don't want to become a *vyèy fi*, a spinster, do you?" Madame retorted, feigning deep concern.

"Oh, no," I mocked, unable to contain my laughter.

"If you stay faithful and remain virgin, you will become a *veyèy fi*," she warned me.

"But, Miss," the young man asserted, "you may be able to make your own babies, but you will never make a Haitian baby."

"That's right."

"And do you have husband?"

"No, I am *placée*."

"Oh!" he exclaimed, somewhat taken aback. "But look at you here in another country. You know that men like to chase skirts and yours will certainly leave you."

The whole family was in the hut with Bicare, only Larian's brother crouched outside, entertaining Vivien. Slowly the hut grew darker as the sun sank below the horizon.

※

I returned home to sit at my small wooden table by the window. Marie sat across from me, sewing. As time went on in Mare Rouge, I seemed progressively more fanatical about writing down every smell, word, and sound. It was a strange codependent relationship. I was here to write this story yet, in a sense, the story was writing me. Everything that I couldn't get from the world around me the notebooks gave to me. I connected with the women, but in a way that felt like I was on an island with the great sea of humanity swirling around me, tossing me about at times. The notebooks were my anchor.

When I traveled, I wrapped the notebooks carefully in plastic bags, another luxury item. They went in the middle drawer of my red pack where I felt they were safe, guarded on both sides by underwear, blue jeans and toiletries. Like my passport, I always knew where they were stashed. In this, my father raised us well. A US passport is valued around the world. Never lose it. Never let it be stolen. It was a religion in our family. The notebooks, like my passport, were my ever-present emblem of freedom.

But this day, the notebooks didn't work their magic. I couldn't fathom what I had heard from Larian, what I was seeing. I felt crushed and stiff inside like something had locked up within me. I needed to get away from the dust, the heat, the *grangou* and, most of all, from my helplessness. In my dreams I was Black and standing by a river, staring. I could see little hands, feet, sometimes a head popping up and down as the river's current pulled the bodies downstream. I had the urge to fly but I could feel my feet turning to rock.

There was only one place I knew to go to truly get away from the *grangou*. And that was Rebecca's house. The idea that I could escape so easily back to my almost painless life gave me such a sense of relief that for a moment it covered my shame.

# Port-au-Prince

To get to Port-au-Prince, I had to walk about two hours on a rutty dirt road. I had a day backpack with my notebooks and a few clothes. Little groups of *marchandes* passed me, nodding and crossing themselves in the belief that I was a nun, the only Whites they ever saw in this area. By the time I reached the town, I was covered in dust and sweat, but the dust was just another layer over my mottled skin.

The only way to Port-au-Prince from this town was in a tap tap, a large truck with benches in rows across the truck bed. If you were lucky, the tap tap would have a canvas roof to protect you from the boiling sun. All the tap taps were hand-painted with intricate, colorful images of religious figures, scantily dressed girls, and even Che Guevara. Epitaphs, usually religious ones, were painted across all of them. The front of the Port-au-Prince tap tap had *The Throne of God* painted in bold red and yellow letters. On the back it said *In Memory of My Brother* on a light blue arc. Various versions of Jesus and Mary appeared on the truck's sides and inside across the dashboard. Bags of charcoal were stacked on the roof, and a peasant sat on top of the bags, a goat tied up by his side.

The driver seemed to pity me or perhaps he was merely conceding to the Blan, but he let me on first. I knew it would be a long, bumpy ride so I sat at the far end of one of the hard benches so I could lean on the sideboard. It wasn't long before I was smashed up against the truck wall, a chicken at my feet, two filthy children in rags standing staring at me, their tiny hands on their mother's knees that were so chapped they were shiny. She had no shoes and her feet looked like claws, toes turning over at the edges with long yellowing nails. There were already ten people squashed onto the bench that would normally hold about seven. But a tap tap won't leave until it is filled with customers. Of course, the driver's notion of "filled" and mine were two separate things.

Suddenly, there was jostling on the front bench. People standing up, moving around, some jumping off. I didn't pay much attention because yelling and chaos were part of normality here. People scrambled, making way for three Tonton Makoute. They climbed on board and sat down in unison on the front bench, sending a woman and two children to the back of the tap tap. The Tontons sent alarm into the air. Before I left for Haiti, my father had warned me about them—Duvalier's army of terror. And they were everywhere: dressed in blue jean jackets and dark sunglasses, guns dangling from their hips or slung over their shoulders, their expressions impenetrable, hidden by the shades and their calm indifference. Dedicated to Duvalier, they would do anything to terrorize in the name of fighting communism.

It was in this very town that, a few years later, one of the many massacres by Tontons occurred. Peasants like Candid had organized land reform actions and were ambushed and macheted to death by Tontons. Around 1,000 people died and the peasants' bodies were hacked so badly that you couldn't even identify the body parts. The Tontons left the hacked body parts along the mountain trails or threw them into the deep ravines that surrounded the town.

The Tontons sat upfront, one of them smoking, another one with his hands folded in front of him as if in prayer. The tap tap pulled out, spraying bystanders with dust, and I leaned against the truck wall, settling back for the ride. Even though I was running away from Larian's world, a part of me felt at ease with the danger and the chaos. I had been exposed to so many different worlds as a child. One thing that gave me confidence was my upbringing. Maybe in a sense my parents had been neglectful, but they were always confident that I could cope with any circumstances, even when I was young.

※

My first school was an Arab–French school in Morocco during its brief revolution against the French, the Arabs fighting to regain sovereignty of their homeland. Every morning I ran out of our house to catch the school bus to first grade. However, at one point, instead of a school bus, a truck sat waiting for my sister and me. Its motor churned while young French soldiers armed with M16s sat waiting for us. Even though it was a nearly bloodless revolution, the French government felt my sister and I needed protection.

*"Bonjour sallops!"* I would cry out then race behind my sister, a string of curse words following behind me. Young French soldiers would lean out of the truck laughing, only to incite another string of obscenities from me as I climbed onboard. And off we went to school.

This scenario was so normal that the only reason I remember this strange entrée into academia is that years later I'd hear my father, over a scotch and water, laugh and brag to his friends, "… and these French soldiers taught her French so that by age six she knew enough French obscenities to fill a small dictionary!"

But my learning didn't stop at school. In every country, mentors appeared to help me adjust to the new situation. When we moved into our big white house in Morocco, Mohammed and Maloda lived in the house, Mohammed in his *jalava* and a burgundy cap, Maloda with a white veil across her face and light blue long robes just like the Virgin Mary. We heard the grownups say they "just came with the house," but we kids saw something else.

We learned quickly that being with Mohammed and Maloda was far more interesting than my parents' cocktail parties or even my dollhouse set on our back porch. They kept animals in our tiny backyard, chickens, a donkey, and a sheep. Every morning they'd fuss over those animals, stroking them, inspecting their water dishes and studiously measuring their portions of food. Now I know those animals probably represented a little extra income, but back then we figured they were just like us: they simply loved animals.

Maloda and Mohammed were married, and their wedding was my initiation into how to politely eat unfamiliar foods such as "the sweat soup" the Haitians later fed me. When we were invited to Mohammed and Maloda's wedding, my father warned all of us kids: If they give you anything strange to eat, you smile, hold your breath and swallow. So, taken as I was by Mohammed and Maloda, when I was offered a sheep's eyeball, it slid down my throat like water.

At home, Maloda fed, clothed, washed, and sang to all of us in Arabic and French. I would go to her house, a garage, where we'd eat warm couscous followed by a sticky treat dripping in honey. Early in the morning, she and Mohammed prayed, responding to the eerie calls of the minarets.

Some of these little chants drifted through my head as the tap tap jostled down the road to Port-au-Prince. I thought of the places where we lived, the men and women along the way who had fed me, clothed me, brought me to markets. Entertained me with songs and dance, showed me how to care for chickens, donkeys and dogs. Spoken to me in their language and lovingly pretended to understand mine until I mastered enough of theirs. I could feel some of that same lovingness in the people of Mare Rouge and some of the deprivation that fed the revolution I experienced as a child. I bumped along in the tap tap exhausted, fed up and frustrated; but my parents' love of adventure and the memory of my past guardians gave me the gumption to keep looking.

※

A marine was sitting behind the counter at the US Embassy in Port-au-Prince. His face was so clean that his cheeks looked like polished, chiseled marble. He wore his United States Marine Corps cap, a long-sleeved khaki shirt with a badge, and dark-blue pants with a red stripe running up the leg, everything cleaned and pressed. He stared out, his blue eyes peering through wire-rim glasses that tapped against the cap's black visor. Above the visor, against the cap's white material, was a gold braided marine insignia. The marine sat tall and straight between two flags, the US flag on one side and on the other, the Haitian flag with the inscription *L'Union C'est la Force*—Unity is Strength—and its insignia of palm trees, cannons, and drums. A royal palm grew in a huge ceramic pot beside the flag. The room felt so cool and clean that even the air felt like I was back home in the States. When the marine nodded and relaxed enough to smile at me, I was surprised. Embassy soldiers don't smile. Yet later, when I saw myself in the mirror, I surmised he was actually trying to suppress a laugh: I looked like a scrawny hobo.

But he smiled and I was grateful. Suddenly, I had stepped into a world where water was readily available, and people took showers and ate pizzas while they watched TV. Where people spoke English and probably smoked Salems when it was hot outside. It was a safe, quiet, and predictable world. The soldier handed me my mail, letters from my parents, a couple of close girlfriends, and one that had an Australian stamp on it.

Instead of happiness, I immediately felt downcast. I knew what that stamp meant. My boyfriend had given up on me and gone home to Australia. I had that sinking feeling you get when you know you made the wrong choice, that you had lost something precious. But I couldn't bear to read the words, so I put it out of sight to be dealt with later, if ever. Instead, I ripped open my mother's letter and read it until I could almost see the golf course, my mother's friends laughing over gin and tonics. And though not much about my brothers and older sister, there was the image of my younger sister, a pencil stuck behind her ear, studying for grad school, her body, tanned, lean, and healthy, her debutante dress hanging neatly in the closet ready for the Très Bien Ball in a few weeks.

Those images traveled with me as my taxi zipped through the city. There was a stench of open sewers and even through the taxi window the city tumult was almost deafening.

The taxi inched its way above the clamor to the city's hillsides where the Haitian elite resided. It charged past the Oloffson Hotel where, they claim, Graham Greene once sulked in the bar's dark corners over gin and tonics. The taxi climbed into a world of flowering gardens and gingerbread houses where Haitians and expats mingled. These were Haitians who, despite their fierce pride in Haiti as the first independent nation of the New World, spoke only French, smoked Gauloises, and drove Renaults.

✳

When Rebecca opened the door of her home, she didn't even blink seeing me standing there. She just peered at me through those green-rimmed glasses. Nothing could ever really surprise Rebecca. Both her parents were doctors and she had been raised in Southeast Asia among a sea of people visiting their home and she, too, had lived through her own tight spots in revolutions and wars. No, nothing surprised her and especially not me at her door. She just chuckled and said, "You're back!" like I had been out to the grocery store.

You could tell she was used to ragged waifs materializing without notice because she led me straight down the hallway to the living room. Her small hands worked quickly, dipping into the ice bucket, the ice clinking into the glass and then the whiskey, which I swallowed in one shot.

The beauty of her home calmed me. There were large picture windows that looked out over the garden and onto the city. To the left of the garden was a pool filled with water that reflected the moon and city lights. There was order in the sleek clean floors, the dining table set with flowers and fresh bread, salted butter, and a bowl of fresh fruit. Fresh fruit! Most delicious of all, later, the shower, the hot water, and the mirror seemed to bring my disjointed parts back together again.

Rebecca was a beautiful poet. We sat in the garden until late at night, drinking wine as she read her poetry about the Mekong River. My spirit felt at rest. A softness was filling up in me again. There wasn't just a blazing sun but shadows and light interplaying.

✕

Rebecca's friends invited us to their yacht. It was a sunny day. About eight of us were on the boat where glasses clinked, champagne flowed. Fresh shrimp with sprigs of parsley and platters of an assortment of cheeses were set out for us. People splashed in and out of the aqua blue waters beside the boat, then couples leaned on each other drying off in the gentle tropical wind.

The conversations were quick and especially witty in English or French after I had been stumbling along in Creole. French stimulated a dormant side of me. Suddenly I could critique the latest book I had read: *The Life of Chopin*. And I was free to drink, tell jokes; better yet, in English, my natural sarcasm emerged. Here was a place I could speak about literature and politics again. This was my world. I loved parties and entertaining people with stories, especially funny stories.

Pierre stood beside me. He was small, in fact shorter than me, and spindly and smart. He was a doctor and had worked in the rural countryside so I knew he could appreciate village stories. I wanted to talk about Mare Rouge, but not the truth of it because I wanted to be unchanged by it, to remain the party entertainer, the flirtatious girl I had always been. I spoke rapidly, trying to stuff it down, but it sat there inside of me, a sort of beast ready to jump out at someone. I tried to make him laugh by telling him about the village prostitute selling Anite and me a table for the workshop. We bought the table, dragged it to the workshop, when out of nowhere a man came pounding in, yelling at us. The woman had sold us his table. Oh dear. Pierre laughed at my story and I could see he liked me. He was the type of man who could appreciate a woman working in rural Haiti.

His interest encouraged me. I searched for another funny day out in rural Haiti. "Well, one day," I told him, "I was standing in front of a hut with Anite. There was a wedding celebration. A pudgy man with sunglasses on walked up and literally threw me over his shoulder and carried me into the hut. He put me down on a chair and told me, 'You are going to Môle with me to a fete, a party.'" As I told the story to Pierre, I mimicked the man throwing me down on a chair. Then I imitated my refusal, by sarcastically telling the man, "I don't go anywhere with a fat potato." Anite and I had laughed about this response for days, but Pierre's demeanor changed. He didn't seem to think it was funny at all.

"You are lucky you aren't Haitian," he told me. "The man could have taken you. It sounds like he was a Tonton." His response made me think I was starting not to like Pierre after all, that he knew my secret—what I had been living—and I no longer wanted to talk about it. And maybe he sensed that because he leaned back on the rail beside me and spoke about it, but in the bigger picture.

"Just think about my country," he said earnestly. He had dark eyes and very long lashes, and as he spoke, he blinked a lot as if he, too, were trying not to remember something. Instead, he brought me to a larger plane, a plane where I could see the horizon, gain a perspective. "No one would trade with us for a hundred years after we won the revolution against the French. They were afraid of us, of savages! But like the French we replaced our Black leaders with mulattos who ran the government and the army until 1957 when the very black Duvalier rose to power. The mulatto government officials, and even the US, helped Duvalier rise to power because they thought they could control him as he was just a mere country doctor. But no one could control Duvalier. No one!" Silently he poured us more champagne. "Francois Duvalier, Papa Doc, took over the country. The way he did this was by forming the Tonton Makoute."

"You have to understand," Pierre continued, "Papa Doc always admired the Nazis. Everyone, including your government, knew that about him. So, he modeled the Tontons after them, creating these militias to make sure he remained as president for life." Pierre paused, looking at me, assessing whether he still held my interest. And he did. Like Rebecca, he was a good teacher. "At first," he said, "Tontons were called Cagoulards after a French fascist group, mainly funded by L'Oreal cosmetics, and who also used to wear black executioner-type hoods over their faces as they maimed, murdered, and bombed enemies—in this case anyone perceived as Duvalier's enemy. Duvalier first recruited Makoute from the bourgeoisie then later powerful vodou *houngans*, priests from the slums and the countryside. Do you know what Tonton Makoute means?" he stopped to ask me.

I knew that Tonton meant uncle, but nothing else. So, Pierre went on to explain, "The name Tonton Makoute comes from a children's tale. It's about a man who at night sneaks in and grabs naughty children and stuffs them in his straw bag, his *makoute*." He explained that many of the Makoute were also vodou priests. Most of the Tontors I had seen wore blue jeans, denim hats and sometimes sunglasses and red bandanas, but I didn't know that those clothes could also represent the agricultural god, Cousin Zaka. Even in the uniform, fear and faith mingled treacherously together.

Pierre signaled me to follow him to the bow of the boat where we could sit in the sun, sipping another glass of champagne and speaking about the Duvaliers without being heard by the others. Although Papa Doc was no longer alive and had been replaced by his son Baby Doc, Jean Claude, people were still afraid to speak freely.

"Duvalier murdered countless enemies. He closed the military academy then built up the Makoute until it was bigger than the army, so he controlled the army as well as the entire country. From that point on, Duvalier alone was the elite, or as he put it in 1964: 'I shall be Lord and Master.' He even rewrote the Lord's Prayer."

I thought I misunderstood Pierre. "Rewrote the Lord's Prayer? What prayer?"

"Yes, the Lord's Prayer, the one we all know. You know, Our Father who art in heaven. He rewrote it."

The notion was ridiculous to me. Maybe Pierre had had too much champagne at this point.

"Yes, it's hard to believe." He was squinting into the sun, so he moved beside me but continued speaking. "But it's true. In 1964, Dr Duvalier issued the Catechism of the Revolution, which included his version of the Lord's Prayer." Pierre folded his hands in prayer, tilted his head and, like an altar boy, recited Papa Doc's prayer:

"Our Doc, who art in the National Palace for life, hallowed be thy name by present and future generations. Thy will be done in Port-au-Prince and in the countryside. Give us this day our new Haiti, and never forgive the trespasses of those traitors who spy on our country each day. Lead them into temptation and poisoned by their own venom, deliver them from no evil."

"Oh my God! And what did the church have to say about that?"

"Well, eventually the church excommunicated Duvalier. They also didn't like his promotion of Haitian vodou. Like one time he even spoke from his balcony dressed like Baron Samedi, a Haitian spirit who wears a black suit and a black hat. He told the crowd that he was 'the personification of the Haitian fatherland.'"

"Well, he's dead now," I said glumly, as if that mattered. In fact, the champagne was taking its toll on me and I wanted to get back to the party.

"Yes, Papa Doc is dead, but the Makoute is still strong and Jean Claude, his son, is now president for life. He used to be called Baskethead by his schoolmates and with good reason." Pierre rolled his eyes. "In fact, he's so thick we wonder who is really running the government. Is it the Makoute or the US government leading Duvalier? Or could it be Baskethead himself?"

It wasn't until later that I learned who was really in charge. But that day, I had enough of Pierre and his explanations. I didn't want to think what could have happened with Fat Potato or what I knew happened to Larian. His words were making me feel edgy, whereas the sun and the champagne had eased me back into this world where I could at least imagine that Tontons, *loa*, and *grangou* were all made of mythological fabric. I needed to plunge into the fresh, crisp ocean water, to clear my head of Haiti, then to feel the sun drying my skin. Pierre dove in right behind me.

✳

I didn't go out much with Rebecca's friends again. At Rebecca's house I could be alone. After Mare Rouge I recognized that solitude was a privilege of the wealthy, a privilege I now relished. I would sit on the balcony and stare at the pool, refreshed after a plunge. I didn't want to go out to the nearby streets lined with gardens overflowing with flowers and the well-built houses, streets that led eventually to rutted roads and teems of skinny, hungry children. I walked around and around the pool. In the distance I could hear voices, dogs, and sometimes children's laughter. The sun blazed down on me as I walked then sat, sometimes reading under a well-placed umbrella.

The first day that I didn't leave the house with Rebecca, the maid came out to see me. She was concerned I was sitting there alone. I had just read Mark's letter and I must have looked sad, as my fears were confirmed. It was only a short note telling me he was going home and to "remember yourself." I was thinking about his cryptic message when she asked me, "Would you like some lemonade?" Her brow furrowed.

"No. Thank you."

But like Marie, she decided what I needed and brought me the juice anyway. I put away the letter and sipped while reading a book. I had chosen Isabel Allende's books because in them I was always certain everything would come out right; and Tony Hillerman because his characters all had fine values and he'd bring me to a world I loved, the Navajo reservations set in the stunning New Mexican desert.

When I tired of reading, I would walk and walk in Rebecca's garden. I kept walking and thought about my life. It all seemed almost fantasy compared to the DeVrai family. I could see my parents' home in the US and my boyfriend and me sitting in a café talking. Images came to me, then floated away from me. But one thing became clearer. I knew I had to go back to Mare Rouge.

✶

In the evenings when Rebecca returned from work, we ate fresh fish, homemade soups and all types of salads served by the glistening aqua blue swimming pool. Her brother was visiting. A strong, stout young man, his quick wit and intelligence reminded me of men I knew in Washington DC. He had a reassuring presence. The three of us had long political discussions, sipping on our glasses of red wine. Sometimes Pierre joined us. That's when they explained more of the Duvalier background to me.

Jean Claude was only nineteen when his father died, and he inherited the presidency for life. But he was playboy stock rather than president material and he feared the position would interfere with his shenanigans, so he offered the presidency to his sister. She turned it down and instead his mother and advisers ran the show. Later, Jean Claude married Michele Bennett, a beautiful girl from a struggling mulatto family. As soon as they married, her father's coffee-trading business took off. He acquired Air Haiti, the national airline, and the Hertz car rental concession in Port-au-Prince. Her brother and other male relatives ensured more family wealth by getting into the drug business. Her brother was eventually arrested in Puerto Rico and later convicted of cocaine trafficking.

Michele threw herself into her life of glamour and wealth, spending millions on her wedding, various homes, cocaine abuse, interior decorating, million-dollar shopping trips to Paris and New York. No one complained publicly because the Makoute threw outspoken journalists are thrown in jail, others left to rot in prison.

I had already witnessed this silence in rural areas like Mare Rouge where, if the Makoute raped your daughter or stole your land or demanded money, no one spoke out. In fact, instead of complaints, I heard compliments. But why, I wondered, was the US, a democracy that upheld human rights, putting up with this corruption? We were a country that helped other countries. I had seen with my own eyes, roads, schools, and medical clinics the US set up in devastated countries. Through the United Nations, the US also helped countries with food and medical assistance all over the world, including Haiti. Why support someone like Duvalier, a merciless killer and thief?

It was simple, Rebecca explained, pushing her green glasses back on her nose. The US wanted Haiti to be a dependent, economic colony. Haiti would produce coffee, fruit, and processed food at cheap prices to export to the US. The Haitians were also a potential cheap workforce. Later in the US, I worked with farmworkers and witnessed our fields and factories being run by undocumented workers, many of them Haitians who had fled Duvalier's iron fist. Even our charity in Haiti was a covert backbone for US industries. US-donated food supplies flooded the local markets so Haitian peasants could no longer live off their tiny farms and were being forced to flee to Port-au-Prince or Miami for work. They could make money by assembling goods like tomato paste and baseballs for export to the US, profiting from the cheap labor, proximity to the US and lax regulations. Haiti was even advised by the World Bank to cut down on social and health programs and use money saved to build up infrastructure so export businesses could operate efficiently.

I wondered what social and health programs they were referring to. I hadn't seen any. Policies like that, it seemed, were already successfully in place.

# Return

By the end of the week, I was rested and ready to head back to Mare Rouge. I wanted to help Anite finish setting up the workshop. And there was a pull toward the DeVrai family. Rebecca once again organized transport for me and left me at a CARE truck where I squashed in the front seat with a man from the States on his way to see his missionary brother. This driver had actual keys but when he turned on the truck, a cloud of black smoke and gas fumes billowed into our cabin. It was sticky hot and sweat glued my arm to the man.

When we stopped midway in Gonaives, we saw beggars and Malheureux everywhere. Young kids tugged at my shirt. They looked like they were starving; their skin shiny as if a thin sealant was lacquered over their bodies; their black hair had that rust-red color. It was dusty, scorching hot and I couldn't stand the sight of these children or bear their tugging at me. I was callous and tried to slap away their hands or yelled at them.

But the American man wasn't so thick-skinned. He worked in advertising and when we got back in the truck, he started weeping. His body racked in sobs as he asked me over and over, "What is my life worth? What am I doing with my life?" He was older than me. I tried to look away, give him privacy by looking out the window. "What am I doing advertising vacuum cleaners, cars, and RVs? What is that worth when you look at this? When you see the spectrum of things? What am I doing?"

I was ashamed of his indulgence. In this world there was no time for hopelessness. Families like the DeVrais faced *grangou* straight on. They worked hard, prayed, joked around. They cared for their family and God and worked ceaselessly. They put one foot in front of the other.

The truck made a lot of stops, so I didn't make it to Mare Rouge that day. Instead, I slept in Jean Rabel that night and in the morning started my long walk back to Mare Rouge. It was early dawn and slowly the sun illuminated the countryside, first bathing it in a splendor of soft colors, then revealing its true character in craggy rocks, dead trees, and endless eroded land. I walked through it and thought about the world inside Larian's hut and Larian doing the unthinkable: contemplating leaving her baby behind so she could make money in the United States. Willing to take the risk of the treacherous ocean, or of capture and the notorious prison, Fort Dimanche, where rape and probably starvation awaited her.

When I finally got to Mare Rouge, I walked past the market with rows of *marchandes* and their mounds of wheat, a few eggs and vegetables, and small bundles of raw tobacco. The women sat straight, stiff-backed, lording over their wares, their dresses tucked between their legs, leaning over, sucking on their wooden pipes stuffed with green tobacco. Its strong, piquant aroma filled the air. Their bearing was determined and cocky, an attitude that I loved.

Someone laughed in the distance. The dirt, the earthiness of the huts, the way the Haitians laughed so boldly and loudly came back to me. The laugh is so loud that the sound grips you and grabs you, so even if I didn't understand the joke—although it usually referred to sex or some wry political twist—I laughed, oftentimes hard and long. An arm would flop over the shoulders or a hand would hit my thigh while someone screeched, laughing, *"Mezanmi!"* And if you were the one saying the joke, you felt like you had pronounced the funniest thing ever said.

✳

After my return from Port-au-Prince, I spent many hours in the hut smoking and talking with Madame DeVrai. Larian, she told me, was in Bicare's village. Who really knew where Larian was?

One morning as I approached the DeVrai's hut a great excitement was stirring among the Malheureux. There was shouting, handclapping, chickens skittering erratically between scorched palm trees. Clusters of people were leaving the village.

"Clémence, Clémence," Madame DeVrai yelled, running toward me as I approached the hut. She was waving her arms in the air. "They are fishing in the pond. Do you want to come?" She explained that the pond was two hours away, but she wanted to go because broth made from the eels could help her sick sister, Atilia. I was grateful for the opportunity to hike. Plus, I knew that soon I would be leaving the village for Guatemala and relished any excursion with Madame DeVrai. Madame took my hand and yanked me toward her, the warmth of her skin fusing to my own.

We began to work our way through the village, crossing the vacant lot that served as the market, and entered the vast array of dusty paths.

It was silent, an eerie silence because of the absence of birds or animals.

Madame DeVrai followed an obscure route, nimbly overcoming rocks and crevices in our path. Her feet instinctively found the perfect niche while I tried to keep up with her brisk stride. Haitians in the Northwest walk everywhere, no matter how many pounds of merchandise on their heads, and always move at a swift clip.

Madame pointed out the remote huts of her relatives. Mothers stood immobile at hut doors. Children sat beside them, just staring out into space. The big taste. Yet, even in these obscure corners of this inferno, the Haitian proverb endorsing politeness, *Bonjou' se paspo ou*, Good morning is your passport, held true. All the Haitians we passed greeted us in the traditional, courteous fashion, offering us a place to rest, a bit of water, or a blessing to protect our journey, ever faithful to their value of politesse.

Madame DeVrai was proud that she was repeatedly hailed. "You see, Blan, my family is very large. Anywhere I go, I have family, so I never worry about a place to sleep."

Over jagged boulders and ancient riverbeds until I began to falter from over-exertion. We suddenly came to a hidden canyon. She halted at the edge to casually light her pipe, her face vacant.

Below us were rows of tomatoes, eggplants, carrots, cabbage, lush coconut palms. Much of the bountiful tomato crop had fallen to the ground to rot. My God! Utter desolation for miles around and here, over the ridge, lies the Garden of Eden. Madame DeVrai seemed unmoved. She wordlessly absorbed the scene, then leaped forward down the path.

"Who owns all this?" I demanded in pursuit of her descending figure.

"Jean Antoine," she stated without turning around. "It's Jean Antoine's. He has the water, and no one can use it."

"Why, you can't even get this kind of food in the market!" I was astounded.

"It's Jean Antione's. He eats it. He sells it in Port-au-Prince. It's Jean Antoine's."

We hopped onto the canyon floor. Defeated by her statements, I was quiet as we strolled between the rows of succulent vegetables. "Well, at least why don't you take some tomatoes off the ground for your family?"

"They aren't mine," she said and turned away, abruptly trotting off across the field as though some demon was snapping at her feet. I followed, cursing her stubbornness and fear. Why couldn't she at least take some tomatoes left to rot on the ground? Then I remembered the fatal vision cupped in the sunglassed eyes of the Tonton Makoute.

But my thoughts were interrupted by the appearance of a cement house surrounded by chickens, goats, and pigs. Outside sat a solitary man in a torn blue sweater. His face was pockmarked, pouches under his eyes. Like so many Haitians, he moved with a graceful confidence to greet me. Despite his clothing, he didn't seem to be a Malheureux. My suspicions were confirmed when he greeted me in French, then ordered me to sit in the chair beside him. Without a word, Madame DeVrai squatted on the ground, then onto a ragged mat.

He kept speaking French then reverted to Creole so Madame could understand, "You know, I own all the land in the village."

I glanced at Madame DeVrai who stared back at me, drawing deeply on her pipe. "It's true," she said. "He owns all the land. He even owns the houses." I wasn't sure why she had brought me here.

"You know the house where you live," he said, "That's mine and I own all the neighboring land where there are gardens. I was the one who constructed the few irrigation canals that are still there. I was the town president for ten years. It was Duvalier himself who appointed me." He continued to brag. "I struggled hard for that village. I have retired to enjoy the quiet life, but I still work in Port-au-Prince to support my children. Three children go to school in Port-au-Prince. My other two are in Switzerland and Paris. Anything you see of value belongs to me."

Sitting there, next to Madame DeVrai on the mat, I remembered Anite talking about this man and I was aware of his relationship to the Tonton Makoute, his power over many *houngans*, and most of all, the dangerous and absolute authority he wielded.

"And how did you become such a success?" I asked.

"I worked very hard, and all my family worked very hard."

"You must have been rich already," I said. "In Haiti, the Malheureux work but don't seem allowed to advance."

"They don't advance because they are too lazy. They don't want to work. And they just don't have the heads to work day after day. They work, then spend all their money. Just like ti mouin, like little people. They don't know how to save. They need to learn this. If they could learn to save and to work hard, they would progress as well.

"You see," he continued, "our problem in Haiti is we don't have enough industry. We need investment capital to create it. We need more money, more aid from your country." He leaned toward me, scrutinizing my face, then furtively glancing at my breasts. "We need people like you to write articles, so our country can receive more assistance. I, myself, give to charity, but we need more substantial assistance. People like you could publicize our plight."

"But whenever anyone dares to write about Haiti, they're killed or exiled like Pere Antoine. He worked here for twenty years and was expelled for a few words."

Jean Antoine's eyes narrowed. "And do you know what the first sentence of his book was? 'When I got off the boat in Haiti, the smell of shit hit me in the face.' Excuse the language," he said in flawless French, elevating our conversation beyond Madame DeVrai—out of her provincial Creole world and into the sophisticated realm of Port-au-Prince.

"In that single sentence he totally discredited Haiti. It was an unforgivable offense. We do have problems, but no foreigner is qualified to judge our country. Maybe you in the US can accept such an insult, but we can't. We are small and still quite young. Calling our country a pile of shit hurts too much." Jean Antoine fidgeted on the edge of his chair. Madame DeVrai gazed straight ahead, elbows resting on her knees as she puffed on her pipe.

"And do you know what else he said? He called us a nation of beggars. Now, what do you think of that?"

"From what I see ..."

"Well, I'll tell you. Haiti has its Malheureux, but we are not a nation of beggars. At the very most, twenty percent of our people beg and live in misery. The rest are middle class."

"Middle class?" I was stupefied. "What is the middle class to you?"

"Why, people like me," he answered simply.

"But everywhere I go people are hungry ..."

"Oh no," he assured me. "Have you seen Cap Haitian? Lambi? In Port-au-Prince there is the Oloffson, the Habitation Leclerc."

"But those are resorts for the wealthy of your country and mine!"

"No, it's only a handful of towns where you see beggars. The rest of the people live well. Anyway," he said, chuckling under his breath, "I can see that like so many young women, your opinions are philosophical rather than analytical. What is a pretty young woman like you doing out here all alone?"

"Just looking, Monsieur," I extended my hand. "We have to keep going, Monsieur. It was nice meeting you." Madame DeVrai stood up immediately in response to my cue.

"Why don't you stay longer so we can talk some more?" he suggested, edging closer to me.

"No, no thank you. We have to go."

"Go? Go where?" he asked, still holding my hand, drawing so close I could smell cigarette smoke.

"Over those mountains. Madame is showing me the countryside," I answered firmly, unsure of whether Jean Antoine should know our destination. Between vodou and the Tonton Makoute, I was often unsure what was public information and what should remain behind a veil of secrecy. "Good, bye, Monsieur." I had pulled away my hand and moved to Madame DeVrai's side. The sweet smell of vegetation engulfed us one last time as we left Jean Antoine to his gardens. His world faded like a mirage behind us while my thoughts were instantly cremated by the blazing tropical sun. Silence. The crunch of our feet. The sun.

"Blan, you know we work hard in our family."

"Yes, I know you do, Madame."

"And you know some people never profit from their work. Every night I lie awake, worrying that we won't have enough food to eat. The Good Lord makes things this way, just like He made your fingers different sizes: the long ones are the rich and the short ones are the poor. What He planned was for the little fingers to be helped by the bigger ones and we could all be even. We have to help each other." She swung around to face me, her breathing heavy. I didn't like how she looked, her chest heaving and her dark eyes intensely on me. She turned away and we began to ascend the canyon wall, sweat dripping off our bodies.

Soon, our destination popped into view: a shallow pond that looked more like an evaporated swamp. The pond was already crowded with people stripped to the waist, leaning over with baskets to scoop up the mud and grab hold of the eels. The circumference was encrusted with gooey black muck.

Madame DeVrai halted suddenly at the edge of the thick black muck, her lean body trembling. With a stiff and cold hand, she latched onto me.

"What's wrong?" I asked, hoping that maybe she too found the black mire disgusting enough that we wouldn't have to join the crowd inching through it.

"You see, Blan," she whispered hoarsely, "I came here because the big taste is grabbing my family and I need to help my sister. We haven't eaten for days. But there are *Simbis* in this pond who may take me." *Simbis,* I knew, usually have multiple braids. Under Madame's *mouchoir* she had splotches on her head where braids used to be. The pantheon of *loa* or *mistès* is so large and confusing, I was unsure of their exact power or even what they looked like exactly, but Marie had warned me that these creatures, spirits of rain and magicians, could be tremendously helpful and equally dangerous.

She insisted, "The *Simbis* live under this mud and that's why Candid doesn't like me to come here. I only like fish from the ocean where the water is pure, but these will keep my family alive. I'm here because the fish only rise today, and my family must eat. And if I get some for Atilia I can make her a special broth that might help her live. She needs food." Her powerful hands felt clammy in mine.

"Well, Madame," I solemnly offered, "even if there are *Simbis* in this pond, you don't have to worry as long as I'm around. They like me because I can swim. They'll never touch you if you are with me."

The frightened woman looked at me skeptically, fingering my braids, disappointed ... only two braids.

Cautiously, we stumbled forward, the sticky mud oozing between our toes. We passed a teenage boy scooping with his basket. I watched as the mud drained away to reveal a squirming ball of eels. Other men and women groped with their bare hands to capture these slimy, greenish creatures. I dug in and pulled one out, but it was so slippery, it immediately wiggled through my fingers. I started humming now to relieve my revulsion of these intestinal creatures. *Malheureux* hiked here from all over the surrounding countryside. It was a sort of *coumbite*. Everyone sang as they slowly waded from one end of the pond to the other.

✳

I had become increasingly fearful of Anite's spitting. There were so many diseases I could catch, but her spitting frightened me the most. TB is a dreaded disease. I persuaded her to travel with me to Jean Rabel to visit the clinic.

The evening before, we went to bed early in preparation for our journey. Lighting a candle, Anite strode over to our bedroom. She moved the basin closer to the bedside as we both lay down. The candle shed a dim light that gently played across Anite's face, fading in and out of the darkness. Drums pounded sporadically in the distance, and we could hear St Jerome singing plaintively as he walked down the road. "Help me mother! Help me mother!" The shadowless earth absorbed his pitiful pleas.

"I always told my mother," Anite kept talking, though I wanted to go to sleep. "Even if I never got married, I would have a child anyway. I'm not afraid of staying single. I have waited a long time, Blan, to find a man who won't treat me like his servant."

"Hmmm," I replied, too drowsy to speak.

She leaned over, the saliva drooling from her thick lips to the basin. She paused, breathing heavily beside me. I was too tired to respond and her loud voice, the constant jabber of Creole, had worn away on my nerves.

"Anite," I pleaded, annoyed, "put out the candle and go to sleep. We have all day on the way to the hospital at Jean Rabel to talk." I rolled over.

She remained silent but made no move to extinguish the candle. "You know, Blan," she said in the weighty voice of a person with something to confide. "I never really understood you before. First, you only wanted to wear two braids. I thought, 'Only two braids? Doesn't she like braids? Then you traveled by yourself,' and I thought, 'Isn't she afraid of being alone?' I got angry because you never ate enough. Then, at the workshop I noticed you weren't a strong person. You couldn't lead the others very well. And I thought, 'So, we have a Blan here who can't even give orders.' But then I liked the way that time you called that Tonton a fat potato! I'm glad you're here, Blan. God never gave me a sister, so maybe we can be sisters."

Tenderly she took my hand, sending a current of emotion through my arm. I looked at her, slightly surprised that that one small incident should bring us so close. She gruffly cleared her throat to spit. Our shadows, cast by candlelight, were swaying on the ceiling.

"Tomorrow," she firmly declared, withdrawing her hand. "I'm not going to visit the doctor in Jean Rabel. I've already been to the doctor."

"But Anite, you may have TB," I implored and grabbed a cigarette for comfort, lighting it with a candle. "Well," I offered, ignoring my intuition, "you can check things out twice, you know."

I could no longer distinguish her face in the darkness, just her white teeth, the gold ones glimmering. I felt her staring straight ahead.

"You're pregnant," I suddenly proclaimed. She had spoken a lot about her boyfriend Jean.

"Yes," she admitted with relief. We both burst into laughter.

"That's great, Anite! That's fantastic. What are you going to do?"

"I am going to get married quickly and secretly."

"So, Jean already knows?"

"Yes, but you can't tell anyone. I could get fired."

"So, you are going to continue to work."

"Yes, Blan, my work comes first."

"What did Jean say when he found out?"

She looked away. "Oh, he was happy, very happy. But he was worried too. 'I'm still in school,' he said. 'I don't work yet. What are we going to do?' 'That's all right,' I replied. 'I am working, and we can use my money.'"

"Oh Anite, you must be so happy."

"Yes, I am. You know, my mother is all I've ever had. My father and brother died in a hurricane, and this will give me my own family. I was scared at first though. I'm employed as a teacher and if the administration discovers I am not married and pregnant, they'll fire me. They act like it's a crime, trying to make you feel guilty for something that's so natural. They're all men, of course, and I don't think they understand that anyone can get pregnant. So, don't say anything, Blan, nothing."

She spat again. It slid down the edges of the basin.

"But you have to go to the doctor about the spitting, Anite. What if the baby ..."

"That's because I am pregnant."

"You mean the spitting?"

"Yes."

"And you've been throwing up in the morning without me knowing it?"

"Throwing up?" She was confused.

"Yes, pregnant women often get sick in the morning."

She laughed, exuberant, patting down the blanket. "Well, maybe that's true in your country where there's plenty of food. But here? Never! We only spit!"

"Are you sure? That's very strange. You never even heard of women vomiting because they are pregnant?"

"No, Clémence, women don't get sick from pregnancy." Now it was Anite's turn. "Go to sleep, Blan. We can talk all day tomorrow."

Suddenly, Anite, despite her large bones and muscles, despite her strong personality, looked very fragile as she drifted into a deep sleep.

# Lavi, Lanmou—Life, Love

It wasn't long after that, word came that Madame DeVrai had sad news. Atilia, her sister, had died. Madame, grieving for Atilia, squatted by the fire next to me, holding my hand, staring into the fire, its radiance highlighting her bold face.

"It's the big taste and this wind that killed her," she told me hoarsely.

Madame DeVrai didn't seem the same since my return. Her vitality was drained and now the death of Atilia. Larian was still missing. Not a word from her to her family. In fact, Larian's absence was hardly even mentioned, nor was my impending departure. Everything felt like it was falling apart. The wind, Larian's disappearance, Anite, and perhaps her TB. I felt attached to it all but knew I had to leave.

Madame again repeated to me that Larian had taken the baby and gone to Eaubonne with Bicare. Vivien was outside playing in the dirt. If I asked about Larian, Madame would say, "She will return," then drop the subject. I wondered if Madame actually knew the truth but was too afraid to share it with me.

I tried to make my questions about Larian light-hearted and even added in a few about the marketplace in Eaubonne, hoping not to reveal anything. I felt swollen by my silence and I was sweating hard, anxious to know Larian's true whereabouts. But, of course, Madame always brought the subject back to her sister, Atilia.

"Her body was soft. Her arms hung down at her sides," said Madame DeVrai, recalling her sister's final hours. "She couldn't drink water or tea. She wouldn't even pee pee. And every so often she brought her hands up like this," Madame DeVrai folded her arms over her face, her muscles trembling, "to fight off death. So, we went down there and gave her a bath to clean up. But we knew she was going to die. Still, a person must care for the dying."

A cold front had hit the village and the biting, pitiless wind tugged at our shoulders as we walked to a nearby hut where family and friends had gathered to honor the deceased. Approaching the hut, I heard women wailing and deep groans from the men. The *Malheureux* were all crammed inside the hut to mourn their dead. Even the children, clustered outside of the hut, wailed like a pack of dogs.

"If she had a good *oeuvre* on earth, she will go to heaven," Madame explained. "And if she has done evil, she will go to hell. But my sister was a good person. A good person."

One man led the rest in song and, as night fell, a throng of tearful faces huddled around a solitary kerosene lantern. It sat at the end of the table where some young men played cards. Others squatted or stood or leaned against the wall, their faces forlorn. The carpenter was among them, solemn and quiet, sitting by the wall. The leader's deep male voice carried a melody that women's voices shrilly followed. I crouched beside Madame DeVrai, who didn't sing. Her blue bandana was tied in a turban around her head, her tattered dress tucked between her legs. She looked almost regal, so motionless and sad while others began to clap all around her.

Madame DeVrai took me by the hand and led me to Sylvain, Atilia's bereaved husband. A white cap was smashed onto his head; one eye peered out and the other was sealed shut with thick scar tissue. His good eye roved, focusing on my face momentarily, then shifting up and down uncontrollably. He would be scary if his handshake weren't so friendly, his hands so warm.

He led us into another hut, lit up with row after row of candles. The space was jammed with people, many dancing to the pounding of two large tambours. Close by, St Jerome was leaning against the wall, staring straight ahead. In one corner, two enormous skinned pigs hung from the rafters between the thatch, the layers of muscle, tendons and dried blood illuminated by the candlelight. They rotated slowly, their hooves unscathed and still covered with hair. Dancers brushed lightly against the carcasses, spinning them in midair.

In a loud voice, Sylvain announced us as if we were royalty, "Here are Madame DeVrai and Madame Blan." Women slid over to greet us, embracing us and kissing us. A young man invited Madame DeVrai to dance, the tambours pounding out a rhythm different from the ones I had heard. "This is the ancient dance for the dead," he explained to me as he took her by the arm. "The dead will walk among us here, but you won't see them. They're invisible. They come here for the prayers we sing in this dance."

I was unsure who this young man was, but he and Madame DeVrai appeared to take an important position in this wake. He led her into the crowd where they held each other at arm's length; she swiveled her hips, her head raised high. He backed away from her, then as he moved forward, she wrapped the edges of her skirt around his waist. The musicians started to crowd round them as the young man raised Madame's hands to the ceiling. The musicians formed a tight circle round them, shaking their rattlers up and down, up and down the course of their bodies. I watched their arms twine together high above their heads and saw two shiny coffins suspended from the rafters. Although one was for Atilia, no one would tell me the purpose of the other. Madame kept dancing, even with tears rolling down her cheeks.

※

For the first time since I came to the Northwest, an enormous bank of clouds was filling the sky. The workshop was busy when this new phenomenon attracted our attention.

Everyone stopped to stare with amazement at the towering, black thunderheads. During the course of the workshop, the people had debated for hours over the remote chance of rain, yet no one ever really believed such a miracle was possible. Today, however, as the sky grew steadily grayer, they began to drift homeward, claiming, "If we don't leave now, the paths will be too muddy."

"It's going to rain, Blan," Anite uttered in a hushed whisper.

"Nonsense," I replied. "That's just everyone's dream. It hasn't rained here in years."

"Heh, you'll see. The whole town believes it will rain. I can feel it too."

Two hours later the rain poured down in torrents, pounding against the dried earth in a hard staccato rhythm. Thatched huts bent under the deluge. Faces peeked out their doors intermittently as this providential rain put life back into the parched soil.

Anite and I retreated to our hut and wrapped ourselves in blankets, paying silent homage to this long-awaited deliverance. We sat for hours in the cold, our shivers a sort of hymn of gratitude for the rain. Everyone's teeth were chattering, but the plants probably rejoiced. The *Malheureux* shivered around their feeble fires. For once their crops might survive.

Anite sat beside me, furious because she had been reprimanded by the local pastor for being pregnant and unmarried. "I don't understand those people. They call themselves Christians, but they create a theater out of me getting pregnant. Thank God, they didn't lecture me on moral doctrines! But I know how they think. If a girl gets pregnant and wants to marry, they won't allow the ceremony in the church. I guess they do that to set an example for the other young girls, but it doesn't work. There are more and more girls pregnant every year! Haitian women have always lived fine without their moral doctrines and that is the way we will stay." Anite gripped her bandana and stared into the candle. "Anyway, Blan, I know what's really happening. They're afraid of my progress with the people. The people are working together more every day and those others, with the money and power, are afraid. One day they may ask me to leave or the Tonton Makoute may come for me. But I don't care. I am Anite and what interests me is to see this misery lifted." Anite leaned her head back, jaw clenched, still glaring at the blank ceiling. Then she spat in her basin. And we sat.

After a week of being confined to huts, the market no longer functioned so there was hardly any food left. We, the fortunate ones, had three tomatoes, four oranges, an egg, and some wheat. We sipped the flour mixed with water. We ate it boiled. We fried it. It filled our stomachs and helped to keep us warm.

"Blan, what time is it?" Anite suddenly asked.

"It's precisely nine minutes after nine," I replied, closing my eyes, "and nine seconds."

"It doesn't make any difference anymore, does it?" She eyed me knowingly.

"No," I answered. "It's always the same time around here now ... it's funny."

"It's not funny!" she gruffly protested. "The people are suffering. There's no market, no work. We just want this cold to go away."

I sat on the bed next to a chair that held the lantern, my notebook and my pen. The hut's shutters were closed but the persistent mist seeped through. Despite my trusty lantern, a haze obscured every word. Anite hadn't washed or combed her hair for days, so it resembled a rat's nest. Real life rats were invading us from all sides, darting brazenly across the floor and even over the bed. Pretending to read aloud from her Bible, Anite praised the Lord and didn't flinch at the sound of their scampering.

Neither of us could muster the courage to budge beyond our bed. I sat wrapped in a blanket; she sat with her spitting bowl beside her. Marie brought us mashed wheat, a viscous yellow mush that clung to our ribs. We spent our days like prisoners, locked inside our hut, waiting for meals, commenting occasionally on the rain, shifting our embryonic positions closer together and farther apart. No one in town set foot outside. Red mud oozed down the deserted street and paths like molten lava.

Marie saved the day by crushing a tin can, balancing it on three rocks and stacking it with burning charcoal. I finally left the bed and slid onto a squat bench nearby, suspending my legs over the tiny fire. Warmth at last! The smoke clogged my nose with black mucus. Anite pulled up her chair, still wrapped in her blanket.

"This is what we needed. It makes us like a family." She smiled, patting her ballooning stomach. Lethargically, we watched the burning charcoal that stared back at us like a great red eye.

"I feel so close to Gaston already," Anite muttered.

"Gaston?"

"Yes, that's the baby's name. It was chosen by Jean."

"And if it's a girl?"

"Nadine. That's an Indian name."

"Hmmmm."

Anite looked deep into the coals again. "You know," she pondered, "I've heard there's a lot of discrimination in your country."

"Yes, too much. And it creates many problems."

"I know what you mean," she nodded. "If you're always on the bottom, like some people in Port-au-Prince, you turn to violence. It's a cruel world and you feel like stealing. You don't have anything, while others live in luxury. It depresses you.

"The Blacks who do make money in this country are too proud. They have been held down so long that, when they finally do get some power, they are arrogant. Then there are plenty of Haitians who reject their Blackness, who say, 'I'm White. My grandmother was White.' I get angry. I yell at them. I say, 'Listen, you are Black just like me. You have a history. You should be proud of your race.' I like my skin, but I like you, too. It doesn't really matter, does it, Blan? We're all God's children." At peace again, Anite leaned over to stir the burning coals.

"Aaaaayyyeee!" A ghastly cry pierced the air.

"Aaayyyeee!"

Anite opened the door and I saw St Jerome drenched, standing in the center of the road. He shivered as he mumbled his prayers, a wooden cane locked in one hand and an empty begging can in the other. His face was shriveled like an old monkey's with protruding cheekbones and fat lips. His ratty eyes quivered, twitching his greasy skin. The low graying sky wrapped around his stooped shoulders.

Anite invited St Jerome inside. He entered, smiling like a politician, and sat on the floor. He took out a matchbox and shook it in a pulsating rhythm. His stench burrowed through our haze of charcoal smoke. He bowed his head in profound devotion to the Almighty. His eyes folded submissively, his weathered hands clasped as he sang.

*I went into the House.*
*The Large House in the sky.*
*And I returned to tell you,*
*my friends,*
*have pity on your poor*
*wicked brothers.*

The melody unwound into a discordant hum. Anite's shadow expanded with the breath of the flames, slowly crawling across the floor until it reached his crouched form. His wide flat fingers traced it deliberately until he giggled. Anite gazed at him thoughtfully. Then her hands, like the smoke, curled round his bent head, through his hair. Tilting her head, she smiled inward and deep, fixed as though she was made of dark stone. St Jerome's glassy eyes looked upward at her, smiling as she began to softly hum his tune, her gentle music seeping through the hut, quickly consumed by the spent dark hills.

※

The frigid wind plus the lack of food and water quietened the village for weeks. People stayed inside, crouched by their fires, too exhausted to challenge fate. Larian remained absent during these cold weeks. One morning, the DeVrai family, like everyone else in the village, was hovering around their fire. There was a gaping hole in the wall where they tore out some thatch to burn as fuel. I was there to say goodbye.

They crouched by their small fire. Everyone was sick and shivering. Candid had the grippe and squatted near the fire under a ragged straw hat, wearing his same brown pants, the remains of a woman's slip wrapped around his head for extra warmth. No one mentioned Larian. Vivien was lying across Madame DeVrai's legs, her little hands reaching up and rubbing her grandmother's powerful, broad face. A boy around her age stood beside them.

"This is Calabash, Vivien's cousin," Madame declared, still staring at the fire.

"It's nice to meet you, Calabash. I'm Clémence."

He smiled.

I took a banana out of my pack, the only piece of fruit I could find in the village and handed it to Vivien. "Please share it with your cousin," I instructed her. She grabbed it, jammed it into her mouth and chomped voraciously.

"Give some to Calabash," Madame cried.

Calabash raced over and violently yanked on one end of the banana. The tender fruit was soon squashed in their tug of war, but the boy snatched what remained. Vivien squealed hysterically, but Calabash was even chewing on the peel. Normally the silent one, Vivien pounded her fists on the ground, screaming out her hell, shreds of mashed banana still wedged between her teeth.

I sat down next to Madame DeVrai, who seemed to be in a daze. Her head drooped, then jerked up. There was a queer twist to her smile. She had a rag wrapped around her head.

"I haven't moved all day," she muttered. "You can see that my feet have no dirt on them. When there's no food like this, I can only sit by the fire and sleep. Vivien sleeps in that basket over there. We do nothing. There is no work, no market. We just sit here all day and try to keep warm. Friends come to visit and talk with us to make sure we don't die of the cold."

Her hands swiped at the air as if she were brushing something away. Then she scratched at her face. "My feet are warm," she chuckled, "but I can't feel the back of my legs."

I offered her some bread that was almost swallowed whole. Staring at the ground, Candid sucked his piece of bread slowly. There was silence among us while the ferocious wind kept pounding outside. Madame DeVrai's cackling laugh broke the silence as she slapped my leg, pointing at me.

"You're going to fall asleep, aren't you? Aren't you?" There was alarm in her voice. She thought I was dying, like her.

She scratched at her face, her mood shifting again abruptly. "If only there was work. Work is so beautiful, so beautiful. I love it, like when I go to the garden and turn the soil. I plant seeds and they grow. Or I take all our clothes to the river, wash them. I love it when I can work."

I handed her a cigarette. There was no more tobacco for her pipe though she sucked on it out of habit. "Sometimes I go to the garden and pull out some beans or potatoes. Then we boil water and cook the food. Only then is there traffic in this kitchen." She leaned over to poke at the fire's mounds of cinders, causing a healthy flame to leap up. The family laughed at this distraction, exchanging comments about the fire, rearranging themselves around it.

"You are leaving," Madame said to me, glancing up from the fire. "You should wait. Larian is in Eaubonne with Bicare by now, but she will be back," Madame said. Smoke curled around her face, bringing tears to her eyes. "Bicare, bah," she spat. "I wish my little girl, my little daughter, would be any place there is work, beautiful work." She glanced at me out of the corner of her eye and I felt she knew where Larian had really gone, but she quickly added, "You know I don't like Larian's union with Bicare, you must know that! What can that boy do? He gives her a necklace, milk and food, but he doesn't have a house. He lives with his family. I don't like that! When a man takes a woman with a baby, he must build them a home with a little table. That's what Candid and I did."

Candid edged toward the fire, clinging tenderly to Vivien. "Yes, we were married years ago," he said dreamily.

"Yes, I wanted to marry him, and he wanted to marry me," Madame said confidently, contradicting her previous story. "We will stay together until we return to the earth. If he dies first, I'll bury him but, before long, I will be lying down beside him. If I die first, then he'll bury me.

"I already had six little people by the time I was married. They all died, though. Some when they were this high," she held her palm three feet off the ground. "And others when they were still here." She pretended to rock an infant, stroking its imaginary face. "I had my first baby when I was still a mademoiselle, but he died too. I don't know why. He just died."

Vivien leaned against her grandmother again, tears running down her grimy cheeks. She crouched, separate now, quite alone. Madame

DeVrai began to chatter so rapidly I couldn't follow her. She laughed at a fly, at the fire, at me scratching my leg. Then she reverted to smoking thoughtfully, leaning on her knees, her eyes glassy.

She set a pot of water over the fire to boil, then slowly began grinding the handful of coffee beans she got at Atilia's wake. I squatted beside her, uneasy, knowing that despite the family's needs I would again be the recipient of their generosity. The three rusty tin cans that served this family as drinking cups were brought out and cleaned over and over with murky water.

"Coffee!" she proclaimed in a louder voice. "Coffee is important. We serve it when someone marries and when someone dies. And now we will serve before you leave, Blan. You should drink coffee every day. If you don't, you'll get a headache. Coffee is expensive, though. It costs five gourdes a pound, but a friend of mine at the funeral gave me this. It's nice to have sugar in the coffee but we don't have any, so we'll drink it plain." Madame DeVrai dumped the freshly ground coffee into a makeshift *passoir* then poured boiling water over it. The steaming brew filled our cups. Candid smacked his lips just as the fire seemed to revive.

"Heh, heh! Ha, ha, ha!" Madame DeVrai cackled, swiping at the air. "Yes Blan, the big taste can hit any one of us. Then we die. A man named Vernesse died just this morning. He lay in bed as still as this ground for three days. Ha, ha, ha, ha!"

She swatted again at the darkness, maybe at the smoke. "You see Blan, when you die your body becomes soft, very soft. Your friends put you in a box and weep as they carry you off to the cemetery. They dig a hole in the ground and cover you up with dirt. Your body falls apart in the ground. Then animals come to eat you. If you lie there for one year, they'll chew you up pretty well. After two years you turn to dirt, like this …" She scooped up a handful of dusty soil and let it trickle through her tough fingers. She sucked on her empty pipe, scratching her face, then her knee. "That's how it is in my country. That's how it is in Haiti."

I tried to follow this droning monologue. She mentioned religion, childhood friends, the market; then a comment about a fly, an itchy nose—the same kind of commentary I had heard from the beggars. But it was just the big taste. Even Vivien edged away from Madame DeVrai as she was drawn deeper into the dark logic of her own desperate need to survive.

I rose to leave and the family, one by one, embraced me, blessed me with a mixture of *loa* and Catholic saints. They touched my forehead, my hair, patted my hands, and rubbed my arms encrusted with red dust. Candid gave me advice not to travel alone, to pray to God every morning for protection. Madame repeated his advice and reminded me not to forget them.

Now she was crying. She had heard of Miami. Miami, the symbol of the rich world that I came from, but I had been a stranger. We hugged again. I dug into my pockets, kept twenty dollars, and handed her the rest of my cash. And finally, I stepped out the hut door, thinking I'd probably never see her again. After a few steps, I looked back at the DeVrai hut, dilapidated, crooked, crumbling.

I looked at the hut and could hardly believe I could walk away so easily to return to my life, to my security, to my glasses of wine by the pool.

When I first met Larian, my impressions were mostly what I had been told. But in that hut the truth was laid bare. Somehow our democratic policies succeeded in answering the desires of the few while other lives were mere grist for a mill. So many people, and especially women, were forced to live without money, painfully struggling every day to answer to the most basic human need.

Yet there was another side to that truth, to that battle for survival. I now understood what was behind Napoleon's loss. The Haitians had taught me about a hope that refuses defeat. Larian's refusal to recognize borders spoke to this hope. No wall or obstacle could stand up to her determination to have her children survive, to have them learn something she couldn't learn. Somehow she faced all these grim circumstances with hope.

I started to walk back to my hut to collect my things to leave. I could see its outline, the outhouse cornfield, the basin alongside the doorway. The sun hit my back. As I stepped into the hut, I saw my pack and laughed inwardly at the uselessness of so many items I had brought to Haiti. I stuffed the last of my clothes into my red backpack, leaving my emerald-green dress, my black blazer for Marie and white shirt for Anite, then started out the door.

It was a two-hour walk to the next town where I could get a jeep or a tap tap. I started walking, knowing I would hear Haitians along the way call out to me, Blan! Blan! To make sure I was all right because no one should ever walk alone, because *Yon sel dwet pa kapab mange gumbo*, One finger alone can't eat gumbo.

The red dust kicked up around my feet.

# TWO

# Teresa, Guatemala

*Tierra de Eterna Primavera*

(Land of Eternal Spring)

# Mayans, Ladinos, Gringos

I flew to Guatemala from Haiti and landed just as the sun was setting. From the airplane window, I recognized the jagged spine of verdant mountains cutting through the center of Guatemala, with over thirty-three volcanoes scattered between their edges and Mayan temples hidden in their folds. I could see the Pacific coastal area where forests and people were hacked down long ago by the Conquistadores to make way for sugarcane, coffee, and banana plantations. And to the north was Peten, a large chunk of almost inaccessible wilderness covered with dense hardwood forest where I had worked on an archaeological site, Yaxha. I loved working on that dig, far in the jungle, but it was after I worked there that I ended up in jail.

I was arriving in Guatemala again. This time, I went directly from the airport to a guesthouse in the middle of town. Archaeologists used this small hotel because it was clean and well-situated. I knew I was safe here. Plus, it had hot water and the café served cappuccinos and grilled cheese sandwiches. The only drawback was that it sat across from the National Police Headquarters, an ivory-white colonial building where soldiers strutted back and forth, holsters hitting against their hips and rifles flung across their backs.

I decided to stay in the city for a few weeks. Maybe I was finally frightened and hesitant to go out to the countryside again, though I never admitted my fear. Or maybe I just wanted to ease into the Guatemalan world by remaining in a city surrounded by familiar ways of living—telephones, refrigerators, cafes, and department stores. In any case, my body felt tight, anxious about my plans. But when I was following my gut and walking those city streets, seeing the tortilla ladies, hearing the shoeshine boys call out, and watching the Indian men and women trot by, I felt I was in the right place. I wanted to understand this world buzzing around me. I wanted to return to the world of Mayan women.

※

A few weeks later a billow of black smoke trailed behind a run-down bus from Guatemala City. The bus jostled its way into the mountains, stopping at villages where Ladinos disembarked and Mayan Indians got on until I was surrounded by Indians wearing ill-fitting sombreros, their machetes dangling dangerously by their sides. Women held their babies and young toddlers clutched their mothers' arms as we swerved past villages. The roads were narrow, coiling like springs round the steep cliffs, and so I, too, grasped onto the seat in front of me, trying to avoid crushing the Mayan beside me.

I was heading out of the city to see about a job in San Lucas Tolimán, a Mayan village on the edge of the waters of Lake Atitlán. San Lucas Tolimán wasn't unknown to me. I had been there with Mark a few years ago on a day trip to hike in the mountains. And I had never forgotten that town. Maybe it was the Mayans or the beauty of the lake, but there was something about it that felt familiar to me, that called to me.

San Lucas Tolimán, only three hours outside of the city, was populated primarily by Mayan Kaqchiquel Indians, the same Indians who had worked with me in the jungle and impressed me with their knowledge. They could identify all the parrots, imitate their songs, track a wild boar, carve a dugout with a machete. There was an insect that would plant itself in your skin, then eat you up from inside out. They knew the sap that would kill it and they knew about the cinchona leaf that could be boiled to stop fevers.

Centuries before, when Pedro Alvarado rode through these very mountains, he didn't realize what he was up against with the Mayans. He was a strange, red-bearded man prone to fits of laughter, and he had left behind him a trail of slaughtered Aztecs as they performed their sacred ceremonies. The Mayans, dressed in their finery of feathered headdresses and hand-woven cloth, welcomed him with open arms, not realizing what they were facing was a lust for gold and land that would change their lives forever. The very land that gave them life would be seized by the Spaniards and those after them—from petty military dictators to multinational corporations like the United Fruit Company backed and outfitted by the US government. Guatemala quickly became Alvarado's personal hacienda. Slavery, mutilation, starvation, and bullets were his weapons. But he didn't understand what he was up against.

The Mayans lowered their eyes, followed commands, but beneath, something untouchable, almost immutable nourished them. Little did Alvarado, or later, John Dulles, expect the tenacity behind those enchanting, hand-woven costumes that the Mayans wore. Who could understand them? Why didn't they just give up and become like us? What held them so strong, so confident despite obvious failure to hold onto their land, their temples, and their mores? It was the same poise and tenacity I had seen in the women in jail. These were the Mayans that stood up to the Spaniards until the very end. Until today. Their resistance was sometimes covertly nestled in their insistence to wear their *traje* and pay homage to *Maximón*, a hybrid saint. I thought if I understood something about them, I might understand something about the depths of humanity and fortitude. I had questions about my own life. San Lucas felt like it might have some answers.

The bus left me in the heart of the small town where the Ladinos lived. The dusty streets were lined with cement blockhouses. Little stores dotted the plaza where bored policemen would stride back and forth all day in front of the Municipalidad. Next to it an old colonial church stood, its mere presence exerting firm control over the little township. The Mayans lived farther away, down a network of paths that fanned out from the plaza. Along those paths were rows of thatched huts, many crumbling into hedges of flowers and maize. Not far from the huts, were the Volcán Tolimán and the Cerro de Oro Mountain where both Ladinos and Indians claimed treasures were hidden, but no one had ever found them.

There was only one small mail boat visit a week and a dirt road leading into San Lucas. Outside influences had trickled into this long-established Indigenous town, transforming it into an uneasy amalgam of the traditional and the modern. In San Lucas many traditions were merged: the Kaqchiquel dialect and Spanish, traditional Mayan *traje* and manufactured clothes, Catholicism and ancient rituals. That fusion, rather than pure Indian tradition, was more typical of Guatemala. Nonetheless, the town itself was separated into two main sections, one for the Mayans and one for the Ladinos.

As I scoured the small town, that sense of the familiar stayed with me. I walked past the Ladinos, working on the police force, running the shops, landowners, running the government; the Mayan Indians, the women weavers and the men who marketed their labor on nearby coffee *fincas* so they could rent the *fincas'* discarded land, rocky soil on the sides of volcanoes, to cultivate their own *milpa*, corn field. Some say the rocky land is so steep, they have to tie themselves to trees to till it.

The other people in the town consisted of the invaders, people like me. One set were travelers, like a German baker or an American artist who lived in town, and the few travelers coming for the day to climb the steep volcanoes. The other set was the Catholics, four nuns and two priests from Minnesota who ran a community project. I didn't feel a part of either group but, after my isolation in Haiti, there was a comfort being around them both.

Walking down a path to the lake, I could see Mayan women bent over, washing clothes on rocks as slick as glass, the waves gently tapping against their bony legs. Dugout canoes, carved out by razor sharp machetes, dotted the lake. Men dressed in woven clothes identical to their ancestors' garb leaned over to haul in their nets. It looked like a world that was guided by ritual, tradition, and routine. A welcoming world after the ruckus and confusion of Haiti and Guatemala City.

I walked to the edge of town to see the experimental farm the priests and nuns had initiated fifteen years before. Looking around, I felt at peace. There were medicinal plants, a bee-keeping project, animal husbandry for families for food and their own cultivation, reforestation efforts, a medical clinic, a school, coffee-exporting projects, and the orphanage. Most importantly, the farm collaborated with the Mayans so they could buy homes and land. Since the day Pedro Alvarado stepped foot in Guatemala until today, the land, so significant to Mayans both as a basic need and spiritually, had been pillaged from the Indians. In San Lucas, the scenario was slowly changing. Many Mayans were now small landowners.

One of the nuns offered me a position in the orphanage, developing a multi-age educational program. The orphanage housed about fifty children of all ages. There was a stone house with a small apartment, including a shower, where I could stay, and a dining room where staff and visitors ate common meals. The beautiful Lago Atitlán was nearby. This seemed to be at the heart of Guatemala, Land of Eternal Spring, the home to Mayans, those very people whose astronomers once mapped stars and galaxies through pure discernment. I could live among the Mayan descendants in the peace of this quiet rural town. But I had misgivings about working with the church.

Since Guatemalan Independence in 1824, the elites had used the church as a means of social control. It preached the will of God while representing the will of the government. The experimental farm seemed to represent a change in the church, but I left San Lucas weighing the situation.

Sometimes coincidences happen that seem to point you in the right direction and that's what happened when a woman named Kathy offered me a ride back to the city. She was a yoga teacher on a day visit to San Lucas. That's what she told me at first. But none of it was true.

Instead, through time I learned she was actually an ex-nun, on the run from a felony charge in the US for her anti-war activities and persona non grata in Guatemala. I never did know her real name. "Kathy" and her husband, both Maryknoll missionaries, were expelled from Guatemala for their involvement with *guerrillero* groups fighting for land reform.

"For us," she told me, "and many other nuns and priests, bettering the lives of the poor, even if it meant taking up arms alongside of them, meant more than the heavenly salvation we preached. We couldn't and can't continue to just sit in our churches watching the destruction of the Indigenous people." She explained that she believed that only warfare against the government would result in social justice for the Indigenous people. "And isn't that what Jesus was actually striving for?" she asked me. "Many nuns and priests now equate their mission with human rights, not with the values of tradition and the hierarchal authority. The government claimed we were communists, but we felt violent revolution was justified by the teachings of Jesus Christ."

Having been raised in the old-fashioned Catholic Church, I was shocked at this perspective. Listening to her, I understood that the San Lucas land titles pointed to many motives behind the experimental farm.

I accepted the job.

# Land of Maize

Three Mayan women worked with me at the orphanage. The cook, Elena, was fluent in Spanish, and basically ran the show. There was an older lady, Teresa, and her daughter, Tina, who made tortillas for her in the morning, then would leave to work in a private home. Juana and Bobdelia worked directly with the children and me. They both spoke a mixture of Spanish and Kaqchiquel. *Lengua*, they called it, meaning Kaqchiquel language, as if it was the only language in the world.

From the start, they were both oddly standoffish and affectionate with me. We worked in an open room with one large table and no chairs. As much as I pleaded for their input they, instead, stood like statues across the room. Their thick black hair braided in satin ribbons fell past their chests covered by tightly woven *huipil*s. The *huipil*s were decorated with embroidered dogs, spiders, cats, birds all symbols used by the San Lucas Kaqchiquel to tell where a woman was born, what man she married, whether she worked mainly in the house or the fields. The *huipil* tucked into a *corte*, a piece of hand-woven material with shiny threads throughout so when they walked it resembled a waterfall cascading down their skirts. The *huipil* carried messages to be read by strangers, people like me, outsiders. But I had no idea.

Instead, I tried to speak with them, involve them with the kids. No matter how many times I told Bobdelia I didn't speak *lengua*, she always answered me in Kaqchiquel. She'd laugh at me while I stood before her like a mute, resenting her as she rattled off her language, knowing she could just as well speak Spanish. But most of the time, she wouldn't. Now I know she was showing me something, but back then I bristled at the way she stood against the wall, arms crossed at her chest, watching me until I felt awkward and incompetent. She'd stand so still, staring like I was a movie she was watching. Other times, she'd confuse me by striding over and kneeling on the floor beside the kids, painting, sewing, coloring. Then she'd stand beside me, lean her head on my shoulder. Or she'd wrap her arm round my waist like she was my sister or a very old friend.

The older Mayan woman, Teresa, and her daughter, Tina, who worked in the kitchen every morning, were the only ones consistently friendly with me. They were my antidotes to the spurning I felt from most of the Mayans. As soon as I walked into the kitchen, Tina smiled and brought me a steaming cup of coffee. Then later in the day, I'd see them at their afternoon job in a private home, a sprawling cement ranch house owned by well-known Ladino family, owners of the town's biggest store, a veritable warehouse of everything from needles to saddles. Tina and her mother were employed there to make tortillas in the house's outdoor kitchen. Whenever I passed the house, Teresa, an older, thin-boned woman with big horse-like teeth and a halo of braided gray hair wrapped around her head would nod a hello to me and laugh. One afternoon, she called out to me in Kaqchiquel, then sent her daughter, Tina, to ask me a question.

"Is your name Teresa?" Tina asked shyly, covering her mouth with her shawl.

"No," I answered. She had already heard my name at work. "My name isn't Teresa."

From the kitchen, her mother rattled off something in Kaqchiquel and Tina looked at me perplexed. "Isn't your name Teresa?"

Confused, I looked from her mother to daughter. Perhaps I wasn't understanding. "No, it's Clémence," I told her.

She took my hand and gently led me over to her mother. Her mother told me in broken Spanish, "A *gringa* used to work in this town and her name was Teresa, just like mine." She looked up at me. Her eyes were watery and had droopy bags beneath them. "My name is Teresa."

The daughter was still standing beside me. She pointed at her mother. "Do you understand what my mother is saying? She doesn't speak Spanish very well."

"Come and sit down," Teresa suddenly ordered, pulling me by the elbow and guiding me to the one small childlike chair in the tiny kitchen. Then, she ignored me. She turned her back to me and began to work again. From the back both Teresa and her daughter looked identical in their red-and-white-striped *huipil*s, traditional blouses. Glossy embroidery threads were woven tightly together in bright wavy lines to resemble the shifting waters of the lake.

Teresa carefully rolled white dough, mottled by flakes of yellow corn skins, into a ball. She clapped her hands rhythmically. I sensed a steadiness in her, then reproached myself for being overly romantic. She was just an old Mayan woman with a young child, both made mysterious by their *traje*, traditional dress. She leaned over to stoke the fire, smiling at me and muttering in Kaqchiquel. Her hands felt warm when she gently patted my own, placing a fresh tortilla between them.

"Eat," she ordered in awkwardly accented Spanish. She cocked her head to one side, observing me. I noticed her ears stuck out a bit and looked incongruous with her *traje* and stately way of holding herself. "And where is your family?" Her question was harsh in Spanish, her second language. She, like most of us second language learners, said words with an effort.

"In my country."

"Aye, *pobrecita*," She touched my cheek to comfort me. "And aren't you married?"

"No."

"Do you have a *novio*, a sweetheart?"

"No."

She shook her head, looking at Tina as if my replies made me suspect. "Well, that's not good, not good at all. You should have your family or a *novio*. That's why you are so skinny," she said. "But don't worry. You stop here every day and I will give you tortillas that will fatten you up."

She paused, considering me as if forming an idea of my value or purpose.

"Your name?"

"Clémence."

"You are Clémence"—her old hands reached for more dough to make tortillas— "Clemencia."

"Mincha," she finally concluded with my only familiar word in Kaqchiquel, my same name from jail. She patted another warm tortilla into my hand, enfolding it with both of her hands.

It was when we were in the orphanage's line of shower stalls, washing lice out of the kids' hair, that Bobdelia finally decided to befriend me and asked me to her house. She wasn't wearing a traditional *huipil*; instead, she wore a lime-green one with the San Lucas symbols. I was scrubbing the head of Verline, a little boy who had been left with us by his father. His head was literally teeming with lice, so I was trying not to look as I washed. Bobdelia was working on Geraldo's head. Everyone called him Pescado, but I was never sure why.

"Yes, Mincha," she used the name Teresa had given me and I

wondered if they had spoken about me. "Verline is like these other children. None of them have mothers."

I poured more of the acid-smelling shampoo over Verline's head that was tilted downward, his eyes clenched tightly. His little six-year-old body was modestly stripped down to underwear, but mine wasn't. Fully clothed, I tried to dodge the spouting water while I scrubbed. "None of them have mothers?"

"No, but some of them still have fathers. Like him," she nodded toward Verline. "The mothers die, and the fathers make so little money that without a wife they cannot take care of the child. Who will watch him all day? Who will cook the food and wash the clothes while the man is at work? If a man has family still alive, they will take some of the work, but in the very poor families their time is already occupied with living, so the man is left with a house filled with dirty children, food to cook, clothes to wash and work, work and work."

Verline stood stiffly before me, water cascading over his thin body. Usually with lice, little eggs catch on the strands of hair or there are a few almost microscopic bugs scurrying around. But Verline's head was quite different. It was alive with a nest of bugs that had clustered on his head. It must have itched horribly, but he stood stiffly with an old man's patience, the acidic shampoo running down to his shoulders.

Bobdelia continued to explain that when Verline was first left at the orphanage, his father didn't just abandon him. The father went through two months of questioning before the child was accepted into the orphanage. Many fathers visited their children each week and took them home after a couple of years, when the man had a new wife or raised his income so he could hire someone to help him.

"His mother died of TB," Bobdelia continued. "His father has it and is dying. Verline has it too but maybe we can help him. His father is a good man, but he is drinking too much. Verline could have died. You see how skinny he is? He has TB but he has worms, too. At first, he couldn't even eat, and he just cried in a corner." Then she abruptly changed the subject. "You should meet my son. I will take you home so you can meet my son. He's same as Verline, only he has no father."

✳

At the end of the day, Bobdelia and I walked down the dusty streets of San Lucas to get to her house. We reached a street that looked more like a path partially destroyed by an avalanche. I could see the lake a block away, outlined by lemon and mango trees near the white limestone huts with thatched roofs. Women trudged back and forth from the lake, balancing water or laundry on their heads, packs of children trailing behind them.

Bobdelia's house was a hut too, but in shambles. The inside walls were covered by old calendars and newspapers. Bobdelia grabbed my hand and led me to the courtyard strewn with pieces of old wood, the ruins of an old hut, and scattered plants of tomatoes and corn. She wanted to show me the rooster, a fat black rooster. The whole time, she chattered in Kaqchiquel, so I simply nodded, not knowing what I was agreeing to. Since the Mayans had been treating me with detachment, I felt pleased that at least Bobdelia was welcoming me.

She then led me to what I discovered was her sister's house. Her sister's house was a hut of misery. Seven filthy children were hiding under a shield they made of plastic and cardboard. Ten dirty cups sat in the mud in front of their makeshift playhouse. Her sister Juana was inside, sitting in a smoke-filled room, breastfeeding a baby while another was strapped to a macramé cradle that stank of urine. Her face was streaked in black from smoke and dirt. It was a filthy place. A young boy, Carlos Roberto, Bobdelia's son, was snoring next to them.

Bobdelia spoke rapidly to her sister in Kaqchiquel. Kaqchiquel was a unique sound—sometimes guttural, other times melodic. It had no root in any language I knew, so I expected it to be a challenge to learn, but I wanted at least to learn the rudimentary words and I thought that I could help out the family. I asked Bobdelia, "Can you teach me Kaqchiquel?"

They both stared at me saying nothing. "I can pay you. Or your sister."

"Yes," Juana stirred, still holding the infant. "I can teach you." She answered in a broken Spanish. She seemed eager, so we agreed I would return in three days.

Three days later, chickens squawked as I approached the house. A large black bird swooped down close to me. Just as I got to the courtyard, I saw Juana slipping into the hut. Then I heard whispers to six-year-old Carlos Roberto. A large black dead tree sat outside the hut and Carlos

Roberto came out and stood next to it like a grown man, like a soldier guarding his home, bravely lying for his aunt, saying in Spanish, "My aunt is not home."

✻

Later, when I complained to Bobdelia and Elena the cook, they were standing by the fire in the kitchen. Bobdelia answered, "She is afraid of you because you only speak Spanish."

"Yes," Elena agreed, "All the Indigenous people are afraid of you because you only speak Spanish. People who speak Spanish look at us like animals. Like animals in the zoo," she added, more worldly than Bobdelia. I started to protest that I was trying to learn Kaqchiquel, but I realized it was a Catch 22.

✻

I learned some rudimentary Kaqchiquel, but I knew language wasn't the main problem. I actually had to change myself; to change my way of going about things, my instinctive way of functioning, which was to converse, to ask questions. How are you? How many children do you have? These questions were fine, but I could see, instead, the Mayans used silence, observation to get to know a person. They paused and watched. They drew on their instincts by observing. They evaluated until their silent watching almost drove me away. To me, their silence was a rejection.

The only thing the Mayan women did consistently was to ask me about my family, my marital status, and then they'd smile at me. But I could always feel their burning gaze on me. They always knew where I was and what I was doing. They watched how I walked, interacted with people, how I swam in the lake and how I spoke. I thought the observations and evaluations of my person were totally based on the exterior, the superficial. I didn't know at the time I was being watched from the inside, that point of stillness, of inner calm. They stood distant and silent, just their eyes following me everywhere I went. Along their paths, their singsong voices would call out greetings, Adios, they would sing to me, always polite, always gracious but forever on the other side of the world, their world. It hurt. I felt misjudged, then isolated, as I faced a wall around their world. But finally, I tapped into my own instinct, which told me to wait, to stop trying. And then, just as I started to consider possibly leaving San Lucas, the wall started coming down. Perhaps the news of my efforts spread in town because people began to greet me in *lengua*, to lift their eyes from the ground and smile at me. Perhaps it was an act of compassion because they always seemed to pity me. Or maybe it was just watching the honesty of my relationship growing with the old Mayan lady and her daughter.

# I'm Kaqchiquel

After work I always stopped by Teresa's and sat in the little kitchen, watching Teresa and Tina pound out tortillas. She talked incessantly about the weather and the drudgery of her work: day in, day out, tortilla after tortilla. I felt bored and unsettled. I longed to be immersed in the Mayan mystical traditions and lore I had imagined when I read about the great Mayan civilization.

I was watching her making tortillas one day when the church bells started ringing midday because of a wedding. "Eh," she snorted, flipping over a tortilla. "Let them get married. I walk alone and fight alone. My life is more tranquil this way." She had never spoken so forcefully before. She looked over at me as if for reassurance and then confided, "I got married when I was fifteen. I knew the man, but I didn't want to marry him. I fought and screamed, but my parents forced me." Then she contradicted herself, something she would do frequently. She softened as she spoke.

"You see, when my husband first fell in love with me, he sent me notes about his love. He can write a bit, you see. Well, I can't write, and I can't read, so I didn't know what the notes said, but I knew what he meant, and I thought, 'Ah, he doesn't mean that! There are so many women for him to love. He is handsome. How can he mean that?' He was too shy to come speak with me.

"Well, after a while we would be more and more together. I would go get water and he would follow me there and we'd walk home together. On the way home, we would always stop where there was a fence, and I would turn and stare at the fence. Yes, Mincha," she added as she bent over to poke at the fire, stirring it to life. "He always stood behind me. He'd still have his sombrero on from work, but he wanted to see me right away after work. It didn't matter if he was dirty. He had to speak about his love for me. I was so young, just like Tina. But I never looked at him, I just listened because I liked his words.

"After a while we went away together and we spent about four happy years together, but then he started going after other women and my sadness grew. All the men do that. They have to go after other women." Tina was sitting beside me watching, listening intently too, and I wondered if she had ever heard this story. Or perhaps heard it too many times.

"But at the beginning, I knew he loved me because when he wasn't working, he was always there waiting for me to leave my house and he'd walk me wherever I was going and leave me there. If he saw my mother, he wasn't afraid, and he'd keep talking with me. In those days I thought about whether I liked him. When I knew I did, then I kissed him. A kiss might be after walking with a boy for three weeks or that might be after walking with him for three days. It depends on the woman. When I was first kissed, I was down by the lake and Pablo had followed me there. I knew he was going to kiss me because you can just feel that in the air. Well, he kissed me, and I felt happy. Too happy," she added cynically.

"One day Pablo said, 'My friend, I love you. Will you be my *novia?*' I agreed, so after some time, Pablo and his parents visited my home with lots of kusha, moonshine. All of us," she continued, "got very drunk while our parents discussed the marriage. They finally decided it was a good idea. We kept working hard until the days of marriage. Then we got married.

"When you are first married, you work for your mother-in-law and that is ugly. In the beginning she is kind but then she grows accustomed to you and starts scolding you for this and that. You are used to working for your own mother, so it's not nice working for a stranger. So, the next months I went and worked at his parents' house. I worked for his parents making tortillas, washing clothes, everything. He worked for my parents, cutting firewood. Finally, we were able to move into our own house.

"After a while you and your husband finish building a house. You fill it up with children and your life becomes happy again. If you have a good man, he can be like a father. He tells you what to do and takes care of you when you are sick. He gives you centavos for the house. You are quiet together and he sits by your fire while you make tortillas. Those are happy days. I was also happy as a mother to my son Miguel. When he was a boy, he used to come over to me and rub his hands on my arms and kiss my cheeks saying, 'Okay, Nan. Oh, Mother.' Now he doesn't kiss me, maybe because he drinks.

"Anyway, people here don't kiss much. I don't kiss my sister or my friends. Kissing is only for a man and a woman. His father, Pablo, was a good man until he went after another woman. He still comes every week and gives me a bag of corn and maybe some centavos." Then she added with a sneer that reminded me of my older sister, talking about her ex. "But I could do without his corn! Now I just look at him and wonder sometimes why I gave up my freedom for him."

"So, does that mean Tina will get married soon like you did at fifteen?"

"*Dios*, no," Teresa answered for Tina. "I want Tina to wait until she's about twenty-five and knows about life. You must learn about life first because a man can leave you."

Teresa stroked my hair, smoothing it down over my shoulders. "I am alone, but I have Tina and Miguel, so that is my happiness. Miguel works in Santiago, the other village." Her thin chest heaved. "But" she exhaled strongly, "there is too much work. I want to quit at the end of the month and just work at home. I miss my animals and my little fire when I am here. I love my animals. My dogs, my cats, all my animals. I love them just like my mother used to love her animals. I'm only paid ten *quetzales* a month so maybe I can earn more by selling *tamales* on the coast." Her free hand swung through the air, indicating the coast, far away. The actual coast was far away, especially if you had to walk. But the coast, I learned, for Mayans in San Lucas, was anything south of the volcanoes.

"I can make money at home and not be with these people." Scowling, she nodded her head toward the house. "Especially during the fiesta, there is work I can do in my home. Have you been to the fiesta, Mincha?" she asked with sudden eagerness.

"No, not yet Teresa."

"Oh, it's happy. The town fills up with people. People from all over the country come to drink and dance. In the plaza there are vendors selling everything! But you know there are always people who die during the fiesta. Mostly from drinking too much. I drink too. Sometimes I drink until I fall. It usually takes me three or four *octavos*, small bottles, for that to happen. Before I fall, though, I get hot and feel like dancing. So, I go out there and begin to dance."

Tina and I both laughed at the image of this woman dancing drunkenly at a fiesta, but Teresa reproached our laughter. "People can die at fiesta." Her tone was uncharacteristically sharp. "They die from hangovers. I get worried because my son drinks too much and he could die." She paused in her work and stared at me for a long quiet moment then added as proof, "Last fiesta two men died."

"From drinking?" I prompted her.

"Oh no. It was because they weren't happy," she answered, again contradicting herself.

Tina was watching her mother very closely, almost as if she was afraid of something.

"You see, San Lucas is a powerful saint," Teresa explained. "One of those men, a merchant, was sad. He said, 'Why did I come here? I'm not selling anything. I'll leave this shit town and go to Santiago where I can make mountains of money. But first I'll go swimming.' So even though he was sad, he went to the lake and drowned because our saint that protects us, San Lucas, doesn't like you to be unhappy or to be with those people from Santiago. If you are sad the saints will kill you.

"Other men have gone down to the lake and disappeared. Some fishermen say when they go out at midnight, they see a huge serpent living in the water. That snake can grab you, so you have to watch out."

I had already heard stories about the lake beside this old town of San Lucas Tolimán. Tolimán means "where the reeds are gathered" because reeds are collected from the lake's coastline to make the *petate*, the mat the Indians use for sleeping. Whenever I looked at the lake's deep sapphire-blue waters, I couldn't help but believe what the Indians said about Lago Atitlán. They claimed the lake was bottomless and went down to the end of the world. The water did seem to go to the depths and then stretch out, flanking the coast where three volcanoes towered alongside fearsomely steep, rocky cliffs where the Mayans planted their corn, their *milpa*, their staple for hundreds of years.

"But isn't it rich to bathe in those waters? You get so clean. You can splash water in front and in back. You go to the lake often, don't you Mincha?"

"Yes, I do," I admitted offhandedly, as I was still trying to digest her bizarre tale. The lake did have an enchanting, almost hypnotic, quality. The waters were soft, caressing, seeming to release a peaceful sense of freedom from one's very pores.

"Will you take me with you to the lake?" Tina suddenly pleaded. She was leaning against me, caressing my hair, then my arms. "My mother won't let me go." She became still and looked at the ground as if ashamed.

I looked at Tina, heard the earnestness in her voice. A royal-blue satin cloth was woven in the traditional manner into her thick black braids. Her brightly embroidered *huipil* hung over her *corte* that swept around her young body so tightly it made her walk with mincing footsteps. Her entire *traje* was a shield that protected her, that gave her something I would never have: a place in the world she knew and where she was protected by rules defined long ago by her own people. Rules that were handed down generation after generation. Again, she begged me to bring her to the lake. I knew she didn't know how to swim, but she wanted to at least play in the water. Her requests were so familiar. After all, behind her *traje*, her endless work with her mother, she was just a child.

I could feel the weight of Tina's history on her, holding her back from swimming freely in the water. Held back and held up by rules made long ago by her ancestors.

I had no sense of belonging to my own society, yet I never felt isolated, or abandoned. I always felt a connection because of my deep sense of belonging with my family, especially my brothers and sisters. They were a fierce and indestructible safety net in a changing world. My father's work had brought us to many new places, new cultures, new languages where we had no friends or familiar ties. But we faced these situations cheerfully because we faced them together, almost like a team. Then, as we grew more comfortable with our new lives, we moved apart from each other.

Sometimes that sense of belonging was carved out by the need to protect each other. My little sister was only in first grade when my parents put us in a Catholic Puerto Rican School. It wasn't easy for us in that school. The nuns only spoke Spanish in my sister's grade. Though this sister was always a quiet and respectful child, the best behaved in our family, once when she didn't understand orders, the nun took it as disrespect and wacked the back of her legs with a ruler. After that, I'd sneak down to check on her—as if I could do anything. But I loved her, and we counted on each other in our new lives. Every morning we had to go to mass, but at that time unstable people weren't institutionalized and there was a woman who would barge into the mass waving palms, singing about *Dios*, sometimes ripping at her clothes. She was a fearsome woman. When she grabbed my sister, yanked her from the pew, then started heading toward the church door, I ran over, unsnarled the woman's hands from my sister's skinny little arms and dragged my sister back safely to the pews. I protected my sister then, but now she was the one, reliable and steadfast, I can always count on.

※

A few days later, on my way to work, Tina caught sight of me. She called out so the three of us could walk together to our workplace. As we approached the town center, women walked by us, loaded down with armfuls of beautiful white wildflowers, tiny flowers with shiny stems so it looked like the women were walking with snowflakes suspended in front of them.

"Where did they get those, Teresa?"

"At the market."

"Let's get some."

She was very hesitant. "People will think you are going to get married if you get those flowers."

"They will?"

"Yes."

"Oh well, let's get some anyway."

"Yes." She agreed but now I wondered what it meant to her to break a marriage rule. Or perhaps those flowers were used for other occasions as well. I followed her into the market. The smell of *horchata*, a sweet thick drink of boiled rice and sugar, hit us. We walked past the small stalls of satin ribbons, plastic glittery jewelry, mountains of plastic basins in blue, red, and yellow.

Teresa led, Tina followed, and I was at the end of our single-file line curving round Indian women squatting beside pyramids of fruits and vegetables. Teresa stopped in front of two women to say hello. As if she was my marriage broker, she explained in her broken Spanish that I was the young woman who didn't have a *marido* or *novio* but had had one before—an introductory spiel I heard frequently. The ladies giggled and said something about me in Kaqchiquel. They seemed a bit cruel. They pointed and laughed and talked, and I couldn't understand a word. I laughed back falsely but I was glimpsing a world just beyond my reach, just like Teresa did when she didn't understand Spanish.

We entered a hall filled with flowers—lilies, purple and yellow carnations, reddish purple wildflowers and thousands of the tiny snowflake flowers. Teresa and I stood before them, oohing and aahing like schoolgirls. "Look at it," she instructed me, tenderly holding up a flowered stem so I could examine it, all the intricate work that intertwined into its beauty. Teresa insisted that each flower had to be regarded separately and complimented for its color or shape. Nothing was to be taken for granted. Nothing overlooked. I mimicked her as she paused, as she relished each moment. All those moments made up her life, so filled with struggle but complete with beauty as she paused to inhale what was placed before her—each of life's blessings, a gift bestowed upon her. Finally, we left, laughing and happy, weighed down by flowers, a running teasing commentary trailing behind us from people giggling at the sight of the lean, ancient Teresa carrying love flowers.

⁂

"I don't know what's wrong with me," Teresa complained a few days later. Every time she poked at the fire, she gripped the thatched wall like a crutch. "Two months ago, I lay sick in bed for eight days. Most people get well after three days, but I just kept lying there until Chula, lovely Tina got worried. Now, once again, I'm sick with that same pain in my head." The sunlight, streaming through the thatch walls, mottled her face so she looked sickly. "You know, it's this work. Those people always wanting more and more work from me."

"Work, bah," Tina snapped, then clicked her tongue against her teeth. "Not work," she repeated, again clicking her tongue against her teeth, a familiar sound Mayans used to show disapproval. "Bah, my Nan was drunk last night! That's why she has pain." The young girl closed her eyes tightly as if she couldn't bear to look at Teresa, then turned her back to her.

"It's true," Teresa admitted, "last night I got drunk. I went to the *cofradía* to pray and to hear music and the man in charge gave each woman two drinks of kusha."

The San Lucas *cofradía* was a small one-room rancher. The *cofradía* is an offshoot of the Catholic Church, created long ago by the Spaniards as a sort of religious propagation tool used to convert and control the Indians. It was a world housed separately from the main church so through time, away from the eyes of the church, the Mayans integrated their own beliefs with Catholic rituals and symbolism. Slowly the *cofradía* became their haven of spiritual and political power. The San Lucas *cofradía* was small but always had a traffic of people milling around. Its windows had no panes; a series of metal poles barred entry into the room that was always crammed with holy statues, flowers, candles, flower petals strewn across the floor, fruits, crosses, photos, and medallions. It was usually smoky from the copal, a resin that the Indians burn as incense. And in one corner stood the statue of Maximón, the saint Teresa prayed to frequently.

Maximón is a saint-like figure who is a defiant trickster. Mayans all over the country appeal to Maximón for spiritual guidance. His wooden effigy appears on *cofradía* altars, but never in churches. His favorite offerings are alcohol, money, and tobacco. And like the *cofradías*, he resists assimilation into the Ladino culture and instead is protector of Mayan rites. Some say he was a Mayan *ajq'ij*, sacred leader, who resisted the Spanish conquest. The Spanish pursued him, but he repeatedly evaded capture using his transformative powers. Finally, he was caught and either hanged or torn to pieces, only to miraculously come together again. Yet another version states that he was captured by the Spanish and locked up for continuing to practice traditional Mayan spirituality, but he escaped mysteriously from his jail cell several times before finally being put to death. He even returns in the modern version of him fighting in the armed struggle to regain Indigenous lands. In each version, Maximón is somehow dismembered and re-assembled, usually donning scarves that symbolically hold together the pieces of wood representing his whole body, which remains indestructible and subversive.

It seemed strange that Teresa would get drunk in a *cofradía*, a sacred community. Many parishes looked down on the *cofradías* for what was called their pagan rites. But San Lucas Church had veered from the religious hierarchy and supported the Mayans' choice of prayer. The feeling was that the two religions were not that far apart. Both religions emphasized ritual purity, had ceremonies enlisting sacrifice and used fasting as a means of purification. Even confession and baptism were practiced by both. The difference was the Mayan religion didn't focus on achieving salvation, but instead strove to balance the vital energies shared with all living beings and the Earth. The Mayan religion is, moreover, a felt sense of life rather than based in dogma like Catholicism.

At one time, the village was run by the *cofradía* leaders and *ajq'ij* shamans who acted as judges and decision-makers. The government tried to put an end to that system when the *cofradías* aligned themselves with cooperatives and trade unions. Both groups were attacked with every form of violence under the guise of fighting communism but, nonetheless, the *cofradía* remained a stronghold of the Mayans, a pathway to eldership and a safe hub of community rituals for people like Teresa.

"We prayed and drank but after we drank, all we wanted to do was dance and dance. Oh, our heads were spinning fast. The only problem was, there were just two men and a lot of women. So, we all danced with those two men."

"And then my Nan fell asleep," Tina added resentfully, still looking the other way.

"Yes, Chula Tina says I became tired later on and fell asleep right there at the *cofradía*, sitting next to the wall. Well, I was too drunk to walk home, so I went to the man in charge and said, 'Tat, father, forgive me for this rudeness, but I am drunk and ask you to let me sleep on your floor with my Chula Tina.' He agreed and it turned out I wasn't the only one who needed to sleep there. The next morning the floor was lined with women on their *petate* mats. Worst of all, that man has so many children and they carry lice. So, all morning I've been scratching my head. Isn't it ugly to have lice?"

Teresa's gnarly fingers dug furiously into her scalp. "Oh, ooooh," she whined. "I feel one louse eating my head over here and then running over there and, oh, I can't get away from them! But it was pretty in the morning. I helped make breakfast for everyone, even though I couldn't eat. I felt like I was going to die and couldn't even go to work. No, I didn't want to. Oh oooh!" She hid her face in her hands.

"It's all right," I consoled her, wrapping my arm around her shoulders. "It's all right. Everyone drinks too much once in a while. I know exactly what it's like the next day."

"You feel like a pig after you drink, don't you?" she blubbered, dropping her hands from her face to hold onto me. "I just want to lie down all day with my head turning and spinning. I can't eat or work; all I can do is drink Fanta or Coke. I already drank three bottles, one right after another, because the bubbles help me. Oh, what shame the way we drink! And what do we want to do when we drink? We want everything! We want to dance and sing and scream and cry. So many men and women cry. Who knows why? That's what drink does to you."

Tina stood close to her Nan. Suddenly, we heard the *patrons* talking inside the house. As soon as Teresa heard their voices, her body jolted, their voices like sharp needles pricking at her to return to work. She jerked herself back to her bag of *elote*, dried corn. Her fingers began nipping out each kernel by the roots. Just the rhythm of the task began to calm her. Afterwards Teresa soaked the corn in a huge plastic tub of water. When the corn got mushy, she rinsed it again and lugged it to the mill. Sometimes, when the mill machine was broken, like this morning, she ground it into *nixtamal* herself.

Grinding the corn by hand looked like long tedious work to me but it was an act of love in Mayan homes. Every aspect of maize was precious and had always been central to the Mayans who for centuries served it together with beans. They deduced from experience that this combination was not only a perfect protein but also prevented pellagra, a disease caused by niacin deficiency. It was *nixtamal*, this dough, and the process of making it, that prevented sickness.

Today the Mayans use the same process. They soak the corn in ash and lime before grinding it. The ash and lime are readily available and cheap. The alkaline wood ash releases niacin into maize while it also softens the corn kernel hull. Every bit of the corn is used: maize stalks around town for fences, feed for pigs, and the husk of the maize is tenderly wrapped around *tamales*, sweets, and other foods. Maize has always been central to life. Even in the ancient texts of the Popul Vuh, the only sacred book not burned by the Conquistadores, men and women were said to be created from maize.

"It isn't hard work," Teresa insisted as she ground the corn, "you just swing your body back and forth with the stone. When I was a little woman like Tina, this stone was all we had. There was no mill. You should have seen me grind." Droplets of sweat trickled off her forehead as she rocked rapidly back and forth. "I mashed ten pounds without getting tired. I just spread the corn over the stone and poon, poon, poon. Then pass it through another time to make certain all the kernels are flattened and the little *nixtamal*, maize dough, is ready for tortilla making."

Winded, she stood to stir the pot. Tina jumped into her place. Leaning over the *metate*, wearing the same colorful *huipil* as Teresa, the same *corte*, grinding the corn the way she learned from her Nan. It wasn't hard to envision Teresa as a young girl or to envision the women who came before her. "When I was young and used the stone, it was so easy. Now I can't arrive. My Tina has to do most of the work because I'm too old."

"How old are you, Teresa?"

"I am fifty in the morning," she snickered, "and 150 by nightfall." Her eyes, spry as a bird's, quickly checked out my reaction. "God knows, I must have lived a hundred years by now. Just look at my hands and face. Look at my gray hair. It looks ugly and only reminds me that I'm old, that soon my mouth will be filled with dirt." Snorting, she turned to the fire, her leathery hands poking at the coals.

"When I was young, how you would see me work! Every day on the *finca* I made tortillas, washed clothes, and cleaned the house for the señora, then I went home and did all my own housework." Teresa's voice deepened as she reminisced. "Since the señora only paid me seven quetzales a month, I had to find more money. I opened a little store in my house where I sold soap, combs, gum, cigarettes, and kusha to the other *mozos*, the workers. I owned a little radio, so we had music at my *tiendita*, my little store, and listened to marimba. Life is sad without music. Oh, I used to be a rich woman then. Maybe five or seven quetzales would come into my *tiendita* a week. Now my poor little money bag is always empty."

She wiped her thick hands across her *corte*, then grabbed the wooden spoon again, slowly stirring the corn. She squinted into the smoke. The constant smoke dimmed her eyesight. As with so many of the Mayan women, her eyesight would eventually fail.

"Bah," Tina interrupted angrily, leaning over the *metate*, her back to her mother. "Your bag is empty because you buy kusha!" She looked over her shoulder toward us, an expression of complete disapproval on her face.

Teresa didn't listen, instead continued with her own saga. "I had something once, but I gave it all away for Pablo. He kept chasing women all the time, so what could I do? I worked and sometimes I cried, but finally I said, 'I'm not afraid to be alone! I have brothers and sisters. I have my friends! All this can go to shit!' Because it was shit. So, I sold all my possessions—my radio, my bed, my little table that he made for our marriage. I sold all my things and left him to go to shit with all his women.

"Well, when I left the *finca*, I was crying and so were the people there. 'What are we going to do without you?' they cried. 'You are the best people we know! You sell us food from your store and watch our children for us. What are we going to do without you?' But now I'm happy that I left the *finca*. Life is better here in town. At first, I wanted to open another store in San Lucas, but that's all you see around here. You walk down one street and there are stores. You take another street and there are more stores. No, it wouldn't serve to have another store here."

The town was indeed overrun by the sort of store that has one tiny counter crammed with glass jars holding chiclets, candies and *pan dulce*, sweet bread. Maybe in the backroom, where the storekeepers lived, there were dusty buttons, nails, some other useful odds and ends. But Teresa was convinced that San Lucas was a bustling metropolis. "So, I left Pablo and the *finca*. He still visits us every Sunday to see his Chula Tina and Miguel if he's around. Pablo always brings us corn and centavos and even yells at Miguel for drinking. But" she added with a sneer, "I can live without anything from him!"

Teresa lifted the tub and slowly poured off the water until only mushy corn remained at the bottom. Tina leaped to attention, placing a cloth ring on her head while her mother carefully hoisted the tub on top. Tina's sleek black mane hung down to her slim waist as she stood erect, then headed toward the welcome sound of the mill's gasping engine.

Teresa went back to work, grabbing a gob of dough that Tina ground into a smooth texture. "The *patrón* only gives us a few beans and tortillas to eat," she said, leaning over to tell me as if it was a secret. "My son Miguel helps us. He came by last night to give us some money."

"Good, Teresa!" I said, happy to hear something positive.

"He isn't drinking anymore so he had seven quetzales. You should have seen Tina! She was so happy. She cries and cries when he's drunk because she is afraid someone will hurt him. She loves him like a brother."

"Like a brother?" I asked surprised. "Isn't Miguel her brother?"

"Oh no. You see, I took Tina into my home as a baby. I was having my own children then, but none of them lived. I don't know why, but they would always die, even before they had any spirit. Their arms withered up like little sticks, their bellies grew huge and then they died.

I had two boys who grew but then they died. I don't know why, but that is my sadness. Well, one day Tina's *pobrecita* mother died on the *finca* where I worked. The poor lady worked herself to death. Her father had too many children to care for alone. I had no little woman, so I took Tina into my home. My husband let me do it, but he wouldn't carry her because she was a little woman, and he was a man. Who knows why some men think that way? Sometimes men are even angry when you give birth to a little woman because all she does is eat and work in the house. Well, I like having a little woman, so I took in my Chula Tina."

"And what about her father?"

"Her father was still living in Santiago where Miguel works now. He already had five other children and couldn't take care of Tina. Then a worse story happened in poor little Tina's life. One day her father came to town to sell fish and buy maize. He got drunk and when he tried to get into his *lancha*, his boat, he fell backward in the water and drowned."

"Oh no, Teresa, poor Tina! She must have been so sad."

"Oh no, Tina was just tiny, and she didn't understand. That is why she is happy when Miguel comes to see her. But when her real brothers and sisters visit, she says, 'Pffffft, I don't want to see them.' They wear different clothes, you see, and in Santiago there are only bad people."

"And what's so bad about them, Teresa?" I asked as I added more wood to her fire.

"Oh, those people only live for themselves. They are just another people. They wear different clothes, and they just aren't right.

"They don't know how to do much, those people. They only want to make tortillas and beans for their own children. You go to that town and ask, 'Where can I buy a cup of coffee?' or 'Where can I buy five centavos of tortillas?' They look at your *traje* then everyone tells you, 'Not here. We don't have any.' Poor Miguel, what can he do over there? He only works with men so if I send him a pound of coffee, he has to make it himself. He doesn't wear his *traje* now. He just wears white, but they still know where he is from. What can he do without a woman and only those people around? I don't like them. They can go to shit."

The force of her conviction had a whole history behind it and her clothes marked the boundaries of an ancient conflict. The towering volcanoes marked other boundaries. The Tolimán volcano shadows the home of the Mayan Kaqchiquel Indians. The other volcano, Atitlán, guards Santiago, the town of the fierce Mayan Tzutuhil nation, the last of the Mayan Indians to be conquered by the Spanish. Long before the Spanish arrived, the Kaqchiquel and the Tzutuhil nations had a tradition of conflict and feud. The volcanoes represented a border that divided the two nations. The man or woman who dared stray beyond that boundary would be killed by border guards camouflaged in the bushes. The two towns were barely eight miles apart and out-and-out warfare no longer existed, but just as Teresa expressed, mistrust remained. Now the *traje*, traditional dress, was the boundary line. But Miguel, like so many young men, removed his *traje* in order to work. No one in Santiago would give him a job if he wore his San Lucas *traje*. And if he turned to the Ladinos for work, he would be mocked and scorned. So, he abandoned his *traje*.

Teresa flapped another tortilla onto the *comal*, her brows knotted with worry. Tina appeared at the doorway, serene as she lifted the basin from her head, smiling at her Nan.

"Anyway," Teresa resumed, "we will go visit my sister one of these days. You should see her. She is so different from me. She's fat and pretty. Her husband and children give her centavos, and she works peacefully at home making tortillas, washing clothes, and sweeping. Her son is a *mozo*, a worker at Pompolah, the same *finca* where I grew up. To reach there you get off the bus down the road and then walk, one hour if you are a man and two hours if you are a woman.

"I don't know what I would do without my sister and my friends. I talk with them about Miguel, about money, about food. We tell each other jokes. You know, in this life there can be so much suffering. I wouldn't be anyone without my women friends. Without them I would die from sadness and worry."

The thatch walls suddenly started to vibrate, interrupting her story. Emaciated dogs sniffing around the edges of the hut rattled its fragile walls. Teresa hissed like a snake at them, then affectionately muttered, "Poor little things." Rushing to the doorway, Tina shouted in an angry mixture of Spanish and Kaqchiquel until the mongrels cowered and retreated to the hedges. As soon as Tina turned her back on them, they edged forward, whimpering and mangy.

Teresa clicked her tongue and whispered furtively, "I love the poor animals but the *Patrón* gets angry so we must keep them away. I don't know why the *Patrón* doesn't like animals. They are my friends. I love both my dogs, Lucero and Paloma. God gave animals to us and they help us and protect us. Well, the *Patrón* is just another class of people." Tina hurled more epithets and rocks until the dogs raced away, their tails tucked between their skinny legs. "Poor animals, they keep you company too, and guard your house like friends."

With the dogs finally out of range, Tina and Teresa returned to work. Teresa shuffled back and forth between the fire and loading tortillas into her hand-woven basket. The sun reached its zenith in a clear blue sky. The day was hot, but a slight breeze ran through the sleepy village, cooling women as they trudged to and from the lake bearing jugs on their heads. The men plodded along, eyes lowered, often with huge loads of wood on their back, held in place by a leather strap across their foreheads. Outside I could see small Indian boys and girls scampering over rocks, broken glass and logs. The little girls, dressed exactly like Teresa and Tina, scampered along together laughing, holding each other's hands. The boys raced around together, kicking a ball through the dust. Only the eternal sound of tortilla-making broke the noise of child's play.

Eventually the sun sank behind the volcanoes and smoke from the dying fire drifted out of the hut. The day was done, but before we left, we sat to sip some watery coffee Teresa brought from home. Tina swallowed her coffee in a gulp so she could sneak out for a few moments of freedom before heading home with her Nan, where the entire work ritual would be repeated, from gathering firewood and making tortillas to washing clothes.

Teresa leaned against the wall, eyes drooping with fatigue as she primly sipped her coffee. She could relax now that her work was done, but as if she was my professor, she was intent on explaining two subjects today: the tortillas and Miguel.

"You see Mincha," she confided after first asking about my family again, "what happens to my Miguel is he drinks so much, his desire for women is taken away. How does Miguel think? He thinks like a *burro*, as if the bottle was his woman. So, he stays alone and makes my Tina cry. But do you know why, Mincha?"

She didn't wait for my answer. "He loved the wrong woman. That's why he drinks and there's no cure. Poor little Miguel. When he was seventeen this woman began talking to him. They weren't united yet, but they were together so much that I said to myself, 'Well, this is good.

My Miguel is becoming a man with a woman walking beside him.'

"Well, one day there was a fiesta, but Miguel said, 'I better not go because I don't have any money.' So, he stayed home, sat by the fire with me and thought and thought. Then he said, 'Nan, I may not have money to take Manuela to the fiesta, but I'm going anyway just to walk around.' Well, what did he see there but this woman walking with another man! The man had his arm wrapped around her and Manuela didn't say a word when Miguel walked by. I think Miguel wanted to kill himself at that moment because he started a fight with that man who was so big. He finally returned home with his arms twisted and his face looking like worms chewed it.

"Then Miguel started to drink and drink. But did that woman care? Miguel drank and his sadness kept weighing on him until one day he came to me and said, 'Nan, I'm leaving this town. I'm going to stay with my father!' I cried and cried, 'Oh no, my son. Don't go from here. Here we have work.' 'Nan, I am leaving,' he told me over and over. So, I said, 'If my son leaves then I will go with him.' 'Yes, Nan,' he replied. 'Pack up your clothes and we will leave.' 'But what about my dishes and animals?' I sobbed to him. 'What about our belongings?' 'They'll be safe,' he answered. 'The neighbors will watch them. Just gather your clothes together and we'll leave tonight.' It was late, very late at night, maybe around eleven o'clock, but he wanted to leave right then."

She leaned over the fire to pick up her white tin coffee pot and with a quick nod, ordered me to take more. She poured out my portion daintily, not losing a drop.

"Tina was just a little woman," Teresa continued, "but she helped me pack. The tears filled our eyes. We walked through the dark to his father's house, crying as we carried our bundles, so afraid to be out like that in the night. Then it was so ugly arriving at Miguel's father's house. I left Pablo so many years before and when we first arrived, he told us to leave. I just sat down and said, 'No. This house isn't yours or mine, it belongs to my Miguel and here he will stay.' Pablo and I argued until we started screaming and all the neighbors could hear us. Finally, Pablo agreed. 'Yes,' he said, 'this is our son's house.' So, we began living with Miguel's father again.

"Ah, it was so ugly for me to live there again with Miguel's father. I thought I had lost all my feeling for him, but his new woman was the lady living right next to us. Well, she smiled at me every morning, but I never said a word to her. Miguel's father worked in the fields and came home very late after dark after he had seen her, so we never talked. In this way I grew very sad. I had walked with him for so many years that I felt strange, even jealous, when he was with Elena. He wouldn't even eat my tortillas, only hers."

Church bells began to toll in the distance, this time marking the day's end. Teresa squinted, looking toward the plaza. "After three months I grew so skinny from sadness I said to Tina, 'My little woman, let's go to Sololá and find some work there.' Tina was young in those days, but she agreed. Then I told Miguel and he said, 'Yes, my little Nan, you should go to Sololá because you are too sad here. But remember, you walked with my father and, although he's gone to shit with another woman, you cannot walk with another man. If you do, I'll never speak to you again.' At that time, I was so filled with hate for his father and other men that I promised to never walk with another.

"So, Chula Tina and I packed our clothes, walked back to the lake, and took the boat to Sololá. There I found work in a *comedor*, a little restaurant. Yes, that was my best job. The owner was a Nan who gave Tina and me a room with a *petate* to sleep on. Every day there was food left over, so we ate and ate until my sadness finally disappeared. Yes, I soon grew fat and life was happy again.

"That's when I met a man named Chepe. He used to come to the *comedor* and talk with me every day. At last, I understood what was happening and said to myself, 'Well, this man is talking to me too much. He must want to walk with me.' So, I thought and thought about it until I realized that I wanted him too.

"One day he came to me and said, 'Nan Mother, I would like to marry you. I can give you a house and land, and you can cook all day in your own home and never have to do any other kind of work. You can even keep a girl in the house to help you. I want to marry you, Teresa, because I can see you are a good woman with your Chula Tina, and I want both of you to come live with me on my land. When Chula Tina is older, she can even go to school. You can live in peace in your home.'

"'What a wonderful life that would be for me!' I thought. Chepe was a good man. He didn't drink. He knew how to love a woman and worked hard. He always brought Chula Tina and I presents and always talked to me. Even when he was angry, he could sit and talk with me. I liked him and wanted to marry him.

"Then I remembered my promise to Miguel 'If I take my happiness with Chepe,' I thought, 'my son will punish me. I'll never be able to see my poor little Miguel again.' So, I told Chepe, 'No, I can't marry you. My son will punish me.' And Chepe said, 'Nan, your son will punish you at first, but I will give him a home, too. He will get used to me and begin loving you again. You should marry me, Nan, and I will give you a better life.' Finally, I said no. I refused that man because I was afraid my son would punish me."

I resisted the urge to interrupt. The rules guiding Teresa's life seemed to me so contradictory—sometimes protecting her and other times limiting her and Tina. But she told the story without rancor toward her son. No, instead, her love for him quashed any self-concern as she continued her story.

"Then my friends who came to the market from across the lake began telling me, 'Your poor son is drinking all the time because his Nan lives so far away.' I listened to these stories and cried. Tina would look at me and start crying too. So, I thought if my Miguel is sad to be alone, then I'll return.

"God knows, if I had married Chepe my life would be easier now. If I had a man, he could fetch my firewood or give me centavos for food. If I had a man, the house wouldn't be so quiet. But it's difficult for an old woman like me to find a man because the older ones are already married and have their own children."

Teresa concluded her story with a giggle, resting her head affectionately on my shoulder. But then she surprised me with a new revelation. "Now," she sighed, "there's another man who wants to marry me. He has a piece of land that he's trying to buy little by little. He works for the *Patrón* like Pablo, clearing away bush or picking coffee, only makes sixty centavos a day. That isn't much but those poor little centavos help. He keeps asking me, 'Nan, Teresa, when will you marry me?' 'No, I won't marry you,' I tell him. 'I'm just an old woman who can't change her ways.' I know there's acid in my heart and I also think, 'Bah, what happens when you walk with a man? All his promises become nothing.'"

Suddenly the squeals of spying children disrupted her.

"Mincha! Nan! Mincha! Nan!" Tina teased us from outside, her nose wedged between the cracks of the thatched hut. Two other children joined in taunting, laughing and exposing their teeth, rotted straight up to the gums. Teresa hissed in their direction, so they dashed away just like the dogs. Teresa laughed at them but then became serious again as she gathered her goods. The tiny coffee pot, the woven napkins to cover her tortillas, her metal cups, all piled neatly in her basket.

Teresa stooped down and picked up the cloth ring used to steady burdens on her head. Her earrings trembled as she lifted the basin until it was squarely set on top of her erect frame. Tina lingered by the door, still relishing her freedom, giggling with her friends, her lanky arms swinging beside her. The instant her mother left the hut, however, Tina's face tightened and with tiny precise footsteps, she obediently fell in place by Teresa's side, carrying an identical basket on her head.

Teresa lived in a little wooden house she got through the experimental farm. Her neighborhood, on the edge of town, was in a cluster of houses behind Casa Spencer where I lived. After you walked past a large cornfield, then a smaller one and a vegetable garden, you would find yourself surrounded by chickens, dogs, babies, women weaving or shucking their corn, cleaning out beans, carrying water, spending much of their day working in total silence.

No wonder the Mayans seemed steady. There were so many daily rituals that brought them into the present moment. Their weaving, with ninety-six threads per inch, demanded concentration, their nimble fingers picking through the threads to weave embossed embroidery thread through into designs. The mere act of making their tortillas, the repetitive thump, thump, thump of the ball of *nixtamal* leaping from hand to hand, slowly flattening into a soft round tortilla. Hoeing and harvesting and planting and even carrying water to and from the lake. All these were repetitive movements that guided the soul to a state of stillness.

Teresa and I stood in that stillness, undisturbed for a moment, on the two short steps leading up to her house. We stared out at her thatched kitchen hut, the coffee trees, the cornfield, the neighbor's door shut tight. Her black dog, Lucero, had come out to greet us and now nuzzled her *corte*. He was a well-formed dog, free of the mange and skinny-to-the-bone look of most San Lucas dogs. Another one, a white one, Paloma, dove, rested by her feet. Teresa stroked Lucero's head and promised him she had a bundle of tamales waiting for him in the kitchen hut. So, the dogs waited as we went into the sleeping hut.

The sleeping hut was crammed with Teresa's hodgepodge of worldly goods. There were two planks, covered in *petates,* used for beds. A string of candles hung from a wall and beside it dangled a huge calendar left on January with a glossy photo of a blonde woman and child walking across a field. But instead of turning the pages, Teresa marked time in her world by harvests, the fiesta, Christmas, Holy Week, and the personal life experiences common to all of humanity: her period, childbirth, great illnesses, deaths, droughts.

Two cats slept together under the calendar. One was a mother of two kittens. Teresa quickly mixed up some oatmeal from work and fed it to the kittens. Then she went over to the corner of the hut where there was a cage next to the firewood neatly lined up against the wall. Beside the firewood was a haphazard clutter of cardboard boxes, clothes and unfinished weaves that gave her home an uncared for, forgotten look. But Teresa just inched her way around the mess, to titter and talk with a soft gray bird with red eyes and a beak shaped into a fine point for digging out insects from rotting bark. She stuck her twiggy finger in the cage and the bird sang, then jumped on it and Teresa looked back at me pleased, quite enchanted by her home filled with her companions, these animals.

We went over to her kitchen hut that leaned at an impossible angle, gradually deteriorating into a heap of cornstalks, thatch, and worn *petate* mats. I gaped at the ruins, but Teresa saw it differently: "Oh, it's so much better for me to make tortillas at home," she said, leading me into the cooking hut, "My little fire is on the ground so I can kneel on my *chula petate* to rest while I work. Come on," she urged me, "Tina will start the fire and my cat, Rosa, the black one, will sit on my lap. She's so happy when I come home." Yet another set of cats in the cooking hut.

Tina had already started the fire with kerosene. A small bottle of it cost them thirteen centavos, but this pair had no time to collect kindling. Tina, kneeling in front of the fire, was already rinsing corn by dropping large handfuls into a metal pail filled with water. The corn soaked momentarily before she carefully poured the contents into a plastic basin. She repeated this process over and over, laughing playfully when we arrived.

"My brother Miguel is coming!" Tina announced to her mother, clapping her hands. She was happy, but Teresa flew into a panic, rummaging frantically in the dark corners of her hut.

"I must get this place cleaned before Miguel comes home or he'll be angry. He's like any man. He expects everything to be perfect for him, as if we had nothing to do but cook and clean all day. Oooooo," she shuddered, stooping here and there. She stooped so much I was surprised she wasn't a hunchback by then. She was straight as a pin, especially when she knelt in front of her fire.

"Look at all my dishes!" Teresa exclaimed as if seeing them for the first time. Dented pots and pans, basins and water jugs, and rusty barrels full of brackish drinking water filled the room, so much stuff it was nearly impossible for her to move around the tiny ramshackle kitchen. She leaned over to sort her dishes, arranging them in an order discerned only by her. Tina grabbed a machete and began chopping up a huge chunk of brown sugar for coffee.

Teresa moved the dishware on top of a heap of string and old rusty cans. Then she spotted something else. "Just look at this," she whispered excitedly, "this is what makes my home so happy." She dragged a cardboard box out of the shadows. Inside were ten gleaming, new pots. "They cost fifty quetzales, but I pay only three quetzales a month. If I even miss one payment the merchant will take them away from me. I never use them because the fire turns them black and that would make me too sad." She lifted the pots out of the box one by one, inspecting their aluminum sheen like a jeweler. She counted them aloud, turning them over, carefully placed them back in the box, then shoved it back into the dark corner.

"I hide that box whenever Miguel drinks," she confided, "because he could sell them. He already sold my radio! That man thinks like a *burro*!"

"A *burro*," Tina whispered furtively to her Nan, pointing to Miguel's silhouette framed by the doorway. Despite their ceaseless talk about him, their restless anticipation before his arrival, Tina and Teresa only mumbled a polite hello as he entered and tenderly touched their shoulders. Then they returned indifferently to their tasks. When he shook my hand, his square working hand held mine loosely. He sat down on the only chair, a miniature child's version no bigger than a footstool that allowed him to sit comfortably by the fire. When Miguel took off his sombrero, he revealed a bold, strong face with a shock of black hair that hung down almost concealing his eyes. His languid gestures and soft-spoken manner made this already attractive man even more appealing. A rope bag bulging with fresh fruit for his Nan and sister tumbled to the ground.

Instantly his hands were filled with tortillas and coffee, as were mine. I was moved, watching the family reverently making the same gestures I had witnessed in jail. They kissed their first tortilla, thanked God for the blessing and then again later, they thanked each other after they'd eaten the last tortilla. Then family chatter ensued, speaking earnestly to each other in Kaqchiquel. Teresa, as usual, seemed worried or upset as she spoke with Miguel. As if to calm her, he caressed his mother's shoulders. Later Teresa slid some *tamales* into his rope bag, then trudged out the door toward the *molida*, the mill, a basin of corn on her head.

As soon as she left, Tina and Miguel reverted to Spanish. Tina imitated Teresa, putting an exaggerated worried frown on her face, hands on her hips, she mocked, "Chula Tina! Don't sit there! Chula Tina, say your prayers! Chula Tina, don't sit that way, that's a sin!" Tina scoffed, taking a piece of fruit from Miguel's bundle. "And she doesn't want me to eat this fruit because it will make my stomach sour. But I will!" She bit into it and, still chewing, continued to mimic, "My mother wants to me to do this work and that work, but she won't let me go to school."

"You see," Miguel leaned toward me, his hard mannish fingers touching my shoulder as he spoke. "Our mother is afraid Tina will become a Ladina. For my mother that is the worst thing that can happen. But you see, we must change. Everywhere we go, the Ladinos own the land. The Ladinos run the governments. So, if we want to live, we must change. My mother is afraid of the dark, of spirits, of everything! My mother!"

Rosa, the cat, climbed on his lap as he spoke and Tina playfully tapped on his arm, so he gently stroked his sister's head, giving her the attention she sought. The other cat climbed on Tina's shoulders, and we all sat quietly content next to the fire, the smell of *nixtamal* curling around us.

"But Tina needs to learn to read," Miguel continued. "Tina can wear her *traje,* but she has to know how to read, how to sign her name. This is the only way she will protect herself in the future, because my mother is right. Life is dangerous for us near the Ladinos. But we can protect ourselves in many ways, not just the old ways."

Smoke was floating between us toward the roof, through layers of spiderwebs and soot. We fell back into a comfortable silence. I sipped on my coffee, then placed the cup on the floor beside me. Tina jumped up and grabbed it. "No, no! Never put your cup there!"

"Why?" I wondered aloud.

"That's a sin! A sin!" she cried, placing it higher on a rock by the fire. Looking around I saw everyone's cup was off the ground, away from their bodies, a practice Tina must have learned from Teresa, and Teresa from her own mother. But it was difficult for me to navigate through this web of Ladino and Mayan practices. Tina sat back down, calmed by moving my cup, bringing order to the visit.

The visit consisted mainly of sitting by the fire together in a comfortable silence. Finally, Miguel gave Tina the rest of the fruit, then stood slowly, his big hands holding onto his bag. Shifting his weight, he shook my hand formally, then turned on his heel to leave. The hut was vacant, more silent than ever it seemed now that he was gone.

Within moments Teresa returned, breathless. She lowered the basin of corn slowly to the ground as she spoke, "The *molida* was packed tonight. You should have seen it! Ugh! All the Ladinos bending their heads over the pipe, trying to dump their corn at the same time! Oh, it was terrible! They acted like horses, their hooves kicking backward and their noses pushing forward in everyone's way. Oh, I can't stand it! How they grab at your skirt and your arms!"

"Oh Nan, aye mi Nan," Tina mocked. Emboldened by Miguel's visit, she chomped on the forbidden mango he had given her. Teresa was so disturbed by her visit to the *molida,* the mill, that she didn't notice.

"And I met a *pobrecito* friend there who told me how dangerous the capital is. You see, there was this truck driving down the road," a pained expression contorted Teresa's face as she explained the latest gossip, "and the driver lost control. He drove straight into a house, knocking down all the walls, and right into the room where people usually sleep. Well, thank God no one was home. The woman had gone to the market to buy food and the man had left for work. The poor little man. There he was just like after the earthquake, standing in front of his house that was totally destroyed. He just stood there and stared at it. The woman stared at it, too, and they both cried, knowing they would have to rebuild their home and knowing, if they had been there, they would have died."

She knelt on the *petate* beside the *chula* fire, one arm wrapped around her waist, the other holding her chin. "You see how dangerous it is to live in the capital?" She looked at Tina proving her point to an old argument. "You see what I mean now? I would never live there. And no matter what, my Chula Tina will never go to work there. Yes, there is work in the capital but all the Indian girls who go there as servants have to put themselves with the men of the house. Either they put themselves with the father or the son. Sometimes they must be with both men. Well, then the *pobrecita* Indian servant gets pregnant and the wife gets angry and throws her out on the streets. No, it's dangerous to live in that capital. Our women go there, lose their *traje* and end up living with one man after another. I don't like that capital. And I have been there once."

Shaking her head again, she shifted her knees on the *petate*. I nodded in agreement, disconcerted that I had heard this story of vulnerability over and over again from women of all walks of life. Tina put her head on my lap, retreating from the conversation. She'd heard this story before too, anytime she mentioned going to the capital. But Teresa continued talking and working, happy to be home by her own fire, with her big black dog Lucero by the door and her cat settled on her lap.

Teresa's tongue clicked as her hands patted out more tortillas, spreading them across the *comal*. "No, the capital isn't good. I am used to the *finca*. Everything happened to me on the *finca*. That is where I became a woman. It was a bad day for me, the day I first started going by *catit,* the moon. It scared me so much. I was working in the kitchen when I noticed blood all over me. I started to cry because I thought I was going to die.

"The *Patrón* asked me what was wrong, and I told her. It was then I first heard how a woman, any woman, had to go by *catit* each month. Well, the *Patrón* was a Ladina, so I wondered if she was lying just to keep me working. 'Look,' she kept saying, 'this happens to every woman in the world. Now you have to watch out for men. They sense when a woman has changed and can become *enferma*, sick, and have babies.' I felt sure I was dying, that the *Patrón* just wanted to keep me working anyway because bosses are like that."

Staring at the fire, I tried to absorb her story, but I belittled her fear of Ladinas. She exaggerated everything, I thought to myself. She was so scared by Ladinos that she couldn't even absorb facts. Suddenly, I could relate to poor Tina. Anything that isn't Kaqchiquel frightened this woman and limited her world and, worst of all, Tina's world. Only later could I understand how justified her fears were.

Teresa continued, "Well, I went home to my mother and told her what happened. And do you know what she did? She got angry, like I was to blame for the whole thing. 'Now you start this,' she screamed, 'and I have to watch you, or you'll be running off with some man!' I ran away into a cornfield and began to cry and cry. I thought a *brujo*, a witch, put a curse on me. It took me a long time to realize that other women were just like me, and I wasn't sick. As you get older you learn to live with it, but you never like it. You just think, 'Well, this is my fate, going by *catit* and having blood come out of me.'

"My husband told me that when men reach fourteen, a sickness grabs them too that makes them want to take one woman after another. Some people say you can cure that sickness and others say you can't."

"The men, Teresa?" I started to protest then I couldn't help but laugh inside of myself at this notion. In fact, I wondered if she was teasing me, especially when she half smiled as she cocked her head to look at me. It wouldn't have been the first time that she or any of the other Mayans played on my ignorance.

"It's true! And there's another sickness, too." As she spoke tortilla after tortilla fell from her hands. She stopped to nibble one, feeding bits to her cat. "Down on the coast where we pick cotton, there are plenty of pretty girls because there are so many handsome boys. Those girls love money so much. They'll walk with anyone including old men. After they take an old man, they take his son. These women pass a sickness you can only cure with a penicillin shot. The shot costs eight quetzales, so what happens? The man keeps the sickness, gives it to his wife and who suffers? It's the children, I tell you, that's who! The children will be born with the same sickness. Sometimes I think that's why it's hard for a woman to take pleasure lying with her man. She lies there with him and begins to think, 'Well, this means I am going to be pregnant, or my children will have that sickness.'"

As the moon rose to a sky brimming with stars, Teresa finally tired of her work and thoughts. She covered her basket of tortillas with a hand-woven cloth and shook Tina awake so she could go to sleep on her *petate*. Eyes still glued half shut, Tina stumbled through the doorway.

Teresa accomplished her final chore, setting the corn to simmer over the fire. She hung over the metal cauldron and swatted it with a cornhusk, commanding in a raspy voice, "You stay here! You stay here!" She slapped it with her cracked leathery hands, scolding it like a child.

"What *are* you doing, Teresa?" I asked.

"That," she declared as we headed out the door, "is so the *nixtamal* will cook even though we are gone. If you don't do that, its heart will follow you and it won't cook. Its heart wants to follow my heart."

I tried to accept that Teresa did not look at the world as I did. She didn't separate the universe into parts. There wasn't a sacred and a profane world for her. No, an elder at the *cofradía* had explained to me how a Mayan experienced the Earth as one living entity giving all the elements significance, so that even daily life, with all its mundane tasks, was a pathway to the spiritual world or God. What she was doing sounded illogical but had some significance I couldn't decipher. I stepped outside and Teresa followed me. We both gazed at the moon, so silver and clean in the sky.

"Oh, the moon," she murmured. "*Catit, catit* is so *chula*, so darling. You feel soft with *catit*, don't you? *Catit*, our grandmother who protects us in a special way when she is full. When *catit* is full, I remember my dreams. I dream I am walking and then I'm picking coffee, or my mother comes to me and talks.

"But more often my brother comes to me. Who knows why, but when our *chula catit* is fat, my brother comes in my sleep to talk and that feels so happy. He is so real, and we always talk beside a river, a beautiful huge river. It is so real, that when I open my eyes again, I'm frightened to see Chula Tina lying beside me. Who knows why we dream that way when we are sleeping? *Catit* helps us think like that. The *chula catit*, always watching the world."

# Los Naturales—The Natural Ones

Teresa sat on the church steps with me after a day's work. She had quit her job temporarily to begin preparing for the Day of the Dead. Plus, she told me coffee season begins soon so she and Tina would still be able to make their "little centavos." The town, enlivened by the annual fiesta, stretched out before us. The plaza was packed with townspeople, people from distant villages and the mountains.

We sat on the church steps, close to the evenly spaced niches around the perimeter that sheltered sacred statues of Teresa, Mary, Joseph, St Francis, and, of course, San Lucas, St Luke, the town's patron saint. The sunset's glow inched across their robes, then their hands, strong and tiny like Mayan hands, curled in prayer.

Teresa and I entered the church. The thick stone walls emitted a chill, obliging Teresa to tighten her colorful *rebozo*, shawl. It was a Catholic church but unlike one I had ever seen.

Indians crowded into the different naves while exuberant children dashed up and down the aisles. Dogs roamed freely, pausing occasionally to sniff at mothers kneeling or sitting in prayer. Some women had infants on their backs or others were breastfeeding, their lips still moving in prayer. Teenage girls strolled around the church as if it were the plaza. They tilted toward each other, whispering and giggling, sometimes holding hands or each other's waist. There were old women kneeling in the pews, murmuring prayers. Ladinos stood close to the altar, responding to the priest's Spanish liturgy. Most Mayans stood behind the Ladinos mumbling prayers in Kaqchiquel. Others, scattered throughout the church, offered rose petals, fruits, copal incense, and candles to the statues of saints. Their mumbled prayers were interrupted sporadically by a clang of coins going into the collection box.

Teresa murmured prayers beside me, and I wondered about her god. What was the pull of Christianity for her? And for the other devoted Mayans in the church? She always mentioned God—but who knew what god or gods she prayed to? She was reacting to something beyond the modern church that I knew. Instead, it was as if she were living in the era where early Christians showed love in the face of hatred and when slapped, they simply turned the other cheek; when it was believed that the meek shall inherit the earth. Her god was a god that loved Mayans, fallen women, illegitimate children. It wasn't just being a Mayan that gave her such a sense of self, but it was also her faith.

Teresa rose, went to a nave to kneel before her personal saint, the saint of the town San Lucas, a stocky doctor and miracle worker. Then she chanted monotone prayers. After a while, her body became alert and erect. Unlike Maximón, whom she spoke to in Kaqchiquel, she reprimanded this saint in Spanish. I could hear her scolding him for not taking better care of her Tina and Miguel. She even threatened him, "Well, if you don't start helping my Miguel more, I won't burn any candles! You must do your work!" Soon she shifted from admonishing him to thanking him for her *pobrecito* tortillas, for her Chula Tina. Her eyes were moist as she headed back to the pew beside me.

When we finally returned to the plaza, we could still feel the warmth of the sun. From our observation post outside, the clamor of fiesta hit us. We could hear male laughter and shouts escaping from tents stocked with foosball tables. Not far away, a cluster of kids gathered round a jukebox brought to town especially for this occasion. It sparkled in the afternoon sun and beat out marimba, Mexican love songs, and American rock. Women strolled by, stopping at stands to buy gooey homemade candy or fiddle with plastic earrings. Out of the crowd, a tall Ladina woman walked at a crisp pace toward us, then stopped in front of Teresa.

"Teresa, I had a fight with the butcher," she declared, ignoring the customary greeting. "Go get some meat for me."

Teresa got to her feet, nodded, and took some centavos from the lady. I thought this must be her boss, whom I had only seen at a distance. The Ladina stood waiting with her son close by. His shirt strained at the buttonholes, so he stood out in the crowd of mainly thin Mayans with machetes dangling by their sides. His mother fidgeted, pulling at her hair, tapping her foot, sweat drizzling down on either side of her face.

Teresa soon returned with a pleased look on her face. Eyes lowered, she handed the Ladina a bundle of meat.

Suddenly the woman was shrieking, "What is *this*? This is pig's food! How dare you get me this?"

Teresa stepped back, eyes still lowered.

"How can you be so stupid? You, Indian, like a pig yourself!"

"But they won't …"

"Pig! Bringing me pigs' meat!" the woman screamed, infuriated. Teresa crossed her hands limply at the waist of her *corte*.

"Stupid Indian!" the woman threw out again as she turned to stomp off with her son. He lurched in quick steps behind her.

Teresa sat down on the steps, silent as the church statues.

"That woman is crazy!" I told her. "Is that your boss? She's…"

"Ay, *pobrecita*," Teresa interrupted me. "*Ay Dios*. That poor little Ladina," Teresa said in a near whisper as if she was talking about a terminally ill person. "The poor little Ladina had to scream so much. She doesn't understand that they only give Indians the worst meat. Ay *Dios*."

But I didn't feel the pity that Teresa seemed to feel. "But Teresa, she was so rude! She treated you like a child and you sat there like one!"

She paused and watched me closely.

"*Ay*, poor little Ladina! *Ay*, poor little *gringa*!" Now I was doubly surprised to also be put in Teresa's compassion stew. "Poor little *gringa*, don't you see?"

"What do you mean, Teresa?" Even Teresa's tone frustrated me now. There was so much I struggled to understand about her. She held herself with such dignity, worked so hard, had such a strong community behind her, yet reacted with shame to a bully. So much of what I didn't understand was related to her cultural mores, but surely, this incident was obvious to both of us. The woman was rude.

Teresa smoothed my hair over my shoulder. "Don't you understand, Mincha? Poor little *gringa*. I greet all the Indians, but when I walk by a Ladina, we never speak a word. The Ladinos own the stores and the *fincas* and the markets. We Indians are the servants who work in their homes. Or we pick their coffee. We are apart. I don't know why, but we are apart. We are another people. But the poor little Ladinos don't have anything. They don't have a *traje*. They don't have *lengua*. They don't have our faith. Don't you see?"

But I couldn't see. I couldn't understand her lack of rancor.

"You see, the poor little Ladinos don't have our *traje,* so they don't know where they are walking. The Ladinos always walk away but they don't know where they are going. *Ay Dios, Ay Dios*," she muttered, patting her cheeks as if to soothe herself.

I responded with a stare. This was what the women in jail told me too. However, I wondered how can someone so racked with fears and superstitions and so put down by society, be so confident? Was she really confident or was this just passivity? Yet as she spoke these words, I felt them to be true. I could see it in her, in the way she looked steadily while the Ladina yelled at her. She sat beside me straight-backed, surveying the plaza as if nothing had happened. "God is with us," she concluded quietly. "God is with us."

She took my hand, "Let's leave this talk. Come on Gringita, let's go see the fiesta."

On one side of the plaza, a tinkling marimba led Indians, tired from fieldwork, to dance to a repertoire of delicate melodies. In the town hall across the plaza, a rival electric band summoned Ladinos to a similar escape. Teresa dragged me over to the Indian dance, held inside a one-room adobe building. Within this smoky, sweaty chamber Indian couples decked out in their *traje* were locked together in a dance that seemed to mimic the way they walked, back and forth, back and forth. Women danced with women, so I invited Teresa to dance. But she didn't want to go inside.

"Tomorrow," she warned me, "is the Day of the Dead and we must prepare. We can't dance. There's too much work to do, too much work ..."

Still, she agreed to peek in on the Ladino dance. Both halls were crammed with drunkards and lovers, except in the Ladino dance the walls were also lined with old ladies. The young women wore shiny cocktail dresses with spaghetti straps and there was a scent of perfume hanging in the air. Some of the Ladino men wore suits and others had printed shirts tucked into tight-fitting, well-pressed pants.

Besides dancing, the major event was *paseando*, simply promenading through town. Passersby walked as if they were a walking fashion show. Indian girls in newly woven *huipil*s and young men in new shiny pants strode around the plaza, staring at each other then pausing to watch the dancing or huddling together to gossip. We stopped to have a *caliente*, a hot chocolate, that for hundreds of years has been the traditional drink of Mayans. We barely spoke, instead just gaping at the colorful sights of new *huipil*s, fishing games and drunkards ricocheting down dirt roads.

Suddenly Tina burst through the crowd, nearly tripping inside her tight-fitting *corte*. Tears streamed down her cheeks as she spoke rapidly in Kaqchiquel. The word Miguel punctuated her speech. The fiesta blasted in the background as we scurried down one dark side street after another until we found Miguel sagging limply against a limestone wall. Teresa spoke softly to him as she tried to straighten him out, while Tina propped her brother on one side, tears still trickling down her face.

Blood was smeared across a gash on Miguel's forehead. A thin layer of mud formed a crust all over his white pants. His steely arms were transformed into blubber and an odor of urine and kusha clung to his sweaty clothes. Teresa on one side and myself on the other, we lurched forward, dragging him to his tiny room in the center of town.

"Teresa Nan. Chula Tina," he yelled out as we lugged him through town. We pushed through the crowds, ignoring friends who called out our names. Miguel howled at times, sending forth some desperate pain into the cool evening. Braving an obstacle course of clotheslines and snarling dogs, we reached Miguel's shack in total darkness. While we heaved him over the doorway, we conversed in whispers as if he was asleep. But he wasn't.

As soon as we entered the room, he stood to attention, blubbering half Spanish, half Kaqchiquel. He wanted to go have another drink with us. Yes, another drink, wouldn't that be fine! Join the fiesta, he told us, then he pushed us away, careening toward the door to escape. Drool of spit and blood sprinkled round the room as he swayed beneath a naked light bulb. Then he suddenly quieted and seemed to be straining to listen to his old mother admonishing him.

Two beds were crammed in the room. On one, an Indian man lay crumpled like a dirty rag. A disheveled mat of hair drooped over his unconscious face. When we could finally guide Miguel to his bed, he toppled over like an infant then immediately passed out. His feet, vulnerable and naked, flopped over onto his roommate's lap. Teresa studied him and then held Tina's hand to her chest. "What can we do but accept him tomorrow when he comes for food. You have a special love for your children and even when they are bad over and over again, love makes you take them back."

※

Every week at Casa Feliz, the orphanage where I worked, a child would be dropped off, the parent weeping, the child skin and bones but undaunted. It was surprising how quickly they fitted into the group, how brave and well behaved they were. Still, their situation was distressing.

One night I had a dream: I was working with kids in the orphanage on collages. They were hungry but then as lunch came there was not enough food to go on their plates. I became frantic. It reminded me of the dreams I had in Haiti.

The dream disturbed my sleep and I lay there listening to sounds. It was still dark, and I heard footsteps tromping by, some very quiet laughter. It wasn't long after that that light moved across my ceiling and birds started bickering outside.

In the morning, I sipped coffee in the kitchen of Casa Feliz, and I told Bobdelia, "I am tired."

"You're tired, why?" she asked me. She was standing at the kitchen table working.

"I woke up at four in the morning," I complained. Then I told her my dream.

"Don't worry about the children, Mincha," she reassured me. "We will take care of them. But you woke up at four. At four in the morning? That's early. I am still asleep then. I sleep and sleep and still I could sleep more."

Bobdelia looked up again from the vegetables she was chopping, green chilis strewn across the large table. It was then I noticed her eyes. Lusterless eyes. Even the beauty of her lime-green *huipil*, her strong features didn't hide the fact she was sad. Her usual olive-brown skin had the hue of a sick person. Or a sad person.

"How are you Bobdelia?" I knew by then it was appropriate to wrap my arm affectionately around her waist.

"Fine Mincha, fine." Silence. Staring at the beans eternally cooking on the fire.

"Why do you look so sad?"

She looked directly at my face, hotly, evaluating. Tears began to roll down her slightly plump cheeks. Tears, one by one, moved down her cheeks, curving toward her mouth, following the smile lines left from other days.

I asked her but then I felt myself retreat, something inside of me pulling back for cover. In a way I didn't really want to know what was bothering her. Maybe I was afraid some issue of violence or hunger would emerge, something I wasn't prepared to handle.

"It's my life. I just think and think about my life. Carlos Roberto, my son, is sick today. Last night he was very sick, and I had to watch over him. What is my life now and what can I do to change it? Sometimes I think, why didn't I just stay with his father? I would have suffered with him and been unhappy, but I would have had my own life, my own house. You see, I have a sister who turns against me and talks to my father. She says mean things about me to my father and then he yells at me. Oh, not about anything in particular, though he calls me a woman of the streets because I have a child without a man now. How could I know what was going to happen with my life?

"She tells my father lies, that I am a woman of the streets, that she saw me talking to a man who is already married. I've only been talking to one man and he isn't married. Oh, why does she have to be like that? I haven't done anything wrong. I try to fight for my centavos, to feed my child."

I said a few consoling words.

"How can it be that I will always live alone? I have to talk to a man here and there because I have to get a *marido*, a husband, that way when my son is sick, I can stay home and care for him while my *marido* fights for the centavos. Life isn't so bad for me. It's Carlos Roberto I think of. He grows up alone. Even his mother is hardly in the house. Then my father is angry with me.

"Oh, last night I stayed up just crying and crying because I had all those thoughts in my head, and I didn't know what to do with them. I cried. Yes, I cried but those thoughts still stay with me. Yes, my mother is kind to me. She helps me and she understands I'm being good, but what can she do when my father is angry with me, and me, who has to live in his house. She knows I fight for my centavos and I always help her with a few centavos each week, but here I am alone and alone with these thoughts and nowhere to go, to stay away from my father. How can I raise Carlito there? But where else can I go? These are my thoughts. They make me cry."

Elena, the cook, popped her head in the door, and said something in a rapid Kaqchiquel. Bobdelia answered with her head down as if absorbed by the vegetable cutting, wiping her tears with a dishcloth, acting as if she was wiping away sweat. Elena didn't notice anything or pretended not to.

It was time for us to work with the kids. "Let's take them for a walk instead," I told her, hoping it would cheer her up. Out in the bright sun, walking by the lake, Bobdelia began to relax. Verline walked on one side of me and Jeronimo was on the other. I had to keep an eye on both these fighters. Jeronimo was a cripple and a braggart. His parents died when he was around four, but no one took him in, maybe because he had a bad leg. So, he roamed the countryside stealing and begging. Finally, he was taken in by a person who had pity on him, but he had to work side by side with men. He learned from them how to fight, how to protect himself despite his handicap. He never had a childhood so fighting replaced playing. When he arrived at Casa Feliz, he wouldn't stop fighting. Every two minutes he picked a fight with someone. Plus, he was a braggart. He'd say to me, "If I didn't have this bad leg, I'd show them. They don't know how to work at all. I'd show them. You should have seen me on the coast helping with the cotton. Now that was work!" he told me, then five minutes later punched a kid. Still, after a month, he started to calm down. It was when he started to protect one of the little kids that he learned he could cuss out his anger rather than hit.

We skirted around dugout canoes set along the shore and past fishermen untangling their nets. Bobdelia suddenly pointed to a man and called out to Verline. There was his father, helping with the nets. He was dressed in his *traje*, but it was filthy.

His face was gaunt and his eyes feverish. "Verline," he cried. He squatted down and with a strong feeling, he hugged his son. Then he let go and ran off and returned with peanuts and candy for all of us to share. We sat on the rocks in the sun, pleased with ourselves and happy to see Verline sitting so close to his father.

✕

As I walked up to Teresa's house, I could see Lucero, her black dog, pausing by the house. He looked at me and trotted over to the edge of the path and sunk his teeth around an empty can someone had thrown there. The can grasped in his teeth, he scurried by me past the house. Two minutes later he returned. Teresa was standing by the door, watching. He sniffed the edges of the path until he came to a small mound of discarded cornhusks that he clamped onto and again trotted off. "It looks like he's cleaning up your path," I called out to her. Teresa laughed as she walked toward me.

"Yes, he's such a good dog. He cleans up all our trash."

"He cleans up your trash?" I thought I was imagining it. "Did you teach him that?"

"No," she answered, looking fondly toward him as he arrived, this time stopping by her side. "He just loves us," she explained while petting him. "He watched us then he did it. He is a dog that always wants to help us." She petted him again then leaned over to say goodbye.

We headed out through the thick mist drifting over San Lucas and along the path from Teresa's hut to the plaza where we would catch a bus. Teresa stood firm that we had to go to a nearby village to buy some special goods for the Day of the Dead feast. She wanted to walk, but I insisted on treating her to a bus ride, a little rest from her normal routine.

We wove down the path lined by cornstalk huts, surrounded by lush green hedges and *milpa*, cornfields. Teresa said hello to everyone we went by. She called out to men working on houses, carrying wood on their backs, riding bikes or strolling through town. The women peered out from their weaves or stopped making tortillas as we passed by. They called out Adios Nan or Nica Nan in a singsong voice to us. Teresa responded, a smile across her face as we trudged through the Mayan section of town. As soon as we entered the plaza, her expression became stilted.

The bus was crowded, thick with gas fumes. It wound down the roads stopping at each *finca* where weary *mozos*, workers, still stinking and steaming with sweat, got on the bus. Everywhere we stopped a pack of skinny dogs barked furiously as the bus pulled out. Teresa gripped the seat in front of her. She was sitting bolt upright anxiously looking out the window. It was when she started breathing rapidly that I asked her, "Are you all right?"

"Yes," she nodded, gripping the seat even tighter. "I used to be afraid of riding buses but not anymore." Her tight grip told me differently, but I listened as she reminisced, "I remember when I saw the first truck come down this road. The people thought it was Judgment Day. They called to us in the coffee fields where we were working, 'Watch out! Watch out! The lakes and the rivers have opened up and are flooding the earth!' Well, we began to shake when we heard the noise of the waters taking the earth. Then we saw the truck and the men called out, 'Watch out! Watch out! That is a thing that eats people!' All the people ran away from the *pobrecito* fields and into their huts. All the women began to cry, and everyone began to pray. It took me a long time before I could ride a bus or a truck anywhere. Now I'm not afraid."

Her thin lips were pasted together. Teresa's eyebrows scrunched together while the bus rattled on. As she anxiously scanned the horizon, she diligently recited the names of *fincas* we passed, dousing Tina and me with memories of the days she worked on the *finca* as a servant girl.

The bus stopped to pick up more *mozos* and some women with babies strapped to their backs. Mayan men from San Lucas sat in front, straight and still, on the left-hand side of the bus. The Ladinos sat on the right-hand side. Teresa claimed this wasn't a rule but "just the way things are."

The Mayan bus driver's eyes focused solely on the road, veering round potholes. Tight muscles quivered under his thin shirt as he turned the heavy wheel. Teresa still clenched the seat in front of her. Her ears seemed to stick out more ridiculously than before. Suddenly the bus jolted to a stop, and she slammed forward, her chin bumping into the steel railing. The bus driver jumped off the bus as yelling drifted through the windows to the passengers.

"You goddamned fucking driver. You are supposed to keep a schedule or not drive," a fat Ladina and a man yelled while tumbling out of an old Buick that had pulled up in front of the bus.

The bus driver, apparently prepared for this routine, offered her a sheaf of papers. "I am on schedule. It's on these papers. But you aren't the owner of this bus." He seemed confused.

"Don't you talk back," the Ladino yelled, snatching the papers out of his hands, his own hands trembling with rage. "Just listen to her, you son of a ..."

"This is a business," the woman screeched, interrupting the man. "You must be on time, or you will ruin our bus schedule. You won't have your bus driving if you can't be on time."

"But those papers say I am," he replied mildly.

"Shut up with your papers." The man approached the bus, waving the wrinkled papers like a pennant in the air.

The bus driver stared at him and answered again in a quiet, firm voice, "Don't yell at me. Talk to the *patrón* of this bus. This is my schedule."

Teresa had finally let go of the railing but looked uneasy, uncertain about the outcome of this dispute. Some of the Indian women surrounding us were clicking their tongues against their teeth, shaking their heads. I felt a rage welling up in me as I listened again to the Ladinos.

"What do you know about schedules? What do you know about driving buses? You shouldn't be in the driver's seat anyway. You're just an Indian who doesn't know anything."

The Mayan replied firmly, "You are the one who is making me late. This is my schedule."

The man tossed out more curses to the air. His belly hung over his Levi's, rippling as he ranted. The woman shook her head in agreement with his accusations, making low rumbling sounds.

Inside the bus, a young Kaqchiquel dressed in traditional *traje* suddenly leaped from his seat and leaned out the window, shouting, "*Sho!* Shut up lady! Listen to the man speak!"

Immediately, the Indian women began clicking their tongues like a flock of frightened parrots. I felt relief. At least the young Mayans wouldn't let the Ladinos treat them like shit. But an old man wearing clothes identical to the young Kaqchiquel turned around. He stood up gently facing the Mayans behind him, his eyes focused on the young man.

"Quiet my fathers, quiet now. It is they who think they have the rights here. It is they who will not listen to words." The people were silent. His voice drifted out the window and the Ladinos were quiet for a moment too. Only the engine of the Buick cut the air.

The old man continued quietly. "Stay calm. Even in a storm and winds, stay calm. Their fear can't destroy a calm heart."

"Shut up old man and listen," the man bellowed, remembering his rights. The woman began her tirade against the bus driver again. Teresa glared steadily at the road. Another wave of rage welled up in me. I wanted to climb off the bus and fight back, kick, scream. Wanting some confirmation, I glanced at Teresa again and then at the other women, but their faces were unreadable. Even Chula Tina just stared ahead.

Finally arriving at our destination fifteen minutes later, the Mayans descended from the bus, still silent. We sat in the shade of a Nancy Tree, covered in little fruits. Centuries before, when there was a drought, the fruit from the Nancy Tree is said to have saved the Mayan civilization from starvation. After seeing and hearing so much violence against the Mayans, I wondered what would save them now. Relaxing under the tree, I asked Teresa about this morning. She tittered and explained in a whisper, "*Pobrecito Tat. Pobrecito Ladina*. Poor little Ladina has so much to scream about. Poor little father has to receive so much screaming. *Dios*." Anger welled up in me again. Why did this woman waste her compassion on such buffoons? Teresa clicked her tongue rapidly, then shook her head.

"Pobrecito Gringa. Don't you see? Even before I was born there were Ladinos. And the Ladinos have always been the ones who owned the land, the *fincas* and the towns. I know my people once ruled this land. We weren't a bad people. We were just ignorant. When the Ladinos came, or whoever they were, my people didn't know how to fight. We didn't have good weapons. We just worked for our *chula* maize. We didn't think about weapons. So, you see, we were just ignorant, and the Ladinos took the land easily. Since then, the Ladinos have been in a higher place. The towns and *fincas*, all the *fincas*, are owned by rich Ladinos, especially the family Hernandez. If there is a decision to make in town, they are the ones who make it. They run the Municipalidad. We don't. The rich make the decisions for themselves and don't think about the Indians. They only want more for themselves.

"Life wasn't like this before. When I was young, people traded and didn't use money. That's how it used to be on the *finca*. We used to trade a chicken for some beans and some beans for a chicken. That made people softer with each other. Now, with money, people worry more and talk meanly to each other over prices. I don't like that. No, I don't like it when people raise their voices loudly. It makes my ears and stomach hurt. But no matter where you go, the world stays the same. The Ladinos on the top and the Indigenous people on the bottom; that's how it will always be. If the whole government is Ladino, how do you expect anything to change? That just can't happen. I have heard about good things Ladinos do for Indians and I've heard of bad things, so I just don't think about it. I think about my son, Miguel, and Chula Tina.

*Ay Dios, Ay Dios.*" She clicked her tongue and repeated the name of God over and over again, resting under the Nancy Tree. As she spoke, I felt the strength of her history in her words and my admiration for this superstitious, hard-working woman grew. But my admiration wasn't just for her. It was for all the people who had been on the bus with us; and for all the Mayans who came before them, who built this sense of identity and community.

My ancestors were so different. Our rules were pliable and often just disregarded. My ancestors would do whatever they had to in order to forge ahead, to be the winners. In fact, our Irish family insignia is a bloody hand, and the story goes that my ancestors were in a boat approaching Ireland when the king declared the first person to touch the shore would be proprietor of that land. So, my great-great-great-grandfather chopped off his hand and threw it to shore. Thus, we became part of the landed aristocracy.

"*Ay Dios,*" Teresa mumbled, bewildered and unhappy. "What life can bring you." Tina was back with the goods and laughed at her mother, then took her hand to help her up, "Come on, Nan, the bus will be returning to San Lucas soon."

When she finally got off the bus in San Lucas, Chula Tina ran ahead, her long black braids flying behind her. Teresa walked slowly, avoiding ruts in the path without looking at them. An elderly Indian man greeted her.

"Hello, father," she answered softly. He was dressed in a short black jacket and red-and-white striped shorts. A San Lucas man.

"*Chuac Chic* Nan," he called out as his shiny chapped legs pattered quickly down the path. Another man soon approached. "*Chuac Chic,*" Teresa called out in a sing-song voice.

"You see, Mincha," she told me, "there's not a person I don't know in this village. I know them all, their wives and their children. And that's why I hate to leave. I know who I am here. Just think of having only two children and being a stranger somewhere else, even in the next village. Oh, the dear God could have given me worse fates."

Teresa stopped suddenly, smiling fondly at a friend kneeling in front of a basket covered with leaves.

"Hello, Nan, how are you?" The woman looked up. She was dressed exactly like Teresa, except her thick gray hair was wrapped in luminous satin cloth and fell straight across her back to her waist unlike Teresa's, which was braided into a crown on her head.

"Hello, Mother, how are you?"

"Fine and how are you, Teresa?" The woman's question mingled with the sound of children's laughter and a machete clanging against something.

"Fine, but I need some food for my Chula Tina and me. What do you have there?" She peered into the woman's basket, delicately sniffing the air filled with the smell of cooked bananas and tacos.

"Chuchos at two cents or at five cents," the woman replied, unraveling the green banana leaves and exposing a mound of soggy, wet cornhusks wrapped around small fistfuls of wet, cooked cornmeal.

"Yes, Nan, would you give me three for two cents? One for me, one for Tina and one for this *gringa*." The woman leaned over the basket, swatting the nose of an emaciated dog that scrambled away over to a circle of children playing nearby. Teresa watched indifferently as they began to torture him by poking him with a long stick and throwing clods of dirt in his face.

"Here you are, Teresa," said her friend, interrupting the sideshow and handing Teresa two simmering bundles. I reached over to pay but Teresa stopped me.

"Sit down and talk a while, Teresa," the woman requested.

"Oh Nan, I am so tired. I have to get down to my house and start my fire and make my tortillas for dinner," Teresa apologized. "We will talk later, Nan."

They waved goodbye, giggling at each other as if some supreme joke had tied them together in that conversation.

"I always feel more comfortable with a woman in San Lucas *traje*," Teresa explained as she left her friend, perhaps sifting through the memory of the bus trip. "At least I know they aren't going to rob me or beat me, and they know who my husband was and that I am going to the same paradise our people go to. Sometimes these clothes cause trouble, though. So many men can't get work because of their *traje*, or young girls laugh at the boys wearing their *traje* when they walk down the street. But we will never leave our *traje*!"

She plodded ahead until she finally reached the cornfield in front of her hut where she cut through a neighbor's yard and was greeted by Lucero and Paloma.

# Mis Ancestros—My Ancestors

Teresa's hut looked beautiful. She had spent hours carpeting the floor with pine needles, adorning the door with marigolds to keep out spirits, and lining all her dishes against the wall. A straw basket was filled with warm tortillas and a cauldron of squash soup was ready to share with friends when they stopped by the next day for the Day of the Dead. Like our Halloween, they went house to house, but instead of candy being given, soup and tortillas were served in refashioned gourdes. Tina was angry because Teresa didn't want to go from house to house.

"No," she decided for us all. "We won't go out in the street. No. It's not good for us to be walking here and there at night."

"*Ay*, Nan," Tina whined.

"No, Tina, men will take women they find in the streets and abuse them. That's why I always walk with a stick," she declared, although I had never seen her with a stick. "I remember once we took Miguel home and when Tina and I were walking back a man jumped out of the dark and attacked us. We picked up rocks and began throwing them at him. Wham, wham, wham, those rocks hit that man on the head. He ran away yelling like a dog. Usually," Teresa continued, "we just walk out there in the dark with our sticks and pray to God that nothing happens. We are too weak and don't know how to close our fists against men.

"Right now, the streets are very dangerous because the government and some *gringos* are stealing people. Sometimes they hold onto them, sometimes they kill them. Who knows why? They're even stealing people during the day at the market where there are crowds. They stole one of my cousins from the market and forced him to work on a road. When my cousin and his friend complained saying, 'No, we can't work so hard just for these tortillas,' they said, 'You're political,' then took them down the road and shot them. That is what the government does here. They steal children too. Some children go up to the market with their mothers, then disappear. Those children finally end up far away, working on a road. It's the government and the *gringos* who do that. People say *gringos* steal babies because they can't have children themselves."

"Oh, Teresa," I couldn't resist responding to her conjecture, "*Gringos* can have children. My mother had me!"

She studied me, then added, "Well, some people even claim that *gringos* like the taste of our brown skin, but I say that is shit. I know *gringos* do some strange things and some bad things to our people. But whether it's the *gringos* or the government who steals the people, it's all the same."

Everything Teresa said seemed so exaggerated, yet I had heard these same stories repeated throughout the town and even back in the capital. There were reports that soldiers had entered a nearby town and murdered fifteen Indians who they thought held leadership positions. In the past, San Lucas was protected by a strong Catholic Church. But it was said that because the nuns and priests challenged the ruthless killings, they also were killed, jailed or forced to flee. It was hard to know what was true in Guatemala, although clergy confirmed the dangers to me. In San Lucas, women always walked at night in little groups, or they stayed home, perhaps imprisoned by their fear.

Teresa served us soup in the gourdes. "But what I am afraid of most are the earthquakes," she confessed. "Many friends died in that earthquake, but San Lucas wasn't hit as hard, thank God. Some houses fell down but not many people died. In other places, thousands of people were killed. That's what they said on the radio, but here, no."

She slurped from her gourd then began her story, 'I was in bed, but I was awake. I was staring at the ceiling and thinking, the way you do sometimes before you fall asleep. Well, all of a sudden, I heard this big noise. It sounded like a truck crashing into the mountains. I thought, 'Oh *Dios*, that *pobrecito* truck!' Then came another huge noise and this time *pobrecita* Tina woke up too. She began to cry because of the crashing noise. Then the ground began to shake, and we ran out of our poor little house. Our neighbors were already screaming at us, 'Come here! Come here!' They were crying too, out of fear. We all wept for hours. The earth was shaking and making such terrible noises until even the volcanoes started thundering.

"We squatted by our neighbor's house and prayed as we bawled like little children. I'll tell you, many people started praying that night who never, ever prayed before. When we lived on a silent earth, they would say, 'God, who is he?' And they would walk through their day without saying, 'God, my Father, I thank you for my water.' Or 'God, my Father, I thank you for my tortillas.' They just never thought about that. But when the earth began to shake you could see those people praying on their knees to God. I was afraid, but my *pobrecita* Tina was more frightened.

"Poor little Tina kept crying and saying, 'Nan, Nan, we're going to die!' and 'Where is my brother Miguel? *Ay*, Nan!' And we prayed our Miguel wasn't dead. We went on like that for days, because Miguel was working in Santiago and I didn't know what happened to him. But three days later he walked into our village. You should have seen Chula Tina. She jumped up and down yelling, 'Look, Nan! Look, Mother! Here's my brother Miguel!' Many people were killed in Santiago, so God blessed my son.

"Everyone stopped working because when you stood in the fields, your *milpa*, cornfield, began to bounce. How can you grow maize on an earth that shakes? I was walking through a coffee field and the earth began to shake like the Great Dog. I had a full basket on my head and thought I was going to fall. I grabbed a tree and held on as tight as I could. Oh, the Great Dog! I would have been thrown down if I hadn't grabbed that tree. Everything was shaking and the crashing began again. I thought, 'Well, this time we will all die.' But we didn't.

"The men claim the earth trembles because there are bad people here, robbers who only pay a few centavos for a day's work, people who force you to become a soldier or kill you. The radio says that's not true, that our government works for the people, that the earth would still shake whether there were bad people or not. But I know the fate of my people and I say the radio lies. You should thank God every day if you've never known a shaking earth. It makes you cry and cry.

"Well," Teresa concluded, "we shouldn't talk about these things anymore because soon it will be midnight and the Day of the Dead."

Tina clasped my hand and added, "Yes, and you know, Mincha, my dead mother will come and try to grab me. But she can only take me if I say her name."

"That's right," Teresa agreed, her eyes darting round the room as if looking for someone lurking in the shadows. "Yes, tomorrow is the day our parents and all the other dead people will come out of their graves. You can't see them, but they are everywhere. If you leave the door open, they will walk right in. That's why I put marigolds on the door, it keeps the bad ones out. The other spirits are glad to see those flowers shining like a thousand suns all the way around my door.

"The air is filled with spirits. Whether a person died fifteen or a hundred years ago, they will return tomorrow. My own mother died a long time ago. She will walk right into the house and watch us. Tomorrow I can't repeat her name because that would call her closer and she might steal me away. Yes, the spirits watch us to see how we are doing, but they would like to steal you, too, and take you to whatever place it is that dead people go. The best thing you can do tomorrow is not think. You see, if you walk down the road with your head full of thoughts, those spirits will grab you. You must keep your head empty like a big cauldron and be happy. If you're sick, they can easily grab you.

"My older brother will walk in here too. He was a carpenter, you know, and his wife was a midwife. That gave them a little bit of this." She sticks her hand into my face, her fingers curled into a claw, the sign for money. "But he died anyway. He just puffed up all over his body. His ankles, his arms, his face, everything grew fat and he lay in bed for two months. When I asked him if he wanted to visit the clinic, he said, 'No, I'm staying in my own house.' So, in the end, he died in his own house. This is the same brother who comes to me in dreams all the time. You see, once, when we were children, we went down to the river together and I slipped. He caught me just before I fell in. My head, though, hit a rock and started buzzing. I still hear that buzz on the side of my head and that's why I always dream of him next to the river." She poked gently at the fire until a flame leaped up, lighting up the room.

"My father died when we were still very small. None of us even remember him. My mother took care of the whole family herself. My mother—you should have seen her work. She made tortillas and coffee to sell, plus a special kind of candy. She took two pounds of chamomile, removed the flowers and leaves, and put them into a big pot. Then she added a lot of brown sugar and boiled it all together. That made little drops of candy that she sold for one *centavo*. She worked and worked. Then, she died. I don't know why, I guess she just worked herself to death."

Teresa stopped her story abruptly. A cold draft seeped through the thatch walls and she grabbed a piece of garlic, kissed it, waved it once over her head then passed it to Tina who repeated her exact movements. When I asked about this gesture, they just shrugged—perhaps too tired to answer or maybe, as is often the case, it's a gesture that was passed down, but never explained. The fire's rosy coals were just turning gray when they finally left the hut to get some sleep.

※

The Day of the Dead finally arrived, and we were in Teresa's cooking hut.

"And what is that?"

"That is special food for the Day of the Dead. You let it boil and boil until it turns black and ugly."

"Well, it certainly looks ugly," I snickered.

"Every now and then you stir it with this." She held out a great wooden spoon with a charred handle. "If you taste the squash and if it's sweet, then you say it's sour, otherwise it will turn sour. You lift off the top of the pot and say, 'Oh, how ugly! This squash isn't good to eat, let the pigs have it! It's so sour and ugly!' And that will make the squash sweeter."

"Hmmm," I mumbled, too tired to do anything but accept Teresa's logic. Tina finished her job, then rested on the *petate* beside the fire. Soon, we were all slurping down the sugary soup.

Suddenly a woman poked her head in, her rapid-fire Kaqchiquel disturbing our peaceful morning. Her head vanished as quickly as it appeared.

Teresa was already standing. "Miguel is drunk again. He's down by the soccer field, shouting like a crazy man. He lost his *pobrecito* sombrero the other night when he was drinking. He found it again this morning on another man's head, but now he's lost his own head!"

She ran her gnarled fingers through her hair, then decided to sit down again on her *petate*. "I never thought he would be like this when he grew up. I had no idea, although he was always an angry child. Who knows why? From the beginning he wanted his way and just yelled until he got it. That's when my mother was still alive. When I had Miguel, she was there helping me to make hot water and comfort my pain.

"I cried and cried, but I never screamed. I guess because I always worked so hard, I could just have a baby quietly. Some women scream all night. My mother took care of me for those fifteen days that I stayed in bed after I had Miguel. All the women rest for fifteen days after they have a baby. Every day my mother brought me my tortillas, coffee, and soup. It was so peaceful resting in bed with my little son. I was alone most of the day in that dark room and it was so nice to be quiet. When else in my life can I be so quiet and alone?

"Then my friends would come to see my little Miguel and tell me I looked fine. They sat next to my *petate* and talked. If it got dark, we lit a candle so I could see the person talk instead of staring in the dark listening to a voice. Those were my days of peace and rest next to my mother. When you have a baby, you just want to be with your mother. Every woman turns into a child again.

"Only later, when Miguel was growing up, sometimes I didn't want to be near her. You see, my mother never learned to weave. She took care of animals instead. Oh, that house was filled with her animals— chickens, birds, dogs, cats, pigs. Everything! Well, when I was just a little girl, I saw the other women weaving with their *chula* threads and I said, 'I want to weave too, even if my mother doesn't.' So, I thought and thought of weaving. Until I finally began to dream about it. Then one day I woke up and I wove.

"No one ever taught me anything. Many women are like that. They just learn in their dreams and by watching other women weave. Chula Tina learned to weave through her dreams too.

"Anyway," Teresa continued, "as Miguel was growing up, I strapped him to my back and knelt to weave for hours. My shoulders used to hurt so much, but I would keep weaving. It was so beautiful, but my mother would get angry. 'What do you think you are doing?' she used to ask. 'You kneel here and weave when you should be taking care of your baby.' She didn't care if my weave went to shit. 'That baby is more important than your weave,' she would yell. Oh, she became furious sometimes. She even threw my threads across the ground. I cried and cried for my poor *chula* threads, but I listened to her and stopped. And what good did that do? Here's Miguel who drinks until he's in the mud like a pig."

Teresa leaned over to stir the great pot of squash, calling it ugly but smiling when she sipped a bit from the wooden spoon. "But Pablo loved my weave," she continued her story. 'Yes, you should weave,' he used to say. 'I will buy you some *chula* threads.'

"But then he started with another woman. I still remember the first time I saw them together. My cousin ran into the house, shouting, 'Look up the street! Your husband is kissing another woman!' Well, I went to look and there he was kissing her right in front of everyone! I just walked by. You know, most women would have grabbed her by the hair, thrown her to the ground and beat her. But I just walked by.

"For three days my husband didn't kiss me. Finally, I said to him, 'Look, I know you have been with someone else because you haven't kissed me.' I told him I was going to leave, and he begged me to stay, not because he loved me but for the sake of our son. I gave in. 'All right, I'll stay,' I said, 'but where's my kiss?' He laughed and we became friends again. But it kept happening over and over. We would fight and make up. Fight and make up. I got married so young; I didn't know about the world. I didn't think I could take care of myself. So, whenever I wanted to leave him, I'd be too afraid.

"He got angry sometimes and came home to eat his tortillas without talking to me. How does a woman feel in front of a silent man? To work all day making tortillas and *caldo*, soup, then he barely says hello to her.

"Anyway, I was too afraid to leave Pablo. I have other friends whose husbands beat them, but they are scared also. Only their brothers can help by saying, 'Father, don't beat my sister.' Then the man will stop. Most women believe they must stay with their husbands because they have nothing to call their own. I finally left Pablo and now we are friends. He is still shit sometimes but he always brings me my corn and some centavos, and sometimes he even yells at Miguel for drinking. Some women say, 'Nan, don't give Miguel food when he comes here after drinking.' But he comes with those eyes, and I always give in."

※

Teresa and I left to find Miguel. We walked through town along the dusty side streets. Women glided past us, their *cortes* shimmering like water as they walked. Often, they stopped to speak softly with Teresa, their voices conveying an earnest concern for her family. Then they scurried away, the dust twirling round their bare feet.

As we approached the town center, we had to skirt around a group of children taunting a drunken young man, an Indian wearing San Lucas *traje*. The children picked up rocks and sticks, then pelted them at the man. He stood rigid, his black matted hair in tufts across his forehead.

He bent over and charged from one side of the street to the other, then halted abruptly. Again, he charged so fiercely, I wondered what hallucination the kusha had set in motion. Growling like a rabid dog, frothing at the mouth, he threw his head back and forth, grabbed hold of his machete and slashed at the air again and again. The machete moved quickly and steadily, then crashed against the stones.

Indian people, dressed in their finest *traje*s for the Day of the Dead, stood around watching him. A flutter of *Ay Dios, Ay Dios* was heard moving up and down the crowd. Suddenly, a tall Ladino stepped into the circle, grabbed the young man from behind and hauled him off to the *preso*, jail. The Indian's dragging feet left a trail of dust alongside the lonely machete, coated with dust. People stared at it. Even the children stopped their jabbering momentarily. Then the crowd quickly dispersed, some rushing back to inform the Indian's family, others to visit the cemetery and some, like him, to soothe their own distress with kusha. Teresa grabbed my hand, muttering about her Miguel. After all, couldn't he be next? Same *traje*, same fate.

We continued wandering through the labyrinth of dirt roads and paths. Finally, we spotted Miguel loitering along the roadside. He was with a group of men wearing sweat-beaten sombreros, bragging to each other, their white pants spotted with earth, their dark eyes like hardened pellets. Miguel gripped his beer bottle.

"Miguelito," Teresa approached timidly, unsure of herself before these men. "Miguel."

He slung his arm over her shoulder and followed her to the side of the road. "Si, Nan," Miguel answered.

"Miguelito, watch out," Teresa began weakly, "you had better watch out, my son. Today is the day the spirits come out!"

Miguel threw his head back and laughed, his Adam's apple quivering. "Ah, sí, Nan," he laughed. "I just met one of them up the road!"

He repeated his Nan's verdict to the men who also laughed, but there was fear lurking behind their mockery. Their hands gripped the bottles a bit tighter as they shifted uneasily from foot to foot.

Teresa resigned herself almost immediately and left, confiding in me, "He doesn't believe me," she explained. "But at least I know he is protected. The spirits won't grab a drunk man."

✳

As dusk approached and a cool breeze whistled through the trees, we returned to Teresa's.

"Now," she declared upon reaching the hut, "is when the spirits will try to enter the house." The words hardly left her mouth when Tina jumped up to greet us, grabbing her Nan around the waist.

"Nan, I am so glad you finally returned," she cried, burying her head in Teresa's *huipil*. "I was so afraid of being here alone. I could hear things move. I was so afraid here alone, I finally brought Lucero in to guard me." The big black dog sat next to the fire, his eyes glowing, his coat glistening with the fire's rhythm. Teresa wrapped her arms around her Chula Tina and together they knelt by Lucero, close to the fire.

"Ugly," Teresa pronounced, glancing into the cauldron of simmering squash. "So ugly we can eat it now. But it will taste sour." The mushy black soup was soon floating in our gourdes, syrupy sweet, the lumps tasting like candy. Lucero edged closer, the cats slinked in from behind and even the chickens in the courtyard seemed to squawk louder. Satisfied with her soup, Teresa caressed the cat next to her thin chest, gazing round the room. Tina knelt beside her holding another cat, cast like a reflection, a miniature replica of Teresa. "Yes," Teresa mused out loud. "My mother will be happy when she visits my home today. She will see that I live just like she did, with lots of animals."

"And will your grandparents come? Even your ancestors?"

"My *chula* grandparents will come and so will my ancestors, though I don't know very much about them. I know they planted maize just like we do. We work the earth that has rocks but no matter what, we must plant out *chula* corn. Corn is what we eat but also corn feeds our spirit. We plant corn and thank God for our beautiful corn.

"Pablo grows corn," she continued, "on a small piece of land he owns down by the coast. He and Miguel still go there every year to plant, but only out of love of the land. It's a tiny plot and it doesn't produce anymore. But they go there and pray and burn candles and copal to thank God for life, to thank God for the food we eat. Land is so beautiful. People want their own land, but what can they do? Some Indians try to work and buy good land, but they never can. Others put themselves into politics. But I warn Miguel to stay away from politics. You see, the only thing that ever happens to those people is they are shot. How can that not be so?"

She stared glumly at the door, her hooked Mayan nose silhouetted by the fire. "So, my ancestors mean something, but this government means nothing to me. It can go to shit. You know why? All the politicians come to the plaza and talk. The president even speaks Kaqchiquel, but he still breaks every promise. No, the government can go its way and I will go mine. Whatever they do has nothing to do with me. I can't vote because I can't write. But I still have to eat. In our village the Ladinos go to town meetings and the Indians don't. Why? Because the Ladinos never listen to what we say. Even if the Indians went, we wouldn't say much because we're afraid of being killed. I wouldn't give any of my ideas to the president or any of them.

"You see, all the Indian people used to wear their *traje*. Many no longer do because they're laughed at wherever they walk. Ignorant people mock them, so the men have changed their clothes. When I was first with Pablo, he always wore his *traje*, but finally he took it off and threw it away forever. A young man who wears his *traje* won't get any work. He can look and look but he won't get work if he wears his *traje*. *Ay Dios*. Little children will even throw rocks at him. I begged my Miguel not to wear his *traje* so he could live in peace. You see, Mincha, it is dangerous to be an Indian.

"That's how it is here," she concluded sadly. "A lot of people have their heads filled with darkness and you must protect yourself. In the town of Chela, the Ladinos even fine you if they hear you speaking *lengua*, Kaqchiquel. But we women will never give up our language or our *traje*."

A fine for speaking her own language? But I suppose a fine is a step up from the original practices when the Spanish colonists attempted the Ladinization of the Mayans. In those days instead of a fine, the Mayan was publicly lashed for speaking *lengua*. Plus, they weren't allowed to use their own names but were forced to adopt Castilian names. Even the towns were redesigned to fit the needs of the colonists. They felt the traditional villages where Indians lived were too scattered, so it made it hard to convert or indenture them. The Mayans were forced into towns, designed in the Spanish style, with a church that faced a plaza. The towns were compact so the people could be easily controlled. But again, in San Lucas, there was that quiet, steady defiance. The Mayans remained scattered in hamlets throughout the countryside, while the center of town was populated mainly by Ladinos. The Mayans spoke *lengua*, prayed to Maximón and wore their *traje*. An unshakable, stealthy defiance.

Tina sat up straighter, her slender hands softly smoothing out the folds of her *corte*. "No, we love our *chula* weave and *huipil*," Teresa continued. "We know our clothes are better than Ladino clothes, and we women will never give that up. We understand how important our *traje* is." Teresa had access to Western clothes. Shirts, skirts, pants were all sold in the market. But she didn't buy them even though a *traje* could mean a loss of work. She just didn't seem to even consider changing. She jabbed at the fire. The night air rushed in cold around us. Hungry dogs howled plaintively in the distance while footsteps crunched outside, approaching the hut. A murmur of voices. I was startled by a loud clanking sound, like a clanging of rocks in cans. A rustle of thatch wall.

"Don't worry, Mincha, they make that noise when they are coming for our ugly squash," she whispered.

"Who, Teresa? Who is coming?"

The shuffling feet came closer and closer.

"And do you have anyone dead, Mincha?"

"Well, yes, my grandparents."

"Good, good," she smiled.

The refreshing smell of the pine needle carpet beneath our feet drifted upward. There was a knock. Teresa jumped up, answering the door bent over like an old crone. Two men stood outside, rattling their tin cans. They extended their hands for the gourds of soup, their faces hidden behind blood-colored, stained masks, their white pants soiled by earth. Machetes dangled by their sides, moving menacingly to the rhythm of their eating. As they slowly walked away, their bellies filled with the richness of Teresa's food and tradition, her prayers, her pine needles, her marigolds and her happy thoughts, Teresa stood by the doorway knowing that countless women, dressed exactly like her, were standing watch over identical departures, bathed in the gentle sensuality of this windless night.

Teresa stood, then stooped again to pick up her canister filled with pine needles and handed me another one filled with food. "Come on," she ordered, lifting the basket to her head and walking toward the door. "We'll visit the cemetery while Tina watches that ugly squash."

✳

The cemetery was already packed with people decorating the graves. Just as in San Lucas there were two worlds—the Ladino world and the Indigenous world—and both intersected in the graveyard then branched off into separate sections. The Ladinos' dead were in great cement mausoleums painted light yellow, turquoise or white. Some of the wealthy families built theirs to resemble small Roman temples. Farther away the Mayans spread pine needles over the ground. Teresa claimed this kept the bodies warm and gave spirits a fresh smell as they rose from the earth. Other mounds were adorned with homemade wreaths fashioned from paper flowers, holy statues, and even some toys.

A marimba played at one corner and the people danced right there between the graves, marked and unmarked, Ladino and Mayan. Men with guitars sang holy songs and once in a while someone stood up to sing praise to the Lord. As the night progressed, kusha-drinking guitarists crooned sentimental love songs to their dead wives and girlfriends.

"There are plenty of dead wives because the men just screw them to death," Teresa said in a neutral, factual tone that made me laugh. Screwed to death! She sobered me up quickly by adding, "But there are even more dead children because there is never enough food."

We started walking toward another part of the graveyard that preoccupied itself with bingo, called *lotería*. Colorful flashcards with drawings depicting boots, flowers, horses, corn, pretty ladies, and cavalier men were used instead of numbers or letters. After paying a *centavo*, the players covered their square with pebbles. Teresa and I roamed around, sympathizing with the bereaved, listening to the marimba, eating ice-cream, and playing games. Then we went back to the Indian part of the cemetery.

The Indian dead were mainly at the back of the cemetery, buried in shallow graves that swelled like living things from the earth. Across the earth there was a faint outline of bodies: a small child, a woman, a man. Entire families were buried, but it was impossible to tell their exact location because many of the Indians hadn't marked the graves in this cemetery. There were some crosses, a few headstones but mainly there were mounds covered in green grasses, tonight surrounded by fresh flowers.

Teresa ran back and forth, confused about where her parents might be. "*Ay Dios*," Teresa puckered up her face. "*Ay Dios*, I can't remember where my mother and father are buried. Where are my two boys? I just can't remember which place." She started trotting up and down the rows, past people gambling and others weeping. "What can I do? I know they are here but where?" Her *corte* swished, her basket nearly toppled. She raced up and down again; then with a pleased expression on her face, she lifted a basket, grabbed a handful of pine needles and began tossing them in all directions. With each handful she mumbled an apology to her parents and children, begging God to protect them. "May He take their souls in peace."

Then she finally chose a mound and sat down and began placing the food carefully on the grave. In one basket were pine needles, in another, plates of food—some sweet rolls, a mound of rice with some black beans, cooked squash. I imagined that we would eat in the graveyard, but we didn't.

"You don't eat the food?" I asked her.

"A little," she told me. "But the food is for my sons, my brother, my mother, my past people." She placed the spread of food carefully on a nearby mound for her lost loved ones. Then for us she pulled out one of her exquisite woven cloths and unwrapped it to uncover a stack of warm tortillas that we ate with salt.

Most people were very content sitting among the dead, but an Indian woman nearby was crying next to a mound, a child's mound. She had decorated the mound with beautiful white flowers. At the head of the mound, a plastic statue of a Virgin Mary teetered beside a plate of sweet breads and hard red, blue, green, and yellow candies coated with sugar.

Teresa leaned over and whispered in my ear, nodding her head to indicate a skinny woman on the other side of us. The woman's eyes looked gummy but then I realized those were tears, little wells of tears just resting below her eyes. Teresa's whispering was urgent, "They took her son and cut off his fingers." A bit of her spittle landed in my ear when she added, "He still didn't give them what they wanted."

"What did they want?" I tried to whisper back, still staring at the woman.

"They ask you things," she whispered back mysteriously but then went silent and didn't want to talk about it, or didn't know the answer.

But later, as if she couldn't resist the urge to finish the story, she gave in. She was looking at the ground as she made the sign of the cross a few times and said quietly, "Finally they left his poor body right there near the plaza. Some people said he didn't even have eyes."

The woman was sitting in the Mayan version of cross-legged. Her legs tucked tightly under her. Her hands swiped across a mound on the ground, shifting the pine needles to and fro as if caressing her son below. I could see her lips moving and I imagined she was mumbling prayers.

Later when I got back to the States, I would learn how people in this region had been killed in gruesome ways. I was in an apartment in Washington, DC, when I met the first of the lucky ones who had fled, escaped through Mexico, then walked all the way to the US. He was a Mayan from the highlands. He looked at the ground while he told me his story.

"The soldiers came into our village. They told the women and children to go into the Municipalidad and we men stood out front in a group. Then three soldiers went into the building. For a long time, we could hear some women screaming then the gunshots and it was silent. Then I saw two soldiers take babies and hit them against the wall. The other soldiers walked over to us and shot all the men. The men fell dead on top of me and I stayed there very quiet. I was on the bottom, but I could see the soldiers stealing everything out of our little store and drinking all the beer. They sang and drank all night and then they burned down houses. They burned down the stores. They burned everything, then left. After many hours I pulled myself out and I knelt by the bodies and I prayed for their souls, for my brothers and sisters. I prayed, then said, 'God, my Father, I don't know why you decided for me to live but I will help.' And I got up and walked here," he told me as if walking thousands of miles to the States was like walking around the block. "Yes, *Seno*," he lifted up his eyes and said, "That is my story and God kept me alive so I could tell it."

I heard this story over and over again because it was a strategy the Guatemalan military had learned in the School of the Americas. They called it the Scorched Earth policy, the most effective means to eradicate unwanted human beings.

That night at the cemetery was a very long night for me. Teresa was worried about me. She wouldn't let me go home to sleep because she was afraid for me to sleep alone in my room. Anything could happen to me on that night. She wanted me to sleep on the floor next to her and Chula Tina, so I did. In the morning I felt like I was drunk from sleeping in a strange place and eating all the *tamales*, the *jocote*, the soup, the tortillas, and bread she piled on me.

# Fincas and Kusha

"It's time to pick coffee," Teresa told me weeks later. "Not here, but in the nearby *finca*." She eyed the farms' groves thick with blossoming, emerald-green trees bending low under the weight of the blood-red beans. "We are going to pick coffee," Teresa repeated and so did Bobdelia and Elena. Everyone was excited for a change of pace, for the money they would earn.

But at dawn when I went to meet them, Teresa and Tina were sitting on the house steps, weeping.

"My poor Lucero was killed by another dog." Teresa's tears spilled down her cheeks. "Oh, my poor dog," she moaned. I sat down next to her and put my arm around her. Tina leaned against me, sniffling. "The dog just tore him apart, poor Lucero. We buried him over by the trees." She pointed to the place behind the house where I'd see Lucero trot off with trash.

"We'll all still go and pick coffee, but we have to beware," she cautioned, her voice heavy with warning.

"That dog was born to watch over the house," she grieved. "He would bark and bite to keep robbers away. From the time he was a pup, all he wanted to do was help me. If I sat by my fire and dropped something on the ground, Lucero would pick it up, the bit of paper, and give it to me. Then he would sit beside me. That's how that dog was. He helped me in everything. If I cried, he sat next to me, looking at me, his eyes crying. And now he is dead. *Pobrecito*. Someone cursed us, Mincha. Someone is trying to hurt us." She was sure it was a curse. I tried to talk her out of it, but she only got angry.

"No Mincha, you are wrong. I know because another evil also happened last night. My other poor dog, Paloma, was roaming in the field next door when a huge snake came down the mountains. A snake about this fat," she indicated six inches with her fingers. "That class of snake has never come so close to the village. This one wrapped herself around Paloma's legs and began squeezing my poor dog to death." Well, Paloma was lucky because my neighbor saw what was happening, ran up with his machete and killed that snake.

"What I know now," she claimed her voice getting stronger, "I know that someone has gone to the *brujo*, a witch, to hurt me."

"A *brujo*? Teresa? It was only an accident," I protested again.

"No, no! You don't understand! You see, there is jealousy in this world. People see I have a pig or a chicken and think I am a rich woman. Now I should visit the *ajq'ij*, the spiritual leader, and bring him to my house to say prayers with me. I know this is true. Something else happened."

I waited thinking perhaps now she would mention the cats were also harmed and that would convince me that indeed someone was trying to hurt her. But she didn't talk about cats. Instead, she told me she got a splinter under her third finger's nail when she was putting some wood into her fire. She couldn't get the splinter out and had to walk to town to get a safety pin because you couldn't use a needle to remove the splinter. When I asked her why not, she said they were from the same family, the same type, no, you had to use a safety pin. The neighbor removed the splinter, but that night she had a dream that Tina's *huipil* was being eaten by rats. Oh, I said as she ended her account of the dream. Yes, she told me, the rats were jumping up and down, trying to eat her *huipil*. All of these events, people and animals were somehow related.

"Yes, I have to go to the *ajq'ij*," she repeated. "I don't have the centavos for that, neither does my Miguel, so I must say my own little prayers to protect us. After we work in the coffee, I will buy candles and we will go to the *cofradía*." Tina's tears changed to sniffles as we stood up to leave but Teresa's old eyes brimmed over with tears. Her quiet weeping made Tina and me stare at the ground, afraid to look at her. We all thought about how Lucero normally followed us halfway from the house and then trotted back to guard the little homestead. We walked slowly through the morning mist to the place where a truck picked up workers to transport them to the coffee groves.

As we rounded the bend, we spied a cluster of pickers waiting for the coffee truck; Teresa changed her tone and became quiet. She joined the shivering workers huddled together against the chilly mist still blanketing the countryside. Everyone talked in hushed voices until finally the truck clanged down the rock-ridden road. Young men raced alongside the truck, yelling and banging its sides with their fists until it finally stopped. A Ladino nonchalantly unhitched the tailgate of the dilapidated wreck so men, women, and children could pile on board, squashed in together, rope bags loaded with tortillas and salt swirling from men's sides.

The tailgate was wedged shut again and the truck took off, bouncing down the road past mountains and endless groves. The women gripped each other and the sides of the truck until their knuckles turned white. There was a strong, sweet aroma of *nixtamal*. I was grateful the women close by smiled at me and chatted with Teresa. Somehow it felt normal to me to be crammed in this truck side by side with these Mayans, not really knowing where we were going.

When we reached our destination, we tumbled out. Impatient youngsters raced ahead to collect burlap sacks, baskets and rope straps for the work. The Ladino supervisor pointed out several rows and pickers dispersed into the shade of the trees. Then he pointed to me.

"Who is she?"

I thought Teresa was going to go into the normal spiel that I worked at Casa Feliz and didn't have a husband. But instead, she replied, "She makes tortillas for me." Her answer made sense. It was true and defined exactly who and how I was in that moment. It was how she understood me. I walked with her. I made tortillas for her. It was the truth of that moment. But, of course, this made little sense to the Ladino. I was a *gringa*. The Ladino rolled his eyes, then laughed incredulously, directing us to another row.

Everyone tied the huge baskets to their waists and started combing the trees. Each bean had to be discovered among a tangle of branches. When the tree was full and ripe, the task was easy. The rest of the time, I strained to keep my balance, plucking gently at the beans, trying not to break a branch. Tina was the first to carefully pour her full basket into our burlap bag.

The trees were endless and came in all sizes and shapes: some sturdy, others puny, some lanky, others stubby. The ones on flat land were easy to pick but sometimes on the hills you had to stretch, and it was dangerous. Some of the trees had a scent of deadly pesticides. The sun climbed higher and our hands became glazed with the sticky brown juice of the beans until they looked like they had been dipped in tar. Row after row. Another row and another. Sweat poured down our faces. Teresa's hands were calloused but mine were soon cut and stinging. My fingers looked nicotine stained.

Basket after basket was delivered to the burlap bag until this became the single most exciting event. The pickers barely conversed but mumbled or joked with each other. The men kept up their spirits by whistling constantly as they moved from row to row, stopping now and then to help out a friend. Although they whistled separate tunes, the melodies seemed to harmonize, lending a pleasant rhythm to the work.

When the sun reached the zenith, Tina started a small fire by the side of the row and warmed coffee and tortillas. I sprawled exhausted across the prickly grass, my hands throbbing. Teresa and Tina knelt before the fire like they were still in their hut. All around us people knelt beside their own fires, chatting among themselves. Tina handed me a tortilla with salt and some coffee.

I took a sip of the sweet brown liquid but dreamed of an ice-cold beer, a sandwich, anything to relieve this heat and hunger.

"Well," I exclaimed with feigned cheerfulness, "at least we can have all the coffee we want."

Teresa looked at me startled. "No Mincha, no coffee."

"No one will know if we take a few beans," I laughed.

"No, no Mincha!" she whispered frantically. "You'll go to prison. You'll pay a fine. Maybe you'll even be killed for stealing coffee."

"No, Mincha," Tina echoed, her forehead furrowed. "Listen to my Nan."

I relented quickly to their pleas. "Well," I proposed, "at least the coffee will be cheaper in the market now."

"No coffee in the market," Teresa stated glumly. "There's never any coffee in the market."

"What do you mean?" I finally sat up.

"There's never anything in the market. It all leaves in big trucks. Our coffee is made from burned tortillas."

I was certain this was a joke. Once, teasing me, they told me they saw a *gringa* buying lice in the market to eat.

Teresa explained. "You take the burned tortillas, and you mash them up. Then you cook them with water and sugar." She continued while munching on her tortilla. "This coffee is better for you anyway, Mincha. If you eat burned tortillas, then you won't be afraid of the dark."

Suddenly the panorama of endless rows of trees made me dizzy. A boy walked past us, his sister tagging along behind with a load of firewood. I asked them and they agreed with Teresa, "Oh no, that's not coffee. The only coffee you can buy is Nescafe but it's too expensive."

She handed me another tortilla that I stared at, disgruntled. Teresa surveyed the grove where boys and girls chased each other under shady trees. Music from a transistor radio drifted over the grove while young men stalked the area, shyly eyeing the young women. Even Tina was part of this spring fever. She took her time collecting firewood or going to the burlap bag; I noticed there was always a handsome boy waiting to help her. She usually looked to the ground instead of at him. But occasionally, when Teresa wasn't watching, she mumbled some teasing remark. Coffee-picking time unleashed some simple pleasures—but for all its hard work generated little income.

At the day's end, all the burlap bags were collected and carried over to the Ladino manning the scales. These were tense moments. No one could actually see the scale, or the numbers recorded on paper. Plus, there was always the suspicion that the scales were rigged in favor of the *Patrón*. The sun set behind the crowd, the pesticides still burning their skin. Still, whenever a high number was called out, everyone applauded and cheered because someone, at least, had triumphed over the scales' stern neutrality.

During one session, a tall Ladino inched through the crowd and took me by the arm. "You're a *gringa*, yes?"

"Yes," I answered casually, but feeling uneasy.

"We have a machine here with instructions written in English. Can you translate it for me?"

"Well, yes I can try." I turned to Teresa who nodded while Tina gripped her *corte* tightly.

The Ladino led me to a small utility room about fifty feet away. Inside it was damp and dark, the cement floor littered with rubbish. On a table sat a nondescript electrical appliance, looking incongruous in this setting. I was used to these requests. Everyone thought because I was a *gringa* that I would know how to do just about everything. Once I was even asked to deliver a baby. This, however, was a task I could manage.

The Ladino stood close to me. He smelled of fresh soap and Vaseline while my body seemed to exude all the wretchedness of dirt and sweat.

"Right here!" He pointed to a tiny label. I slowly began to read it aloud while he fiddled with the knobs. Apparently, it was a sterilizer of some sort. The operating instructions were in technical language that I barely understood in English, so we bumbled along making little headway.

"Sssssst, sssssst," I heard from behind me.

I turned around and saw no one.

"Sssssst, sssssst." I looked at the Ladino who seemed deaf to the sounds.

"Just a minute," I told him.

I peeped out the door and found Teresa and Tina crouching in the corner. She snatched me. "Come on Mincha, come on! Don't go with that man!"

"But I'm only translating something for him, Teresa."

"Ssssst, Sssssst." I looked behind her and there stood five young Indian men, friends of Miguel's, their faces sober. They gestured me to their side and repeated Teresa's warning.

"Sssssst, Sssssssst," Tina was now hissing, so frightened that she was teary-eyed. Bewildered by their reactions, I went back inside and informed the Ladino, "I'm sorry but I can't read anymore. That's all I understand."

Outside again, Teresa bounded to my side. The young Mayan men walked behind us like bodyguards. "After you left, my Nans said no. My Tats said no," Teresa explained. "You can't go with that man. He is not a good man. He might steal you. The Ladinos will steal you!"

"Oh no, I was just going to ..." My protest faltered in front of their blind terror as we headed back to the truck. Men's leathery hands reached out to help us onto the truck where our sweaty bodies soon glued together, Teresa snug against me. As we bounced along, I wondered if maybe she wasn't right. She and those young men knew something I didn't know, protecting me from an unpredictable and dangerous world.

※

After a couple of weeks, the day finally arrived that the pickers had been waiting for. Husbands, wives, children, young men and women, Tina and Teresa, they all lined up in front of the *Patrón*'s estate to receive their pay. A restless anticipation stirred the crowd, each person wondering what their pay would be.

A name was called. The person disappeared into the *Patrón*'s office and returned; each person was given a tiny paper party basket of mint candies along with pay. After fifteen days of working from dawn to dusk Teresa and Tina earned twenty-four dollars and, of course, three baskets of candy, including mine.

As we jostled home in the back of the truck, the young Mayan men were unusually rowdy, imitating the *Patrón*'s voice and gestures. "Such delicious candy! Maybe next year," they mocked, "the *Patrón* will give us balloons to eat!"

Over the road, over the truck's stuttering engine, the young men denounced him and then sang, the children humming along,

*The contractors ignore our poverty*
*and don't do their job.*
*They only want to cheat and rob.*
*The coffee finca ignores our poverty.*
*We earn fifty centavos a day.*
*Not enough to buy a drink or some pants,*
*but what can we say?*
*The butchers ignore our poverty.*
*They charge us one dollar just for a bone.*
*Then send us out for a loan.*
*The barbers ignore our poverty.*
*They charge us one dollar just to cut our hair ...*

※

"This morning, a man with green clothes came to town!" The woman babbled shrilly, her scrawny head poking through Teresa's dark doorway. "He searched all the houses and wherever he found bottles of kusha, he took that person away. So, your son Miguel is now in jail." Then she launched into a stream of Kaqchiquel.

The news froze Teresa in place. The next minute she was mumbling prayers, frantically grabbing her shawl to run to the jailhouse.

Scuttling down the dusty road, she gasped to Tina and me, "Miguel will stay in jail at first, then he'll be sent to the prison in Sololá for maybe two months. There's nothing he can do but sit there like a bird in a cage and wait for his release. Oh, our poor little lives!"

Her pace accelerated. "All my poor little Miguel does is work and drink, work and drink. He doesn't have time to make kusha! Oh, our poor little lives." It was late afternoon as we zigzagged through a maze of dirt roads outlining the town. "You see, a friend accused Miguel of making kusha. How can that be? Anyway, the friend was about to be arrested by the men in green when he said, 'Wait, I'll show you who brought the kusha here.' He led them back to Santiago where they found Miguel at work. But Miguel denied everything. 'No, I didn't make kusha, it's you who did!' Then the friend picked up his machete and tried to kill my son, but Miguel's boss stopped him just in time. You see, this man thinks Miguel has been seeing his wife—that is why he wants Miguel in jail. Now my Miguel is in jail because of that man so filled with lies."

In no time, it seemed, we were standing under the dark eaves of the Municipalidad. A soldier loitered nearby, cracking his gum.

"Let's go in and find out what's happening," I urged her.

"No, no!" she protested, twisting her head back and forth like she was caught in a noose.

Teresa prowled around the perimeter of the dusty Municipalidad. A light from inside spilled over her feet. Through the half-opened door, she could see Miguel sitting on a bench.

"I must go in and speak to the magistrate," Teresa concluded.

"Yes, go Teresa!" I encouraged her.

"No, I can't," she sobbed, tucking her head into her shawl. "I'm afraid! I'm afraid!" Her head popped out again as she strode courageously to the entrance. Then at the last moment, she spun around to face us.

"Go, Teresa," I insisted. "Talk to him now before anything else happens!"

"But they might take me too," she moaned.

"But they might take my Nan!" Tina panicked.

"I'll go with you Teresa," I tried to bolster her.

She began pacing back and forth again. "*Ay Dios, Ay Dios,*" the words rolled from her mouth, "*Ay Dios.*" Would her pleas be heard? Who could help her now? Of course, it was the curse. She should have gone to the *ajq'ij*, the shaman. Anything could happen to Miguel now that he was in jail.

"Please, Teresa, I'll go with you." Tina pushed forward as I spoke, her head also buried in her shawl. "Miguel just looked up," I told her. "He wants to see you."

The eavesdropping soldier snapped his gum, bored. "I'm so afraid," she whined. "Will it help? Will they take me?"

The judge walked by the open door, a black shadow standing there. Teresa inched toward him like a whimpering dog. "My son, Miguel," she pleaded. "My son, he can't do anything but drink and work." Her big feet plodded closer, more certain with each step, more confident each time she uttered, "My son." The shadow backed off and Teresa followed it into the cavern.

"Oh, our poor lives," Tina started to whimper. "My little Nan. She's all I have in the world."

I walked over to the door to see what was happening. "Come on, Tina."

A damp musty smell hung in the air. Time felt suspended within these yellowing walls, just like the Municipalidad walls I once knew. And probably the same fortresses of corruption. Miguel's body was slouched. Teresa was cowering in front of the judge who leaned over a wooden handmade desk that wobbled. The negotiations moved quickly.

"Don't worry," he comforted her in Spanish, a fatherly tone. "Don't worry about your poor son. He'll be fine. I'll take care of everything. I know he only drinks and drinks, works and drinks. Don't worry, Teresa. He'll be taken care of tomorrow. Just warn him not to drink anymore because that man will try to kill him." So, the judge knew the town gossip and Teresa. Everything could be settled with money. It seemed this wasn't the first time she had been inside these walls.

By the time we left, it was night, but she insisted on walking the length of San Lucas to get money from anyone she could. I showed her my travelers' checks, promising to help if necessary, but she eyed them skeptically, resuming her quest. We walked another five miles to her husband's house. For hours that night we tramped through the cold mountain air, over a mountainous trail where scruffy dogs bolted out at us and snapped at our feet. Teresa and Tina were constantly teary-eyed.

"The magistrate will never listen to my son," she explained. "He is only young, and his accuser is a Ladino. A Ladino. And he is older than Miguel. So why would anyone believe my poor Miguel? The older man is the one who makes the kusha, not my poor little Miguel. Only God knows what will happen tomorrow. Only God knows."

Tina tugged on my shirt, then whispered hoarsely, "My poor brother, Miguel. My poor little Nan. Now all she'll live for is drink." But Tina's prediction was lost in the night as we trudged along.

I walked beside Teresa, but it all seemed hopeless. Yet as a mother, like so many mothers, she couldn't give up. She'd pay his way out of jail. She wanted to save him, but how? If he was an alcoholic, this would happen again. Then the mere fact of being a Mayan man could land him back in jail. I was finally grasping that Teresa's fears weren't exaggerated at all: low wages, poor soil, ill health, the racial hatred, and the massacres taking place in villages.

Even though Teresa was terrified to be out at night, she pushed on, Tina by her side, willing to walk the paths, pounding on doors of friends, begging for help. She walked to another village despite her fear of spirits, of kidnappings, and things I didn't even understand. Her hope, her love, her duty quickened her pace. She walked so she could beg her husband for help. She believed her love would save her son, or if not, God's love would intervene. Like any mother, she'd do whatever was needed to save her son.

She mumbled prayers as she briskly walked through the night. I offered her money again, but she refused adamantly. Me, the *gringa*. Before tonight, I had bought things for her, but never offered any money and she never asked for any. But I wanted to help, yet she wouldn't take any money from me, not even in this emergency. Perhaps her pride held her back. Or maybe because I, too, was "another people" wearing a different *traje*, and this was the moment when only one's own kind could be trusted. She realized what I didn't want to admit but knew to be true: I belonged to the Ladinos. I was somehow part of the system taking away her son, driving her son to drink, and pushing her to walk from village to village.

I knew what she thought was true. I could reach down and feel my travelers' checks, my symbol of power, of where I came from. I was willing to relinquish part of that by helping her with money, but the power of my education and resources went way beyond that small handout. No matter what I said or did, the world remained fixed, boxing our friendship into closed, tight definitions beyond our doing. I felt frustrated but I knew walking beside her was the best I could give then. So, we walked and walked, her love and sense of duty driving her on.

The next day Miguel went to court. After five minutes, Miguel was sentenced to five years in prison. In another five minutes, the judge's palm well-greased with all the money Teresa had collected, Miguel was free again. I figured all along that with money, Miguel would be set free. I had seen the system in action myself, and it was that experience that made me ask deeper questions about the world I lived in, that made me want to discover for myself the true circumstances of so many people in the world and women in particular. It's what had eventually led me to Teresa.

✳

As soon as Miguel was free, we all headed to Pompolah, the *finca* where Teresa was born and raised, where she had Miguel and was given Tina. For the family it was the site of the most important fiesta of the year.

It began innocently. A celebratory event.

Teresa, Miguel, Tina, and I walked past the foul-smelling water reservoir that marked the outskirts of Pompolah. After hiking another hour and a half we finally spotted the shacks for *mozos*, workers, the tiny white church and the *Patrón's* sprawling ranch house. Ramshackle stands selling snacks and trinkets were erected everywhere. The night smelled of pine needles, incense, and kusha.

"Here," Teresa laughed slightly through the shawl drawn over her mouth, covering her big horsey teeth. She was happy now that Miguel was free and by her side. A fiesta seemed like just the right place to be. She halted in front of a small hut that also served as a *tienda*, a store.

"Together we will have a drink, right, Mincha?"

"Right," I replied eagerly, taking out money to buy a round of kusha.

She chattered to women dressed just like her and soon we had gulped down our first little bottle of kusha. It tasted like kerosene, so for the first round we bought a Fanta chaser, passing the bottles back and forth. We sat against the thatch wall, the radio playing marimba. Occasionally, we heard a man hoot at the moon, or someone stumble past, or another pass us hanging on the shoulders of a woman. Skinny dogs sniffed the ground around us. We laughed at everything we saw. We were so happy, felt so free sitting together, listening to music, the night crisp and clear.

I bought everyone another round.

And Miguel bought the next.

Now we drank it straight, reeling over to join the dance. People turned to greet us, offering us more food and drink. The little room had a heady aroma of kusha; dust flew, bodies collided, Nans danced with Nans, holding each other tight. Couples shuffled to and fro, stiff and awkward. The marimba players tapped out their sweet-sounding music while the kusha continued, with fierce precision, to split open our heads. While we sat and leaned against the wall, we watched as two young men picked a fight and young lovers sneaked out the door. The kusha transformed the world into a fog and gave us an escape that was perilous—both enjoyable and extreme.

In a drunken stupor we staggered to Teresa's cousin's thatched hut. More kusha splattered. I dimly perceived Tina skirting around us protectively. Teresa and I fell down beside each other in a heap, our mouths filled with dirt, our ears still ringing with the sound of marimba.

✳

"My head, my head," I whined as we headed home in the chilly morning air. We had been drunk for two days, most of which I couldn't remember. My head hurt but Teresa and I were still slightly tipsy, so we laughed at anything. Tina, sober, looked sour and pinched. Miguel had long since disappeared with some friends.

"Over here," Teresa called out excitedly, leading us down a narrow path to another hut.

"We'll drink a little bit of kusha to clear our heads."

"Ugh," I protested, slightly nauseous.

"No, this will clear your head, Mincha. It's the best medicine."

I downed a shot. The throbbing in my head faded, the mountains and Teresa's dress became mysterious again. Tina tugged at my arm and yanked me out of the hut, out of Teresa's earshot.

"My Nan is going to drink and drink," she was worried.

I patted her on the head, "Don't worry, Tina. Even in my country this is how we cure a hangover."

Finally, we arrived at Teresa's hut in San Lucas. Almost immediately she ran off to fetch water while Tina lit the fire and soon, we were sitting beside it, calm again, recuperating from all the excess.

Teresa rushed back into the hut without any water. She reached inside her *huipil* and pulled out another little bottle of kusha. "More, Mincha?"

"No, I can't Teresa. I can't." The kusha smelled foul. This diet of alcohol and no food had me nearly hallucinating in this already hallucinatory world.

Teresa, however, gulped it down like soda, munching on a tortilla. After a few more she raised her head to the ceiling, prayed drunkenly to God, cried for her mother, conversed with Pablo, reprimanded the *Patrón*. She delivered herself to oblivion.

✕

"Give me more money, Mincha," Teresa demanded, "so I can buy more maize for my Tina."

"Kusha," Tina hissed. "She already sold the pots."

I refused and Teresa turned on her heel to borrow money elsewhere.

Tina shrugged while Miguel, sitting beside her in the shadows, watched sheepishly. Their Nan soon returned, her blood now kusha, freed at last from anxiety, freed from her world of Ladinos and Indians. "*Aye, Dios,*" she moaned, kneeling by the fire. "*Aye, Dios,*" she repeated then laughed hysterically. Her eyes watery, her lips slack, she methodically rubbed her knees then began to sing,

"I wake from my dreams. Thinking of you. I wake from my dreams ..."

The verse wound round and round the hut as she swayed before her fire. Her cats retreated toward the shadows. Mumbling at the fire, she raised her head. Drooling like a child as she mumbled and began to sway. "*Ay, Dios,*" she repeated.

I walked out in disgust, sick of kusha, sick of watching this woman disintegrate, and of my helplessness before it. I strode through the plaza, seeking the cool waters of Lake Atitlán. Tina came running up behind me. "My Nan is dying," she cried. "My Nan is dying! Miguel hit her! Oh, she is dying!"

We raced back to the hut and found Teresa sprawled on her *petate*. Her thin chest heaved. Her right eye looked like a purple golf ball. A dark streak of blood trickled from her mouth.

# Katok Ki—Helping Each Other

Worry and hunger compressed Tina's young face, so she looked almost ancient. Teresa's fat sister sat weeping by the clinic bedside where Teresa's body, close to lifeless skeleton, lay sprawled out before us. Tubes for intravenous feeding entangled her arms. An odor of urine and kusha rose like steam from her clothes.

For three days Teresa remained semi-conscious. The young volunteer doctors from John Hopkins told me malnutrition and kusha don't mix.

"Teresa will die," people in the village repeated. "Teresa will die." "She vomited blood. That means she will die." "Anyone who goes to the clinic dies."

Tina looked desperate. "My mother will die," she said, scanning my face. I didn't want to look her in the eye. I felt so ashamed that I was the one who bought that first round. "My mother will die, and I'll be left alone in the world."

But she wasn't alone. There was an endless stream of women, dressed just like Teresa, walking in and out of the clinic, their eyes downcast, carrying bundles of warm tortillas, hot soups, herbal remedies. They whispered to each other, and one always remained behind, sitting straight-backed like a sentinel, lips barely moving in constant prayer, guarding Teresa. I watched how the people nourished Teresa and each other with food, with comforting words and smiles. They murmured prayers and their love of God and the saints fortified them. It was real nourishment for them and for Tina.

No, Tina didn't have to ever worry about being alone. It wasn't just the women, coming in and out of the clinic, who were her security. No, it was the traditions and the rules passed from person to person, woman to woman, generation to generation. The most important thing for them was each other, maintaining each other through their traditions. Some of the women cried, sitting by Teresa's bedside, watching her thin chest barely move up and down.

On the fourth day a rasping noise erupted from Teresa's throat. She began to rock back and forth. Tina slowly prodded, then propped her up in bed, where she fed her sips of *atole*, a drink made from maize.

Teresa's bruised eye opened slightly, blood-red tears rolling down her cheeks. She finished her *atole*, and then slipped down between the sheets, an intricately woven scarf wrapped round her head.

"I close my eyes," she croaked hoarsely, "and I'm in my house. I open my eyes and I'm in this clinic. I close my eyes and I am in the groves picking coffee. I open my eyes, and *Ay Dios*, I'm back in this clinic. Sometimes I'm standing in a large field in front of a mound of dirt and a huge pile of ripe tomatoes. A crowd of people starts rushing toward me. I wave my hands, but they keep coming and coming. Then I open my eyes and ask poor Chula Tina, 'Who are those mean people attacking me?' 'Oh Nan,' she tells me, 'There is no one. You're in the clinic.' I lay back and I still see those people grabbing at me. Then I see a huge brown dog running over the beds. 'Chula Tina, Chula Tina,' I yell. 'That dog! That dog!' Tina holds me tight, saying, 'There's no dog here, Nan. Don't worry. Just lay down and rest.'"

So, Teresa rested some more, soothed by Chula Tina. The stream of women continued. Her fat sister came to visit again, weeping shamelessly under the naked light bulb.

Finally, Teresa started propping herself up in the bed, eager now for compassion. "It was my son Miguel. He hit me in the face."

"Oh, Nan, that can't be. You poor little thing."

"Yes," she said, pleased with the attention, resting back on her elbows. "And he hasn't come to visit me or sent me any money. Only his father has."

"Oh Nan, you poor thing, your own son. A son can't hurt his mother."

After Teresa heard "Oh you poor thing" a hundred times, she was satisfied and fell back into a deep, sometimes terrifyingly deep sleep. Days passed and she reverted to her old worried self, anxious to leave the clinic's sterility.

"Mincha," she whispered. "I must leave. I must return to my little animals and fire."

"Wait, Teresa, wait until you are well. Tina is taking care of the animals."

"No, Mincha," her eyes darted back and forth, "I have to leave now." She leaned her old body toward me, pausing to spit in her precious scarf. "What are these things stuck in my arms? I tell you what they are. The Ladinos are putting water in my blood! I must leave." Always her old fears returning, injected into her by history, by experience. The pull of nourishment and safety among her own.

At the end of the hall, a Ladina nurse bent over a tray of food, flies hovering above, steel dishes clattering.

"Teresa, those are vitamins for your body. You need more vitamins."

"No," she shook her head fiercely. "You and Tina must get me some Alka Seltzer and Coke. That's what will cure me."

Tina looked at her Nan, weak and thin. There were no fires, no animals, no *nixtamal*. Oh, the clinic was a bad place, a place where people only went to die. She darted out the door to find the "real medicine" for her Nan. It was all so frightening. Teresa leaned back, exhausted by her fears, the Ladino's water pumping into her system.

Soon, the intravenous feeding tubes were removed. Teresa could walk. Despite the doctor's warning, and all of our arguments, she meticulously gathered up her scarves, her Alka Seltzer, the tin cups, and tortilla basket Tina brought from home and lifted the bundle onto her head. Tina frolicked round her, happy.

Teresa plodded out into the morning mist that still lingered over San Lucas Tolimán. Tina and I walked beside her, passing the rows of crumbling huts hedged by flowers and maize. Once again a deep sense of shame overcame me that I helped her start a binge that almost killed her. But it didn't kill her because she had her community, her tradition, and her responsibilities to return to. Her spirituality guided her moves, brought her respite, and shielded her. She was confident of what she had to do.

Watching her made me want to explore something deeper beyond all the noise and movement. Teresa walked beside me. She seemed to have a sense of confidence that was built on knowing you are valuable in and of yourself. There was a seed of that in me. Despite the drunkenness, the illogical explanations, Teresa had shared that sense of self with me and awakened something in me that I hoped would grow.

I watched her re-entering the network of tree-lined paths that met in the dusty plaza. Men tromped by her, bent over with bundles of wood on their backs, machetes swinging by their sides. She followed the path and joined her Nans who trotted by balancing jugs of water or *nixtamal* on their heads. Soon she knelt by her fire, Tina beside her, and began the familiar sound of tortilla making, the steady rhythmic sound, the life sound in all Guatemalan villages that has existed for hundreds of years.

# THREE

# The Walk, Guatemala to Mexico

*Solvitur ambulando*

(It is solved by walking)

# Paso a Paso—Step by Step

After Teresa's episode, a loneliness slowly came over me. I ignored it by working more in the orphanage, comforted by the company of children, especially Pescado and Verline. They liked to walk by the lake to collect colorful rocks. Sometimes they acted out little stories for me, especially ones ridiculing drunks. I also relied on Bobdelia, who was always affectionate. She'd walk with us by the lake, her arm around my waist, sometimes singing church songs. Or late afternoon I would sit by Teresa, absorbing her motherly gestures. Letters from home were tucked in my backpack; I reread Mark's letters, trying to read between the lines. I perused books of all kinds, spiritual, historical, philosophical, looking for answers to unspoken questions. But it wasn't enough. I longed for my one place of belonging: my family. I wanted to go home.

I struggled with the idea of leaving, until one image kept haunting me. It was a simple image: the image of women walking through mountains, a sight I had seen frequently here in Guatemala and in Haiti. Walking. I decided to walk, at least part of the way, back to my family.

I had known for a long time that walking was critical to the lives of the women I had met. I felt I couldn't know Teresa or Larian, or any of their friends, until I knew more about what walking meant to them. Both the women in Haiti and Guatemala walked as a means of transportation. They walked from relative to relative, village to village, market to market. Often, they carried huge bundles on their heads or herded animals to sell in the market. Back and forth to the creek or the river, they carried laundry or water in ceramic pots made from clay gathered in open rivers and mixed with ash. Sometimes they walked for days. And some walked for weeks to reach El Norte. Walking was independence. It framed the way they looked at the world. Perhaps it would help bring me insight into both them and myself.

I decided to walk from the outskirts of Guatemala City to the Mexican border. I didn't explain my plans to Teresa as she worried. Nonetheless, Teresa and Tina spent days fretting over my departure. Teresa gave me a bright red and gold necklace and a red-beaded bracelet. The red beads were like wearing a prayer, the color red was a protective shield among the Mayans. Tina wrapped warm tortillas and *tamales* in a hand-woven cloth from San Lucas. They walked me to the edge of town. Then Teresa and Tina waved goodbye to me as I boarded the bus back to the city. They waved goodbye in the traditional manner: their hands reversed toward their faces, waving me back into their lives, urging me to return. The bus pulled out and they grew smaller and smaller, standing close to the coffee groves, the thatched huts, while men and women dressed in *traje* walked past them, on their way to the lake.

After the quiet and natural beauty of San Lucas, the city felt like quicksand, sucking me in with smells of sewage and perfumes, the racket of cars, the hawking of vendors and shiny storefronts. I elbowed my way through the crowd at the bus station, settled into the guest house, and then left for the map store so I could plan my walk.

But the map store in Guatemala City could only provide me with one huge map of the country. The map was sold in sections. And the center section was missing.

"This map needs another section," I told the man. He was a Ladino with bushy eyebrows and glasses that hung on a chain round his neck.

"That's the only map of Guatemala that you will find."

"But it's not complete," I insisted, pointing at a blank space where Alta and Baja Verapaz, and a portion of the Peten, would normally be—the exact area I was planning to walk through to get to Mexico.

"Is there another map store where I can get an entire map?"

"No," he replied curtly as he turned back toward his shelves of maps, geological books, compasses, and ropes.

I thought he was probably lying. He just didn't want to lose my business to his competitors. So, I left. I quickly discovered that not only was there not another map but there wasn't another map store in the entire city.

I returned and our argument ensued again. It was urgent for me to have a map to help guide me. Finally, he told me the truth.

"The Guatemalan government does not allow us to publish that part of the map."

"What? Why not?" Suddenly I could feel Teresa's influence. The Ladino was doing this on purpose. Maybe he just didn't like Americans.

At first, he wouldn't answer and just began refolding the map. He looked over at me, blinking rapidly then said, "The government doesn't want *guerrilleros* to use maps, so we can't sell the entire map to anyone.

And," he paused and added, "you never know who is a *guerrillero*."

The information slowly sunk in. "Just sell it to me then … like it is."

"You want to buy it?" He stood there with the map folded in his hand.

Even in its entirety, it would be a ridiculous map to take on this journey. It was a general map only indicating main roads, some elevations, and a few rivers. But I believed I needed maps only for general directions. For specifics, I could rely on the local people. Living in San Lucas Tolimán gave me the conviction that villagers scattered throughout the other regions would assist me.

"There are *guerrilleros* all over that area," he warned me.

"I know." I was fishing into my purse, wanting to pay him.

He leaned over the counter and, like a friend reassuring me, he put his hand over mine. "That means there are soldiers too."

Sliding my hand out from under his, I thanked him and put a ten on the counter, grabbed the map, and walked out the door.

✳

I was very low on money, so I sold my red pack and folded my few belongings into a blanket that I tied round my back and carried. The pack was stained and had grease spots, but it was functional, with four compartments rather than one large pocket so you could easily organize all your worldly goods. I sold it to a young Canadian traveler who I knew would bring it on many adventures, but it hurt to watch it go. As I handed it over to him, I remembered my mother at the camping store with me, buying the pack. I could just see her leaning against the counter then saying, "Here, put this in the top pocket, make sure it fits," She handed me an army-green mosquito net.

I obediently jammed it into the top pocket.

"And this too." She gave me a bulky flashlight, but the young salesperson interrupted, "No, not that one. It's too heavy. How about this," he handed her a little red flashlight. He was smiling. She had a knack with people, and he was already her friend.

The young salesperson was staring at us. Maybe he wondered about her. Mothers in this neighborhood usually bought debutante dresses for daughters, not Swiss Army knives and backpacks. I had my own misgivings about the situation, but I felt I had to be brave. I was kneeling by the red pack inspecting it. A snake-bite kit sat on the counter beside my mother. As I zipped open each pocket of the pack, I could still feel a sort of panic running through my body. The Peten, the Guatemalan jungle. Mayans.

She watched me closely as I stood up. "You know your uncle told me not to let you go, that *banditos* could kidnap you." Then she smiled and walked to the counter. Watching her pay for my equipment, I knew she wasn't afraid for me, so neither was I.

✳

I started from Sacatepéquez, a Kaqchiquel town outside of Guatemala City. I left on the main road that was so dusty I tied a bandana over my mouth, so I looked like a robber tramping among the Indians. The familiarity of their dress, the rhythm of their gait somehow reassured me. It wasn't until the second day as I passed the last of the villages, crossed a small river, and the throng thinned out, that I started to question my choice. The road had thinned out to a path, then became a dirt road again. With each step the insanity of my quest was more apparent, especially without detailed maps and the added threat of *guerrilleros* or soldiers. What was I doing?

With each footstep I felt more doubt—a little voice telling me: turn back, turn back. The ground was hard against my feet, pushing against something deep inside of me, pushing against what had been the backdrop of my life. Yet as the day's end approached, I wiped dust and sweat from my face, and felt more assured this physical challenge would restore my perspective on the world. I had witnessed so much poverty and struggle but now I was headed to a world where I felt I was going to face a different kind of poverty. With each step I knew that something deep within was shifting, that I needed to examine things, to understand what I valued now. Things that once seemed worth struggling to achieve were becoming a backdrop. Walking would be my transition, my meditation.

I walked by villagers. Sometimes, the women scurried into a hut and peered out at me between the wall's stalks. Other times they stood like stone statues, rigid at the edges of tilled fields, only their eyes following me, the world around them quiet except for the crows swooping down behind, pecking at the turned soil, dark and volcanic. Sometimes a hut would be a little *tienda* like the one Teresa once had on the *finca* and I'd sit on a rock smoking, relishing a lukewarm orange Fanta and a piece of dried bread. A few times, when I rested beside a path, a Mayan marched out bravely to escort me to a dark hut where I was given a few tortillas and beans.

I soon forgot about the Ladino's map store and instead of feeling fearful, I had the growing sense of being guarded and passed along, hand by hand, village by village. Protected even as I slept under trees, beside fields, or one night, when I was too tired to walk farther, by a little cemetery. Perhaps it was another rationalization on my part, but in all these months with Mayans, love and protection was all I had ever known. I kept moving at a relaxed pace.

※

I walked and walked through the mountains, under crisp blue skies. Yes, this was the Land of Eternal Spring. A few mountain passes were steep, but the landscape was green and fertile, the air cool and fresh. When I wasn't on a dirt road, I followed paths that were well trodden, but soon there were fewer and fewer people in sight. Every now and then, there was a small adobe hut or a clump of four or five adobe homes with chickens out front or skinny dogs barking at the village edges. I stopped at the villages to buy hunks of bread or even a simple meal. A few times I slept in a family hammock, but mainly I was satisfied sleeping outside, under the stars, tranquility all around me.

After a week of walking far into the mountains, I saw two White men in suits walking toward me. They carried briefcases and wore white sparkling shirts. They had straight backs, short hair, and clear skin that seemed untouched by the sun that was turning my skin bark-colored.

"Hello," I called out as I walked by this strange sight in the middle of nowhere.

"Hello," they answered. And they paused for a moment and explained to me, "We are here to help the Indians, to bring them the word of God." They explained their mission in kind, steady voices and had a patient way of speaking, but as they walked off, I looked at their backs and hated them, the steadiness of their walk and their confident talk. The combination of their quietness and their mission felt brutal. Patronizing and intrusive. But of course, that's how the Mayans in San Lucas first saw me. However, if that was true along this trail, the villagers never let me know.

The map allowed me to tell people the name of the next village so they could point me in the right direction. The mountains got steeper and I followed close behind local people. Once I scampered behind a man and wife or a family; another time, behind a small group of workers, machetes tapping their thighs, hoes swinging off their shoulders. I studied how the Indigenous people walked. They took short quick steps, never leaving their center of gravity. They didn't try to use giant steps to climb the steeper, higher mountains. No. Always the same pace. Always the same amount of space between their footsteps. Feet close together, never having to lean forward or backward. This also seemed to represent the way they lived. A steady pace that would get you there. A straight-backed body that doesn't leave its own center of gravity even if there is rain or wind. Even if there are massacres or drunkenness. Always remaining in your own center of gravity.

As I climbed a steep, rocky path, the walking quietened my thoughts. I savored the growing sense of inner calm. Following their example, I tried not to lose my own center of gravity. Each footstep brought me closer to a sense of space and peace and eternalness, a deep sense of interconnectedness, because the earth and the humans work together and live for each other.

All this replaced the personal fears driving me as I headed back. Fears about what profession to follow, where to live, whether I wanted to have a family someday. The walking quieted that swirl of thoughts. I savored a sense of inner calm.

And then it started to rain.

It started to rain just as I got low on food and passed fewer and fewer huts. I only had a bright-blue sheet of plastic to use as a tarp to cover my blanket and clothes. It was almost impossible to keep dry in the slow drizzle that formed little streams along the path's edges. I was wet and cold. I wanted to turn back but I was far in the highlands. I must turn back, I thought. I must. But there was no way to turn back. I only had Incaparina, government-issued gruel, to eat. I had started my period and it weakened me more. I must turn back or arrive someplace. I started to feel exhausted and trembled from the cold. My feet slipped in mud as I climbed a very steep mountain and then there on the top, like a vision from the prophets, was a small white adobe chapel. I went in, sat on the bench, and started to weep.

✕

The next day, a husband and wife showed up in the little chapel where I had slept. But these were not Kaqchiquel Indians. These people were Quiche Mayans, so I knew I was in Verapaz, closer to the jungle and the river that would take me to Mexico. I knew they were Quiche Indians because the woman didn't wear a *huipil* like Teresa's. Instead, she wore a traditional white lace *huipil*. She seemed confident and not surprised at all to find me there, dirty and hungry. She looked me in the eye and said, "*Pobrecita*." This seemed to be the refrain I always engendered among the Mayans. This time I knew it was well-deserved—my uncombed hair, my muddy clothes.

The woman walked to the chapel door and squatted outside to build a small fire. Then she put some kind of receptacle on it. I was still sitting on the chapel bench. Her back was turned to me so I couldn't see exactly what she was doing.

The woman didn't invite me over, so I just sat there dumbfounded at these apparitions: a tiny adobe chapel, a roof to sleep under, a bench to sleep on, and now two Mayans. Finally, she strode over, her face ageless, her gaze confident. Like a well-trained pet, I obeyed as soon as she nodded for me to come and sit close to her. Then a bowl of steaming hot soup was carefully placed in my hands. At first, I just stared at it. Steam. Warm food. Nourishment. Gratitude. For a moment I paused, absorbing her gesture, a sort of holiness surrounding it.

I took a sip. "Good God," I thought, resisting the urge to spit it out on the floor. "I can't drink this." It was a thick, brick-colored gruel: pure chili. It burned through my tongue, my gums, my throat. I felt it scalding my stomach. She nodded and she had that look I'd seen with Teresa: this is what you must do; no other options exist.

Little by little I sipped it until the bowl was empty. My body wanted to throw itself on the ground, hurl itself against the wall. Then muscles unclenched, slackened until my body calmed when it recognized it had absorbed a powerful food.

I looked over to the couple. They lit candles, knelt, and prayed together in the tiny, damp chapel. When they were done, they murmured to each other in their *lengua*, clicking their tongues while I gathered my belongings.

On the track, I could hardly keep pace with them as they trotted over the mountain's backside. As we descended the precipitous path, I could see in the distance where the land flattened and melded into the jungle. We moved quickly, me often stumbling behind, until we finally arrived at our destination: a small cement blockhouse on the bank of an olive-green river. A little hotel for government laborers who worked in the jungle clearing land, drilling for oil, and God knows what else.

For almost a week, I lay collapsed in a hammock on the veranda. It overlooked the gateway to the jungle. It started to rain again, but this time I was pleased. It was a quiet soft rain that lulled me into a sleep that gained me passage to the next stage of my trip.

After many meals of rice and beans and daily cold showers, I learned about dugout canoes going up the river to deliver merchandise. I was fearful to walk any distance in the jungle and decided to get rides on the dugout canoes with Mam Indians. The government was promoting settlement in the jungle, so there were tiny settlements of two or three huts scattered randomly along the river.

So, I paid my way to sit among the stocks of bananas, bolts of cloth, and cans of gasoline as a man paddled up the river. The dugout sank halfway down under the weight but oftentimes the pilot stood at one end with a paddle, whistling as the Mayan men had in the coffee fields. The canoe moved along slowly, languidly, while flocks of scarlet-red parrots hurtled through the sky.

It took time to get up the river, stopping in small villages where I spent a few nights until the next canoe came by. Up I went, until I hit the River Usumacinta that followed the border of Mexico. There I boarded a flat boat with big wooden boxes stacked all around us, piles of oranges and bananas, thick ropes, chickens in cages and dogs lounging in the sun. In a corner was the luxury of a little kerosene stove to make some coffee right there on deck. It seemed like a sprawling huge boat after the dugout canoes, but it was as tight and functional as a minivan. By then the rains had stopped and the sun blazed down, finally warming my bones as I stepped onto land again. There was an old Ford, engine churning, already crammed with people. Men with swagger looked me in the eye. They milled around a small *tienda* blasting *rancheros*. I could see a calendar advertising *Pan Bimbo*. Mexico. It felt so familiar. I was already home.

※

When I finally did get to the outskirts of Washington, DC, where my family lived, I opened the door to our home to find a stranger standing in the hallway. I smiled, pleased that my family remained so hospitable, figuring that this was a family member's friend. But the man looked startled.

"Who are you?" he asked aggressively, as if I was an intruder. After some confusion, we realized that during my long-extended absence, my parents had sold their home to him and they moved. I was exhausted, shocked and began to cry. But the man tried to comfort me and reassure me, "Don't worry, we can find them," he said kindly.

"No, you don't understand," I told him. "My family could be anywhere in the world."

But I was wrong. They had moved only a few blocks away.

# FOUR

# Jayla, The United States

*... the home of the free and the land of the brave*
— Francis Scott Key

# The Richest Nation on Earth

I spent months in my family's new home, a brick colonial house that overlooked a park. Every day I'd walk through the neighborhood to visit the local library. The huge old elm and oak trees edging the streets shaded me as I passed houses that took up almost a block. The neighborhood was quietly elegant, filled with interesting, powerful people from the Supreme Court Justice to bestselling authors and journalists. This enclave of hushed streets was protected by a private police force that could boast a mere two robberies in seven years.

The neighborhood wasn't unfamiliar to me. It had been a three-year stopover for our family between Morocco and the next jaunt to Puerto Rico. But as I walked past the well-tended lawns, I found myself wondering, as I had as a child, where everyone was. No one on the sidewalks. No animals. No dust. No one under the trees squatting before fires, making sweet mint tea. The only sign of life, an occasional car driving by. As a child, the lifelessness of it frightened me so I'd climb up a cherry tree at the end of the block, my hidden sanctuary. My other refuge was my brothers and sisters. They were my tribe, the intermediaries between me and this neutral world. And once again, as I returned to the US, they ushered me back into their world. When the library was becoming a hiding place rather than a resource, my sisters took me out for dinner and dancing. They helped me find an apartment, jobs working with children and as a bike messenger.

My sisters helped bring me back into this old familiar yet unfamiliar world of mine. None of us mentioned jail, Haiti or Guatemala yet it remained with me and flavoured everything I did. When I opened the refrigerator and gazed at the meats sitting between Brie cheese and diet soda, angry thoughts emerged. A frenzy of thoughts racing through eras of my life, sprinting past lives I had seen, dashing past all the wealth and opulence surrounding me. The thoughts led to feelings of despondency and guilt. I wanted to banish those perceptions and return to the safe haven of my ignorance. Yet I couldn't drown out the confusion of thoughts. This was my world. And the reason I was free, out of jail, was because I belonged to this world.

Jayla, a friend from work, lived downtown, just a short ride down the pristine street of Connecticut Avenue. She would show me, once again, how a sense of belonging can be an anchor or an ax.

✳

Jayla lived right in the heart of DC. She lived close to the broad, tree-lined boulevards that stretch out all the way from the Capitol. I could ride my bike down one of those wide streets near Jayla's house and in ten minutes or less, be right smack dab in front of the White House.

Her street was noisy, littered; disco music blasted all day from a bar and men loitered on the corners. Most seasons of the year it felt humid and hot and year-round it had a threatening quality. The sense of danger was different from Haiti or Guatemala. There were no M16s or sunglassed Tonton Makoute. Here danger was more like smoke circling round you, the threat of fire, hidden but close by.

I hadn't lived in Washington DC for any length of time since I was a young child. Crossing the border in Mexico, I sensed that I was crossing into other borders within the US. And that's what happened to me when I met Jayla, a young African American woman, working as a receptionist, safe within the cloistered walls of Rose Hill School.

It was surprising that Rose Hill School was in this area where Jayla lived. It was a bilingual institution that catered mainly to children of diplomats and to young families convinced that bilingualism was a promising educational strategy that prepared their children for bright futures. Jayla was working as a substitute receptionist, hired because of the director's efforts to employ welfare mothers. All day Jayla worked answering the phone, greeting visitors, and leading lost children back to their classrooms. She sat behind a great wooden desk, surrounded by memos, directories, and paperclips. She seemed so at home there, I hardly noticed her except for an occasional explosion of boisterous laughter.

I became friends with Jayla because I was looking for someone to type up all my journals and notes from Guatemala and Haiti. I had moved to the area, and my new roommate, a Rose Hill teacher, suggested I might ask Jayla to help with the typing. The teacher also hinted that Jayla was quite a character and had a story to tell.

One day after work, I stopped at Jayla's desk to formally introduce myself and ask her about the typing. She accepted my offer immediately. She would transcribe my notes in between her other chores at Rose Hill, the receptionist job being subject to periodic lulls. As if to make sure I felt comfortable with this arrangement, from time to time she would show me the drawer where my notebooks were kept.

Jayla seemed mature and strong for her twenty-four years, with a large tree-like body, thick and powerfully built. The skin on her round face looked soft while her arms were brawny. She was friendly and we got along from the start. We chatted frequently. I liked her sense of humor and she responded to mine.

But for weeks our relationship remained on a businesslike level, me giving Jayla another notebook, she handing back typewritten pages, and me handing her the pay. Despite her semi-professional allure, the typos and slow work betrayed her lack of professional training. My little bit of money was going down the drain. Some of the problem, of course, was my handwriting, barely legible to anyone. However, her enthusiasm for the work, combined with my curiosity about her life, persuaded us both to continue. As she read more and more of the journals, she began to comment about their content. When she typed up Teresa's story about her children dying but her persistence in looking after her family, Jayla said, "Now that woman has some strength the Lord must have given her!" She was astounded that these women who lived "God knows where" had dreams and troubles similar to her own. Plus, she was impressed by their physical and emotional strength.

Her observations convinced me that this woman had her own story to share, and I was eager to listen. Still, I made no mention of my hopes of learning about her story. I waited. I already knew from her moody silences and temperamental nature that Jayla was both reserved and proud. And so was I. Plus, a class and racial bias separated us that neither of us knew exactly how to handle, so we didn't mention it. It wasn't until she interrogated me more than usual about Haitian women that I frankly invited her to share her story.

"And those Haitians! Looks like they can survive just about near anything," she'd repeat in admiration. She plied me with questions then tenderly remarked about the Haitians, "Why Clem, they call their children little people, don't they?"

"Yes," I confirmed, glad she could appreciate their world.

"Well, ain't that cute," she said, smiling from behind her desk.

I recited terms other mothers used for their children—*mamita, papacito, choufleur*—then haltingly proposed that Jayla's own life be added to the collection.

"Me?" she protested. "You know my life ain't been nothing to brag about."

"Well, neither are the lives of the other women. But they still have a lot to give, don't they?" Listening carefully, she nodded as I continued, "My problem is that so far, they're all from other countries. I want a woman from the wealthiest country in the world to have a voice."

Shifting her thick body uncomfortably in the chair, Jayla's face remained blank. "So, you gonna write about that place too?"

"Yes, and that woman would be you."

"You know I ain't no rich woman."

"But you live in the richest country in the world."

"This place?"

I stared at her, suspecting she was playing me for a fool.

She gazed back, no doubt wondering the same thing about me.

"Yes," I told her. "This is the richest country in the world."

"And who says so?"

"Experts. People who study this stuff. The US has more money per person than any other country."

She cocked her head to one side, watching me closely.

"Lord, girl!" she blurted out. "Have mercy on those other countries!" Suddenly angry, she shifted her papers from one side of the desk to the other. "I'll tell you, ain't nobody ever showed me that!" Then she laughed—a cruel, bitter laugh. "The richest country in the world! Ooh, ain't that something! I'll tell you." Her laugh grew louder. "Look like the more I think about it, the funnier it gets. Them so-called experts have something to learn, don't they?" When her laughter died down, she realized I was still waiting for her answer.

"Well, yeah," she decided hesitantly. "Maybe if people see someone like me pushing on, they won't want to do away with themselves. Lord, there have been times in my life when I felt like dying was the only answer. But the Lord's touched me now, and people might learn from that. And just maybe," she added, growing more at ease with the idea, "people will see my mistakes and avoid doing the same thing."

At that moment visitors looking for the director cut our conversation short. It wasn't too many days later, however, before the topic was resumed. Jayla and I accidentally ran into each other in the deserted faculty lounge. We sat side by side that day on the tattered sofa, looking out at the playground. The hectic rhythm of the school day had subsided in the late afternoon. Muffled shouts of children climbing over monkey bars could still be heard. Teachers with tired smiles gossiped under the trees, waiting for parents to collect the last stragglers.

"Let me get you some coffee," Jayla offered, hoisting her stocky body from the couch. I nodded gratefully as she reached for the Styrofoam cups. "I'll get *you* some—but not that other teacher!" She paused, waiting for confirmation that I was listening.

I looked up. "What other teacher?"

"Lord, I don't know, one of them other teachers. I fetch her a cup and she don't even thank me. I swear how some people can be. Walking round with their asses on their shoulders. Lord, they got some kinda attitude!" She carefully poured out two coffees, her thick eyebrows knotted together, still mumbling half aloud. Normally an attractive woman, anger contorted her face.

"Well, most teachers here aren't rude," I rationalized, accepting the cup.

"No, I can't complain too much about this place," she smiled, accentuating her high cheekbones. "Most people here is nice and there ain't no racism. It's like one big happy family here and that's okay. Nobody wants a boss saying, 'Do this! Do that!' No, I can't take that. I'm too much of my own woman."

Sitting down beside me, she sipped her coffee before leaning back on the couch. "But" she added shyly, "I ain't gonna have this job for long."

"Why, Jayla?"

"Well, you see, the lady I am substituting for is coming back from Jamaica."

"That's too bad."

"Too bad is right. Now I'll be living off that damn welfare again unless I can find myself another job. I should be so lucky!" She lifted her gaze to the ceiling, then back at me to emphasize her point. "It's hell trying to find a job. You go searching and searching, answering this ad and that, wasting money you don't got on buses. Lord have mercy!" She shifted in her chair, her belly bulging from her black pants. "It's something I've had to get used to in my life, Clem, always looking for work. And it ain't like I can go after just any job. I don't have the right clothes, but I try to make do with what I got. Now I'm studying for my GEDs, so that'll help.

"Anyway, the work I done for you has helped me learn more typing and brought in some money. Every extra bit helps, you know. And like I told you before, it's interesting what you are doing, writing about women. I told my friend about it last night and she said, 'Well, if she does write the story of your life, Jayla, then she sure has got a story!' And that's true, I guess. It's been something else 'cause, you see, I never even knew my mother. Guess she couldn't take it or something because she just left me to die sitting on top of a garbage can. That's right. She left me right out in the street. That's already starting out on the wrong foot if you ask me. Then I just went from one foster home to the next 'til I finally landed in this place called the Village Conference. It's a place for all kinds of teenagers, you know. And let me tell you, there was *all* kinds a teenagers, you know! Yeah, there were all kinds! Drugs, violence, and so many lesbians there, I was scared to go to sleep at night. It was bad!" She bowed her head.

"In those days," she continued softly, "everyone would say what kind of a bad kid I was, but I wasn't. I just never had no mama saying: 'Now Jayla, do this!'" She shook her index finger at me. "Or 'Don't do that!' No, I wasn't a bad kid. I just wouldn't listen to no one.

"Well, when I was seventeen, I got pregnant. I was underage so the people at the Conference told me, 'Either you get an abortion or we're gonna take that baby away from you.' I wanted to have that baby bad. I needed somebody in this world who would love Jayla. But then I thought, 'Well, I ain't gonna be fat for nine months just to lose my baby. No, I ain't,' so I got an abortion. It was sad, very sad, but there wasn't nothing else I could do."

Jayla's voice tapered off as she fell into a gloomy silence. Young voices repeated a playmate's name until a clamor erupted in the hallway, followed by a slamming door.

"Anyway, while I was at the Conference, this woman, Mrs. Simpson, got to liking me or something, because she said I could come live with her. So finally I left the place I hated so much. Everything was fine, living there with her, 'til I started seeing this dude named Abe. Well, you can guess what happened next." She flattened her blouse over her stomach, leaning forward slightly. "I got pregnant. Even after I had Dora, everything kept going fine 'til Mrs Simpson decided that she didn't like this man. He'd come over for dinner and she'd say something like, 'Look, this is your baby girl and you ain't even paid one cent for her milk.' Abe couldn't take her mouth. After a while, Abe asked me to come live with him. He had a room for sixty dollars. It wasn't much but he was footing the bills and everything."

She paused to make sure I understood, then shook her head in a way that indicated to me the end wouldn't be happy. "Well, you know how it gets with men." She glanced furtively around the room, her foot tracing small circles on the floor. "After a while they start bossing you around, putting themselves in all your business. Well, like I said, I ain't having no one boss me around. We fought like cats and dogs. Sometimes he'd hit me, but mostly we just yelled. Finally, he left. There I was with the baby, the bills, and no job. Before long I was evicted. That means, I come home one day, and all my things was piled out in the front hall. There I was with nothing."

Drawing a deep breath, she continued her story. "I called my past foster mother. She's the woman paid by the state to watch over me. She said, 'Okay, don't worry. I'll be right over.' Well, I waited and waited but she never came. It turned out she was too busy playing cards! Can you believe that?"

Stunned, I stared at her, dumbly nodding my head as if I could truly understand such a situation. Her voice grew harsher with each new desertion. "Well, I called Mrs Simpson again. It just about broke me to do that, but who else could I turn to? I stayed there until I found another place, a basement apartment, and it happened again! I got pregnant by this other man. At first, he was real nice, bringing Dora little presents and all. But soon he got bossier and bossier. He'd come over drunk and hit me. I finally told him to walk and he walked! Now he lives up the street with his real old lady. He don't help me with nothing, I mean nothing! He ain't even seen his little girl but a few times.

"One time I asked him for money to buy her a winter coat and a pair of boots. I'm ashamed to say this, but you know what that man did? He said I had to go to bed with him first. I must have been real low and it was getting cold, 'cause I did it for my little girl. He gave me ten dollars.

Ten dollars! Can you imagine, Clem? See how people is!"

Jayla glared at me, her chin jutting forward, "After that," she resumed in a stronger voice, her jaw clenched, "I said, 'No more! The only thing I got is myself and I ain't going to sell it for no cheap price!' But you know how life is, Clem. Sometimes you bend a little, 'cause you just ain't got enough in you to hold it all together. But that's the human life, isn't it?"

"Well yeah," I agreed tentatively, a bit confused by the whole story. "But it seems like your life has been, well, pretty severe."

"Maybe so, but the Lord has pulled me through this far. But back then," she sighed, "things got a lot worse before they got better. The wires went bad in that building and started a fire, so the whole place was condemned. The Red Cross put everyone in a hotel 'til we could find someplace else to live. They gave us money and food in the meantime. But I was pregnant with Denise plus I had my other baby, Dora. I looked at that money and thought, 'I got to find a place to live.' Well, by the time I found another apartment, there wasn't no money left!

"There I was out on the street again, pregnant with no money, no job, no nothing." She looked me straight in the eye and frowned, her thick lips puckering. "I couldn't call Mrs Simpson again, so I called my friend Ada and told her about my situation. 'Jayla,' she said, 'you come over here and stay with me. I'm going take you down to Social Services.' And that's how I got on welfare. I've been living off it practically ever since because I don't have no real education. Plus, I got my kids, so how am I supposed to find a job? I hate that welfare 'cause the state has been supporting me since I was a baby. I want to support my own self, you see what I mean?"

Again, I nodded mutely, disturbed by her story but entranced by the easy flow of her storytelling. She let out a huge sigh that heaved her chest. Her voice was shaken by the weight of the memories. "Anyway, I lived with Ada and her kids for a while, but I ain't going to live with another woman again. She walked around with her ass on her shoulders 'cause it was her place. I kept staying there though, 'til her man moved in. I don't know, I just felt like he didn't want me around, so I went looking for another place. That's when I found the apartment where I am now."

Jayla leaned back on the couch with a relaxed expression, having apparently reached the happy part of her tale. A station wagon rumbled out of the parking lot with hectic sounds of kids screaming, excited farewells. I heard the teachers down the hall, moving tables and chairs as they chatted amicably.

"I liked the apartment the moment I saw it. You know," she pointed out, lightly brushing some hair from her forehead, "it's right next to a drug store, a supermarket, a post office, and a bank. It's sure convenient, but lots of problems started up for me there. Right after I moved in, Denise was born. Like I said, her pappy wouldn't do nothing to help me out. I loved that baby, but it was money problems and loneliness all the time. It built up on me. Never getting a job. Bills coming at me. All alone. It kept just building up inside of me. Money problems, loneliness. I loved that baby, I swear I still love her. Well, one time, before she was a year old, she just got on my nerves. I grabbed her and started shakin' and shakin' her. She fell on the color TV."

Jayla hesitated, then rolled her eyes, adding sarcastically, "I don't know why I kept that TV,' cause it never worked. Her pappy gave it to me." Nervously, she brushed her hair from her face again. Her hand froze there, tugging lightly at the ends that glistened with pomade. "She fractured her skull."

"Christ!" I whispered hoarsely under my breath.

"That's right, Clem. It was bad, real bad. The state took Denise away from me. Now she's got foster parents just like I did."

"And how long has she been with them?"

"Since she was a baby," Jayla replied dryly. "It's like I don't even know her anymore. I don't even know my own baby."

"But she visits you?"

"Ah, they let her come for short visits," she looked out the window, her face strained again. "It just ain't the same. Whenever Denise is with me now, all she does is scream and cry. She don't act that way over there with them! She just ain't used to me anymore, Clem. My older daughter, Dora, is and my baby boy, Glennie."

"Another baby, Jayla! After that ..."

She closed her eyes and nodded her head as if in church. "Yep, I got a little boy too, but I ain't going tell you about his father now. That man is too much! I had his baby 'cause when the Lord came into my heart, I just couldn't think of no abortion. It's murder for sure, and I'm a sinner already without that on my cards. Glennie ain't no trouble anyway. Plus, I don't have Denise in the house no more. I've been thinking about giving her up legally. I mean she's happier in that foster home than she is with me."

"It's hard, Jayla," I muttered, unsure of how to respond. Part of me thought, "Yes! Give her up!" But I faltered, wondering if the vicious cycle would be repeated again with Jayla's other daughter.

"It is hard," she readily agreed. "But sometimes you got to let go of what you love if it's better off. I swear I wanted that baby so I could feed her, care for her, watch her grow. But I got problems, Clem."

"Is anyone helping you out with them?"

"Oh yeah, I go to a shrink and that helps some. I understand now that I can't give loving to a baby the way other people can, 'cause I ain't never got it my own self. And don't never fool yourself." She leaned close to me. "People got to learn how to love. It don't just come naturally.

"I got Glenn, who's helping me with that now. He really loves me and, thanks to him, I'm learning something. But he is in prison," she added casually, "for murder and armed robbery or something like that."

"Christ!" I gasped loudly, exasperated and shocked. I was starting to think that I was in over my head.

"How about that?" she continued in an even tone. "I swear, it's like a pattern in my life, one guy after another and, sooner or later, they all land in prison. All I ever wanted was a husband so I could raise a family, a real family. Maybe Glenn is that man. He's good with the kids and we can always communicate. But he got taken away. I don't know, I feel like it's different with him, but we just got to wait and see. Ever since I was a little girl, I've dreamed and dreamed about getting married and having a family. Now, is that too much to ask?"

"No, of course not Jayla. Maybe in time ..."

"I don't know, Clem," she interrupted me, rising to leave. "I just seem to fall in with one bad dude after another. But you know what? I keep trying, 'cause I still believe my life could be better, sharing it with a man. If that don't work out, then at least I can say I tried!"

She picked up our empty cups and tossed them in the wastebasket. "Sometimes I feel like giving up, but you got to either deal with your problems or finish yourself off. So, I guess I just take mine on, 'cause believe it or not, I've moved up in my life and I'm trying to now. It's pretty tough," she admitted with a slight grin, "but we're going to make it, ain't we?"

Encouraged by her sudden optimism, I smiled back. "Well," she declared abruptly, "we'd better get out of here before they lock us in." Grabbing her maroon coat, Jayla headed for the door, but stopped and chuckled by the window. "Is that your bicycle, Clem?"

"Yeah."

"Ain't that something! You ride through all that traffic on that. I'd be scared to death!" She shook her head with a look of sheer amazement. "Guess that's why you be so skinny, and I stay fat!" Laughing again with the whimsical self-assurance that I noticed before, she threw open the door and we stepped into the crisp autumn air.

✳

Weeks later I veered my bike through a trail of broken bottles and debris that led to Jayla's neighborhood. It was midday and a wrinkled man sauntered out of a disco bar, his baggy pants flopping round him like sails. He greeted me with a drunken slur as I stepped into the nearby phone booth that reeked of urine. I called Jayla's apartment. Now that security measures—locking the front door—had been established in her building, our signal was for me to ring twice and then hang up. "That way," Jayla advised, laughing, "you won't lose fifteen cents."

A fat lady wearing a feathered hat and a coat that fitted like a tent happened to be standing in front of Jayla's building. She opened the door for me, and I bounded up the dark stairwell. The sickly olive-green paint was chipped and neglected. It reminded me of Jayla, who had grown more despondent each day away from her job. Now, she told me she could no longer type at home.

"Too many kids. Distractions. Just lonely. Just can't do it no more."

The outer door to her apartment had wooden shutters with a gaping hole, smashed in by one of her lovers. Before I could knock, the door opened and Jayla stood there, smiling. A surgical top and tight black pants emphasized her broad frame. Dora darted out from behind her. She lunged at me suddenly, her lanky arms round my waist.

"Look at those braids!" I exclaimed, wrapping my arm around her thin shoulders. "And all those barrettes!" Pleased, she stopped fidgeting for a moment so I could inspect her hair closely. A dozen braids jutted out like skinny black licorice sticks.

"Yeah. Well, that's the one thing we got done," Jayla rolled her eyes, and walked toward the living room. "That baby Glennie is bawling all the time, so I don't get much accomplished. Lord!"

She plopped down heavily on the black vinyl sofa. An oblong coffee table sat beside it with a vase of imitation red and yellow roses, centered on a white plastic doily. A telephone, equipped with a push button for hold, was enshrined in the corner. This was the most treasured item in her household. Jayla's link to the outside world, to lovers, friends, opportunities, and threats. It sat there like a modern sculpture, silent and promising.

Dora leaped on the sofa, restlessly touching everything in sight. "Now get out of here, Dora!" Jayla gruffly ordered.

The little girl froze immediately, checked her mother's scowling expression, then slunk obediently out of the room.

"Children!" Jayla sighed, pushing her tangled hair from her face. "Lord, can they get to you!"

"I guess so," I calmly agreed. "I can tell just by working at Rose Hill, and those kids aren't even mine!"

"Why that's right, you don't have no kids," she declared, one arm slung over her stomach. "Well, ain't that something! You must be my only friend who don't. I guess you're lucky in a way. Dora ain't so bad, 'cause she's learned my ways. It's the baby crying all the time that gets on my nerves." Jayla nodded toward the bedroom where, I assumed, Glennie was napping. She reached over the coffee table and flicked on the television. Dora's head immediately popped out of the bedroom, scanning us like an old busybody.

"It's nice having a kid. I love my kids so much," Jayla continued, "but it's something else carrying that baby around for nine months. When I was pregnant with Denise, no one could tell 'til I was seven months and then, whammo, it just blew out, huge-like. With Glennie, it worked itself out little by little. And the bigger it got, the more scared I got. You know what I mean?"

Dora sneaked into the living room and hid beside the bookcase. The shelves were crammed with knickknacks, souvenir ashtrays, and paperweights, a clock, a metal sculpture of a bull, a plastic statue of Jesus, and books. Books that Jayla never read but saved as a symbol of her future. Someday, maybe, when she had the time, when the kids weren't screaming, when she wasn't preoccupied with mere survival ...

"Every woman is like that," Jayla resumed, staring blankly at the TV while Dora slowly approached the flickering screen on tiptoes. "You just start wondering how the delivery is going to come off."

Dora stepped on a creaky board and Jayla spotted her. "Get out of here, girl!" Jayla screamed, lifting herself slightly from the sofa. The instant the words left her mother's mouth, Dora bolted like a frightened mouse into the bathroom. Jayla glared at the empty doorway while I gazed uncomfortably at the television. "The little bitch," Jayla muttered. "She just don't know how to keep still!"

"It's hard ..."

"Hard is right! Lord help me!" She crossed her legs, redirecting her attention to the TV. "That brat is a headache now but having her was easy, almost too easy."

"How's that?" I asked, still unsettled by Jayla's angry outburst.

"You see, when I got to that hospital, they left me alone in the labor room. You know, thinking it was going to take a while. The nurses got sick of hearing me holler and stuff. It's embarrassing, Clem," she confided with great emphasis. "You holler all sorts of things to people you don't even know. I don't like that at all.

"Well anyway," her body shifted as it sunk deeper into the sofa, "It felt like I was going to have that baby any minute. I kept calling for those nurses 'til they turned off the intercom. There I was laying on my back and all of a sudden I feel this gushy thing happening down there. I reach down and it feels all gooey and stuff. I just laid back down, not knowing what to do 'til the nurse finally walked in. 'Why didn't you call us?' she asked me. 'Call you!' I shouted. 'Now how can I call you when you turned the intercom off!' 'Well,' she said, 'you've already had your baby!'"

"Oh my God!" I laughed. "I mean, that was horrible what the nurses did."

"Now, how about that?" she chuckled. "Then that nurse went to fetch the doctor. All he did was cut the cord and clean that baby up. I was woke the whole time ... hollering my head off, but I was woke!" Laughing proudly at my astonishment, she didn't notice Dora had raced back to the bedroom where she pretended to play with her toys. Shuffling two dolls across the floor, the child stared fixedly at the back of her mother's head.

"With Denise, it was different. One morning I woke up and all this watery stuff was coming out. I couldn't figure out what was going on because it was way too early. 'That's strange,' I thought. 'I'm peeing all over myself or something.' I got out of bed, but that stuff kept coming. I called up a friend who already had two kids. I mean, I was scared! She wasn't home but her old man was. 'Girl,' he said, 'you better git to the hospital. You going to have that baby!' I stuck a towel between my legs, put on some pants and called a cab.

"I made it to the hospital all right, but that baby wasn't due yet. They gave me some shots so I would go into labor and, sure enough, there I was, hollering again 'til that baby came out. Then the doctor started sewing me up. Well, I swear, as many times as doctors looked up me, I still can't get used to it. Havin' my legs spread apart like that! Well, that doctor kept working down there till finally I leaned over and said, 'What? You sewing the whole thing up?' He laughed and all the nurses laughed, but he kept sewing and sewing. I'll tell you!"

With an unconscious gesture, her strapping shoulders still shaking, Jayla leaned over to primly rearrange the vase on the doily. Meticulous order prevailed throughout the apartment, each object cemented in place against the shifting outside world. Chuckling hoarsely, her contented gaze wandered over the room, forged and molded by her own thick hands.

"And were the fathers with you during any of the births?"

Her laughter stopped in midair. "Does a cow talk?" she wryly quipped, squinting one mocking eyeball. "Ain't none of my men stick by me. But Glenn is calling me every chance he can. He wants to claim little Glenn as his own once we get married. Or," she smirked, "so he says."

"Sounds like you two are getting serious."

"Yeah, he's in prison so at least I know he isn't messing around!"

"Are you sure?" I teased, nudging her shoulder. "Every minute of the day?"

She looked down bashfully at her feet, suppressing a smile, suddenly transformed from the haggard mother I knew to a vulnerable young woman. "Yeah, well, you know," she stammered, biting her lip. "When he was out on the streets, Glenn was always chasing women. We'd be together and then we'd break up, but we always stayed friends. I mean, there was always good communication between us. Even after we broken up, that man kept calling and calling. But I never thought he liked me much until my friend, Susan, told me, 'Jayla,' she said, 'Glenn must be feeling something for you 'cause he calls here every day.'"

"I figured he felt something too, but he was always saying things to hurt me, like, 'Martha has a nice-shaped body but you don't got nothing.' That really hurt. And then I didn't hear from him for a long time, so I called his mother. That's how I found out he was in prison. I started writing him letters and going to visit him. We had plenty of time to talk and get to know each other. I guess maybe he could think better in there. So now Glenn wants to marry me."

"You are going to get married even with him in prison? When?"

"Not so soon, right now he's up for shorter term. I'm hoping and praying for that, 'cause who knows about marriage?" Lowering her voice, she added, "If he don't change his mind."

"Well, you know what I always say," I answered in a cheery voice, "hope for the best and expect the worst."

A strained silence fell between us as Jayla puzzled, stared at me. "I don't say that!" she retorted angrily. "I don't say that at all! I just hope for the best, 'cause the best is all I want. That ain't too much to ask for after the life I've had. I mean I want a family, a real family. And I believe I mean something special to Glenn. He calls me every Tuesday. His mother talks to me and I visit her sometimes. Right now, he's trying to change prisons."

"Where is he?"

"Lorton," she grimaced. "The same place everybody goes to."

"And where does he want to move?"

"Well, he's just switching to another place inside Lorton where there ain't so many guards. You know, where they live in cottages. Right now, whenever I visit, there are these huge motherfuckers with rifles and everything. Girl, they are scary! It ain't no fun at all! So, I'm praying for the best 'cause it's always been my dream to get married. Now that ain't too much to ask, right?"

"No," I answered slowly as I realized a marriage in prison is as normal to her as going to college sounded to me. Our worlds, so distant, collided in her hopes, making me want to leap up and run away. But there was no getting away from it; our mutual histories cast a shadow over our lives, our civil structures and policies forming those lives. Self-loathing, confusion.

"So," I continued, wanting to quickly change the subject, distressed by my naiveté, "he's not Glennie's real father."

Jayla huffed angrily at the mere suggestion. "No, I don't have nothing to do with the real father." Eyeing me slyly again, she said softly, "You know, loneliness can drive you to do all sorts of crazy shit. I mean you might end up fuckin' some guy like he's a movie star or something, when normally you wouldn't give him a second glance. You see what I mean? Well, that's how I got little Glennie, from a minister who ain't worth nothing.

"Let me tell you about that guy." The sound of someone yelling came through the open windows as Jayla leaned toward me, her voice getting louder. "He comes to me once with this sob story about a battered woman who needs help. So, stupid me, I open my cupboard and let him take what he wants. I just went to Safeway, so I had some pretty fine food. The very next week he comes and borrows ten dollars, promising to make it good when he gets his paycheck. Well, he never paid it back, even when I asked him for it.

"I should have known from that what kinda man he was. But since he was a minister, I just couldn't imagine." Barely pausing to breathe, the words rushed out of her mouth. "Anyway, one day he comes over and I'm feeling real lonely. We go on back to the bedroom and have a satisfying time for ourselves. Well, the next thing, I find out he's married! He comes over again one afternoon, goes straight to the bedroom and starts takin' off his shirt. I turn to him and say, 'Man, you gotta understand we ain't doing that stuff no more. Here you are a minister with a wife and you fixing to commit adultery! I ain't having that on my cards!' He laughed and started in with all that sweet talk, you know how men do to get you all steamed up. I kept telling him to lay off, but you know what that man did? That nigger threw me on the bed and started going at it! Well, I'm a woman with my own needs too—"

Jayla hesitated, inspecting my face to gauge my sympathies. "Once we began, I started enjoying myself. That was the day I got pregnant. And you know what that man said? When I told him about it, he said I better get an abortion. 'What you talkin' about?' I asked him. 'You, a minister!' It ain't like I never had one before, and God knows I am a sinner, but since the Lord come into my heart, I couldn't no more. I just couldn't. Look like killing to me and, God knows, there's already enough of that to go around.

"That minister kept insisting, so I told him to git, that I didn't need him for nothing. He just stared at me and said, 'I know what that body of yours needs.' I pushed him away good and hard. 'Listen you,' I said. 'I know what my body needs too, and I swear I'd rather play with myself than be with you again!' 'That's different,' he said. 'Sure, it's different,' I told him. 'But in the end, I swear it satisfies me more, 'cause there ain't no strings attached!' He got angry then and left. Later, he promised to buy Pampers for the baby, but I told him I'd rather wrap a towel around the kid's ass first. Men can be so damned mean! I don't understand it."

"Some men," I awkwardly tried to comfort her. Then I added, "They're not all bad."

"Oh yeah?" she contended. "Show me one who ain't!"

We both stared at each other until I was forced to look away. "You are so bitter. I mean, I understand how you feel. It's awful what you went through, but it just won't do any good."

"I know," she mumbled, tears staring to brim over. "Look like I had so many bad experiences in my life, I just can't help it. I fight that inside of myself all the time. 'Now Jayla,' I say to myself, 'what's going to happen if Mr. Right comes along? You going to be so damn hard, you won't even be able to love him!' My attitude will ruin the relationship!"

"But you are building something positive with Glenn."

"Well, I don't know. Even that man is so hot and cold, I can't count on nothing. I just want to get him out of that place."

"Sounds smart."

"Sounds hard too, don't it?" she grumbled. "I don't want to be hard, I swear, but I still don't know nothing about love. All I ever asked for is some man, so we could make us a home. That was the one thing I believed in since I was a little girl, but I ain't had no such luck. I got this woman body and three babies and I still ain't got no husband. But," she smiled again, "now that the Lord has come into my heart, I look those problems in the eye and say, 'Don't worry, that Man Upstairs has plans for me!'"

Jayla winked and nodded toward the bedroom door where Dora was peeping around the corner. The girl flicked on a radio and began to swing her hips coquettishly. She watched her mother carefully, testing whether it was all right to be in our presence again.

"That boy still asleep?" Jayla barked at her.

Dora nodded, frantic to please.

"Look like he won't be too much longer with that radio blasting."

Dora immediately flicked it off and turned back to face us, standing at attention, her thin arms hanging down.

"Come here, girl," Jayla laughed. "Come here!"

The girl bounded to her mother's side, slowing down at the last moment to gradually ease onto the sofa between us. Jayla's arm wrapped around her waist while Dora's small head leaned against her mother's large soft breasts, a fleshy cushion of warmth and security. Dora shyly reached over to me, took a lock of my hair and twirled it slowly round her fingers. Her mother's strong frame became a niche for her to relax into and Jayla's voice, something honeyed and familiar, as she hummed a gospel tune under her breath.

※

"Hey Jayla, you want to get together and talk?"

"Yeah, sure. Come on over."

I heard an abrupt click at her end and hung up the phone. Heading east on Columbia Road, I passed a West Indian grocery store, a parking lot, and the imposing Unification Church building. At 16th Street I crossed an invisible border, coolly entering the fragmented world of Jayla's neighborhood. A washed-out empty lot stretched along one side of the street where shards of broken glass winked like eyes in the afternoon sun. A row of somber apartment buildings lined the opposite side, their missing windows patched with plastic and cardboard.

I took a step toward Jayla's building and then balked indecisively. A sleek black sedan rolled by, the young driver leaning out to whistle at me. He stopped in front of the go-go bar at the end of the block where raucous music jostled across the sidewalk at 3 pm. The coarse laughter and clinking glasses were disconcerting beside the littered parking lot. I felt out of place and vulnerable as I stood watching a man, his skin the color of melted yellow wax. He swayed in the doorway, twitching and bickering with himself.

The halls inside Jayla's building had recently been washed. The white floor tiles sparkled against the olive-green walls. But the stairwell was filthy, dank, and dark.

I moved quickly to Jayla's apartment at the end of the corridor. The shattered wooden shutter was sealed now with electrician's tape. I knocked twice and waited, studying the bare light bulb. My sweaty shirt clung to my back as I looked down the row of anonymous dark doors that looked like they led to cells. I knocked again louder. The sound of Jayla's TV set drifted through the door and I could hear her heavy frame moving about inside the apartment.

"Jayla, it's Clem!" I announced. The hallway felt eerie and suddenly I began to bang on the door, calling her name repetitively. The hollow echo of my calls was the only response. A vision flashed through my mind of Jayla standing very still at the center of her apartment.

I rushed outside to the deserted sidewalk, a fierce wind gusting soot into my eyes. A voice inside of me screamed, *Leave her alone! Leave her alone!* But next to the go-go bar I slid into the phone booth. "Hey, babe," a sleazy-looking man muttered, leaning against the phone booth. His buddies were lined up behind him, smirking, and then resumed their banter, swaying drunkenly. Jayla's number was in my hand. Brrr, ring. Brr, ring. Brrr, ring. She's there! I know she's there, but she won't answer.

I looked at the phone booth's chipped paint and nervously began picking at the edges, a sense of rejection and unease growing in me until I felt cemented there. Like I was an easy target. But a target for what? As I opened the phone booth door, I knew the distance between her door and that phone booth was the bitter truth. I kicked some litter out of the way and told myself: Don't take it personally. And I don't know if it was Jayla's story, the rejection, or the mere weight of our histories, but I started to cry. Right there on that fucking littered street, just like I did in Haiti and Guatemala, I cried like a kid.

✕

"Just make yourself at home," Jayla sighed, leading me to the sofa, "while I fix the kids something to eat."

A week after the incident, Jayla called again, inviting me over to meet her second daughter, Denise, who was spending the night. When she opened the door, I asked about the aborted visit, but she merely shrugged, looking at me with "No Trespassing" eyes.

Denise and Dora were huddled around the kitchen table, anxiously waiting for their late dinner. The kitchen itself was more like a closet, stuffed with a sink, stove, refrigerator, and cupboards. Though spotlessly clean, it was dark and uninviting. Jayla dutifully attended to her children, her leopard-skin bathrobe swinging to and fro. Glistering with Vaseline, her hair stuck out straight from her head. Little Glennie slept beside me on the sofa.

"Now you two just sit still and behave yourself," I heard her instructing them as she leaned over to kiss the tops of their heads. The TV blared in front of me. Jerry Lewis was conducting his annual telethon for muscular dystrophy. His strained, contorted smile bounced around the screen as Glennie breathed softly in his sleep. The baby's mouth puckered occasionally as though he were still sucking milk.

"Well, we ain't got no hamburgers, Denise, so shush up and eat your Cheerios." Jayla's brittle voice was drowned out by Jerry's hysterical pleas. Sweating profusely, he stomped back and forth across the stage, lighting the wrong end of a cigarette, then tossing it away.

"Just fold your hands and thank the Lord for what you got."

Footsteps creaked across the ceiling above, then a toilet flushed, vibrating the pipes here below. Perspiration trickled down my sides, the closed windows spawning a humid air. A constant pressure seemed to exude from the walls, as if the already congested space were shrinking. Yet I felt safe among the treasured, meticulously arranged clutter of Jayla's home. A human sensitivity lingered in the begonia, flowering delicately in front of a crucifix bathed in sunlight. The cramped apartment was a paradise compared to the world outside those windows, though no window could hold it out.

Spoons clattered against plastic bowls as the clock ticked away the minutes, hours, days. It ticked along with the clocks in other apartments, while other mothers, separate and isolated, often frightened, reached bravely for the Cheerios to nurture their simple dream, the ancient task of motherhood. Jerry and his desperate antics, the flashy commercials, and the next episode of *General Hospital* also connected their worlds.

Glennie's tiny feet suddenly kicked as his dark eyes opened, innocent and unfocused. His lips puckered, struggling to communicate in the only way he knew how, with a piercing wail for his mother.

"See what I mean?" Jayla moaned, approaching me. "If it ain't one, it's the other." She picked up the baby and propped him on her shoulder, tapping his backside comfortingly. Collapsing next to me on the sofa, she added in a hoarse whisper, "These kids won't let me out of their sight, Lord!" Glennie's pudgy hand groped at Jayla's face. She kissed it playfully, then let it wind round her index finger. "I swear to God, I don't know if I am going to make it sometimes, especially without no job. There ain't hardly any money for food, let alone the rent." She laid Glennie between us and turned to watch the telethon.

"Nothing's come up yet?"

"Not even a nibble," she answered dryly. "I've been looking high and low but I ain't found nothing yet. Besides, there ain't no money for a babysitter. My friends can't always watch them, they've got their own lives.

"Whenever I call about a job, they always ask what I'm doing now. I tell them what little experience I got, 'cause they'll find out if you're lying. I filled out applications all over this town—in cafeterias, hotels, restaurants, stores, warehouses, schools, offices, just about everywhere. Any time I see an ad, I run over and put in an application. There just ain't no jobs."

"But do you keep calling the people back?"

"I call them back and call them back 'til I don't even need to tell them who I am. I told this one lady I could type forty words a minute and she said, 'Sorry but you don't have any experience.' 'Now you wait a minute!' I told her. 'How will I ever get experience if you don't give me a job?' 'You got a point,' she answered, but she still didn't give me no job. Lord!

"Anyway, I called Metro for a job cleaning buses, but there wasn't no openings. This other friend told me that Control Data was accepting applications. Well, it turns out they accepting applications all right, but they ain't givin' no jobs, they just file your application away. What do I need with that? I don't want a job next year, I want one today! I just ain't got the money or time to be running round town, leaving applications. Then my friend told me that the new Holiday Inn was accepting applications. Well, we went down there first thing in the morning. They hadn't even finished building the place yet! And do you know what? There was a line clear round the block for applications."

"You're kidding!"

"Lord knows, I wish I was. We had to wait in that line for an hour just to pick up our application forms, so I know there ain't no job there."

A sudden clattering noise yanked Jayla away. She charged toward the kitchen as Dora headed for the bathroom, headed for the bathroom.

"Now you pick that up, girl!" she shrieked at Denise's back. "Oh, never mind, I'll do it. You go and play with Dora."

The solemn-faced girl walked away, never once lifting her eyes. A tampon commercial of a woman diving through crystal-clear water drowned out Jayla's grumbling. Before long she stomped heavily out of the kitchen. She glared at Denise, who watched from the bedroom doorway. Struck by her mother's glance, the girl slinked back out of sight.

"I don't know, Clem. Sometimes it's more than I can bear. If I didn't have Glenn loving me, I don't know what I'd do." Poking gently at the baby's tummy, she added softly, "Not this cute little thing, the other one."

"But I got to watch out for Glenn too," she added wistfully. "Last time I seen him, his face was all balled up."

"Oh, no, Jayla!" I cried out, alarmed. The tension in the little apartment was already mounting.

"Yeah." The corners of her mouth tilted downward. "He said he got in a fight and showed the other guy a thing or two. 'Honey,' I told him, 'I'm scared for you. You ought to be thinking about being good and getting out of this place.' That man's got to change his attitude.

"He's got a violent streak that mostly comes out when he drinks. Glenn drinks too much, in or out of prison. The most he does on the inside is usually some herb, but I don't know which is worse. I don't want to preach to him but since the Lord came into my life I've tried to stay straight. I don't drink or smoke no more."

"You used to smoke?" I asked surprised. An incongruous picture of Jayla puffing on a cigarette popped into my mind.

"Oh yeah, when my girlfriend and me got baptized, the first thing we did after leaving the church was light up a cigarette. Well, I'll tell you, we felt really dirty then. It was so bad we never smoked again. But I try not to push it too far. Everybody's got their own ways. I just pray for Glenn, instead of preaching to him.

"Now he says he wants to marry me." She raised an eyebrow, "And I'd like to marry him, but all my friends say, 'Look here Jayla that Glenn is a bad man. He's in jail.' Well, I say those people is just prejudiced. Any man can change, especially if he's got a family, if he's got someone to stick by him. Everyone needs love and Glenn ain't no different."

I sat wordlessly listening to the desperation of her dream, the hurt of her life, the thrashing toward something else. Something better for her children. For herself. What were her options? She was riveted to the TV screen as if it might be an answer to her needs, a promise of a dream come true. "I visit him once or twice a week now with my friend Susan who's got her man in prison too. Last week they had a function, right there under the moon and stars. Glenn didn't want me to come, 'cause he's shy about dancing. He's the type who only dances behind closed doors. So, I told him, 'Look Honey, we don't got to dance together. This is just another opportunity for us to talk and be together.' So, I went and his mother came too. That was the first time she had been there in four months. Now don't that show I got to stick by him?" She glanced down at little Glennie, his eyelids drooping slowly. "I can give him something to live for, he can work his way out of that place. He's already been there for three years."

"Three years!"

"Yeah. You see, his charges was serious—attempted murder and armed robbery. It's like this. Glenn's always hated his father's side of the family. When they was little, that man used to come home and beat his kids. That made Glenn bleed some bad feelings toward his family. One day he and a cousin went over to his aunt's house with a piece, threatening to kill her. They was laughing on the inside, but she got scared and called the police."

I glanced dubiously at Jayla. Attempted murder and armed robbery? Maybe that was the way she preferred to recount the incident, to me; I wondered what actually happened but I didn't ask any questions. I just listened yet she sensed my doubt. "Anyway," she shrugged, changing the subject, "we never talk about that night. I know he's got a mean streak. I just hope if I stick by him, he'll think twice in the future. Every man's got a good side too, and I seen that in Glenn. He's always playing with my kids and bringing them presents. Ain't no one ever been so nice to them kids.

"Still, I got to watch that man. Once, when he was going with a girlfriend of mine, he beat her 'til she was black and blue. I swear, he'd kill a nigger with his beatings! I told that woman, 'See here, girl, you let him get away with that once and he won't never quit!' I seen too much of that stuff, and I say to Glenn or any man, 'If you ain't here to love me then git, 'cause it's loving I'm looking for.'"

She stood and roughly flicked off the TV. "I did have one real bad fight with Glenn. He likes to dog fuck, you see, and I don't go in for that stuff. One day he snuck up and grabbed me from behind and I got scared. I swear to God, I picked up a kitchen chair and smashed it right over that nigger's head!

"Then I ran to the bathroom and hid behind the shower curtain. He found me, of course, and started slapping me.

"'You better be scared,' he yelled. 'You crazy if you ain't!' 'Maybe I am crazy,' I shouted back, 'but at least you know I ain't going to take that shit!' Now I'm sure with Glenn, I won't get whipped bad, maybe just little beatings.

"One thing I know," she added tenderly, "is he loves me." A smile crossed her lips. "He made me this card at Lorton that said, 'To My Leo Lady.' I swear, I put that card and slept with it there every night. I want to marry that man so, even if it don't work out, I can at least say I tried."

"Mama!" Dora whined from the bedroom. "Can we come out and get us some water?"

"You fetch a glass, Dora, then take it back to the room. I can't have both of you out here messing around." Jayla winked at me out of the corner of her eye. Denise stood at the doorway, resisting the urge to follow her sister. Her tiny hands wrung the hem of her skirt as she watched Dora, so worldly and confident, strut across the room.

Jayla turned away from their universe that always gravitated around her: the mother, that tireless, omnipotent being. "Dora's daddy, Abe, is mighty jealous of Glenn," she told me. "But he never did nothing for his family. He's locked up in Georgia for murder, too."

"Hell, Jayla," I laughed to cover up my consternation, "it looks like all your men are staying faithful!"

"Ain't it the truth." Our shoulders touched as we both laughed over these ironic circumstances.

"Yeah, that Abe used to love cocaine. One time he had a couple of lines laid out on the table and this other guy started snorting it, so he shot him. He had a real bad temper, so now he's in prison for sixty years.

My life wouldn't be no better with him."

A watery sniffle drifted over from the bedroom door where Denise sulked forlornly. "Well, look who needs some loving," Jayla whispered. "Come here, girl," Jayla repeated, still determined to hide her tenderness. Jayla gently tapped the sofa cushion as Denise's reluctant feet inched toward us, eyes glued to the ground, half her hand shoved into her mouth. Without lifting her gaze, she moved smoothly onto the couch and Jayla began stroking her hair, then her forehead, stroking out the pain, the confusion, and fear that she had implanted in her own daughter, her own flesh and blood.

Dora grabbed one of her dolls and bounded onto the sofa beside me, her high-pitched squeals begging for attention. At this moment, Glennie opened his mouth and began to wail.

# A Good Man's Hard to Find

It was seven o'clock in the morning and, all over the city, this Monday, alarm clocks heralded the beginning of another workweek. There was no such summons awakening Jayla, though; after months she remained jobless. Besides, little Glennie had kept her up since well before the first buses heaved down the street. Her daily routines were still the same when I returned from a few months out west, but Jayla herself had definitely changed. A plucky rhythm in her gait, an inner glow kindled by an answered dream, all pointed to a profound transformation. Today Jayla was getting married.

I waited in my sister's car at the entrance to Jayla's building. The front door was permanently smudged with the imprints of countless hands passing to and fro. Brown cardboard replaced the missing plate glass. An emaciated man in a fake fur coat hobbled down the street, his knobby knees shaking visibly through his ripped trousers. A transit bus roared by, belching exhaust in his face. A buxom young woman with teased hair stabbed the sidewalk with her high-heeled boots. Hugging a fifth inside her paper bag, she nodded to me, then disappeared behind those battered doors.

I watched the door, waiting for Jayla and wondering. Today she will be married. Like a hardy weed sprouting through the sidewalk, her dream rose amid cold black prison bars and the icy desolation of the slums. Yet another seed had taken root in her womb, the unborn baby already demanding a future from its parents. Only this time the baby would have a name, a home, and a father. Jayla's life-long dream was finally coming true.

"Just a minute," she shouted, waving from the doorway. "Be right there!" An electric current surged through her voice, but I wondered.

I wondered, then I laughed at myself. A chorus of proverbs sprung immediately to mind: Love is blind; Love will find a way; Love conquers all; Lovers are lunatics. It's the story between the lines in all the history books, the ordinary story of man and woman. I laughed at my doubts that Jayla's love could be any less powerful or eternal. It was so inevitable and common, it made me want to weep.

The door swung open again and she sauntered up to the car, little Glennie propped on her hip. Dora and Denise waved from the door, unhappy they wouldn't be driven to Lorton until tonight. Jayla's pleased face poked through the window, her head wrapped in a tight turban, the bright flowers of her polyester shirt singing to the world.

"Hiya, girl!" she cried out, sliding into the front seat beside me. A brand-new raincoat was slung over one arm while Glennie gurgled from the other.

"Where'd you get those clothes?" I asked her brightly, already caught up in the happiness of the occasion.

"My girlfriend bought them for the wedding. Dora and Denise have new clothes too. The only thing I still got to do is fix their hair and my own. I feel like I'm about to burst!"

Our conversation was sidetracked as Jayla guided me through a maze of streets, tracing the bus route she'd memorized through downtown DC and suburban Arlington. Only when we reached the highway to Lorton did she lean back, relieved and eagerly anticipating her long-awaited wedding day.

"What I don't quite understand," I confided amid the roar of speeding cars and trucks, "is how you managed to get pregnant with Glenn still in prison."

Bending over Glennie, she gave a quiet laugh, her broad shoulders shaking. "Well, everyone asks that! He got transferred to minimum security, you see, and there it depends on the season of the year."

I glanced quickly at her, hoping for an explanation.

"When it's winter and the men have to stay inside, it's difficult 'cause the guards and everyone is so close by. But that don't even matter. People still do it right there in the visiting room! You see the women git on the men's laps, I mean, Clem, in positions you wouldn't believe! You'd never know it was possible!"

"Anything's possible in some situations, huh, Jayla?"

"That's the human life," she agreed. "Everybody's got to bend sometime! You should have seen them at the Halloween party. There were six or seven people organizing it out of this trailer. Well, when the guard left them alone for a minute, just one minute, they all went to it standing up!"

With the both of us in stitches, we turned off the highway onto a smaller access road headed for the prison. The rolling farm country was periodically blemished by large green signs proclaiming Lorton ahead.

"Them Muslim women got the right idea," Jayla continued, trying to suppress her laugh. "They wear them big skirts and they're covered from head to toe." She stared at the road, her laughter finally subsiding. "But they still get pregnant."

"It's hard to believe," I observed hesitantly, shaking my head. "You're expecting another baby ..."

"I know, Clem," she answered quickly. "Normally I'd get an abortion, 'cause I like to keep them spaced apart two years. The Lord wouldn't like that, but it's just too much work with two babies. Only, well, Glenn wants this one."

"But he's in prison, Jayla! You're the one taking care of those babies and it doesn't exactly come easily for you."

"Clem," she declared in a grim tone. "It's better for Glenn. This way, he'll really have a family of his own and won't be a man fighting alone. I want to raise his children, his own flesh and blood. I'm through with messing around with other men, no matter how lonely I get. You know, this other dude keeps calling up to tempt me, 'Just sleep with me once, Honey,' he says, 'and make sure you really love Glenn.'"

"Christ!" I snarled.

"You said it, girl! That man thinks he's something, but he ain't nothing! Nothing at all!" Her lower lip curled over, exposing the pink of her gums. "Anyway, marriage or not, I'm my own woman and there ain't no man going push Jayla around! I even told Glenn, 'Listen Honey, I'm not just a wife and a mother, I'm also Jayla. I'm a woman who needs a job. I want to get out of the house. I want to work.' Glenn is kind of old-fashioned, you see, and he don't approve of me working. He can't appreciate the problems I struggle with day after day.

"He can't help me out with money 'cause he works at Lorton as a barber. You know how much they pay him? Seventy-five cents a day! Now what's a grown man supposed to do with that? I bring him what I can, but I swear that nigger always needs money. Sometimes I try to sneak him in some cash. I put it in my shoes or under my tongue, anywhere. I even put it between my legs for him, thinking, 'Now ain't that too bad—he can't enjoy the real stuff that's right there for him.'

"Anyway, he's proud of his barber job, but there's lots of drugs in prison. Sometimes he'll call me on the phone and be really stoned. I mean just blind! 'Honey,' I ask, 'you been smoking that herb?' 'Yeah,' he says. 'That's what scares me about you. You know me too well.' And it's true. That's because we communicate."

The bare exterior walls of the prison suddenly loomed into view: cement, barbed wire, ominous watch towers. "Our marriage is going to be hard, but I'm going to give it everything I got." Jayla's steadfast gumption almost convinced me; she seemed to stand up to so much. "And you know what else? After this baby, I'm getting my tubes tied, no matter what Glenn says."

Lifting Glennie, she slid out of the car and led me toward the trailer. The gravel scraping under our feet was the same gray color as the sky, the walls, the gloomy expression on the guard's face. We stopped in front of one who sat inside a glass box, surreptitiously leafing through a girlie magazine. His pants were too tight, but he looked strong and lean. "Go over there," he said, pointing to a long squat building.

Slowly we approached the structure that turned out to be a deserted cafeteria. Tables and chairs were scattered around inside, an empty rostrum at the far end, all seemed to have suddenly been abandoned. Quite unexpectedly, I heard giggles coming from the kitchen. A turbaned head peeked around the corner.

"There she is! There she is!" the woman gaily screeched. Another woman with orange-dyed hair and a slight mustache stuck her head out and sang, "Here comes the bride, all dressed in white ..." Jayla grinned self-consciously, her eyes lowered to the floor.

"You ready for the big day?" another woman called. "We almost finished with this carrot cake."

"Carrot cake!" another repeated. "Lorton ain't never had it so good!"

"I don't know if I'll make it 'til tonight," Jayla stammered.

"You'll make it, honey," the turbaned woman promised, affectionately wrapping her arm around Jayla's shoulder. "We are going to make sure of that!"

A lightheartedness emanated from the hard-working women. Platters were strewn haphazardly over the counters, heaped with pork, chicken, rice, eggs, a vast array of food in preparation for tonight's feast. Idle, animated chatter enlivened the kitchen as Jayla joined the women, flattered by the teasing and comforted by their support. A uniformed matron already cradled Glennie in her arms, mumbling gibberish to his uncomprehending face.

The women smiled and chatted while their hands worked feverishly to complete their tasks. On this day, at least, the clanging of keys, the bars and handcuffs belonged to another world. Touching her elbow, I bid Jayla farewell until tonight. As I passed the guard's glass cage, it seemed ironic that Jayla should find such acceptance and love here in prison, the home of murderers, rapists, junkies, and robbers. For a fleeting moment the idea struck me as more foreign than anything I had yet encountered in Haiti or Guatemala.

※

By the time I returned to Lorton that night, I was nervous without Jayla's company. The mammoth prison looked deserted. Towering klieg lights illuminated every nook and cranny with a clinical glare. A close, watchful silence hung in the air of this regimented city behind electric fences. I could sense guards standing in the distance, weighed down by their guns. Decked out in my finest clothes, I felt foolish and apprehensive as a black van pulled up beside me in the empty parking lot.

A White man in the driver's seat threw open the door. "What you want, lady?" he leaned over to ask.

"I'm here for the wedding," I stated, shifting my gaze rapidly from a revolver shadowed by a layer of flab folding over his thick leather belt to his face. But he wouldn't look at me.

"Git on in," he commanded, leaning back in his seat.

"Well, I've got my own car."

"Gotta bring you over there," he replied. "Regulations."

As I climbed in beside him, I fumbled with my wedding gift and purse, hoping they wouldn't be confiscated. He still didn't look at me, but narrowed his gaze into the night, deep creases forming around his eyes. Shifting his weight in the seat, he rested his arms on the steering wheel as if preparing for a long wait.

"Okay if I smoke?"

He nodded.

"You want one?"

"Nah." He stared out the windshield.

I watched my smoke curl out the window and fade into the artificial radiance outside.

"Lots of people here for the wedding?" I asked, trying to be friendly.

"Some," he grunted, turning on the motor.

We lurched forward and zigzagged through an assortment of anonymous buildings, the engine running soundlessly. Human beings seemed to have deserted this world. We passed the main prison compound and entered a minimum-security area that had some semblance of the real world I knew. Squat cottages, grassy yards, even a few short hedges.

"Here you are," the driver suddenly announced as he jammed on the brakes. We stopped in front of that same squat building where I'd left Jayla that morning. Or was it another, identical structure? I couldn't really tell in the dark, but I was greatly relieved to see other people milling around the entrance under lights—regular incandescent lights.

The guards at the door dug through my purse, nodding benevolently at the gift. I spotted Dora skipping through the crowd with bright yellow ribbons braided into her hair. As I entered the cafeteria, a sea of black faces startled me with the bitter truth. No wonder Jayla always spoke so casually of prison. Except for a handful of armed guards, everyone was Black.

I stood there alone, gaping until I felt other eyes upon me, long, hard stares piercing through my skin until I began to itch. Quickly I sat down at the nearest table. Red tablecloths and sprigs of wildflowers had transformed the drabby room. The rostrum still stood in front, with a minister pacing back and forth, giving last-minute instructions.

At my table a Rasta with natty dreadlocks gesticulated wildly, two gold earrings in his right ear. His companion, wearing silver plastic sunglasses and a blue denim jacket, nodded but continued ogling me. Suddenly aware of my presence, the Rasta slowed down his speech, examined me. My half smile tightened as I looked away. I studied the crowd and wondered who all these people were. Prisoners from minimum security? Friends and relatives?

Two heavy-set men in faded army jackets advanced deliberately through the crowd in my direction. With close-shaven, army-style haircuts, they looked like bouncers intent on ejecting me for crashing this exclusive affair. Slouched at the shoulders, they stopped about four feet away and stared at me, thick arms folded defiantly as though concealing something under their shirts. Self-conscious, I looked around the room, praying for the wedding to begin, anything to distract them. They leaned over and whispered to each other, then laughed derisively at me. A fat man in khakis slinked up from behind, murmuring "Hey, babe!" in my ear, his hand gently on my shoulder.

Other women were scarce. A few were decked out in suits, their hair finely preened, light makeup delicately highlighting their dark eyes. The Muslim women were more conspicuous, dressed in turbans and long robes that fluttered with a light gracefulness round the tables. Still laughing, the two heavy-set men sat down at a neighboring table gawking at me. I glanced again at the Rasta. He seemed slightly nutty with his beads and bracelets but at least he didn't stare as much.

"Guess it will start pretty soon," I remarked, turning my back to the bouncers.

"Pretty soon," the Rasta echoed, rolling his eyes.

"Are you a friend of Jayla's or Glenn?" I asked, eager to strike up a conversation.

"Both," he laughed. "You see, I live here. Lorton's been my home for a lonnnnnnnng time. I been in the other neighborhood for a while," he disclosed, nodding toward the maximum-security prison. "But eventually they transferred me here. You see, they all upset about some money," he smirked. "Some money I borrowed on the long-term plan!"

He laughed loudly, finally managing to make his turbaned friend smile. I was relieved to be laughing with someone instead of simply staring. "Oh yeah," he continued, encouraged by our response, "I've been on this vacation a lonnnnnng time." He was animated and lively.

The murmuring crowd was suddenly hushed by a scratchy voice surging from an old phonograph, "Here comes the bride, all dressed in white ..." Jayla entered from the back of the room, squashed into a light blue Sears and Roebuck dress, a white communion veil pinned to her hair. She clutched a small bouquet of flowers at her waist, her large brooding eyes pinned to the ground. Beside her Glenn's cellmate, now the best man, walked decisively, staring straight ahead, his tailored suit lending him the air of a lawyer.

As they advanced down the aisle, Jayla jolted to a stop and began to giggle.

"We are off beat," she announced to the crowd. "We gotta start over again."

The guests within earshot applauded Jayla, relieved she hadn't changed her mind. On my left I could hear the bouncers muttering her name affectionately.

Step by step the scratchy record guided them onward, Glenn marching solemnly behind. He was extremely handsome, tall with fine features, a slightly rounded face with bright questioning eyes set against his coppery skin. His thin mouth smiled gently. Finally reaching the end of the aisle, they arranged themselves ceremoniously around the rostrum.

Jayla bowed her head prayerfully while Glenn looked fixedly ahead. The minister's robust voice resounded over the crowd, praising this blessing of love that God had given the inmates of Lorton. He beseeched the bride and groom to nurture their love and family. The Lord would watch over their lives together until death. Then, in a softer voice, he set about marrying them. Jayla's timorous voice sang back the vows while the audience took stock of the union. The ring looked small in Glenn's large hand as he reverently slid it onto Jayla's finger. A sob, then she trembled uncontrollably with strong emotion. A current of sniffles flowed fitfully from person to person. And there, in front of the world and God, the bride and groom kissed.

The kiss stretched on and people began to smile at this great accomplishment of love. Despite the armed guards and electric fences, despite what the rest of the world thought or did, they smiled at this love that belonged to no one but themselves. Close friends rushed forward to congratulate the couple, tears streaming down from the eyes of even the most hardened criminals. Children bounced off their seats, agitated by the baffling sobs and laughter afflicting the adults. Like frisky pups, they chased after each other between the tables, clamoring round trousered legs and past flower-sprayed dresses. Jayla looked regal as she shook hands and kissed people lined up across the cafeteria. A veneer of tears burnished her cheeks. Glenn stood beside her, holding little Glennie, his eyes brimming over.

Once she collected herself, Jayla began directing everyone through the cafeteria line. "Eat! Enjoy yourselves! Eat enough for me too, 'cause Lord knows I ain't in no state to keep anything down!" Laughing and crying simultaneously, she shyly glanced at Glenn. He wrapped his arm around her waist, boastfully showing off "his" son to all. Soon the guests were streaming back and forth, their plates laden with potato salad, roast beef, chicken, and rice. The ominous-looking bouncers joined the Rasta and me at our table, laughing now at the braided bandit bragging of his criminal exploits and cosmological insights.

No sooner did we finish sampling the wedding cake than the overhead lights flickered off and on. The Rasta stood then swaggered to my side of the table. "Well," he said gallantly offering me his arm, "look like the fun's over, sweetheart. But you stop by and visit us some other time, you hear?"

The guards paced anxiously around the exit, waiting for the guests to say goodbye. "Everyone out now!" a skinny one with a pug nose ordered loudly. "Everyone out so the newlyweds can have some time alone!" The lights flickered again. The guests made leisurely progress toward the door, tossing sexual jibes through the air. Jayla and Glenn were left alone, conversing earnestly. Glenn's taut frame towered over Jayla, whose hand rested unconsciously on her belly filled with new life. And the lights dimmed as a guard shut the door, granting them some privacy on their ten-minute honeymoon.

# Trouble's Come Home

It was high noon. The office workers scrambled out of their buildings to eat lunch and enjoy the sun in the grassy square. Women strolled in soft-flowing clothes, clutching bags of sandwiches and fresh fruit. The men walked by, their faces pensive and strained and their gaits as certain and methodical as a computer. They walked through the tiny park called Farragut Square in the center of Washington DC. The square was only two blocks away from the White House, so sometimes traffic stopped while a limousine, guarded by a motorcycle brigade, roared past.

I watched the park fill up with these industrious people from safe, hard-working environments—such a contrast to Jayla's world, to her latest news. I thought about what she had recently told me and so many contradictory feelings arose in me. She was my friend yet what happened was ignominious. I was trying to compose myself before the reunion with her. I hadn't seen her for a while because I had retreated, for half a year, to the West Virginia mountains. I departed, convinced we had shared a fair bit of our lives and pleased to leave her on such a positive note. During my absence she wrote a few letters, sounding fairly happy. She even sent me a photo of Melissa, their new daughter. But I should have known better.

Jayla wasn't one to confess her problems unless you were face to face and she could gauge your receptivity. Upon my return I wrote a brief note, giving her my new address in the city. Two weeks later she phoned to break the news.

I was banging out a story, growing more and more frantic as my words coalesced into a parody. The phone rang, but I tried to ignore it. The ringing persisted. Thoroughly frustrated by my work, I decided to answer it.

"Hello, is Clem there?"

"This is Clem."

"Hiya, girl. This is Jayla."

"Oh my God, how wonderful to hear your voice! Where are you?"

"Well, I moved to Southeast and didn't get your letter 'til last week. The old apartment on Lenmore Street is still under my name, you see, but it's sublet to a friend. I'm living by the Shrimp Boat with my mother-in-law."

"Glenn's mother? Is he out yet?"

"Well, he is in a halfway house now, but he had been out before but was sent back to prison. He just got released last month. Thank the Lord, they let us spend time together."

"And how's everything going between you two?"

"Good, Clem. We're still together and working things out, but ..." she paused for a long moment. "There are some bad things that happened too. You see, I had a nervous breakdown."

"You! A nervous breakdown?"

"And all my children got taken away by Social Services. I have to go to Family Court next week and Criminal Court on the 20th of April for child abuse. You see, they're charging me with fifteen counts, including mayhem. That means attempted murder."

She paused again, but I was unable to speak.

"I might land in prison, Clem. It was terrible when they arrested me. I swear to God, they kept me locked up all night! While I was there, I lost the will to live. My whole life I done what I could to keep out of jail but there I was just the same. I'd still be on the inside if my friend, Susan, hadn't put up her house to bail me out. A $10,000 bond, can you imagine that? Who do I know with ten grand? They aimed to keep me there, but the Lord came to my rescue."

"My God, Jayla!"

"You ain't kidding, girl, God is sure enough what I needed. I don't know what I'm going to do if they send me to prison. Already I can't see my kids. They're all in a foster home."

"Do you have a lawyer?" I asked, wondering what exactly happened.

"Well, I got a public defender. You know, someone the state assigns you if you are poor. But I can't expect too much either. So far, I only talked with her one time. Even then, I had to keep calling her back. Don't ask me why. She ain't got the time to see me before the trial but she promised to call on Monday."

"Hmmmm," I just didn't know what to say. Attempted murder? Her children? Complicated thoughts raced through my mind. Everything felt soft and hard at the same time. Judgments. Support. Love. Courts. I pictured little Glennie and Dora.

"You see, when you're poor, it means you got to be with your kids twenty-four hours a day. You can't get no babysitter 'cause welfare just don't cover something like that. So how are you suppose to look for a job? I asked my friends to take the kids for a while, but you know how people is, they got their own problems, their own families."

Hardly stopping for a breath, her husky voice suddenly sounded like it broke into coarse little pieces, "When it happened, everyone oooohed and ahhhed about those kids. But where was they when I asked for help? It was only afterwards they felt sorry. I even went to the government to ask for a homemaker, but they said I didn't qualify for assistance. Well, I wonder what a woman has to do to *qualify*! Now that same government is paying for someone else to take care of my kids. Yeah, they all feeling sorry for those kids now, but no one's talking 'bout Jayla! No, nobody knows how Jayla felt, that Jayla is more than a mother, that she can't even look inside no school, that she ain't got no freedom or no fixed income. Nobody sees she's got to pay for the rent, phone, and clothes. Now they're all telling me, 'Well, you should handle that! You should be able to handle that!' Well, I *couldn't* handle all that!"

There was no stopping her to ask questions at this point, I could tell. The anger and defensiveness in her voice pleaded for someone to understand, even if she couldn't.

"And Glenn messed up about getting out. He was doing fine, coming out to work every day, but then he got drunk and didn't want to go back behind no walls at Lorton, didn't want to live by their terms. When they finally caught up with him, they slammed him back into Lorton and the little money he was sending me stopped. Then on top of everything I had to drag them kids all the way to Lorton to visit him. You best believe he wants those kids back now, especially Melissa 'cause she's his own flesh and blood. All he's got to do is prove to the court that he's working and has a proper home."

"Well, I don't know about that, Jayla. Even if he has a job, the court may not trust someone with a criminal record." She was silent and I wondered why I felt defensive about acknowledging the truth.

"Ain't nobody got the right to deny him his babies!" she cried angrily. "If they say he ain't a fit father 'cause of a record, then they talking about half the Black population. Everyone's got a record, Clem, but that don't mean they ain't good fathers. We both love them kids and we're in this together."

Her statement felt like a challenge, but I couldn't respond.

"The main problem is," she resumed in a softer voice. "I had two babies, one right after another. You know how they is at that age. They need you for everything. Plus, my boy, Glennie, was jealous of Melissa and he'd start yelling whenever I gave her any attention. Sometimes I'd stick a bottle in his mouth and take her to the other room, but I swear he'd still be crying. Then I'd think, 'Don't that baby ever get satisfied?' I tried to shut myself off, but there wasn't no place for me to go. So, I started losing my nerves."

I listened with earnest attention, but she never mentioned exactly what happened. Something horrible. I could tell by the way she avoided it.

"So, the courts took them away. The babies is okay, but Dora's having a rough time 'cause she's lived with me for the first six years of her life. At least they kept the three kids together and they're still a family. They living with foster parents now."

"And what are they like?"

"I ain't never met them. I'm allowed to visit the kids at a Social Service Center once a week for about an hour. I can't talk with them on the phone yet and that bugs me, but Social Service don't care nothing about their mental wellbeing. Long as those foster parents feed and clothe them, then everything's fine, so they think! And me? I go to a psychiatrist. It helps me understand my feelings and stuff.

"But Clem ..." She expelled air as if her body had knocked against something. Then a sob, "I love those kids. I don't believe a psychiatrist is going to do much good, 'cause it was the situation. It's the situation that's got to change! I'm bleeding some bad feelings, but Glenn is sticking by me. He listens to my feelings and supports me. Everything is different for us now. He's back in a halfway house so we don't get none of that stuff on the side anymore. It's like we is really married. I can fall asleep in his arms and wake up and he's still there. It's good, Clem. He's got a job and he's almost out of that halfway house for good. Anyway at least he can visit me. Come over here and have dinner like a decent family.

"But it ain't perfect," she added. "That man's got his ways too. 'Honey,' I asked him, 'is it true that women is stronger than men?' 'You be crazy!' he said. 'No,' I told him, 'cause if I wasn't stronger I'd be right over that whiskey bottle just like you.' You see, Glenn can't drink just one or two. He can't drink socially. I swear to God, he's a changed man. Normally, he don't talk a lot but, when he's drunk, he'll say just about anything."

"My husband," she said proudly, "don't curse and he usually don't fight. But when he drinks, he's got a temper. I worry about Glenn walking the streets alone 'cause someone could hurt him. They'll kill you for nothing out there! But when I tell him that he says, 'Hey babe, I ain't met the man yet who could beat me.' Well, there's always a first time!"

Still pondering the phone call, I abandoned the park bench and started heading for my sister's truck. An elderly jogger brushed past me. His tennis shoes slapped the sidewalk, scaring away a flock of pigeons. Without slowing his pace, he nimbly skirted around an old Black man scouring through the litter basket. Disco music drifted through the now deserted square from under a tree where a young man sprawled, his dark skin camouflaged against the shady ground. I noticed a dog plop nearby and chuckled to myself, reminded of Jayla's bewilderment before things so familiar to me, as though we were actually from two separate countries.

"I'm living with my mother-in-law," Jayla told me. "And her crazy dog. Let me tell you, this animal drives me nuts. Why, one day I come home, and he was sleeping in the bed with his head on the pillow just like a human being. I swear to God! Glenn's mother, Porky, will sit at the table and just drop her food on the floor for that animal to eat. And dog hairs! That dog leaves hair all over the house and a scent, you know an odor. I swear, if I ain't kid-sitting, I'm dog-sitting!"

Smiling to myself, I climbed in my sister's truck and began driving away from the center of town toward Southeast. I slowed down as kids on rollerblades wove through the traffic. There were people sitting on the front steps of townhouses and clusters of men hanging around the corner grocery stores. As I drove farther from Farragut Square I started to wonder, "Where are the border guards?" I passed from white to black, from genteel movement to restrained frenzy. "Where is the passport station?" I asked myself as buses flew by me, crammed with men and women on their way back from cleaning houses, mowing lawns or applying for jobs.

Before long, I was driving through a residential area of brick rowhouses with tiny, treeless yards. Following Jayla's instructions, I turned onto a quiet street and stopped in front of a nondescript tenement. Upon entering, I walked through another foul-smelling hallway, following the cement stairs to the basement. A door slammed upstairs, and I heard footsteps descending the stairwell in my direction. Quickly I knocked. The door immediately opened, and Jayla was standing there, welcoming me with a smile. We embraced and she invited me inside, jabbering rapidly. A small German Shepherd pranced excitedly around us.

"Jayla," I remarked, "when you told me about this dog, I pictured some gigantic beast. Why, he's just a cute little pup," I murmured, kneeling down to pet him.

"Cute little pup is right!" She backed away from me, sternly folding her arms across her chest. "When Mama's around he's naughty, but as soon as she leaves and we're here alone, he do much better. Just like a spoiled kid. Lord!"

The impatience behind her words stung. The thought of this same testiness brutalizing those children turned my stomach. Standing, I bit my tongue, resolved to give Jayla the benefit of the doubt, resolved to listen, to deeply listen. "You look good," I told her. "You really do. You've lost weight."

"Ain't lost no weight," she asserted. "I've gained some, in fact." Her hair was longer, combed out in a straight bush on top and slicked down close to the scalp on the sides. Despite the light rash across her forehead, she did look more relaxed.

"So, this is my new home," she boasted, extending her arm in a sweeping gesture. I peeked to the right inside a cramped kitchen, quite like Jayla's old one.

"Oh, your faucet is running," I pointed out, walking over to turn it off.

"That ain't nothing," she explained. "It's always been that way and the landlord won't lift a finger to fix it."

I stared at the green groove etched through the enamel by the constant flow. "But who pays for the water?"

"The landlord. Look like he'd rather pay that bill than fix the faucet. I swear, how people can be." She turned to leave but the excited shepherd blocked her path. "Git dog!" she shooed the pup with a feigned kick.

"Come on, Jayla, it's just a pup." I followed her to the living room where she turned on the color television.

"That pup's got a scent," she grumbled, collapsing on the couch.

"All pups do."

"Well, he is a good watchdog," she conceded in a voice that indicated the subject was closed.

A coffee table adorned with family photos sat in front of the couch. Across the room was a dinette set where Glenn, his mother, and Jayla apparently took their meals. More imitation flowers and plastic doilies enlivened the space.

"Clem!" Excited, she clapped her hands together. "I talked to your friend Pete today and he's got me a job in Takoma Park, cleaning some lady's house."

"That's great!" I exclaimed, reflecting her happiness.

"Praise the Lord! I sure hope she likes my work. My husband says not to worry because I am the cleanest woman he's ever seen. And it's true, you should see how I clean! It must be a sickness or something, 'cause I can't abide no disorder. I mean, that was one of my problems with the kids." Her voice rose to a higher pitch, her eyebrows crinkling at the center. "It was hard for those poor kids to even play, 'cause I couldn't stand to see their toys all over the place. Now that ain't right, Clem!

"That just ain't right," she repeated as if momentarily confused. "The other night," she continued in a happier tone, "I was scrubbing the kitchen floor when Glenn was visiting and he said, 'What you doing now, woman? You always washing this and washing that. Sometimes I think you're avoiding me.' He was trying to kiss me you see." She smiled coyly. "And I said, 'Now look here, when you get back from work, you want a messy house or a clean house?' Well," she rolled her eyes. "We all know the answer to that one! Then he says to me, 'Enough is enough, you can't even sit down with me on the couch without first making sure the wrinkles are out!'"

I chuckled, searching through my purse for a cigarette. Jayla immediately jumped up to find me an ashtray. She quickly wiped off a smudge before handing it to me.

"You are a fanatic!" I teased playfully, "But that will be good for the job!"

"I sure hope so. I plan to work real hard, 'cause that's what I like. You know, sometimes when I get depressed, I start cleaning everything in sight. After about three or four hours, I feel worn out enough so I can relax and watch TV or something. When I don't work, I just sit mulling it over in my head. And that don't get me nowhere.

"Also, around here, it's my way of contributing. It ain't right, me living here without a job, 'cause my mother-in-law is always complaining about this bill and that bill. She's got a steady job with the government, but her problem is she likes gambling too much. All her money goes to the horses or the numbers, so she's never got enough left for the bills. Glenn is like that, too. All his money goes to horses and booze."

"He hasn't slowed down yet?"

"Does a cow talk?" she snorted, then lapsed into a sullen silence. "But I ain't complaining about him or Porky too much. That woman and me we got one thing in common—we both love Glenn. So, we got to work at being better friends. It's just that I don't like staying here without giving something. The other day I told him, 'Honey, we got to talk to your mother and find out how much rent we owe her.' 'We don't got to pay Porky nothing,' he said. But I wanted to work something out with her anyway. 'You all just pay what you can,' she told us. Well, when we got to the bedroom, I told Glenn, 'Listen, honey, we ought to give her some money every week.' Well, we figured twenty dollars was about right. Last week we couldn't pay her 'cause we had to buy groceries when our food stamps was cut off. Finally, she asked Glenn, 'Where's the money?' So, I know she wanted something! I try to make up for it by cleaning, 'cause there just ain't no money now. My husband lost his job."

"Oh no, Jayla! What happened?"

She tugged at the hem of her skirt, folding it over her thick knees. "What happened is he was suppose to clean the cafeteria floor and pieces of the mop kept falling off. They said he didn't do a good job. I mean they fired him without even asking what happened!"

"Sounds like there must have also been something else, Jayla."

"No, Clem, he didn't do nothing wrong. They just lost their temper. Of course, he could go back and beg for that job, but he is sure it will just happen again. So, I try to give him some love and understanding. Anyway, something worse happened to him after that."

A cop car rushed across the silent TV screen and screeched to a halt in front of a tenement building. The mouths of White policemen moved, forming words we couldn't hear. Suddenly a door flew open and a man walked out, his arms in the air. The next moment, a blonde woman motioned toward a car, urging the audience to buy it Jayla continued to speak while watching the TV, as though filling in the missing sound. "First he lost his job, then the next night he got beat up."

"Christ!" I moaned. "When it rains, it pours."

"Yeah," Jayla nodded in agreement. "And by five guys. 'I told you so,' I said to him. 'You lucky you ain't dead!'"

"What happened, Jayla? Was he hurt?"

"Well, no, not much. Just banged up his elbow and a few bruises. He had called me up around four that afternoon to say he was on his way back from a friend's. He was already blind drunk. Well, I waited and waited but he didn't show up. After a while I got this real bad feeling in my stomach like I ain't never got before." She held her belly, her brow constricted with pain. "'Lord,' I thought, 'something done happened to that man!' Well, pretty soon a friend called up and told me about the fight. Then she said, 'Glenn says he's going to the hospital, but I just don't know, maybe he's out looking for revenge.' I started getting angry, but she told me, 'Now Jayla, let that man do what he's got to do. There ain't no stopping him anyway.'"

"So, I just kept waiting, looking out the window. Around midnight he finally came home. Sure enough, he never went to the hospital. I poured peroxide over his cuts and covered them with Band-Aids."

"God, Jayla, it sounds like it could have been a lot worse."

"That's exactly what I told him. You know Glenn has a reputation for being a bad man. Maybe this shook him up 'cause it was five men who jumped him, five guys he knew. That man's having some trouble, though, adjusting. He keeps talking about this holdup and that holdup, scares me to death! The halfway house won't do nothing to help him find a job or lay off the booze. Sometimes I think he ain't never going to change, that he'll never adjust to life outside them walls. There's lots of people like that. They'll do something wrong on purpose to be sent back. At Lorton they got beds and regular meals. It ain't the best, but at least they don't have to deal with society."

I sank farther into the couch. "Sounds like serious trouble. Glenn is on the wrong track."

"I know, Clem, and I pray for him. Praise the Lord, he's changed already some since that fight. When we're in bed now, he curls right up next to me like I was a shelter or something. You know, like a kid does when he's afraid and needs affection."

"The man needs a lot more than that, Jayla. Can't you talk to his parole officer or someone?"

She scrutinized me out of the corner of her eye, an exaggerated scowl on her face. "You still ain't learned, have you Clem? I give him love and compassion. Ain't no parole officer going to do that!" Snickering at my naiveté, she continued on a more serious vein. "It's hard sometimes. He's still got a whole lotta bitterness inside. I swear, some of the stories he tells, you just wouldn't believe! When they was not even teenagers, carrying guns and all. That gave him a certain disposition and he can still bleed some pretty bad feelings. When you first meet him, he looks like a mean man."

"Not at all," I countered. "He looks rather handsome and intelligent to me."

"Well," she admitted, looking down at her lap and smiling bashfully, "maybe to you, but most folks get a bad impression. Even I felt that way at the beginning. It took a lot of time and a lot of digging, but I finally found out there wasn't nothing but a puppy inside of him, nothing but a puppy …" Sighing wistfully, Jayla stared at the TV while her large hands patted out the creases of her skirt. The delicate smell of bath powder lingered in the air.

"Still, if I start digging too deep, he says, 'Watch out! You're getting too close!' So, I have to be patient 'cause, you see, there's a shield we all put up to protect ourselves. I was hurt as a child, so I put up a shield, even with Glenn. I had a real big one, 'cause I had been hurt so bad. As I dug deeper into him, I had to dig into my own self and my shield started coming down. Now I feel secure with Glenn. 'Don't ever leave me, baby,' he says. And you know, I believe that man's sincere."

"Come on," she proposed, rising to her feet. "I'll show you our real home."

I followed her down the hall to a small powder-blue bedroom. Crisp navy-blue curtains hung from the undersized window, matching the satin comforter that covered their double bed. A portable TV was perched like an altar at the end of the bed. Jayla fell across the bed and reached underneath to retrieve several flowered photo albums.

"Look here," she said, inviting me to sit beside her. "I got pictures of the wedding and you're in one."

She hastily flipped through the collection, stopping now and then to explain the history of a close friend or relative. Nearly every man she pointed to, old boyfriends, Glenn's cousins and brothers, all had served time behind bars. She mentioned this fact casually, the holdups, shooting and robberies, until I was convinced that the Washington I knew was a myth. Life in the capital for Jayla was more like a cowboy feature, populated by ruthless gunslingers and outlaws, bound by their own mysterious ethics and rituals. I looked at snapshots of ex-convicts, pictures of children visiting their fathers in prison and, finally, her own wedding at Lorton, where she pointed out the blur of my face among the crowd. As she closed the album and stowed it under the bed, I marveled again at the stark contradictions she embodied.

"You've changed, Jayla," I suddenly observed aloud. "You've changed since I first met you. You don't seem so, well, so bitter."

My observation took her by surprise, but then she smiled broadly. "Glenn has a lot to do with it, but so has my faith in the Lord." She spoke slower now, leaning back against the headboard. "I'm a sinner from way back, Clem. When I was seventeen I had an abortion. My life without the Lord was going nowhere. So finally, I met Abe and had Dora. I wanted that baby real bad. I was alone and needed someone to love me. Then later, I met the minister. I thought I was doing right, but I learned the hard way that I was wrong. Look like I got to learn everything the hard way.

"Glenn was incarcerated, so I prayed and prayed and finally decided to tell him that I was pregnant. By the time I got to Lorton, I was trembling all over. I sat down beside him and told him the whole thing. He looked at me and said, 'I always thought this would happen.' I mean, how else did he think it would be? What's a woman suppose to do when her man's in jail? She's still got her body and if she's got to wait for two years, what else is she going to do?" Jayla left the question suspended in midair. "Glenn said, 'I love you and I'm going to stick by you.' Then he asked me to do him one favor—to say the baby was his."

She bowed her head, wiping her hands across the comforter to smooth out the wrinkles. Against the wall was a bureau cluttered with cosmetics, perfumes, deodorants, and creams. The reflection of Jayla's anguished face in the large oval mirror looked like an ancient tribal mask.

"But, Clem, I can't do it. I got to tell my son about his real father or he'll just grow up hearing it from other people."

She bowed her head, weighed down by guilt, the tremendous, accumulated guilt of her years of struggle.

"It's okay," I tried to console her, rubbing her shoulder. "I see what you mean. How could you look at Glennie in the eye if you kept a secret like that? A mother has to be honest with her own child."

"That's right," she replied. "I done enough bad in my life without deceiving my own son, without living a lie. I got to work hard to mend the wounds I already gave them. I'm scared of my own self, Clem, scared about what I done. Sometimes I just lie on this bed and cry like a baby, 'cause I done things that no one but me and the Lord knows about. Whenever I think about my kids coming home again, I get scared. I don't know how they feel about what happened or if they remember or nothing. I don't never get to talk to them.

"Who knows how much more I can take? What if Glenn gets sent back to Lorton and me with no job and no money? I learned something though, this time. I didn't reach out to my friends enough. I asked them for help but I never did tell them how bad it was. I mean, as a mother you want everything for your kids, and I was always too proud or embarrassed to ask for help. I'd see myself spanking Glenn, then hitting him again a little harder. 'Jayla, you got to get a hold on yourself,' I'd say. 'You got to pull yourself together.' Then the other one would start crying.

"I go to therapy now, but I need a whole lot more. Look like I got a long way to go before I understand Jayla, before I teach Jayla to hit the wall instead of my own flesh and blood."

She rocked back and forth sniffling plaintively. "Someday I'd like to get a decent job with a fixed income. You know, working in an office, typing, and answering phones. Look like I got a long way to go, but I got the Lord on my side now. I done wrong but the Lord's taking care of me by sending me the love of Glenn and Porky."

Sitting straighter, Jayla smiled through her watery eyes. Her gaze fell upon the open closet, stuffed with her hand-me-down wardrobe. The tiny bedroom was impossibly overcrowded, but there was a warm, settled atmosphere.

"You know what?" she asked. "I believe I can practice on Glenn 'cause he's as bad as any kid! He's so jealous, he wants me near him all the time. If I'm out in the kitchen cooking, he'll yell from the bedroom, 'Honey, come here and lay by me.' Then, I got to stop my work and lay with him."

"Oh, Jayla," I laughed. "I don't know whether I could take that. I mean, how do you ever get anything done?"

"Well, you see, my friend Susan has the same problem with her man 'cause he was incarcerated too. I ask Glenn, 'What do you do when I'm not around? How in the world do you ever sleep?' 'I dream of you,' he says. 'I close my eyes and pretend like you're there.'" She laughed affectionately. "'Lord!' I tell him. 'What you going do when the kids come back? You going be jealous!'"

"When the kids come back?" I hesitantly inquired.

"If I don't get them, they'll be split up in different foster homes and that ain't no good. I'm going to therapy and parenting class so I can learn to deal with them. Glenn will be out for good soon, plus I got Porky to help now. Actually, the kids won't be decided at Family Court for some time. What I got to go to first is the Criminal Court."

Once again, I was torn between Jayla and the children, between an individual's ability to determine her own life and society's power to crush that freedom. "Criminal Court?" I repeated as if speaking to myself.

"What I done was pretty severe," she quickly explained. "You see, I fractured a skull and broke some ribs. I slapped them around some 'cause I couldn't stand their screaming and crying no more. They was young and fragile so it hurt them bad, real bad."

A deluge of questions cascaded through my head. Was it day or night? Did she call the police or the hospital herself? Was it in the bedroom or the living room? Where was Dora? Question after question leaped at me from the darkness, yet something was frozen inside. I remained silent, focusing on what Jayla chose to reveal.

"I ain't hardly talked to my lawyer. I guess she's a busy woman 'cause I called and called but she won't ever return my phone calls. She ain't spoken to me but once, when I called her! I guess that's how lawyers work. The trial is going to be the seventh."

"I'll go with you, Jayla, if you want."

"Thank you, Clem, thank you. I might need your help 'cause it's a long way to Upper Marlboro and there ain't no buses going out there."

"You can't have the trial here?" I asked with mounting alarm. The DC courts might be more sympathetic in a case like Jayla's. Upper Marlboro was rural and White, not too acquainted with the plight of Black welfare mothers.

"No, it all happened last winter when I was living in Maryland, so they have to press charges there. But I got to call the courthouse again and make sure of the day 'cause of what happened last time."

"What do you mean?"

"Last time my friend got her husband to drive us to court. It's about an hour from here, so he dropped us off and went straight to work. After we got inside, we found out the trial date had been changed. And my lawyer never even bothered to tell me! Lord! So, there we was with no way home. We finally met someone who gave us a ride, but that was luck, and I don't want to go through that again. This time I'm going to call the court myself and make sure."

"Why can't you talk with your lawyer? That's his responsibility."

"Hers, you mean. She's a woman and she don't return no phone calls. So, I got to make sure about the correct date. You see I got eight different counts against me, child abuse, beating, bruising. It all amounts to the same thing with the words changed around. The lawyer says if I plead guilty to one charge, they'll go easy on me."

"Why is that?"

"The one time she spoke with me, she explained the whole thing. You see, when I plead guilty to child abuse, the District Attorney will drop all the other charges. Only I don't get no jury trial. If a jury finds me guilty, I could be sentenced to forty-five years, fifteen years on just one count. By pleading guilty, my sentence is cut down to three years and my lawyer says I won't go to prison, that the worst that could happen is I might have to report to a women's detention home. That means you go to detention on weekends but work on the outside during the week. So many weekends add up to your sentence, let's say six months."

The jarring ring of the phone suddenly interrupted our discussion. Jayla leaped from the bed and rushed down the hallway. Speaking in a whisper, her fingers nervously twisted round the cord. I gravitated toward the door, waiting to say goodbye.

"I'll be right there, Clem," she called out.

After sitting so long in the bedroom, the living room looked spacious and bright with sunlight. I examined some photographs of Glenn. He was smiling in one like a high school graduate, though he barely made it through fifth grade. Another showed him standing next to his mother, a rotund woman who leaned against him, her arm slung round his waist. And there was the inevitable Christmas snapshot of the tree with the presents being unwrapped by children clad in pajamas.

"Clem," Jayla began, walking toward me.

"I have to go now, Jayla. But you be sure to call me again soon."

"We ain't even talked about you! You been in touch with that nice guy again that you told me about? How's your life doing anyway?"

"Not bad, Jayla, not bad. But I think you should get another lawyer. That one sounds a bit ..."

"Clem," she interrupted, gently holding my arm and, as if pleading with me to understand, she continued in a softer voice, "I got the best lawyer of all, the Lord standing by my side. Don't worry 'bout nothing," she fervently instructed me. "Cause the Big Man Upstairs is going to take this case. He ain't going to send me to no jail 'cause I got to be there to take care of my husband and kids. I don't know what Glenn would do out here without me except maybe drink himself to death. And do you know, Clem, this will be the first time Glenn and I really been together without guards or halfway house. No, I can't go to prison 'cause somebody's got to watch that man."

※

Jayla's pick-up point to meet me for the trial was the Shrimp Boat. She referred to this landmark as though it was as well-known as the Washington Monument itself. Tucked deep within Southeast DC, I found the crumbling diner at a busy intersection across from a Kentucky Fried Chicken and an Exxon Station. On the morning of her trial, both of these establishments were teeming with activity while the Shrimp Boat looked deserted, even slightly haunted. Chipped paint peeled from the walls and a gaudy sign over the top announced: SUBS, SEAFOOD, BURGERS. The diner was slightly oval in shape, which presumably entitled the owners to claim it as a boat.

At 8 am, rush-hour traffic was intensifying and the air above the intersection darkened ominously. I barely managed to park my borrowed vehicle. People, mainly African Americans, were either racing off to work or wearily returning from evening shifts, crowding the sidewalks.

I sat in the truck, waiting, worried about the trial and still trying to sort out my mixed feelings about Jayla. I just couldn't seem to untangle my feelings. I hated her crime. I couldn't even imagine the horror of it. Yet I watched the whole situation evolve. Like others, I thought she could "handle it" because I never did anything for her but listen. And she seemed like such a strong, powerful woman. But she was crying out for help the whole time. She laid it all on the table: her financial situation, her lack of social supports, her past history. In fact, she was, oftentimes, painfully honest. But I didn't hear her nor did anyone else. This didn't justify anything, but it gave it context and the context created half the situation. Then, as Jayla herself pointed out, she didn't have the skills to love, to nourish. She herself was only just getting her first deep nourishment from Porky and Glenn and her spiritual life. I sat watching people hurrying off to work, a simple act that Jayla relished. I saw someone wave and spotted her, standing near the Shrimp Boat. She had a neutral expression, like she was waiting for a bus.

"There you are!" I called out to her, laughing.

She turned, clutching her maroon raincoat and embraced me. "You ain't been here long, have you?"

"No, not at all," I assured her, heading toward the truck. "But I wasn't sure at first whether I'd make it. The battery in the truck was dead, but my friends gave me a jumpstart."

"Look like you already well woke up!" she laughed, looking hurriedly both ways before we crossed the street.

Caught up in the spirit of rush hour, we raced to the truck. Jayla climbed aboard, daintily yanking her polyester dress over her knees. Slamming the door, she coughed, then spat into a Kleenex.

"Sorry, Clem," she apologized.

"Got a cold?"

"Well," she giggled, "I thought I got rid of it, but my husband gave it back to me again last night."

"Giving you encouragement, huh?"

"Oooooo yeah!" she tittered gaily, sitting straight up in her seat, the raincoat neatly folded on her lap. "You know the way to Upper Marlboro, Clem?"

"No, but I have maps."

"Let's see ... you just go right down this road." She squinted, pointing east. "We'll just follow the bus route 'til we get on the main road. Look like I don't know the way so good either."

As we passed through the suburbs, traffic wasn't as heavy. All the cars were in the opposite lane, headed back toward the city. The regimented columns of brick rowhouses gave way to a homogenized landscape of matchbox abodes with orderly green yards. Air-conditioned shopping malls surrounded by asphalt parking lots dotted the roadside.

"It's nice out here," Jayla commented cheerfully. "We'll probably see some cows and horses along the way. Before I went to court, I hardly knew people lived this way. You know, all that land and them big houses. Ain't that something!"

Cautiously, she directed me into a nameless residential development. There was a tense moment when Jayla forgot the bus route, but suddenly a sign pointing to Upper Marlboro leaped in front of us.

"Well," she began after we were safely headed in the right direction, "I worked for that lady your friend told me about. I swear to God, I scrubbed for ten hours and must have cleaned the whole damn house. That woman was right there standing over me the whole time. You know, supervision to make sure I kept working and didn't break nothing. That kinda made me nervous, but I guess she had to do that 'cause she didn't know me. She asked me to start with the oven. Well, I swear, that oven ain't been cleaned for years! It was just piled with grease!"

"Ugh!"

"And it wasn't coming off at all. I sweated over that thing all morning and it still wasn't clean!"

"Is that why she wanted you? To clean the oven?"

"That's what I asked her. Finally, I told her I better dust first 'cause that oven would have taken me all day, and the rest of her house was still dirty. So, I opened the cabinets and wiped them all out, then the windowsills. I cleaned out the refrigerator, the venetian blinds and even washed the curtains for her. Then I swept and cleaned every room."

"She wants me to come back. I told her I would, but I don't think I can do that. You see, she's a pleasant old lady but she's stingy. All that work and she only paid me Candy and Cracker Jacks! It sounds like Guatemala! Being paid with little party baskets of candy! But Jayla broke into my thoughts. "I mean," she added with an angry toss of her head, "it just ain't fair to get paid so little and no overtime. But that's how it goes lots of times when you work in houses. This woman only hires someone every other week, so that ain't enough work for me anyway. I appreciate the job, but after I take the subway from my mother-in-law's and then transfer to a bus, it just ain't worth the expense."

"No, that's about four dollars right there for round trip transportation."

"I'm still putting in applications all over town," she continued, "but there just ain't no work. Reagan's cutting out all the jobs, just like he's cutting off food stamps and welfare. That man is crazy! He's hurtin' people bad, real bad. And who suffers the most? Women! Women with kids! Somebody's gonna kill him and I bet it's a woman!"

She spat out the last words, still grumbling under her breath. "Lord!" I could hear her mutter angrily. A huge red barn zipped by us, then a field where cows were grazing.

"Glenn has got a job now," she reported.

"God, Jayla, that's great!"

"It's heavy construction. He calls it manual labor or something. I swear, it wears him out. He comes home and just falls into that bed. Glenn is going to be a mighty dull boy if he keeps that up." Snickering lewdly, she looked out the window. "I mean, when he don't want that stuff, you know the man's got to be tired."

"Don't worry," I laughed, "he'll get used to it."

She shook her head, gaping at the passing scenery. "Well, look at all that land. Just look at it!" Swaying fields of red clover surrounded us on either side, rows of birds chirped contentedly from the telephone lines. "How 'bout that? All this land and hardly no people!"

Queen Anne's Lace mingled with the dandelions and buttercups in a colorful collage. The wind rustling through the trees soothed our senses after the city's clamor. The road bent unexpectedly, and we crossed a bridge, entering the outskirts of Upper Marlboro.

"Keep going straight," she advised me, studying the tiny town. Gift shops, antique stores and restaurants lined the narrow road. "This is Main Street and that's the courthouse over there."

A four-story brick building towered over the small town. A steady flow of people streamed in and out, walking between the clipped hedges. The parking lot was already jammed, the meters lined up like vigilant soldiers round the edge.

"I hope your lawyer comes this time," I told Jayla over my shoulder, locking the truck.

"Well, if she ain't here, the Lord is, so everything is gonna turn out fine." She carefully patted her hair in place, her bright eyes certain.

Silently we walked toward the courthouse, zigzagging through the parked cars. "My lawyer is a big woman," Jayla informed me, watching the ground. "She's nice but it's strange, I just stare whenever she talks." Another tense silence fell between us. "I guess it's the right thing to do, pleading guilty."

"It sounds right to me," I commented, trying to comfort her anxiety. "I mean, you couldn't exactly say your kids did it themselves."

She stopped dead in her tracks and glared at me, looking betrayed. "You sure know how to make a person feel bad."

"Jayla, I'm sorry! Really I am, I didn't mean it that way!"

She resumed walking, slightly ahead of me now, staring hard at the ground. With a shrug, she whispered, "It's okay, forget it," and led me into the courthouse.

A group of policemen stood next to the metal detector, fumbling through everyone's purses and briefcases. The corridors were alive with movement like a bus or train station. As we got into an elevator, people around stood silent and anxious or conversed in terse tones. Down another hallway, in another elevator, the identical scene was repeated. Inside the courtroom antechamber, we watched a dapper young lawyer giving last-minute instructions to a family. "But he ain't told me about that," I could hear the mother plead. I looked around, noting the invisible dividing line that separated the throng into two groups: the accusers and the accused. It was eminently clear on which side the African Americans sat.

"I ain't worried," Jayla leaned against me and whispered. "The Lord is going take care of me. I just know He is. And if He don't," she glanced furtively round the room, "then there's a reason." Touching my arm, she added, "Wait here, I got to go sign in."

Her blue dress disappeared through the door labeled "Criminal Department." The red block lettering fairly screamed amid the prevailing drab décor. I noticed in front of me the one White accused person in the courtroom. There was a tubercular looking gentleman and his teenage daughter with straggly blonde hair, slouched in her tight blue jeans, legs spread apart in a triangle with her toes touching. She chain-smoked from a pack of Winstons, dark circles under her eyes. The balding father wouldn't look at her and stubbornly avoided my searching gaze. They sat together, haggard, depressed and, above all, defeated. I couldn't help but wonder, as with the other accused, what it was she was charged with.

Jayla returned with a tall, robust woman whom she introduced as her lawyer, Ms Bartlett. She was tanned, blue-eyed and had thick sensual lips that were slightly open and moist. Decked out in a starched white suit, her thick ankles plunged into a pair of tiny, low-heeled shoes. As we greeted one another and chatted amiably, I noticed how she smiled, regardless of what was being said.

Although older than Jayla, she appeared younger, for everything about her was impeccable, orderly, wrinkle-free. Jayla wouldn't look at her directly in the eye and instead turned her head to the left or watched the floor. "Yes, ma'am," she answered obediently to every question. As Ms Bartlett guided us into the courtroom, her lively gait clicked assertively against the tiles. I noticed her hands were baby soft with gleaming pink, manicured nails. Jayla's hands hung down at her sides, slightly curled into leathery fists.

Sliding onto the bench in front of me, Jayla folded her arms, staring out to the courtroom like an attentive student. Although a trial was in session, the solemn atmosphere reminded me more of a church service. Attorneys spoke to their clients in hushed tones, milling amid the polished wooden furniture under subtle indirect lighting. An elderly judge in black robes presided. Two flags stood majestically on either side, representing the authority of the United States Federal Government and the Commonwealth of Maryland. The attorneys, clerks, police, and bailiff, all White, stood on the far side of the rail while Jayla and the other African Americans sat across from them.

A defendant, still dressed in his olive-green prison outfit, head hanging low, stood before the judge. "Why did you do it?" I heard the judge repeating. Ms Bartlett chatted affably with the young DA, her breezy laughter surfacing now and then. Tiny beads of sweat materialized across Jayla's upper lip and forehead. I rested my hand over her hand. Was every white face here merely a reminder of the world that condemned Glenn, her boyfriend Abe, and now maybe herself? Was she lost in this sea of white faces, asserting its dominance, the same power she encountered when she walked down one of DC's boulevards, or worked in someone's house, or had a baby?

"Next!" The judge hammered impatiently on the table as the previous defendant was led away in handcuffs.

"Section 43, 170031," the clerk responded in a practiced monotone. "The State versus Jayla Morris."

"Anyone show up for this case?" the judge inquired, distractedly rummaging through his papers.

"Yes, your Honor," Ms Bartlett replied, rising to her feet. "Jayla Morris is present."

With her gaze pinned to Ms Bartlett's back, Jayla lumbered past the railing to stand in front of the judge. Ms Bartlett whispered to the handsome DA in the pinstriped suit. Then she threw her head back and rattled off a stream of legal jargon to the effect that her client, Jayla Morris, pleads guilty to one count of child abuse against Glennie and Melissa.

"And are there any motions pending in the court?" asked the judge, skimming through the indictment.

"All motions are withdrawn."

Jayla straightened her posture with extreme care as though the slightest blunder might jeopardize her case. As she stared intently at the judge, I could almost hear the deluge of prayers swirling though her head.

"Are you under the influence of any alcohol or drugs?" he asked, a slight Southern accent drawling out the words.

"No, sir."

"Do you wish to plead guilty?"

"Yes, sir."

"Mrs Morris ..." he paused, then added, "I assume it is Mrs?"

"Yes, sir."

"Ah-hem!" Clearing his throat, he launched into another legal tirade that was impossible to understand. I only caught the tail end. "You understand that a plea of guilty can only be offered by a guilty party, that 'abuse' means you physically abused your children, signifying in judicial terms that the results are from cruel, inhumane treatment from a parent?"

"Yes, sir." Jayla replied in a self-effacing monotone.

"That changing your plea to guilty is not a result of a misapprehension or deception, that it is given of your own free and unconditional will? Do you understand?"

"Yes, sir."

"That you, in pleading guilty, abandon your constitutional rights including the right to a jury?"

"Yes, sir."

"That you are denying your innocence and claiming that you did abuse your children?"

"Yes, sir."

"That you are waiving your right to a confrontation with your accusers and the right to subpoena?"

"Yes, sir." She tilted her head to the side.

He swirled around in his chair to face her directly. "Is there anything you don't understand?"

She was silent for a moment, evaluating this curve. "No, sir."

"Are you acting in accord with your state lawyers? Have they done everything to make you understand what this plea of guilty means? Have they done everything to help you with your case?"

Another weighty pause. "Yes, sir," she lied in an undertone.

"And do you fully agree with the terms of pleading guilty, with full understanding of the allegations involved?"

I watched Jayla's back.

"Yes, sir."

The state lawyer sprang to his feet as Jayla sat back down. Quickly, as if by memory, he reeled off a list of her crimes: bruising, hitting, intending to kill her children. After each count the judge nodded his head, then swiveled his chair to face Jayla again.

"Did you commit this crime in this country?"

"Yes, sir."

Ms Bartlett and the DA were on their feet at once, reiterating their separate arguments. The date for Jayla's sentencing was scheduled for May 7. There was no pause when the judge pronounced the verdict "guilty" and turned to ask, "All right, what's next?"

The trial was over. No more than ten minutes had passed.

"I got to sign some more papers," Jayla whispered to me as we left the courtroom. "It'll take about a half hour."

She vanished into another office, leaving me stranded in the hall with a crowd of defendants, a gray cloud of cigarette smoke hanging over our heads. The figure of Ms Bartlett walking toward me was indeed a refreshing sight. Her blonde hair swung freely over her broad shoulders, her white suit a flag of sanity in the chaos.

"Thank you for coming," she smiled, turning to walk away.

"Wait," I said, touching her shoulder. "What's going to happen with Jayla?"

"Oh, she'll probably get thirty days in jail and the rest on probation."

"But the District Attorney asked for two years."

"No," she immediately countered. "I'm dealing with him and he'll recommend otherwise. Usually it's thirty days." Standing erect and poised, not a hair out of place, she seemed indomitable.

"And what about vocational training and therapy? Will that be part of his recommendation? Jayla desperately needs work, you know that."

The lawyer looked over my head at the crowd, as though searching for someone. "The state has excellent programs for such people. I'm going to make sure an agency helps her find a job and furthers her education. I've already handled three other child abuse cases this week, you know." Taking a step backward, she added, "Goodbye now." She shook my hand summarily and turned away in haste, her white suit lost in the crowd.

"I was nervous," Jayla admitted, sliding into the front seat of the truck beside me. "But the Lord was on my side."

"I would have fainted right there! You didn't seem nervous at all."

Tapping my shoulder, she laughed, then added seriously, "Well, that's because, when I stand up there, it's a trial before Man, but I'm on trial every day before the true judge, My Lord."

I started the truck, not wanting to look at her.

"So, what do you think, Clem?"

I pulled out of the parking lot onto Main Street, watching the courthouse disappear in the mirror.

"It was okay," I conceded, concentrating on the road. We drove over the stone bridge leading us out of town. "I guess the judge has plenty of documentation explaining the situation." I paused, wondering whether I should tell her what the lawyer said.

"That's right, Clem." The long line of trees shaded her face as we passed underneath. A healthy greenness enveloped us again. "Documents or not, I know the Good Lord is keeping me out of jail. I got to see my kids and take care of Glenn."

"Jayla," I began hesitantly, "the lawyer says you'll probably get thirty days."

Shocked, her head spun around to face me, then she turned away. "She said that?"

I nodded slowly.

"She didn't tell me any such thing!" Jayla cried, panicked. "I lost my will to live after just one night in their jail." She peered out the window as if she was lost and was trying to remember the way. Defiantly, her jaws clamped shut. "Well," she declared, "I just ain't going to think about that!"

The noise of the engine droned monotonously between us.

"What did you think of the judge?" she finally managed in a milder tone.

"He was all right. I wasn't sure if you followed all the gobbledygook. I didn't."

"You ain't kidding, girl," she chuckled. "I thought he was nice, though. He seemed like the kind of man who might understand a woman's situation."

"What was your other judge like?"

"Oh, he was simple, I mean simple! He was cracking jokes right there in the courtroom, smack dab in the middle of my arraignment. Plus, he acted like he was angry at me or something. Can you believe that? Then, right in the middle of the whole thing, he started sweet-talking my lawyer, telling her how pretty she looked and what nice clothes she had on. I mean simple, Clem, just like that."

Jayla stared out the window without speaking. A feeling of gloom had settled over us since I mentioned the thirty days. "It's bad," she finally decided, pensively rubbing a smudge from the windshield. "I get a different judge every time and the new one can't possibly know all the details of my case. Anyway, how's they to know what's going on outside of them courtrooms? Those judges never really understand, not like your friends who see you working up to it every day. They don't hear the kids screaming and yelling when you only got a dollar left. They don't see you dragging them to visit your man in prison so they can have some kinda family. I tell you, I just couldn't handle it no more, as much as I loved my children. You should of seen us! Trying to catch a bus to Lorton with the Pampers, the strollers, the bottles and everything. By the time I'd get up even with the bus, the doors would slam right in my face or I'd have to stand the whole way holding them babies. It was horrible! But they don't understand none of that, sittin' in the courtroom."

Trying to get a grip on her emotions, Jayla hugged her waist, then resumed in a softer voice. "There's so much I don't understand about myself. I got a lot of anger inside. I'm going to a psychiatrist now, but she only deals with day-to-day problems. She can't help me dig down deep. Plus. I don't trust her."

"Why not?"

Concentrating on her answer, Jayla watched the country road swiftly change to a four-lane highway. A shopping mall materialized on the horizon, indicating the city was nearby. A flashy billboard advertised the site of the latest housing development, complete with hot tubs and private golf course, only a half hour from the office downtown.

"Well, she went to my social worker and started talking about getting my tubes tied. I think she should have talked to me first! I already had them tied anyway, but that's my private business. After that, I don't trust her no more. I mean, there might be some things I talk about that I don't want my social worker to know, if you see what I mean."

Jayla shifted her weight, glancing at the gray metropolis shimmering before us. "I don't even know my real age, name, or birthplace. I don't know nothin' about me when I was young. There are so many years I can't remember, it scares me. I don't remember no hugs or kisses from my foster parents. There probably wasn't none, because my foster father was a man who drank himself to death on vodka, but it's all a blank now. Ain't nobody watched me close enough, so who really knows the truth?

"One thing I do remember and that was when I was about fourteen. The director at my institution had sex with me. I was afraid, so I didn't say nothin' at first. Then he kept coming after me. I didn't know what to do, so I told his wife. 'Don't you come round here spreading your dirty lies!' she screamed. She beat me with an extension cord 'til I promised to shut up about it. Now I guess I am too scared to remember 'cause all those years are one big blank. I'm still looking for the answers every day 'cause I want a family. I know I got to learn how to love, and don't ever kid yourself, Clem, loving is something a human being has got to learn. There ain't no jail going teach me that, Glenn and Porky maybe, but there ain't no jail."

# Justice for All

The checkerboard pattern of the floor tiles stared back at me as the hands of the clock paused at eight. Without the normal crowd of witnesses and defendants, the antechamber of the courtroom appeared ornate. For the first time, I noticed the bronze chandeliers, the heavy oaken doors. I could almost feel the ideals of law and order and justice for all in the strong walls and high ceilings. The black and white tiles echoed the belief. The distant murmurs of office workers so early in the morning were reassuring as they wrote out someone's fate. Fate? Well, Jayla's, it seemed, was sealed the moment she was born. I wondered, while waiting on the day of the sentencing, if she ever had a chance to become someone other than who she was. At the most, considering her past, she might have made it through life without having to go to jail. But that's not the way it happened.

I lit another cigarette and suddenly spotted Glenn striding down the hall looking left and right like a person at an airport searching frantically for his gate. "Hey, Glenn!" I called out, jumping up to grab his arm. He stopped and looked at me with a befuddled expression.

"I'm Clem," I explained. "We met at the wedding and we've talked on the phone."

"Oh yeah, Clem. Wait here a minute, they're comin.'"

Anxiously, he peered into the empty courtroom, then swirled around and raced down the hall. He jolted to an abrupt halt as Jayla walked out of the elevator and headed our way, her eyes glued to the floor. Glenn's mother, Porky, waddled up behind, her pear-like body stuffed into a pair of skintight burgundy slacks.

"Clem!" Jayla called out as she looked up, then rushed forward to hug me. "I'm so glad you made it. Thanks so much for coming." Quickly composing herself, she turned slightly toward Porky to introduce us. "Clem, this is Porky, my mother-in-law."

Shaking hands, I understood immediately how she earned her nickname. Her flat broad nose was turned up and her eyes, behind thick tinted glasses, looked squinty and small. Smiling politely, she waved her hand, inviting us to all sit down together. Glenn declined, too hyped up to interrupt his frantic pacing.

"Well, look at you grinning," I teased Jayla.

"That's just on the outside," she answered in a husky voice. "I'm so glad you came."

"I am too," I told her, placing my arm around her. "And besides," I cracked, "it never hurts to take a day off from work."

"Ain't that the truth," she laughed, tugging her dress over her knees. "Especially when it's Friday. Does you nice to have three days in a row. And guess what, Clem?" She squeezed my hand like an excited teenager. "I got a job now too, at the Smithsonian, cleanin.'"

"It's a miracle!" I rejoiced.

"The Lord is surely with me. These people are going to see I'm serious 'bout getting my life together. But Glenn," she hesitated, glancing at her husband. "He's been impossible. He didn't sleep at all last night."

"And you could?"

"I slept fine 'cause I was tuckered out from work. Only now my stomach feels a little queasy." She looked up at Ms Bartlett, who had suddenly materialized before us.

"The judge just called in," she cheerily announced. "The sentencing won't begin until ten-thirty."

She flashed us a wooden smile, then vanished again amid the growing crowd, her white suit fluttering. Glenn paused long enough to study her departing form, his eyes two cold black slits. Formally attired in his blue wedding suit, he looked both gallant and awesome as he spun around to pace the floor, jittery as a cat.

"Now look at you," Jayla scolded. "You're going to wear out them shoes."

Glenn glanced over at his wife, then nodded toward the courtroom. "Heh babe, these floors is hard but they ain't nothing compared to the people running this place!" He stepped toward her, his stern expression melting. "It's usually me on this side of the court. Then, I know what I'm doing. But when I ain't the one being judged, I don't know how to act." Stepping closer, he pleaded in cajoling tones. "Can I switch places with you?"

"No!" Jayla protested, pretending to push away his open arms. "I've had enough of that!"

Glenn caressed the back of her neck, then rushed off, mumbling something about calling his halfway house. He strode down the hall, looking warily to either side as though he were being followed.

"Let's go to see who the judge is going to be," Porky suggested, pointing out a wall of official portraits.

I was reluctant to leave Jayla alone, but Porky was already on her way, squinting at the solemn-faced portraits. "I know eyes," she gravely disclosed. "I know them well. You can read a person's soul through their eyes. Now, take this one for instance; I wouldn't trust him for nothing!"

As I studied the judge's pinched expression, Porky nudged me in the side, whispering, "Look over there, Clem." Behind us Jayla was sniffling and dabbing a Kleenex at her eyes. Already back from making his phone call, Glenn sat beside her, stroking her arm. Shaking her head sadly, Porky turned her back on them. "Look like this is going to be a sad day."

I stood there next to Porky and I could feel how much she cared about Jayla; how willing she was to share the little she had to help Jayla survive. It wasn't just the free rent, the food, but it was showing up today, believing in Jayla, helping her the best she could. It was the same goodness and generosity I had seen in jail and with the women I met in Guatemala and Haiti. No matter what the system said or did, these acts of kindness were a shield protecting their lives and their dignity.

"Let's go inside the court," she urged. "Some people is there already."

"Kodak vs Gonzales," a bespectacled clerk announced as we entered the hushed chamber. A tepid atmosphere permeated the room, crammed with White men in suits. A young lawyer angrily jumped up to argue his case before the judge who, to my surprise, was a woman.

Another nudge from Porky prodded my ribs. "A woman judge ain't no good." Porky's pudgy face was inches away from mine. "Women is always harder on other women." Unwilling to elaborate, she slid primly onto the bench beside me.

"I sympathize with your objection," the judge conceded, addressing the young lawyer. "But both parties should sit down together and compare facts. Forget about theories and take this horse by the bit." She rapped her gavel. "See if you can't settle this whole affair outside of my courtroom."

The judge leaned back in her high-backed Naugahyde chair and smiled, her bushy eyebrows arched. Silver-gray hair encircled her once-pretty face. Jayla and Glenn pushed through the doors hand-in-hand and marched bravely to an empty bench in the middle of the courtroom.

"The Board of Education vs Gleason," the clerk announced loudly.

Two new attorneys leaped to their feet, one immediately stepping forward to present his case. The judge gave him her undivided attention, biting her lower lip with concentration. Jayla's lawyer was nowhere in sight. Time dragged on as we heard case after case involving everything from a breach of contract to corporate malfeasance. Through it all, the judge maintained her smile, carefully weighing every nuance of law. Gradually it dawned on me that Jayla's case had no place among these trials and probably wouldn't be heard for quite some time.

As noon approached, Porky stood abruptly to leave. Jayla squirmed on the polished wooden bench, shifting her weight uncomfortably through yet another nearly unintelligible proceeding. Glenn tugged at his tie with exasperation, then they both departed.

"Lord!" Glenn gasped as we huddled outside the courtroom. "This is going take a while. So why the hell did they tell us to come so early? Damn!"

"I got to urinate," Jayla cried, making a beeline for the bathroom.

"And I got to call my halfway house again." Glenn strode off behind her.

As they disappeared into the crowd I lit a cigarette, resigned to the likely prospect of an all-day ordeal. Of course, it wouldn't be so bad if it weren't for the tension … Suddenly Ms Bartlett tapped me on the shoulder.

"Here," she said, handing me a sheaf of papers. "This is the pre-investigation report. The sentencings won't begin until after lunch, so you can come back then." She turned to leave.

"But when will that be?"

"Oh, around one I suppose." She stepped away from me.

"And what about character witnesses?" I tried to ask, but she had already slipped inside a neighboring courtroom.

As Jayla, Glenn, and Porky straggled back, I informed them of the latest postponement. We muttered inanities for a few minutes, nervously passing Jayla's pre-investigation report back and forth. Finally resolving to grab a bite to eat, we advanced toward the exit with Glenn walking ahead like a guide. Most of the morning had gone and absolutely nothing had happened. Porky grunted and complained as her son bolted out the doorway and dashed across the parking lot toward a small tavern.

"Now you got to watch over me, Clem," Jayla mumbled, rolling her eyes, "cause that man of mine is too uptight for anything. And I ain't much better. Oh Lord!"

An intense sun blazed down on the asphalt, but outside, in the fresh air, everyone felt more relaxed. Porky struggled to keep up with our pace, laughing and reproaching herself for being so fat. Birds scavenged among the scattered bits of litter, fluttering off as we approached.

"It be dark in here," Glenn shouted over his shoulder, holding open the bar door. "Porky, you take your sunglasses off!"

The smell of beer and grilled hamburgers assailed us upon entering. The heavy red curtains and dim lighting created such a darkness, we barely made out the tables. Porky and I stood frozen by the door, waiting for our eyes to adjust. Jayla plunged fearlessly ahead, gesturing for us to follow. Cautiously dodging the low-slung tables, she finally halted next to an empty booth.

"This'll be fine," she decided, sitting down. "Now maybe I can read these papers."

"In this light?" Glenn asked, sliding in beside her.

"And I got to eat something too," she continued, ignoring his hand on her shoulder. "When I get tense I got to eat."

"Just like my daughter," Porky sighed, wedging her portly frame next to mine. "She's like her with the cleaning, too. That woman loves to clean!"

"Yeah," Glenn smirked, leaning closer to Jayla. "Her name ain't Mrs Morris. It's Mrs Ajax!" He unconsciously massaged her shoulder, intently studying her slightest move. As her hand turned a page or reached for coffee, as she sighed, frowned or giggled, he doted on every morsel, afraid it might be his last.

"Grrr!" Jayla snarled, startling our waitress as she poured more coffee, "Now what does 'horrendous' mean?" she asked, her finger stuck on a line of the thick document.

"Let me see that," Glenn grabbed at the paper.

"Now hush you! I got to read this myself." She swatted him lightly with the papers.

"What does 'horrendous' mean?"

Glenn stared ahead, his face perplexed.

"It means something terrible, ick," I explained.

"Well, that's how my therapist describes my background!"

"What does it mean?" Porky asked her son.

"You know the word horror?" He put his face close to hers.

She nodded mutely.

"You know the word horrified?"

Again, Porky nodded.

"Well, horrendous comes from that. That's what it means."

Porky touched her lip for a second. "Somethin' awful, it means something awful," she concluded.

"That's right," Glenn proudly replied, looking to Jayla for confirmation.

Porky stared at her cup of coffee. "I need some sweet," she complained.

"Here," Glenn quipped, "let me stick my finger in it." Playfully, she slapped his hand.

"I swear to God!" Jayla blurted out. "They got my whole life written down. My whole life!" Bending over the report, she read on, following each line with her pudgy finger. "It says here that Jayla Morris 'chose' to have an abortion." As though yanked by a string, her head jerked up, her mouth twitching angrily. "I didn't choose nothin' of the kind! They forced me to get an abortion." Annoyed, she roughly folded the papers, then pulled her plate of fries and burger closer to her.

"Let me see that thing," Porky demanded.

"You can have it! I've read enough. I'm just going to think about the Lord being on my side, 'cause the people sure ain't. You know the investigator recommended that I be incarcerated?" She chomped down on her burger.

"Incarcerated?" Porky's baffled again. "What does that mean?"

I stared at her in disbelief. Somehow this word had bypassed her, even though her sons had been in prison off and on for years. Then I realized she was being ironic.

"It means put in jail," Jayla bitterly replied. "All my other recommendations came out fine, but she still believes I should be incarcerated. She called up my boss, my therapist, everyone said I deserved another chance. When I asked her what my recommendation was going to be, she wouldn't tell me at first. 'Find out from your lawyer,' she said. 'Well,' I answered, 'you're the one who's given it so I want to hear it from you!' So, then she told me. Afterwards, she had the nerve to tell me good luck."

"She never asked me nothing," Glenn snapped, affronted.

"And after I explained to her about my past," Jayla continued, "she went to my social worker and said she thought I was lying about not having any family, that I was making up the story to get her sympathy. That's what kinda person she is! Well, thank God for my job. At least it will show them I'm trying."

"Look at this!" Porky cut in shrilly, her beefy index finger glued to a line. "They use this word 'claim' all the time. Now what does 'claaaaaaim' mean?" She dragged out the word, her thick jaw quivering with an angry tic. "It means you ain't nowhere at all! It says here I 'claim' Jayla don't drink or take narcotics.' Well, I don't 'claim' nothing! I say Jayla don't do that! It says I 'claim' Jayla loves her children. I told them Jayla *does* love her children!"

"Yeah," Jayla agreed sarcastically. "They use 'claim' when they want to make me look bad."

"I don't like that word at all," Porky grumbled with mounting suspicion. She squirted some ketchup on her fries, then repeated even louder, "I don't like that word at all."

"Well, they ain't got no feelings," Glenn concluded, pushing away his plate cleaned of food. "None at all!"

"That investigator listened to my whole story," Jayla nodded, "and never asked no question or anything. She just sat there like a big dummy."

A coin clinked into the jukebox and a country and western tune drifted through the sparsely populated tavern. Our waitress hovered over a nearby table, carefully remaking a place. In a flash I realized that for countless defendants, this tiny bar represented the last beer or coffee they'd share with loved ones for many years.

Yanking at his tie and scowling grimly, Glenn continued, "I know how these people is. You make one mistake and that's all they ever want to hear. They just look at your past and not what you're trying to do for yourself now." Locking his hands together, he leaned over the table. "There was a problem in our family, but that investigator didn't ask me nothing, and I'm the husband! I'm the one who knows and loves Jayla the best! But no one talks to me!"

The waitress walked past our table, carrying two frothy mugs of beer.

Realizing that his anger only heightened Jayla's anxiety, Glenn laughed, throwing his arm around her shoulders. "But that judge is a woman," he crooned. "So maybe if I get close enough and looks at her with these sexy eyes."

"Nigger, you something else!"

"He certainly is," Porky readily agreed. "He ain't been nothing but trouble since the day he was born. Why, I can remember when Glenn was just a boy and I got a phone call from the police. 'We got your son down here,' they said. 'We caught him peeing in the alley and you got to pay ten dollars to get him out!' 'Ten dollars!' I yelled. 'Well, that's too much!' 'What you say, ma'am?' they asked. 'I said ten dollars is too much. You can keep him!'" Our laughter briefly interrupted her story. Glenn smiled mischievously as she continued. "Ten dollars for peeing in an alley, they'll get you for anything! Well, I went to bed and a few hours later he came on in home. 'Porky,' he asked me, 'what you tell those people?'"

Jayla doubled over laughing while Glenn smiled smugly, raising his collar with mock embarrassment. Jerking his head back, he suddenly announced. "It's time to go back. Come on!"

"Man, you is nervous," Jayla complained. "Now, you sure you don't want something else?"

"Just you," he moaned in a husky voice.

"Well, you can't have any of that now!" Edging away from him, she dug some cash out from her purse. "This should cover the bill plus a tip for the waitress."

"I'll give her a tip," he joked, clutching the bills. "A tip of my hat." Still chuckling, he strutted off to pay the cashier.

Porky squeezed out of the booth, mumbling under her breath as she brushed off her sweater. Her purse, a gaudy imitation alligator skin, dangled awkwardly from her arm. Jayla, more composed after our laughter, led us out into the glaring sun. A heavy cloudbank loomed over the horizon but the sunlight, reflected off the concrete, seared our eyes. The odor of car exhaust stung our nostrils. We approached the courthouse in silence until Glenn came running up to us from behind.

"Porky!" he yelled. "Go put some money in that parking meter while I call."

Porky wheeled around with her hands planted on her hips. "Well, look at you!" she angrily snapped. "Telling me what to do!"

Glenn roughly grabbed her elbow. "Lookie here."

"God Almighty!" Jayla shouted, scaring the pair of them. "You people is too tense." Pausing for a moment, she appraised them both with a critical eye. "I got to go to court," she declared, stomping away.

Glenn released Porky to quickly follow his wife. "Honey," he called to her back. "You're right. At all times, we got to keep cool." Jayla halted at the doorway and turned to face him. "Yeah, babe, you're so right. And just remember when we are in there that you are married to the coolest thing alive." He gallantly opened the door as Jayla scowled, then secretly winked at me.

Together, we marched back into the courthouse, strengthened by our temporary escape from this day's ugly purpose. The judge passed us in the hallway, smiling sympathetically when she overheard Porky grumbling about her aching feet. Reclaiming our places in the antechamber, we resigned ourselves to another wait. It was well past one o'clock, but the courtroom was still deserted.

"Now let me see here," Porky mumbled, unfolding a newspaper. She flipped to the funnies, which I read along with her, leaning against her shoulder. Jayla and Glenn cuddled in the corner on the bench. After the comics, the race results, then the advertising supplements appeared.

"Now what's going on over there?" Porky suddenly demanded.

Jayla withdrew her lips from Glenn's. "Oh, we just communicatin'."

"Communicatin'!" Porky repeated, feigning disbelief. "Well, that ain't what I call communicatin'! I call that hanky pank!" Perusing the discount coupons, she added out of the corner of her mouth, "Boy, you musta got that from your daddy." She ruffled the newspaper like she was shaking out laundry. "Well," she said, handing Jayla the real estate classifieds, "you read this 'cause I got to go to the bathroom again. Lord! My nerves!"

Glenn softly caressed the back of Jayla's head. "And I got to call my halfway house," he murmured, then bounded after his mother.

"Come on, Clem. Let's check out these ads together."

I sat down beside her, watching her finger slide over the columns. Occasionally she read the ones from suburban Maryland aloud. She wanted to live there, miles from the District line, so Glenn would be far from the temptation of the streets. Ironically, Glenn was to be a free man the next day, after four years. For the first time since their wedding, Jayla and Glenn would genuinely be together as man and wife, unless … Jayla's finger kept scanning the columns. "Gaithersburg is too far away, if you don't got a car," she mused. "You know, I saw an ad for College Park, a two bedroom for four hundred dollars. Now that ain't bad, is it?"

"Not too bad," I mumbled, looking away as my stomach tightened.

The judge seemed efficient and capable of compassion. Yet, Jayla's lawyer had neither rehearsed her testimony nor asked for character witnesses. I had discussed the case with an attorney friend who was very skeptical. "The bottom line," he finally conceded, "is how much justice a client can afford." Jayla read to herself, her lips silently forming each word. My skin felt hot and flushed from the tension of waiting, from my fear of the outcome. I was very edgy, yet Jayla remained calm. Perhaps because she had been through this so many times with her friends. Perhaps it was her faith in the Lord.

"Someday," she sighed wistfully, "Glenn and me are gonna have our own place. You'll come to visit, and we'll laugh about these old times in court." Chuckling contentedly at the thought, she turned to the employment section.

"Yeah," I muttered. Unable to look her in the face, I stared blankly ahead. Ms Bartlett stood by the courtroom door gossiping with her friend, the handsome District Attorney. Beyond them I could see inside the court, the clerk's hunched shoulders and the windows behind him filling up with gray clouds.

"I really like my new job," Jayla continued chattering. "I got to be there in the morning by six o'clock but, praise the Lord, it turned out a neighbor drives that way every day, so I can have a ride. Otherwise, I couldn't do it." She folded up the newspaper on her lap. "The Lord is surely with me, getting a job just in time to show these people I'm trying."

"And what exactly do you do?"

"Oh, you know, cleaning out the bathrooms and all that stuff. In the afternoons there ain't much to do. My supervisor knows that but we're suppose to stick around. What you got to do is walk around like you're doing something, you know, carrying a mop or a sponge. I only been in trouble once and that was in the afternoon. I stopped to talk to this other woman, you see. She went into the bathroom to fetch a broom when all of a sudden my supervisor came around the corner and there I was stuck! 'Jayla Morris!' she yelled. 'You better look busy!' Well, I learned my lesson and I ain't going to walk around with nothing in my hands no more. I always keep the Ajax or a rag with me now. My supervisor knows we ain't hardly got work."

"Come on," Glenn interjected, taking Jayla's arm. "We got to go inside now. Come on sweetheart."

Porky sauntered up beside me as Glen and Jayla disappeared through the doors. Unlike this morning, the benches inside were empty except for three other Blacks. Just like the cop at the Muncipalidad with Teresa, a bored cop, furtively smacking his gum, lolled by the door to the judge's chamber. The judge, draped in her black robe, peered down at a young Black man flanked by two White attorneys. The room darkened noticeably as ominous thunderheads rolled by the window.

Ms Bartlett, the defendant's lawyer, stepped back as the judge declared, "Twenty-two years old and you do something like this! Do you have anything to say?"

Glenn sat on Jayla's right-hand side while I sat to her left. Porky slid onto the last bench, evidently figuring we'd have to wait a few more hours.

"I want my family back." The young man's voice resounded hollowly through the vacant courtroom. A patter of rain slapped against the windows, tap, tap, tapping away each moment. "I hurt my boy, but I hurt myself worse. I need help but I want to stay with my family. They all I got."

Glenn shot me a sidelong glance. I saw his body stiffening as he sat straighter on the bench. The rain beat more ferociously against the windowpane, mincing the young man's words. "My family is all I got."

"You got aspra?" Jayla suddenly leaned over and whispered in my ear.

"Do I have what?"

"Do you have aspra?"

"An aspirin?" I asked, annoyed by her question. The young man was a child abuser and I wanted to observe the judge's reaction.

"No, do you have asthma?"

"Asthma?" I repeated, chuckling.

"Yeah, you're breathing so hard." She shielded the remark behind her crumpled Kleenex.

"I'm just nervous," I whispered back. "I'm trying to hear what the judge is saying."

Shrugging her shoulders, Jayla leaned back on the bench with a faraway look in her eyes. The lawyers rattled off their closing arguments now, but she wasn't listening. Instead, brooding, she stared out the window at the heavy clouds assembling. Torrential sheets of rain pounded on the glass, a desperate sound. I wondered whether she even heard the judge.

"Although assault is normally considered a serious offense," she began, "for me child abuse is always the worst ..."

The downpour drowned out the rest of her sentence, sweeping me into Jayla's dark moody world. I glanced over at Glenn. He was leaning forward, squinting as if to absorb each word. Beads of sweat covered his forehead. Feeling my gaze upon him, he looked sharply at me, a wordless hatred of the system screaming through his entire body.

"... it is an assault against something weak and defenseless. There couldn't be anything worse. I just don't understand it."

The defendant reiterated his pleas while the cop ambled up behind him, a pair of handcuffs gleaming from his belt. The man's wife, close by, hid her head in her hands.

"And some people say," the judge continued in sardonic tones, "that therapy will help, that employment will help. They say this is a social problem." Drawing out the words, she carefully enunciated every syllable. "Well, I for one, don't believe it. Three years in prison for you and don't ever forget what you've done. Never do it again." She banged her gavel and a sob burst out behind us. The wife bent over as if she'd been maimed. Jayla's name was called while the cop led the young man away, his head hanging limp over his chest. Glenn's hand slid over to grasp Jayla's the moment before she left. Facing him, she smiled.

Suddenly the sky split open, and I gasped. A blazing white streak flashed across the parking lot, then a deafening crash.

Frightened, Jayla stepped back, staring ahead into the near darkness. The overhead lights had gone out, but her name was repeated as if from a black hole. Her silhouette slowly inched toward Ms Bartlett's white suit. The rain beat against the window, rattling it. I sat stiffly, unable to believe, as Jayla's quivering voice resounded through the courtroom, that they thought it possible to mediate justice surrounded by darkness.

"I don't have no birth certificate," Jayla answered Ms Bartlett question as lights flickered overhead.

"And why is that?"

"'Cause I don't got no family," Jayla answered, patches of flickering light moving across her face.

"And you tried to find your birth certificate?"

"Yes, ma'am."

Ms Bartlett's white suit was a steady radiance of light in the darkened courtroom.

"And where were you raised?" The fluorescent lights began to wink back on. Jayla lowered her head, eyes blinking rapidly. "Where were you raised?"

"In foster homes," she replied.

The judge leaned back in her chair, rubbing her chin while Ms Bartlett interrogated Jayla about her past. The questions came at her like bullets while she responded with single syllables, guarding her personal history from the enemy. If only Jayla could speak up! If only she would express her plight! Yet no one practiced this moment with her, warned her what to say. If only she could defend herself!

Ms Bartlett, after her barrage of questions, stepped back. The judge lifted herself in her chair then leaned forward, studying Jayla. A patter of rain was the only sound.

"How do you feel about your children, Mrs Morris?" the judge asked. Her question sounded cunning.

Jayla raised her eyes and looked at the judge. A knotted mound bulged on her forehead as she struggled to concentrate. She licked her lips and replied, "Your Honor, I love my children."

"Now then," the judge settled back in her chair again, satisfied. "How is it that a mother who loves her children can abuse them? That I just don't understand."

Jayla's chest heaved painfully. "Have you ever loved your children," she began now in her normal deep voice, "and found yourself with problems? You want to give them everything you can," Glenn squirmed in his seat, one arm holding his stomach as if he had been hit. Now she will say it. Now they will understand. "Have you ever loved your children and not been able to give them what they need?"

"That happens to every parent," the judge answered flatly.

Jayla stared boldly at her, then hastily looked away. Her large body slumped, defeated by the courtroom. She clenched her jaw, shutting them out as she once shut me out, withdrawing into herself. In a voice coming from someone else, she continued. "That's how it was for me. There was no clothes for school, no money ..." Her voice faded.

The judge nodded.

Soon Porky was called to testify on Jayla's behalf. To the best of her ability, she answered the questions. Smiling politely and sitting up straight in the witness stand, she told it "like it is." Despite her best efforts, her testimony at times was almost too colloquial to be understood in this courtroom. The judge's eyes glazed over. My spirit sank.

Glenn walked swiftly to the stand, impatience tugging at his wiry body. His handsome face was locked in a stern expression. Answering questions in an iron voice, his left eye twitched as he struggled to restrain his deep-seated hostility. The DA asked him a few questions, but when he was finished, Glenn's hand shot up in the air.

"I'd like to say something, your Honor," he blurted out.

"Go right ahead, Mr Morris." The judge moved some papers across her desk, her thin lips pursed. She was prepared to listen.

"Your Honor," he began in a studied voice. "I know institutions and the violence inside of them. I, myself, have been incarcerated for four years." His voice was cool and easy, just like he told Jayla to be. Glenn was employing all the diction he'd acquired after countless legal proceedings. My hopes rose again interlacing with my confusion. "Your Honor asked my wife how she could love her children and still abuse them. Well, while this was going on I was in prison. Jayla was there, alone, trying to manage. She had the problem of her man in prison, of no job or security. There were problems with the children, but you have to work with the family to solve these problems. Yet no one spoke to me or asked about my feelings. Jayla hurt our children, but I am going to continue to support her while she makes some changes.

"My wife, your Honor, is not a violent person." His eyes, usually so watery, were dry, demanding that this woman understand. "She has come a long way, without any family, as a single mother. Since she started living with my mother, Jayla has come to know love. The institutions will only teach her more hatred. She needs the love I am giving to her. Our children have forgiven her and so have I. Your Honor, the institutions are filled with criminals and my wife is not a criminal. Let the family work this out together."

The courtroom was dead silent except for the stenographer tapping away at his machine. Now the rain descended in a slow, steady drizzle. Jayla shifted positions awkwardly, her Kleenex sopped in sweat. The cop walked up behind her.

The judge observed Glenn without a comment, her slender fingers tapping thoughtfully against the desk. "That's all?" she asked softly. "Thank you." Then she looked at Jayla.

"Mrs Morris, I'm going to let you off easy," the judge began. "In my eyes, child abuse is the most serious crime a person can commit. I want you never to forget it." She paused, appraising Jayla's bent head. Then she rapped her gavel, declaring, "Three years."

The handcuffs clicked.

There was a yelp, a painful yelp. Jayla bent over slightly. Glenn leaped up, clutching her purse. The policeman whisked her away by the elbow. Glenn bolted out the door, Jayla's sobs trailing behind. Porky raced out of the room faster than I had ever seen her move. It all happened so quickly. I looked around me at the empty courtroom.

In a moment, I was in the hallway where I could see Glenn standing outside the judge's chambers, still hugging Jayla's purse as though it were her. His eyes were brimming with tears now. He was going to be strong, though. Not here, not in front of the authority he despised. The judge, disrobed and smoking a cigarette, walked out of her office. Porky immediately leaped to her side.

"Your Honor, excuse me. Please, your Honor," her desperate voice pleaded. "I'd like to talk to you."

The judge turned to face Porky. Although nearly the same age, they were both quite distinct in their separate ways. The White woman studied Porky's face, then swirled to leave.

"The decision has been made!" Her high heels clicked against the floor.

"But your Honor," Porky begged, pursuing the judge. "I'm the grandmother of those children." Her urgent requests finally lassoed the retreating woman to a halt. "I know Jayla well and prison just don't help a person like that. I been helping her and now all my work is going down the drain. That prison'll ruin Jayla. Lord have mercy! I'm the grandmother and I know what's good for them kids!"

The judge, a woman dressed like any other, was momentarily

stunned by the passion fueling Porky's outburst. As she responded, the firmness returned to her face. "Everyone knows how I feel about child abuse. They knew that before today's sentencing. The only way your daughter-in-law will appreciate the seriousness of her crime is by being locked up. That is my decision! How else can I prevent her from doing it again?"

"Your prison is going to ruin all the work I done," Porky wailed.

"Did you see those children?" the judge hissed between her teeth. "The baby had a fractured skull and three broken ribs! That is a deadly assault, an assault against a defenseless creature. Do you understand?"

Glenn leaned against the wall, restraining himself. Despite his teary eyes, I was afraid of him. He was quite capable of beating the judge to a bloody pulp. And if he didn't, who else would be mugged instead? He was gray at the temples and starting to have a protruding belly. Porky lowered her eyes. The judge spun around and stalked off in a huff.

Several minutes later, we were all inside Porky's car as the rain pattered across the roof. We waited silently for a letup so I could walk back to my truck. Yellow stuffing poked out of the car seats with gobs of silver electric tape dangling uselessly from the holes. We watched the water roll down the windshield, a gray wall between us and the world.

"No feelings," Glenn muttered. "No feelings at all." The corners of his mouth formed a sneer. He glared at Porky and me, then stared off again.

"I tried to reason with that judge," Porky sniffled. "But you can't say too much. If you go too far, they'll put you behind bars." She patted the newspaper on her lap, leaving the wet imprint of her hand.

"That's right," Glenn spat out. "Ain't no nigger allowed to talk back. They killed the only man who spoke the truth!" His fists clenched, the dark knuckles yellowing. "I never trusted that lawyer and I told Jayla I didn't like her. She never called Jayla or nothing." Suddenly he threw open the door. "I got to go see when the visiting hours are, wait here."

Holding the newspaper over his head, he vanished behind a wall of rain. Porky wiped the windshield meticulously, but foggy blotches remained. The windows on the passenger side wouldn't close completely, letting the water drip through like a leaky faucet. I shivered, folding my arms over my chest. Porky futilely wiped the windshield again.

"I told that judge everything I could. Prison ain't no place for a woman like Jayla. But these things happen all the time and there ain't nobody leading us out of it. No, that man already dead!"

I couldn't answer Porky. The faces of Jayla and the judge swirled through my head as tears streamed down my face. Jayla—what else could she do in her situation? In a motherly gesture, Porky handed me her soggy Kleenex. And the judge, what choices did she have? She couldn't let Jayla off. She couldn't put her in a rehabilitation program because there weren't any. She only had one option: to punish the individual and disregard the massive abuse of society.

"But you've already been through this before," I observed sadly.

She looked at me hard, stopping my tears by staring at me in that fierce way.

"I mean, as Glenn's mother ..."

"No," she countered sharply. "I never done this way before. My son was a criminal and had to be punished. Jayla's a fine woman and she come up by living with us. No, I ain't never done this way!"

The door flew open abruptly and a newspaper plopped on the backseat. Glenn jumped in, breathing heavily, his eyes bloodshot. "Visiting hours ain't 'til eight o'clock," he mumbled.

Porky wiped the windshield again with resigned strokes. "Well," she consoled, "a three-year sentence means she'll be out in six months."

"Porky," he yelled. "I told you to get out of that TV!"

She shrugged her shoulders, resting her calloused hands on the tattered seat. The pelting downpour shattered our gloomy silence.

"Now they're going to have me to deal with," Glenn hissed. "They ain't faced that yet but now they going to have to!"

I began to gather my things, discreetly patting Porky's arm goodbye. "I want to tell you," Glenn addressed me, his voice strangely tender, "I'm grateful you been with us today. I know you learned something and, little by little, we got to learn so we can move out of this world where people ain't got no feelings."

His large eyes still glistened with tears as he squeezed my hand, then opened the door. Outside the rain struggled to erase all the oil stains on the pavement, but they remained. And as I walked away, the radio in Porky's car blasted out the song Upside Down. Diana Ross's voice drifted over to me, singing the words round and round.

Those were the perfect words at that moment. Round and round went so many questions in my head as I left their car, so many thoughts and insights. I watched their rickety car grind out of the parking lot and I thought of another context of Jayla's life. A context from my own life, my own past history, my family. It happened years and years ago, but it set the stage ... or maybe it was the same stage, just a different era.

It was a story about my great-grandfather, James Rollins, who once served in the House of Representatives and was so instrumental in ensuring the continuation of the University of Missouri that he's called "The Father of the University of Missouri." As a state legislator, he worked tirelessly to pass the Missouri Compromise because he was "opposed to all kinds of human merchandise." He helped stop slavery, I was told. And I once read a report that confirmed, even as a young lawyer, he dared to speak against slavery.

The report stated that on August 12, 1853, a Friday, in Columbia, Missouri, a crime was committed just as it was getting dark. On that day, Miss Nancy Hubbard, a fifteen-year-old White girl and her married sister, Mrs Mary Jacobs, with her little daughter, Amanda, were returning from a funeral. Miss Hubbard dismounted from her horse to open a gate when a completely naked Black man jumped out of the thicket and attempted to rape her. Miss Hubbard struggled with her attacker and succeeded in fighting him off. He fled back into the bushes but this scuffle spooked Mrs Jacob's horse. It threw her and her daughter onto the ground. The daughter ran for help into a neighbor's house but by the time they returned the assailant was nowhere in sight. The White community went into an uproar and scoured the neighborhood immediately to protect Miss Hubbard and to find her attacker. They seized then released a number of Black men, suspects, before settling on Hiram, a slave. Hiram's lawyer, James Rollins, was my great-grandfather.

Obvious questions must have faced him immediately. First: was any Black man, a slave in pre-Civil War Missouri, suicidal enough to rape a White girl? Not only that, but to rape her in front of witnesses in the middle of the day? Second: Would a completely nude attacker lurk in the bushes? Answer to both questions: Implausible. Yet that day in August, the White community took Miss Hubbard's tale in earnest and sealed Hiram's fate.

After a week in jail, on Saturday August 20, 1853, Hiram was handcuffed and brought to the courthouse. He had to walk past a threatening crowd, then into a courtroom that was packed with agitated spectators. At about 3 pm, the bloodthirsty crowd outside the courthouse became so enflamed that it burst into the courtroom, grabbed Hiram, threw a rope around his neck and started to drag him out to hang him; but Rollins, his lawyer, managed to slash it off. Hiram was noosed again and hauled over to a nearby wood. Rollins raced after the crowd, stood before them and begged them to allow Hiram a just trial. His eloquence was such that the mob actually listened to him and returned Hiram to the sheriff to wait in jail for a "fair" trail.

But that night, while Hiram was sitting in jail, he mysteriously had a change of heart and "confessed" to the crime. By Monday, when the trial resumed, the rabble stormed the courtroom again. The lawyers calmed them enough that they retreated outdoors to convene a meeting, in front of the courthouse, to decide on Hiram's fate: should he be burned to death? Be hung? Or—better yet— castrated? They decided to hang him. By the time they made the decision, he was back in the jail so they broke into the jail, dragged him off and hung him in a nearby grove.

Rollins had tried to give him a fair trial, but he was also a man of his times and wasn't going to risk his life with the mob.

My great-grandfather went on to represent other Black men and women, with better outcomes. In Congress and in public, he repeated his truth that he was "opposed to all kinds of human merchandise" observing that slavery was "a cankerous ulcer, baleful to the body politic wherever it existed."

Yet in the stories about James Rollins, what no one ever mentioned was that my great-grandfather owned thirty-four slaves. Thirty-four living, breathing human beings. How disgusted and betrayed I felt when I learned the truth about this man. It is a mortifying display of hypocrisy at its worst. And what contradictions he must have lived with. Fighting against slavery yet owning slaves. Was this contradiction lost on him? Lost on the people around him? Yet I understood his stance because I was living those contradictions too. Sitting in that courtroom with Jayla or talking with Larian and Teresa. I tried to help by looking for a lawyer, working in their communities, giving money at times. But like Rollins, I was fearful to take that extra step and I was confused what that step might be, so, like Rollins, I was willing to live with my contradictions. Jayla, like Hiram, was in jail and who knew what could be next for her. The sad fact was that the situation really hadn't changed for African

Americans. Yet how to respond? The problem felt so much larger than any of us. Present-day slavery, climate change, violence against women. We are so embedded in systems that we are born into—the religious, cultural, economic scaffolding that shapes our lives—that it is hard to extract ourselves.

I started up the truck thinking any of us can have the best intentions to change society but how to actually disengage ourselves is a very different question. Sometimes it seems impossible.

# A Visit

Agonizing weeks went by. I only heard from Glenn. Almost every day I vainly attempted to contact Ms Bartlett about pushing for a reconsideration of Jayla's sentence. True to her elusive nature, the lawyer never returned my calls. As far as she was concerned, I presumed, the case was closed. Finally, Jayla called, inviting me to visit her at Jessup's Women's Detention Center. The length of the journey and the stress of seeing Jayla locked up persuaded me to bring my sister Phoebe along as one objective, familiar presence—at least on my initial visit.

"She's written a few letters," I explained to Phoebe as we cruised down the highway toward Jessup. "At first, they only let her make one phone call a week, but now she gets more. Sometimes we're cut off because they only allow her five minutes."

My sister remained silent as she turned onto the exit ramp, slowly passing a dingy truck stop surrounded by idle tractor-trailers. We were deep in rural Maryland now, far from the capital's congested streets. "And when she does phone," I added, "it has to be collect, which means if her friends are poor, they can't afford to talk with her. Not only that, but how could they possibly visit her way out here without a car?"

Phoebe turned onto a shady tree-lined street. I looked out the window. Tiny wooden houses with breezy porches and immaculate lawns zipped by. The sleepy hamlet reminded me of the sort of place Jayla always dreamed of moving to. We passed a field spotted with wildflowers, then a sign for Jessup leaped into view. We made a sharp turn and bounced along a narrow, twisting country road.

"And how is she adjusting to life in prison?" Phoebe asked, concerned.

"It's hard to tell. She hasn't told me much. When she first arrived, they put her in 'quarantine' for a week. She was alone all the time and could only leave her cell once a day for a shower. Then she was put in a dorm with fifteen other women, which was hard on her. Finally, they moved her to a cottage with seven other prisoners. She has a room to herself, which they call 'the closet' because it's so small. It's pretty rough in there, though. One night she hung her blouse up to dry in the bathroom and found it the next morning ripped to shreds."

"God!" Phoebe exclaimed as we pulled into the prison parking lot. She stopped the truck and we stared out the window in silence. A huge storm fence stretched as far as we could see in either direction. Strung along the top was a jagged length of barbed wire glaring like bared metal teeth. Behind the fence was a squat building that resembled an elementary school, apparently used for offices. Across the green, manicured lawn was an old-fashioned courthouse with a white bell tower. An impersonal sterility pervaded the grounds. Everything had been swept and polished, but not a human being in sight. Even the white puffy clouds looked artificial as they lingered over this technological feat. Abandoning the truck, we slammed the doors, disturbing the uncanny silence of the place.

A plump Black man in khaki sat inside a booth next to the enormous gates. He took our IDs, mumbling gruffly to himself as he ran his beefy finger over a prepared list of visitors. Slapping my driver's license on the counter, he muttered, "Sign these papers."

"Is this your real name?" he asked Phoebe.

"Yes," she replied, smiling.

"Well, lady, you can't come in," he informed her curtly.

"I don't under—"

"Regulations," he grunted. "Your name isn't on the list."

"But can't you contact the prisoner," I began to appeal, "and get her permission?"

"Look lady, regulations say no!" He stood up inside the booth and turned his back to us.

"Phoebe," I began.

"It's okay," she assured me, crinkling her nose. "I'll get some coffee in town. You go ahead." Then she added under her breath, "But there's no reason for him to be so rude."

A loud jangling of keys startled me. The guard stood by the gate, waiting impatiently. "You going to come or not!"

I nodded and quickly walked past him, afraid lest I jeopardize my chance to see Jayla. The gate clattered roughly behind me.

I walked to the squat building where I signed more forms and was handed a pass. They sent me through some swinging doors to a large room that resembled a cafeteria. A woman guard ambled up, took my pass and ordered me to sit in the center of the room. Clusters of families and couples were scattered around me, chatting, smoking, and sipping on Pepsis as though they were in their living room. Vending machines were neatly lined up in a row against a yellow wall.

The woman guard returned to her seat by a huge picture window that looked out over the "campus" as Jayla called it. On the opposite side of the room there were lavatories for visitors. A warning sign printed in red marker announced: No Items Can Be Passed Between Visitors and Inmates Under Penalty of Law. Another one warned: Soda Cans Not Allowed in Restroom.

I tried to imagine Jayla's entrance into this world. Before being placed in quarantine, she was strip-searched, ordered to bend over, her body searched then disinfected. Then questions, handcuffs, prison clothes, cops leading her from place to place, then quarantining her like an animal. After days and days alone in quarantine, she finally faced the other prisoners— other prisoners—women who, because of their colour, and because they live in a society which criminalises the symptoms of poverty, ended up addicted to drugs or resorting to theft or violence—victims dislodged by the system.

Suddenly the door flew open and Jayla walked with long, decisive steps into the room. The huge smile on her face quickly transformed into a scowl as she marched up to the matron and handed in her yellow pass. But when she wheeled around to face me again, her pleased expression returned. We embraced and I stepped back, astonished. She looked lovely.

"My God, do they have a beauty parlor in this place?" I asked her, laughing. "You look great, Jayla!"

"Aw, Clem," she answered, bashfully bowing her head.

"Really Jayla! You look so pretty. And you have lost some weight!"

"Well, it's true, I guess." She grinned and I noticed that the familiar rash on her forehead was gone. Even her wrinkles seemed to have disappeared. It was this place, of course. The strain of the children, the unpaid bills, the tiny apartment, the constant job hunting had all vanished. No need to hide the knowledge from herself and others that she had been convicted of abusing her children. "I am happy to see you, Clem. It's so nice of you to come."

Sitting beside her, I prattled on nervously, a deluge of useless information about my personal affairs. She nodded, responding politely to my news report. I felt cautious, like I was visiting a friend in the hospital, scared I might ask the wrong question.

"And I talked to Glenn a few times on the phone. How are you two doing?" I finally inquired.

"Well," she began, looking down at her skirt, "he ain't been able to see me much 'cause Porky's car broke down. He's only come here once, in fact, and that was right after I first arrived." She drawled out the words sadly.

"Oh Jayla, I should have offered him a ride with me."

"That's okay. You see, Glenn gets mad when other people helps me." She gazed at me grimly, twisting the thin belt of her wrap-around skirt through her fingers. "But what the hell is he doing? He ain't even sent me my clothes. He says he's got them all packed but can't send them 'cause he don't have no money. He lost his job 'cause he didn't show up for two weeks in a row. Still, he don't even got time to write me a letter."

Uncharacteristically, Jayla voiced her anger without bitterness. Her body slumped as she shook her head, bewildered. "He swears he loves me, but I don't believe he know how to spell the word! I call him, my friends call him, but he's never home. My friend Susan phoned him at six in the morning and he still wasn't there. He just goes and stays out all night. He says he was running round town trying to get the kids, but I ain't seen them yet, so who knows what's going on in their little minds? Susan arranged to bring them out here once, but Glenn got mad at her and never showed up."

"He's probably on a binge," I told her softly. "After living in prison for so long, he's like a drunken sailor."

"That man got to learn to manage without me standing over him," she shot back. "I don't even want to call him no more, 'cause I got enough on my shoulders already and that just makes it worse. Believe me, Clem, we ain't never gonna fully understand men. I've tried hard since I met Glenn, but I ain't had no luck." She smiled tenderly as her sorrowful eyes scanned the room. A White family next to us munched contentedly on potato chips. "It's really strange in here for me. I got to watch myself all the time or I'll get in trouble for talking to somebody the wrong way. That's why I try to keep myself busy, going to school and religious classes at night. We ain't allowed to make our own food, clean our own place, or even wash our clothes. You see what I mean? I can't be bothered thinking about Glenn all the time."

"You've got someone washing your clothes?" I teased. "I thought they'd have you all hanging over the washboards!"

She chuckled, quickly glancing at my face before returning to her belt strap. "Yeah, they wash our clothes, but I do mine by hand because they make them fade."

"And what about your job? You said you had one now."

"I swear, it's strange. We have to report to the kitchen at two-thirty, but all we do is sit around 'cause people don't come in to eat 'til four o'clock."

"Just like the Smithsonian job, eh?"

"I swear to God! Ain't it strange what they make you do, waiting around all the time, doing nothing! We just sit there and gab. Then at four-thirty we start cleaning."

"Ooooooh," I joked, pinching her side. "You like that cleaning don't you Jayla?"

"Yeah," she answered, giggling. "But guess how much they pay? Seventy-five cents! Then for each day I work, I get out of here quicker. I can buy my freedom!" A disgusted sneer streaked across her lips. "But mostly I read my Bible, trying to keep out of fights."

"You go to church here?"

"Yeah, we got prayer meeting every day and then there's choir."

"I didn't know you sang."

"I really can't," she answered with a timid smile, "but I try. And I say prayers for you too, Clem. Yes, I do," she repeated, nodding her head.

"Well, thank you lady, I know that's going to help me climb the ladder!" We both laughed over my sarcasm, reverting once more to our spontaneous camaraderie.

"I been studying too, but I don't think I'll ever pass those GEDs."

"Of course, you will Jayla!"

"But I never even made it to seventh grade in school."

"Poof!" I scoffed. "You have beautiful handwriting, plus you spell and write pretty well."

"Well," she furtively glanced at her skirt, "I don't know what good it would do anyway. I still can't get no job. They got sewing classes here and I could use that skill, but they're at the same time as my GEDs."

"Stick with the GEDs, Jayla. You'll pass and it helps with a job to have a high school diploma."

"Oh Clem, you just don't understand some things too well. I mean, once you got a record, you don't get nowhere! The girls and I kinda laugh about that 'cause we see girls coming back to Jessup all the time. They release them, you see, and does society try to help them? No, it rubs their noses in what they done. Nobody wants to hire you if you're a criminal." She paused a moment, her chin jutting out with concentration. "Well, I ain't no criminal but I feel like one now 'cause I got a record. And I'm going to keep that record for the rest of my life.

"GEDs can't change all that, but one thing that's helped me is my spiritual studies. Maybe that's why God put me here. I'm helping other girls read the Bible and understand God's word. Most of them come to me and ask for help. It makes me feel good that they can see Jesus living in me, I guess. As long as I am here, God can use me to witness other souls."

She was right again; the system was failing her. Making empty gestures. I shifted uncomfortably in my seat, my shirt sticking to my back. "And what about sports? Are you allowed any exercise?"

She glanced skeptically at me, arching her eyebrows. "There's basketball and once in a while they let us out on campus to wander around. But I don't go in for none of that 'cause that's where the fighting starts. I mean, you might step on a person's toe and a fight'll break out. Some of these girls just ain't regular. You know, like the lifers."

Jayla lowered her voice, looking around the room. "Those lifers just don't care. They might as well just try to escape, 'cause what they got to lose? They can do anything at any time. I try to stay away from them, you see what I mean?"

She quickly looked around again to make sure no one was listening. The matron paced up and down next to the picture window. A Black couple behind us cuddled closer, with a half- suppressed laugh. Jayla turned back to me, mumbling hotly under her breath, "I mean, some of these women is murderers. They killed their husbands or parents or even their babies. I swear to God, you wouldn't believe what they done! But they're all in here for a reason. Why, do you remember about six months ago this nineteen-year-old girl hired four guys to kill her husband? She paid them $100 to do it. Not $100 a piece, $100 between all four of them. Well, she's here. She got natural life. Plus, she's pregnant. Natural life means you got to stay here until you die.

"Then there's another woman who put her baby in the closet for eight years. Can you imagine that? Eight years she kept that kid in a closet, just given it bits to eat! Now I say that woman has something wrong inside of her. I say she's crazy and shouldn't be here! But she is.

"I've come in contact with girls my heart goes out to. I thank God, with all I been through, that I don't have no problem with alcohol or drugs. It would'a been easy for me to get hooked on drinking or shooting, but I never hung around with that crowd. Plus, I was always too poor. Thank God I don't have to deal with those problems too."

Jayla looked at me, shaking her head like an old lady. Then she continued in hushed tones, "I look around here and I see how far I mighta gone. I coulda killed my kids. I heard all about the others and I thank the Lord for stepping in before I put that on my slate. Just think what these women got to live with! Ain't no amount of time in prison going to wipe that memory away. You know, what I done ain't so bad compared to that. But I coulda killed my kids.

"I've been thinking—after I leave here, maybe I can come back and help these women. Now I know what it's like. I want to use my experience to help other women like me. Maybe that's the reason the Lord put me in this place." Despite the brutality of the place, she did look peaceful.

"That's a beautiful idea, Jayla. But," I added slowly, "have you figured out your own feelings? Is there anyone helping you with your own problems?"

"That's exactly what I wrote the judge when I asked her to reconsider my sentence. I need therapy but we don't get none of that here. A child development woman talked to me once, but she ain't come back again and I can't get ahold of her. She ain't called me, so there's nothing I can do. Then there's a shrink. They say he's a ..." giggling, she looked away, whispering out of the side of her mouth, "He's a fag!

"Anyway, I talked to that man once and, even then, he didn't come again to talk with me, I had to ask to see him! He wouldn't say nothing 'cause Glenn wasn't present. Well, I'm the one who's in prison now and I got to work on my own problems! I got to find out about Jayla! So that shrink didn't do me no good.

"That's why I wrote the judge. I told her how sorry I was and that I wanted to learn some new ways. But there ain't no rehabilitation here, there's only violence and more violence. I think the worst punishment so far has been not seeing my kids. I ain't even talked to them by phone. I told that to another woman here and she said she knew what I meant, that when she first came in here, her kids was just babies. Now one of them is five, so she ain't seen them grow or nothing. Maybe she won't even recognize them anymore."

"Well, you'll get out of here sooner than that, Jayla. The teachers at Rose Hill are going to write to the judge too."

"That's great, Clem."

"And you know, Jayla," I reminded her, "you have the right to change lawyers."

"No thanks," she said, shaking her head. "Glenn don't want me doing that 'cause my reconsideration might be delayed. I'll just take my chances with Ms Bartlett and pray for the Lord to be by my side. You see, they might send me to a halfway house and I don't want that 'cause those places ain't no good. The women there is on drugs and stuff, so I'd rather stay here where I already know my way around."

"Well, you look really good, so you must be taking care of yourself. Have you made any friends?"

"I try not to get too close," she warned, "'cause that's how the problems start. There's this one woman who came in the same day as me, about two hours later. We talked and went through processing together, so we sorta became friends. Well, the other day I borrowed a blouse from her. I hadn't cleaned it when her boyfriend came to visit her. So, I was standing there thinking what blouse of mine I could lend her, when this so-called friend of mine walked up. She was working on, what do you call that thing you sew?"

"Embroidery?"

"No."

"Crochet?"

"No, you sew little pictures," she explained, a tinge of exasperation in her voice.

"Ummm, needlepoint?"

"That's it!" she said, slapping her hand on the chair. "Anyway, she's working on this thing and asked me, 'Do you like it, Jayla?' I answer: 'Um, no.' I didn't mean to say that," Jayla chuckled. "I was thinking about the blouse. I wasn't even looking. So, all of a sudden she stomps off shouting, 'Well, kiss my *White ass*!'

"I couldn't believe it. I wouldn't say that to no one. I mean I seen people kill each other over talk like that! That's the lowest thing you can say to anyone and it changed me with her."

"But Jayla," I protested, worried about her safety, "words like that don't matter, not in the long run."

"That's right," she bitterly replied, hardly hearing me. "And then that woman had the nerve to pretend like nothing happened. She came over to sit and talk with me at dinner. I didn't want that! She had disrespected me.

"I couldn't get it off my mind, so one day I asked her to meet me in the bathroom where we could talk. 'Now you ain't ever heard me say those kinda words,' I told her. 'That ain't my way and I expect an apology.' Well, she acted like she hadn't said nothing wrong. Lord! I mean she was shocked that I was thinking about it for so long."

"Some people are like that," I remarked, hoping to quiet her temper.

"Maybe they is, but you don't speak that way to a friend," she retorted. "She apologized, but we ain't the same no more. I just don't trust her!"

"You've got to stay out of trouble," I said, my voice emotional. "What else can you do here? Crochet?"

"Yeah, but I ain't got none of my stuff here."

"They won't let you have it?"

"Yeah," Her voice deepened, "But the needles got to be plastic!"

We both burst into laughter simultaneously. I rolled my eyes, leaning against her shoulder. "I'll get you some plastic needles then. Good Lord! Well, at least it will help you think."

"Jayla Morris!" The matron summoned stridently.

Jayla looked at me with pleading eyes. "Our time is up, but you can sign in again and stay another full hour if you want."

"Oh, I'd love to, but my sister is waiting outside. I'll come again soon though." I didn't budge from my seat. "Oh, this is hard ..."

"You better get going," she muttered. "They don't like visitors hanging around after time is done."

"Oh!" I exclaimed, jumping to my feet. She remained seated. "Well," I stammered awkwardly, "can I hug you at least?"

She nodded, giggling tenderly at my embarrassment. "Thanks so much," she sighed, her eyes welling up with tears. "Thanks so much."

I walked over to the matron who leafed through the passes and marked off my time. As I pushed through the swinging doors, I looked back and saw Jayla, still sitting there stiffly.

# Freedom is Just Another Word

The night before Jayla's long-awaited reconsideration, after an avalanche of unanswered phone calls to Jayla's lawyer, after contacting lawyer friends for advice, then finally the judge, I fell into the bed, emotionally exhausted. The cumulative tension of the past weeks cut across my back like an icy blue streak. Still, I couldn't sleep, and I wondered, watching the ceiling, whether Jayla was faring any better. Did the teachers at Rose Hill actually write to the judge as promised? Most people don't even want to think about child abuse. For them, "mother" is a sacred word. The mother should overcome all obstacles under any circumstance.

I speculated about Jayla's life, still watching the ceiling. As Jayla had told me, the state was now responsible for the wellbeing of those children. They paid the foster parents, all medical, dental, and school bills. Yet when Jayla asked the government for assistance, she was refused. As my eyelids closed, I wondered whether they'd keep her in handcuffs for the ride to the courthouse. She'd be smartly dressed, I knew, anointed underneath with bath powder and prayers.

The next morning, I spotted Ms Bartlett immediately in the empty courtroom, dressed as usual in her lily-white suit. Did she always wear the same outfit, I wondered, or was it somehow attached to Jayla's case? She acknowledged me as I slid on the bench next to her. A chilly silence bristled between us. For a brief instant I felt like walking off in the opposite direction. Evidently, she was as incensed by my dogged persistence in this case as I was by her passivity. We both stared at the clerk arranging legal papers on the judge's tall, polished desk. Unlike the previous courtroom, this one had no windows, yet the paneled walls lent it a warm hospitable feeling. I heard the clicking of high heels behind us as someone entered and sat on a nearby bench. "Is this where the reconsiderations take place?" she asked in a British accent. One glimpse at her thick shoulder-length hair, her bone-brown skin and finely etched features made me guess that she might be West Indian.

"Yes," Ms Bartlett answered with the indifference of an answering machine.

"Is there any time schedule?"

"You can never know when specific cases are going to be heard." The lawyer rose to her feet.

"Do inmates come first?" the woman persisted, an American inflection entering her voice.

Heading for the door, Ms Bartlett paused before answering. Then exasperated, she asked, "Who are you looking for?"

"Jayla Morris."

This was the final blow. "She'll be here," the lawyer huffed, stalking out of the room.

Still squinting at the door, a surge of unadulterated hatred flashed in the woman's eyes.

"That's Jayla's lawyer," I confided quietly. The woman faced me, her eyes dark and angry. "Are you Jayla's friend Susan?"

"Yes, and you?"

"I'm Clem."

"She's mentioned you," Susan replied circumspectly. With the back of her hand, she pushed a strand of hair from her face, the bracelets round her wrist jangling lightly. "I'm nervous as hell," she whispered out of the corner of her mouth.

"Oh!" I said, "Are you going to testify?" The clerk glanced curiously at us, then hunched over her work.

"What good would it do?" Susan snapped. "White people don't care what I think. They'll never understand because they haven't lived through what we have." Her hoarse, angry whisper rumbled past the clerk and over the judge's vacant upholstered seat. "I mean, whites have their own problems too, but when you take the average Black woman, you're talking about a mother, a grandmother, a great-grandmother, all on welfare. That's an entirely different story. Now what White can understand that? Why should they?"

I nodded my head sympathetically, uncertain whether to hazard a reply.

"I can sit here and talk with you," she continued, "but I'd never really trust you, never really be friends with a White. I wouldn't go that far because, in the end, I just can't trust you people." Her dark almond eyes gauged my reaction, then she cast a quick imperious glance at the doorway where clusters of attorneys had begun to gather.

"Well, Jayla ..." I stammered, disconcerted but grateful for her frankness.

"Jayla's a good mother," she declared unhesitant, inspecting her painted nails. "At times, certain times. She loves those kids. I mean, if you could see her with baby Glennie, they're like a good TV show. But she had a bad time with her pregnancy, you know, the minister and all; leaves a woman with a bad feeling about her child. Somehow, she has to find a way to work out those feelings."

"Well," I pointed out, "she certainly isn't doing that in prison."

"That's right. You know, I understand exactly how she feels because I have children too, only they aren't babies anymore. They've grown up to be my friends. But my own childhood was similar to Jayla's. When I was small, I was given away to my godmother. She took me for the money, so there wasn't much love between us. I never learned anything about that so-called mothering stuff, you know like teaching the kids to say 'ga ga' or 'pee pee.' No, my kids learned 'defecate' and 'urinate' right off."

Her tone was brusque.

"Now Jayla's a neat freak like me. But when they reach the stage where they touch everything, I don't tell them, 'No, you're bad!' You should never say that to a child. It isn't the child who's bad, but what he's doing. So, I say: 'Don't touch that!'" Her boney finger waggled at me as a smile finally broke across her face. "Only now, when my older daughter comes in late, I say, 'Girl, I'm gonna shove my fist down your throat!' I do hit her occasionally, but my children are my friends."

"Jayla had the problem of raising her children alone, with no money."

"I know," she interrupted, pulling her tweed jacket around the waist of her designer jeans. "I'm a single mother too, only I think it's easier this way."

"It sure didn't seem any better for Jayla."

"Well, you see, with two parents you've got two separate personalities with two different ideas how to do things. Alone, I don't have to consult with anyone but myself. Anyway, in Jayla's case, I don't think it's going to help having Glenn around." Susan mentioned his name as though the very thought turned her stomach.

"Oh," I suddenly recalled, "you and Glenn had a fight over bringing those kids to Jessup."

"You've got it, honey, and that's not all," she snarled, her upper lip curling to expose her white teeth. We studied each other in silence for a moment.

"Let's get out of here," I proposed, rising to leave. "I'd like to smoke a cigarette."

Quickly scrutinizing me from head to toe, she stood to follow. At this hour we had to push our way across the crowded hallway. Standing among the broad-shouldered men, Susan's petite frame appeared even smaller. I lit my cigarette, elbowing a Woody Allen type behind me. He cringed, fearfully clutching his briefcase. I started to apologize but looking over his shoulder, exclaimed in surprise, "Susan, look!"

"I already saw," she answered dryly. "And I can tell he's already been into something!"

Glenn barged toward us through the crowd, his wedding suit flapping round him like wounded wings. Sour-faced, he stared ahead as he strong-armed lawyers out of his path. And quick as smoke, Susan disappeared completely among the bodies.

"Glenn!" I called out as he blindly elbowed ahead.

He spun around abruptly, his face hardened. "Don't say nothing to me!" Angrily, he pushed onward. Baffled and frightened by his rage, I stared at his back, then frantically scanned the horde for Susan.

"Clem!" Glenn shouted, grabbing me from behind and lifting me in the air. Still confused, I struggled to be freed from his grip. "Am I glad to see you! Oh, babe!" he exposed his yellow teeth. "Ain't I glad to see you!"

His raucous laughter reverberated over the crowd. I tried to smile as I heard the conversations around us fading. What was the reason for this exuberance? We had gradually become friends over the phone, but is this how he deals with anxiety? The people around us began edging away.

"I love you, lady!" Glenn cried out hysterically. "I knew you was a friend of Jayla's!" He leaned over to whisper in a conspiratorial, threatening tone, "I'm doing it my way this time. They better watch out!"

He positively reeked of alcohol, mixed with a scent of cheap aftershave. His glassy bloodshot eyes gaped at me, and I realized Susan was right— it wasn't just alcohol. He had taken something else. Off to the side the crowd parted slowly as two burly policemen pressed forward.

"Clem!" A woman's voice cut through the crush of people. I whirled around in time to spot a familiar figure advancing between the pair of cops.

"Jayla!" I called, reaching to touch her shoulder. She walked with a measured gait into the courtroom, her wrists handcuffed behind her back.

Glenn's fists opened and closed spasmodically. For some time, he stood like a man in shock, a frenzied contorted face. Finally, he revived and lurched forward, stomping after his wife. Luckily, the reverent atmosphere inside the courtroom slowed him down. The judge, already seated, nodded at Jayla's lawyer, who had already begun to present her plea. The bailiff, rigidly upright by the door, surveyed the nearly empty room. Reeling slightly, Glenn scrambled to a bench right behind Jayla.

"Your Honor," Ms Bartlett continued, "Jayla Morris has spent four months in Jessup."

Fitfully, Glenn looked at me, then back to the judge. "I'm gonna do it my way," he hissed through teeth clenched tight. "My way!" he smacked his chest.

"Take it easy," I warned. How could I handle this man? He was under the influence of something. Alcohol? Drugs? If I rebuked him, he might lash out, yet if I remained calm …

"Mrs Morris loves her children," the lawyer stated, "but she could not manage them under the subhuman conditions of her past life."

Her words reached me, but they seemed irrelevant next to Glenn's panting. Ms Bartlett was earnestly arguing on Jayla's behalf. A trace of hope stirred, but Glenn convulsed in his seat, oblivious to the proceedings. Like a caged animal he clawed at his chest, ripping off his tie.

"I'm gonna do it my way," he hissed in my ear.

"Shhhhh," I snapped back. "She's saying the right things. There might be a chance." I grabbed his arm.

"Don't tell me nothing," he retorted angrily, attracting the bailiff's glare. "My wife and family are at stake here. Let 'em lock me up if they want to."

"You'll ruin it for Jayla!"

The judge's eyes seared through us.

Ms Bartlett droned on, seemingly unperturbed. "Mrs Morris needs rehabilitation and therapy. Her good conduct at Jessup has demonstrated her desire to reform." Glenn yanked his arm free of my grip and pulled off his jacket. "And," the lawyer continued, "she has two friends present who will speak for her today."

I was seized with panic! Two friends? That must mean Glenn and me! Glenn brandished his fist as though threatening the judge. Frantic, I grabbed him again. "Stop it! Stop it!" I whispered. "Just listen!"

Glaring back at me, his eyes two pinpoints of hatred, he refrained momentarily. Two friends! So, I was going to testify after all. Knowing me, I'd be so nervous I'd babble. And Glenn? God knows what he'd do! I began whispering at the lawyer's back, warning her not to call Glenn to the stand.

Jayla fidgeted on her seat as Glenn warned me, "I'm gonna show 'em this time. I could kill that judge!"

The judge leaned over her high bench to address Jayla. "Mrs Morris, remember when you wrote me that letter on July 25th?"

Jayla nodded, staring at the floor.

I tightened my grip around Glenn's steely biceps, still whispering frantically to the lawyer. All this ruckus, she must know! Glenn's demeanor shifted to a catatonic stare, his brow bathed in sweat.

"I have received various recommendations ..." The judge, brows furrowed, addressed Jayla in short, concise syllables, "... but you appear otherwise stable. You are ready now and willing to be rehabilitated. I'm going to give you a second chance, Mrs Morris, no more violence. The next time you lift your hand to your children, it's coming down to caress them."

Her words floated over the polished rail. Glenn's mouth twitched uncontrollably, little spasms from a nightmare of booze and drugs.

"Glenn!" I shook him. "She's free! Free!"

His tense body immediately deflated. A painful grimace cut across his face and tears welled up in his eyes. "I got my wife back," he gasped. "I got my wife back!"

Like a blind person, Jayla hoisted herself from the bench, gripping the edge of the table. The bailiff walked up behind, ready to escort her through processing. As if in prayer, she bowed her head and the handcuffs clicked, then she marched out between the policemen. Each held an elbow as if she might bolt out of the room. With brave determination, she resisted looking our way. For a long moment, Glenn sat frozen, blinking back tears. Then tenderly he took my hand to leave the courtroom.

Outside the door Susan greeted us with feeling. "I can't believe it!" she closed her eyes tightly. "I just can't believe it!"

Halting abruptly before her, Glenn transformed again, swearing bitterly under his breath. "I hate you and I love you. I could even kill you, girl!"

"I don't care," she boldly retorted. "Just look at you, Glenn Morris! You get drunk when your wife is sent to prison, and you're drunk again the day she's released."

"I hate you and I love you," he was delirious. His head snapped backward as though his neck was broken and he bellowed, "I got my wife back!" The bystanders turned, some stopping dead in their tracks.

Ms Bartlett wended her way toward us. "Go get her papers moving," she commanded, looking at me. I turned around and Susan had wisely vanished again.

Glenn lumbered forward to embrace the lawyer "You did a good job," he began, but she sidestepped him and rushed away.

Glenn appeared panic-struck. He grabbed my hand and dragged me down the hall to the processing center. With his jacket draped over one sweaty shoulder, he leaned on the counter and posed there like a movie star. "Hey, beautiful," he crooned, waiting for someone to admire his manly physique. The incessant clacking of the typewriter stopped when a young Black secretary looked up.

"Oh you, lovely lady," he said as the woman stood and approached with a stern professional expression. "Lady, can you help me get my wife out?"

"Who's your wife?" she answered in a voice that let him know she meant business.

"Mrs Jayla Morris." He stood at attention, shoulders squared.

The woman disappeared into a neighboring office. Glenn cursed and began to taunt another woman. Suddenly he spotted an old friend and rushed into the crowd. I stood by the counter, growing increasingly annoyed. Glenn must realize things take time. For all I knew Glenn's shenanigans could jeopardize Jayla's quick release. Miraculously he staggered back just as the woman was returning. Still several yards from the counter, he called out to her in a loud voice.

"Okay, beautiful lady! I knew you was gonna help me. Let's get them papers moving."

"Mrs Morris is with the marshals right now," she politely informed us. "You simply have to wait."

"But I got my wife back! Don't you understand?"

"Sorry."

"But lady," he banged on the counter.

"Come on Glenn," I coaxed, taking him by the arm. He immediately broke free and stormed down the hallway alone, fueled by booze, infuriated by his impotence. He collided with a heavyset janitor and spun around, disoriented. Resuming his headlong flight, he barged onward, unaware that he was rushing back in my direction. Suddenly he saw me and stopped dead in his tracks.

"What am I doing?" he asked like a sleepwalker reviving from a trance. "What am I doing?"

"Come on," I decided. "We're going outside."

We jumped in the elevator and Glenn proclaimed Jayla's release to the crowd in the elevator. Exuberant and loud, he sounded like a man announcing his first born's birth. People shifted on their feet and looked away as he repeated her name.

"*I got my wife back!*" he shouted again, this time at the top of his lungs the second we stepped outside.

"*Yahhoooooo!*" I yelled along with him, laughing at his audacious jubilation.

He started to lead me across the parking lot, his face suddenly serious. "Ya know," he began, squeezing my hand, "they would'a locked me up if I did it my way. But I'd whup 'em good before they got me. Ain't nobody ever whupped this nigger."

The courthouse receded in the distance as we wandered among the silent, abandoned cars. The hot noonday sun scorched our backs, sweat dripping from Glenn's forehead and down my sides. "Now I gotta think about my family. Ain't that something? Do you know this is the first time Jayla and I are gonna be free together? Together for real." He paused to contemplate this fact, then ambled on, "I gotta work hard now, you see, but I'm a bad man."

The asphalt sizzled and my hand, glued to his, felt uncomfortably clammy. "I don't like being wicked but it's just the circumstances. You're Jayla's friend, though, and I'm glad about that, babe." He turned to hug me. "I done some mighty bad things," he repeated, pulling away, his bloodshot eyes squinting in the sunlight. "Do you got any idea who I am or what I done?"

"I know a little," I tried to speak casually, but something about his demeanor unnerved me. The parking lot was deserted. I could hear voices in the distance but they sounded too far away if I needed help.

"Well, I've killed people. I murdered so many people, I don't remember them all. That's why I told you I coulda killed that judge." His eyes, lizard-like, became two slits. When they opened slightly, the pupils were dark and coarse looking. "You remember reading about them people in DC who had their throats slit?"

"No."

"Well, I did that. I was paid."

The intense sun gnawed at my neck, the back of my head. He stood up straighter, an exaggerated gravity thickening his voice. "Me and my buddies used to do that. It was even in the papers," he boasted. "Then there were some others I hurt bad so I could rob their money. I done things you can't even imagine, girl. And now ..." His eyes suddenly welled up with tears. The shift of emotion traveled across his handsome face. "I gotta live with my family and I don't even know if I can, I just don't know. Jayla knows who I am. She sticks by me no matter what. I guess she's got her religion and stuff. But me? I don't know what I can do for her."

His heavy eyelids fluttered, blinking back the tears. "I gotta work for her, but there ain't no work. I tried getting a job with Metro, but I just don't know. I need Jayla. I need her standin' by me, but I gotta give to her too. I just can't get straight."

"It's the booze, Glenn. Why not start with that?"

"Get outta here," he scoffed, shaking my arm. "I'm someone you can't even imagine! Don't you breathe a word of this, but since I been outta prison I already killed eight people. There's these people who writes rubber checks, and I take care of 'em, if you know what I mean."

I silently nodded my head, not wanting to hear any more and unsure what to believe. Still, I tried to concentrate, sorting out the truth from the boasts. But what difference did it really make?

"Then there's these other people I get between the first and third of the month." His dark eyes peered down into mine, but I could barely see for the sun's glare. "You know, when they collect their welfare checks.

I mean, you wouldn't believe it, but when some folks gets their welfare checks, others steal from 'em, from old people, cripples, anyone. I'm a permanent, you see. A permanent."

I wasn't sure I understood. Was Glenn stealing checks from welfare recipients or did he consider himself their avenging angel? I didn't ask any questions. I just wanted to leave.

"So, me and my buddies get 'em, sometimes we just hurt 'em. Where I come from there's mighty bad stuff. I'd like to have friends like Jayla's got, but I ain't never had a friend. I've had to fight to survive, just to live! Now I gotta do something for Jayla and my family but I am a permanent and I don't know if I can. You see what I mean?"

He stiffened again, then faintly swayed.

"Let's go," I proposed quietly. "Let's try and find Jayla." I began to walk ahead of him.

"Normally," he continued, catching up to me, "I don't tell anyone nothing. I just keep it all inside because if you start talkin' about yourself, you're bound to become prey."

"How's that?" I asked as we approached the courthouse again.

"That's what happens to the rich folks. They show their power, how they done this and that, so one day they become prey. You see what I mean?" He paused beside an old Buick to collect his thoughts. "You know as well as I do that the rich are prey. That's why I never want to be wealthy, even though there's money in my family. My grandfather was a treacherous man. He owned more houses than a White man, but he led an evil life."

I listened but I was confused. Was he an incoherent drunk or was he talking about real things? Either way, I didn't want to be alone with him, and hurried over to the courthouse. Glenn clamped his mouth shut as we entered the air-conditioned building and passed through the metal detector. This time, we rode the elevator in silence. The halls were nearly empty now and I spotted Susan sitting under a dingy window.

The instant we walked up, she solemnly vowed, "I'm staying here 'til Jayla comes. She'll come right through that door."

"I hate you and I love you," Glenn recited.

Susan responded by yawning, scorning him through half-closed eyes.

"I gotta go home and clean house," Glenn announced out of nowhere.

"Clean house?" My voice was shrill.

"Yeah, I got a lot to do before Jayla comes home."

"Now, wait a minute," I began, but Susan nudged me.

"I hate you and I love you," he proclaimed one last time as we watched him lope down the hall.

"He's too wild for me," I sighed, sitting beside Susan on the windowsill.

"For anyone," she replied dryly. "My husband was with him in Lorton and he's told me about the insides of Glenn. The man just isn't reliable. I mean, look, when he was in prison, I used to take Jayla to visit him three times a week. He only went to see her once."

"But there wasn't any transportation," I offered lamely in Glenn's defense.

"I know men who ride the train to Baltimore and then catch a bus to see their women in Jessup, but not Glenn. He just let Jayla sit there." Susan paused to sip her Coke. "But she'll go right back loving him like she did before because she's always been alone and needs affection."

A ray of sunshine came through the window then crossed our feet. From this window, we could keep an eye on the office at the end of the hall and the door through which Jayla would emerge. All the proceedings had stopped, and the police vanished for lunch.

"So, you're the woman who first met her husband in prison?" I asked Susan, curious about her relationship to Jayla and Glenn.

"No," she hastened to correct me. "I started going out with Russel when I was seventeen. But he was a street person then, and I just couldn't take his violent ways. I kept coming back to him, though," she shook her head slightly as if she couldn't understand herself, "because the sex was good. Then I didn't see him for quite a while and his mother told me he was in prison. I decided to visit Russel in Lorton, but just once. That's where I ran into Jayla and we started going there together regularly. I was the one who got him locked up again because of a ..." She groped for words. "A domestic problem."

"You see, the last time Russel was released he came to live with me. I had heard from a friend that he was into something called 'Bam.' I had no idea what that was, my daughter knows more about that stuff than me."

"What is it?"

"It's a pill they grind up, then heat up and shoot into their arms. Well, he started blowing all my money on Bam, but I didn't realize it for some time. Once I caught on, though, I'd pretend there wasn't any money, not even for food. Whenever I cooked for my daughter, I'd wash the floors with ammonia, so he'd never know."

"Smart method." Half listening, I was still zeroing in on the doorway.

"Yeah, well, one day I came home early from work to find Russel and his friend locked in the bathroom. My daughter was watching TV. 'How long have they been in there?' I asked her. She told me half an hour. 'Well,' I said, 'either they're homosexuals or they're shooting up drugs and I don't want either in my house!' I started for the door. 'Don't, Mom,' my daughter begged, grabbing my arm. 'You don't know how these men will react when they're high. They could do anything!' I agreed at first and just kept pacing back and forth. Finally, I couldn't take it anymore. I started banging on the door with my fists, cursing a blue streak."

"Oh, no," I interrupted her. "Look who's back!" Glenn walked unsteadily toward us, his face downcast.

"And that's when we started fighting," she quickly concluded, "It was all over Bam."

"Can't one of you give me a ride home?" Glenn asked, all sweet talk now.

We both squinted at him like appraisers. A dead silence.

"Well," he muttered, wobbling a bit. "I guess I can just hitchhike then."

Both of us remained silent. I didn't want to ride alone with Glenn, nor did I care to leave without seeing Jayla. Susan crossed her arms over her chest. "It won't be hard getting a ride in that suit." I poked fun at him. "They'll probably think you are a lawyer." I expected to hear Susan chuckle, but instead she frowned, staring at the ground.

"Well, I'll just have to find another way," Glenn shrugged. "That's okay, I'll find a way."

"I'll take you," Susan announced unexpectedly. Then, turning to me, "You wait here, okay?"

"Fine," I agreed, slightly taken aback.

"Goodbye babe," Glenn waved, then winked. They both turned and headed down the stairs.

Hours passed, standing, sitting by the window, then pacing the long hallway. Still no signs of Jayla or Susan. I asked at the counter, but no one had definite answers. By four I was contemplating contacting the judge to ask her to speed up the process, or at least give me some straight answers. But suddenly, Susan was by my side.

"I stopped at McDonald's and saved you some French fries," she reported, handing me a small bag.

"How sweet of you. You had trouble with Glenn?"

"He got into that tough guy act the whole way," she sighed, sitting down next to me. "He said he was jealous of Jayla having friends like you and me, that he never had friends because his life was so hard. 'Look,' I said. 'You're a full-grown man and I'm tired of hearing that sob story. Stop living in the past and do something with what you got today!' Well, he came right back to that love/hate stuff again, so I told him, 'I'm giving you a ride as a favor to Jayla because you might get hurt hitchhiking in the condition you're in. But just keep talking like that mister, and you can walk home! I don't owe you a damn thing!'

"'You sure are a hard woman,' he complained. 'You ain't like you used to be.' I just drove on. Then he started bragging about how he could kill me, so I stopped the car. 'You can get out right here,' I told him. 'You aren't really going to put me out,' he said. 'You don't understand who you're dealing with, girl.' 'Are you going to shut up?' I asked. 'Yeah,' he answered and never said another word."

Awestruck, I stared at Susan, unable to fathom this petite gutsy woman.

"I don't know," I told her sadly. "Jayla might be walking into another mess. That man loves her, but he's so twisted up inside."

The door at the end of the hall clanged open. A cop ambled through first, escorting a column of prisoners. They were all young Black men, handcuffed by twos, their sickly green uniforms pasted to their sweaty bodies. They trudged past us in a solemn procession without uttering a sound. Their march was like a vision from the past, only now they used handcuffs instead of shackles and whip. A second cop brought up the rear, his heels clicking against the tile floor.

"I'd hate to see Jayla like that," I muttered indistinctly, struggling as I absorbed this reality.

Susan turned to me but paused before she spoke. Studying me, evaluating. Biting her lip, she finally answered, "Yeah, and you might say I was partially responsible for Jayla's arrest."

"I guess we all could have given her more support," I replied sympathetically.

For a moment she was silent, her delicate fingers toying with the strap of her leather handbag. "I wish I could have been a better friend."

"I feel the same way, Susan."

"*No!*" she shook her head. "The first time Jayla hurt little Glenn, she called me up at work. 'You're going to have to say you did it,' she told me. 'I already have a child abuse record.' I was pretty angry at first, but finally decided to say my daughter did it."

"Your daughter!"

"Yes, we said it happened while she was babysitting. You see, the kid had some string around his foot tied to the crib so, when he fell, the foot was twisted and broken. Jayla wanted to leave it for a while to mend on its own. But he kept getting worse, so she finally had to take him to the hospital."

I stared at Susan in dismay, unable to speak. A telephone rang but it must have been far away because it sounded to me like my heart was pounding louder. Susan bowed her head like a woman in a confessional and continued speaking softly. "When the agency finally called, I made my daughter answer the phone. She told them I wasn't home, that she was alone there with her aunt. She's a smart kid. Then she gave them the whole story, just the way we planned it."

"God! That poor girl!"

"Like I said, my children are smart, smarter than me sometimes. They went along with the whole thing, but kept saying, 'Mom, you shouldn't do this. You don't know what could happen next time. She might kill those kids!' I knew they were right, but I helped her out anyway."

So, this was what Jayla lived! Someone in far deeper trouble than even the authorities suspected, a slow death, a drowning person dragging her own children down the bottomless pit of hell. The door at the end of the hall was still closed and silent. Outside the late afternoon sun sank toward the horizon.

Susan coughed nervously, then continued, "Jayla was under tremendous strain. She never had enough money, plus she hated welfare. I can understand why. She had been living off public assistance since she was born, and she just couldn't accept that. She wanted a job with a salary like any decent person. Well, she called me again about two weeks after little Glenn came home. She had done it again, slapping the baby and bruising his face. To this day she doesn't know it and probably never will, but I notified the Child Protection Agency."

My body felt fixed, immovable as I sat and listened astonished by the story. I wondered why she was telling me the truth now.

"I called them up and said, 'I want to report an abused child and I can't leave my name. I'm not certain of the address, but it's on Lemore Street. You already have the mother in your files, listed under Jayla Morris.' You see, I had driven Jayla home many times but had never noticed the number of the building. They ran her name through the computer and told me the address. 'Yes, that must be it,' I said. 'There can't be more than one person on that street with the same name and problem.'

"Well, that night they went over to Jayla's apartment, but Glenn was on furlough from his halfway house and he wouldn't let them in. He knew what was going on and didn't want them to find out. Of course, later he resented Jayla, especially after she hurt Melissa, his own flesh and blood. That's when he beat up Jayla."

I remembered Jayla telling me about this fight, both of them crying, her giving him a bloody nose. She never explained how it started and, of course, by this time, after all her crimes, she must have believed she deserved it. Susan spoke on, carefully articulating each word.

"He beat her bad, but it didn't show because she got on all fours and hid her face in the couch. He just punched her all over the back. Well, anyway, that night he tried to protect her from these outside people, but he finally had to let them in. They brought Dora over to one side and said, 'How are you getting along with your mother?'" Susan imitated a syrupy, sweet voice, pretending to caress the little girl's chin with her fingertip. "'Have you been good? You haven't given her any trouble, have you?'

"Of course, Dora is older, so she answered the questions right. Then they checked out the baby who was sleeping on his side, you know with one side of his face on the mattress. Well, all they did was look at Glennie. They didn't pick him up or anything. I mean they didn't do their job! That kid could have been in a coma for all they knew. They certainly didn't see the bruises, so they left. Soon enough Jayla called me up, complaining about the lady down the hall sticking her nose in everybody's business.

"But you never know," Susan stood with a distant look in her eyes. "Maybe if those people had done their job in the first place, all this would never have happened. Then again, under different circumstances, Jayla might have been a better mother. She couldn't leave that apartment, you see, and, oh, my God!" Susan suddenly grabbed my wrist. "Look!"

Jayla was striding toward us, suppressing a laugh at our astonishment. Her gait grew jauntier as she fought the urge to run. Susan rushed forth to meet her, tears streaming down her face, her breath choked with laughter. Eagerly embracing, they spun around like one body. Jayla's arm flew out and I was pulled into their orbit. Still holding onto one another, we zigzagged toward the windowsill, out of earshot of the police, away from the courtroom and the ubiquitous door.

"I can't believe it," Jayla gasped, pulling away from us. "I just can't believe it!" Delicately, she massaged her wrists as though applying a healing balm. "No handcuffs!" she cried, staring in amazement at her upturned palms.

"Praise the Lord!"

Suddenly, as if awakening startled from a dream, she looked left and right.

"And where is my husband?" she asked in a dark voice.

"He went home to clean up," I reported.

"He's high as a kite," Susan chipped in.

Jayla studied our faces. "I knew that the second he walked in the courtroom," she stated glumly. "Afterwards the policeman in there asked me, 'Who was that man?' 'That's my husband!' I told him. 'Well,' he said, 'if your hearing lasted one minute longer I was going to pitch him out on his ass!'"

She scanned the deserted hall again, still hoping to see her husband. "Well, I'll deal with that later," she decided triumphantly. "I'm free to go where I please now!"

Chattering gaily as we strolled toward the exit, Jayla halted, unable to believe she no longer wore a uniform. She gently caressed the fabric of her dress. "I must be dreaming." As we descended the stairwell, tears rolled down her cheeks.

"Look at this day!" I shouted the moment we stepped outside. Jayla's dress billowed in the gentle breeze, her hair flying over her face.

"Breathe the fresh air God made for you!" Susan sang. Giggling like a schoolgirl, Jayla wrapped her arms around our waists. "And God did make this glorious day by answering all my prayers. I swear, no one believed my prayers would work but me. I know Susan didn't believe and Glenn had his doubts. Well, last night I went to Bible class and told the group about today. 'Now Jayla,' they said, 'don't get disappointed if you aren't released. No one ever gets out on a reconsideration.' And I thought, 'Lord! Ain't no one believe I claim my freedom but me!'"

"And now we should celebrate," Susan declared, stopping in front of her car. "I just got some food stamps so we can have a feast."

"But our guest of honor may have a different celebration waiting for her at home," I teased, poking Jayla in the ribs.

"Ain't that right!" she readily agreed. "It's been a long time since I had any of that stuff!"

The county employees were rushing past us on their way home from work. Their idling engines stirred the air as they crept toward the exit, hoping to avoid rush-hour traffic. Jayla watched them with a pensive expression.

"You know, while I was waiting in the lockup to be released another girl got thrown in there with me. She was bawling her head off. I tried to comfort her, putting my arm around her, talking 'bout the Lord and telling her what Jessup was like. But inside I was thinking, 'Praise the Lord, I'm on my way out and not just coming in!' I'll tell you, that took something out of me. I was just about bursting." She shook her head, still gawking at her surroundings. "What time is it?" she asked.

"It's five o'clock," Susan quipped.

"Count-time," Jayla grunted, her jaws clenched.

"What's that?" I asked.

"Well, three times a day they count your heads at Jessup and you got to wait in your room 'til they finish. But it takes a while 'cause they got to call from one building to the next, just to make sure everybody is inside."

"You're telling me!" Susan commented. "Once I was visiting Jayla when they had count-time and it wasn't over 'til six. Our whole time together was spoiled. We couldn't even say goodbye after they finished."

"But never again," Jayla declared. "And no more of that dull food! Lord, I could sure go for some fried potatoes and onions!"

"So now you're going to get fat," I teased her.

"Oh no!" she cried, covering her face. "I just want to eat!"

"Jayla," Susan quietly interjected. "Do you want to go straight home or stop by Jessup to pick up your things? Glenn put gas in my car so I could take you."

"I better go to Jessup and be done with it," she answered, looking at me. "If that's all right with you, Clem?"

"That's fine, Jayla. I have to return this truck."

Her strong embrace encircled me once more as she whispered, "Thanks Clem, thanks for being here. God bless you."

Our eyes were moist, but we parted with a smile. The slanting rays of the sun bounced off their car doors as they creaked open and slammed shut again. Another round of giggling erupted when a Black man driving a garbage truck pulled up behind them.

"Hey, sweethearts!" he yelled, poking his head out the window. "You two better come with us."

His partner whistled approvingly but Susan's car pulled away, and I watched as Jayla turned to wave goodbye.

During the next few months, Jayla and I spoke with each other, but I knew there was no way out. As she was swept more and more into Glenn's world, there was nothing I could do. Before I knew it, she and Glenn had moved again and even Susan wasn't sure where they had gone. Not long after, I was ready to leave the city myself. I had been offered a job to work with migrant farmworkers, a job with "illegal aliens." After my experiences with the three women, it was the only course that made sense to me—to work with people like the women I had met and try to make a difference.

I left the city and took the job working with the farmworkers, undocumented immigrants, but the past stayed with me. Sometimes right before I slept, images would flash across my mind: Teresa running frantically from house to house to get money for her son; Larian saying a final goodbye to her daughter while Madame DeVrai watched, smoking her pipe. Sometimes I remembered the courtyard where I was in the jail, the hot sun, and the Mayan women huddled together sleeping on the floor beside me. I could see all of them so clearly and could feel how love was driving them to do whatever they could for their families.

※

Working with undocumented workers, I found myself assisting an underground railroad of churches and organizations that challenged the law by providing sanctuary to undocumented immigrants. Some of the "illegals" went on to testify to Congress despite the dangers. One day I was driving through rural America to bring such a fugitive to safety.

As I drove, I wondered if I'd finally find Larian here, where Haitians lived in these flat lands that were spotted by clapboard houses—some that looked deserted, others occupied, the windows protected by pieces of plastic. Here and there you'd see some trailers parked under trees, clustered together like animals that had been herded over to a trough.

Undocumented immigrants had come to this area in hordes. If they were lucky and had some fancy fake paperwork, they found work in the poultry plants; dark, dirty, noisy places where if you tried to take a break to pee, you'd get fired. Their labor became essential to the community overnight. A manager at a poultry plant bragged to me: "Those people ain't nothin' but beasts of burden," he chuckled. "You take a Haitian or a Guatemalan—you pay him practically nothing and know you'll still get the work of three people. Those people can work forever."

Two of those Guatemalans were sitting in the car with me as we drove farther and farther into a rural area. Fifteen years ago, Julia Ajmac, one of the Guatemalan women, had come to the United States penniless, wearing her *traje*, speaking *lengua*, poised to work with a family. She cut off her braids, put on a pair of pants, learned English, raised many children as a nanny. She was still a nanny but also worked tirelessly as a human rights advocate, using her status as a US citizen to help the mounting hordes of Guatemalans fleeing violence and hunger. Oftentimes she hid them in her apartment, feeding and caring for them for months. Such was the case with the other woman in the car with us.

Maria, one of the women who would testify, wore her *traje* with all the emblems of a Mayan Kaqchiquel and her thick black hair braided tightly in a purple satin ribbon, then wound round her head like a crown. Bumping along in the front seat of the car, she told us some of her story. We had heard many versions of it: the soldiers found her, grabbed her, took her to the river and raped her and many other women in the village. Then they burned everything. They tied her up but she freed herself, helped by her five-year-old daughter.

We would leave her at a Quaker community, a sanctuary where they'd ensure her case was presented to the US Congress to help convince them to cease funding the extermination of entire Indigenous nations.

I wondered how successful Maria would be telling her story, in helping them understand the truth of what she was saying. The beauty and horror of her life. If this could really change anything.

Yet this woman was ready to risk her freedom to tell this story, to help others like herself. After all, she was illegal, and by telling her story she could be targeted, jailed, then deported. In this quest to understand women's lives, I had uncovered so many untruths I had been taught about history, about our policies overseas and at home, and about civil rights; yet Maria's willingness to speak up pointed to the biggest lie I had learned: the idea that people are essentially selfish. Instead, what I witnessed in Maria and so many others was people reaching out, helping, listening, risking so much for each other. That generosity seemed to be the reason, in the end, why all of us were still alive. It wasn't competition or cunning that promised survival, it was our innate kindness.

I looked at the two women in the front seat with me I wondered why we were even driving in that car. Yet we all knew if we didn't—if Maria didn't tell her tale and Larian didn't make hard decisions and Jayla didn't dream about returning to jail to help other women like her—that it would only get worse. The women's lives had proved to me the indomitability of the human spirit in the face of immense hardship. Faith drove them. Love drove them. Generosity drove them. So, I was happy to be there with them, driving in the car toward Maria's sanctuary, toward doing our best no matter the outcome.

# AUTHOR'S NOTE

*Remember that writing things down makes them real; that it is nearly*

*impossible to hate anyone whose story you know; and, most of all,*

*that even in our post-postmodern era, writing has a moral purpose.*

*With twenty-six shapes arranged in varying patterns,*

*we can tell every story known to mankind, and make up all the new ones—*

*indeed, we can do so in most of the world's known tongues.*

*If you can give language to experiences previously starved for it,*

*you can make the world a better place.*

— ANDREW SOLOMON

In the early 1970s I worked on an archaeological site in the lush Peten jungle of Guatemala. I could barely speak with the Mayans because Spanish was a second language to them as well as myself. However, even with limited language, I was drawn to this Mayan world. I watched how meticulously they worked and experienced their tendency to be very professorial, the way they taught me how to use a machete or trowel was a work of art. They were very serious, formal, and polite until late at night when they shared old songs and mysterious tales about the jungle and spirits they had encountered. I was drawn to them, but since I lacked the language, it was context that started to teach me about their lives. That context and its narrative helped me endure the next ordeal Guatemala presented. I was thrown in jail on trumped-up charges.

After my experience in jail, I became convinced of the need for this book; of the need for people working or living closely with different cultures to gain insight into the context of women's lives—insight that isn't just based on fact but also on the meaning, the dreams that drive people. Insight that could point to the elements deep in the heart, where connection and healing take place.

I wanted to explore how some women actually feel and think—to investigate how abject poverty is so often filled with violence—either direct violence, where soldiers beat people, or the insidious slow violence of hunger, lack of housing, and education. My aim was to depict real people with real stories that only they could tell in their own words; to reveal the faces and voices behind the global statistics and to give the reader the unique opportunity to listen to the group of people heard from least: women at risk.

The choice of narrative style and memoir is a key element of the book. I abandoned the traditional objective, detached reporting method because it was clear to me from the start that the way to really get to know and understand other women was by nurturing a subjective, warm relationship. While painful discrepancies of class and race between myself and the women I talked with could not be erased, this narrative approach created a setting where the women felt heard, safe, and respected.

Likewise, remaining in the story as the narrator, writing memoir and depicting my presence, honestly acknowledges and reveals the power dynamics in our interactions and relationships. It also sometimes draws out different stories. The contrast of my presence can give a distinctive look into the context of such women's lives, rather than just the outcomes.

Cross-cultural experiences have been my world since I was a child. As far back as I can remember I have been enmeshed in different cultures— Moroccan, Puerto Rican, French, Belgian, Swiss, Mexican and, of course, American—and I learned at a young age that understanding language and cultural mores was critical in order to connect with people who were different from me. My whole life, professional, familial, spiritual, has been formed by those experiences and relationships. I witnessed and experienced worlds wrenched apart by colonialism, a force I was part of. But I also observed the heart of Indigenous cultures that remained true to itself, as you will see reflected in these women's lives.

It is a privilege to write these stories—a privilege these women didn't possess for many reasons: a lack of literacy, fear of government reprisals, the demands of daily life. There is no question of the privilege I hold, and I only hope that I have handled it in a way that respects and is as honorable as the women in this book, and spurs healing.

These stories occurred during the late 1970s and early 80s. They are based on hundreds of pages of notes taken over the months spent in each locale, and, in some places, on return visits. Authentic quotes from the period have been used, and readers may encounter language that has since evolved and is now considered inappropriate. I acknowledge this sensitivity and present the material as an unaltered reflection of the era's discourse. The names of many people and places have been changed to protect them, and certain figures may be composite to also allow anonymity, especially in such small villages. Likewise, in some cases, I have used compression to blend dialogue thematically. None of the stories told by the women were cross-checked or substantiated. This is reality as they saw it, as I heard it. I attempted to remunerate the village and women indirectly by working in a local organization. Within those limitations, this is a true-life story, the true-life stories of many women.

# ACKNOWLEDGMENTS

I am deeply grateful to the women in this book for sharing their lives and time with me. For trusting me and, oftentimes, caring for me as I struggled to adopt to new situations far from my own family. They opened their doors and hearts to me, as did many of the nameless people in villages throughout Haiti and Guatemala, bringing context, human understanding, and insight into these worlds. Any mistakes or misinterpretations are mine.

Over forty years ago, the first draft of this book was written as fifteen case studies, drawn from a series of journals meticulously kept during this odyssey. Soon my family life and my professional life as a social worker, advocate, and psychotherapist with immigrants overcame this work. The stories gathered dust under my bed until, years later, Cate Cousland, on a visit to the United States, pulled out the stories and, visionary that she was, she encouraged me to turn them into a book. Later my friend and adopted brother, David Brown, stood many hours in our home office collating and scanning hundreds of pages so I could actually write the book.

Guiding and teaching me about writing was a crew of readers, scholars, writers, and editors. Julie Farrar was the first to read the entire manuscript, and I couldn't have done without her endless encouragement, insight, and book-design skills. Katie Rawson and Rebecca Weldon have been by my side throughout this process and their friendship, advice, and editing have been crucial emotionally and professionally. A deep gratitude goes to my lifelong friends, the Ajmac Cuxil family, whose friendship, knowledge, and humor have fed my life on all levels—especially Julia Ajmac, my dear friend and godmother to my son. Lou Slater's stalwart presence transformed Australia into a home for me, and her sharp eye brought clarity and vision to this work. A special thanks to Graeme Sparkes for his meticulous editing, mentorship, and encouragement which was my fuel to finish. Nicole Bowller's skills in editing and graphic design brought depth to the work while her family gave warmth and nourishment to me. A coterie of indefatigable readers who gave hours of their time to edit and discuss the work include Ingrid Baring, Carmel Ceglia, Nadine Davidoff,

Shelley McInnis, Sandi Nicolaides, and Jodi Stewart. Laura Russo's expert eye gave a deeper form and beauty to this work. Karen Bowller finally polished this work into reality. And to my lifelong mentor, Lieba Kaplan, may her spirit live on.

The original research was partially funded by Church Women United, National Council of Churches, and LAOS, Inc. Tom and Edna Boone added their mentorship to this funding. My friend Pamela Malchin's generous financial support seeded my last days in Guatemala. I am grateful to the Association in Solidarity with Guatemala, which taught me the history and facts behind these stories, and also to the Haitian American Community Health Organization, the San Lucas Mission, and US Quaker Meetings, especially Camden Friends Meeting. Many thanks to Mia Wotherspoon, my niece and fellow writer, for reading early drafts and introducing me to HARDCOPY, ACT Gorman Center where Nigel Featherstone and staff provided training and insight into all aspects of writing and publishing and, above all, created a community of writers who have supported this work throughout its second phase.

The Queensland Writer's Centre selected this work for its Publishable and then Printable Program, introducing me to agents, publishers, and mentors. Julie Postance and her Authentic Authors Program educated me about publishing, publicity, and marketing and supported me all the way to the finishing line.

Nothing would have been possible without the generous support of many friends and strangers along the way who housed, fed, and nurtured me throughout this odyssey, especially Eliza Cutcher and her family who provided my first writing space in their Southwestern hay shed. Thank you also to the Eltham Bookshop, especially the Govil family, whose devotion to literature and community confirms books can change lives. The Dunmoochin Foundation provided a residency in the bushland outside of Melbourne, Australia, giving me the sanctuary and time to focus on finalising this book. Yet all of this support would have gone to waste had it not been for Mark, Thomas, and Clemmie who encouraged me every step of the way.

# GLOSSARY

*Note: These terms are those that may pose questions to the reader. The definitions offered below refer to their use at the time of the narratives offered in this publication, the 1970-80s.*

**Haitian terms**

[Haitian Creole is derived from languages originating in both West Africa and Europe. African people, traded into colonial labor on the island of St Domingo by both the Spanish and the French, developed, over generations, linguistic communication that could be understood by all.]

*blan*  "white" foreigners, regardless of skin tone. A Haitian man is always a *nèg*, even if he is of European descent, in which case he would be called a *nèg blan* ("white guy"), and his counterpart would be *nèg nwa* ("black guy") (ie: blan=blanc; nwa=noir).

*coumbite*  work party (combine/commun/communautaire).

*dokté de fey* (also: *medsen fey*). A leaf doctor/herbalist and shaman who deals with a range of health problems from the aches, cuts, and bruises to more serious complaints. This form of traditional medicine is linked to vodou and to shamans, called Gine, from Africa. In these healing practices, the practitioner works as an expert herbalist and shaman. Most remedies are obtained through experience and traditional local knowledge. Other remedies come through dreams, intuition, or communication with the spirits, especially a family of spirits known as *zanset yo*, powerful healing ancestorial guides. Sometimes these spirits are "inherited" from another healer or family member. (dokte/medsen=docteur/medicin, fey=faies/fates).

*gourde*  official currency of Haiti (Haitian Gourde [HTG]). It is divided into 100 centimes (French) or santim (Creole). Every single coin and paper bill in the country is denominated in Haitian Gourdes. The exchange rate of US Dollars to Gourdes fluctuates with currency markets, but for many years it has been somewhere around: 1 USD = 40 HTG (+/- 5 HTG). (The word "gourde" is a French cognate for the Spanish term "gordo," from the "pesos gordos" in which colonial-era contracts within the Spanish sphere of influence were often denominated.)

*grangou*  hunger; literally the "big taste" (Fr. *grand gout*).

*hougan*  (also: *oungan*) male minister in Haitian Vodou (a female minister is known as a *mambo*). Term derived from Gbe languages (Fon, Ewe, Adja, Phla, Gen, Maxi, and Gun) that originate in West Africa—including Ghana, Togo, Benin, Nigeria.

*kob*  money (translated to the Fr. as "épi", meaning a piece or one in a group of pieces on a cob, a hand of bananas, a tuft of hair, etc).

*lao*  (also: *lwa*) spirits in the African diasporic religion of Haitian Vodou. Akin to the orishas of Yoruba religion and of similar Afro-Caribbean new religious movements, but, unlike the orishas, the lao are not deities but are spirits created by Bondye (God) to assist the living in their daily affairs. There are more than 1,000 lao in Vodou, grouped in 17 pantheons (*nanchon*). Every person is born the "child' of a particular lao. The relationship sometimes formalized through kanzo, an initiation ceremony. This lao lives in the person's blood and guides and protects the person throughout life.

*marchandes*  market vendors (Fr. origin, referring to female vendors).

| | |
|---|---|
| *Les Malheureux* | "the unhappy ones"; signifies poor peasants, the unemployed, beggars, and all rural dwellers. This term stretches back to the nineteenth century but was renewed with vigor beginning in the occupation period through the Duvalier years. (A term often linked to the works of Alexandre Dumas focusing on issues of injustice. Dumas's father was born in Haiti, of a French nobleman and an African slave.) |
| *ti moun* | little person; child. |
| *Tonton Makoute* | (also: the Macoute) a Haitian paramilitary and secret police force created in 1959 by François "Papa Doc" Duvalier. Named after mythological Tonton Macoute ("Uncle Gunnysack"), who kidnaps and punishes unruly children by snaring them in a gunny sack (*macoute*) before carrying them off to be consumed for breakfast. The Macoute were known for their brutality and state terrorism. In 1970, the militia was renamed the Volontaires de la Sécurité Nationale (VSN; English: National Security Volunteers). Though formally disbanded in 1986, its members continue to terrorize the country under new guises. (Also often linked to a play on words: "uncle is listening": "tonton m'écoute".) |

*vodou*  (also: voodoo) developed among Afro-Haitian communities during the sixteenth to nineteenth centuries by blending the traditional religions of enslaved West and Central Africans with Roman Catholicism and Freemasonry beliefs of the Spanish and French. Many vodouists were involved in the Haitian Revolution of 1791 that overthrew the French colonial government, abolished slavery, and transformed Saint-Domingue into the republic of Haiti. After the revolution when the Roman Catholic Church left Haiti for several decades, vodou became Haiti's dominant religion. In the 20th century, growing emigration spread vodou abroad.

Most Haitians practice a syncretism of vodou and Roman Catholicism. Both in Haiti and abroad vodou has spread beyond its Afro-Haitian origins and is practiced by individuals of various ethnicities. Having faced much criticism through its history, vodou has been described as one of the world's most misunderstood religions.

**Guatemalan terms**

*ajq'ij*  a Mayan spiritual guide. According to Mayan spirituality, a person often discovers he/she will be an *ajq'ij* through dreams and visions that come when the person suffers a sickness or accident. The *ajq'ij* Mayan religious beliefs are based on the notion that virtually everything in the world contains *k'uh*, or sacredness, a divine life force of existence in all things. This force creates a sanctity of all human beings, the earth, and the universe. The spiritual guide helps people come into balance with this divine force by fostering emotional and physical healings through offerings and Mayan ceremonies, many of which are conducted in secret. The community also relies on the *ajq'ij* for wisdom, direction and divination. The *ajq'ij* lives primarily from alms although he/she is paid for the materials used in ceremonies.

*caldo*  broth.

*catit*  (also: *ik'ati'*) moon.

*centavos*  cents.

*chula*    smart, lovely or cute (according to Mayan people). Also: a brassy, low-class woman (Collins Dictionary), a flashy woman or girlfriend (Cambridge Dictionary) or a pimp or dandy (PONS). This etymology seems reflective of the colonization and regionalism of language.

*comedor*    dining room; diner.

*cofradías*    religious brotherhoods, an integral part of the syncretic culture of those towns that still adhere to ancestral customs and traditions. Originally established to propagate Catholicism, over approximately five hundred years they have acquired important religious, civil, and political status. The *cofradías*, custodians of ancestral wisdom, provide an insight into traditional community identity.

*corte*    traditional Mayan women's skirt, usually woven on a treadle loom by men. The treadle loom was introduced by the Spanish to Mayan weavers shortly after the Conquest in the 1500s.

*finca*    land; property; farm.

*gringo*    a derogatory term used in Latin America for white English speakers, usually from the United States, in the context of economic, cultural, and political interference. The word is said to originate from the Mexican–American War of 1846–48 and the song "Green Grow Rushes On," sung by US troops. It is also said to be what Mexicans told the US soldiers in camouflage uniforms invading and occupying their land: "Green Go Home!".

*guerrillero*    guerilla fighter; partisan.

*huipil*    a traditional garment worn primarily by women in Mexico and Central America. It is an Indigenous design morphed by the Spanish invasion. The *huipil* is usually made out of three pieces of cotton or wool cloth that Mayan women weave on backstrap looms and sew together at the shoulders.

*indiginas*   Indigenous peoples. The Mayans are the Indigenous people who constitute the majority of the population in the Central American republic of Guatemala. There are 21 different Mayan communities in Guatemala making up an estimated 51% of the national population. Maya are dispersed throughout Guatemala, especially in the western highlands. The largest populations are in rural departments north and west of Guatemala City, most notably, Alta Verapaz, Sololá, Totonicapán, and Quiché. Mayan groups are distinguished by language. The most common of the approximately 26 Indigenous Mayan languages that are still spoken are Q'eqchi', Kaqchiquel, Mam, Tzutujil, Achi, and Pokoman.

*ito*   Diminutives -ito, -illo, -ico are mostly used to refer to a smaller size of something, but also used as a form of endearment. In polite forms, especially when used with adjectives, they soften the importance of a statement, which in some cases may have pejorative or insulting connotations. Example *pobrecito* or *tiendita* = poor one or tiny shop.

*ixtamal*   (Also: *nixtamal*) From the Nahuatl word *nixtli* meaning "ashes," and *tamalli* meaning "cooked *maíz masa*." The resulting product of corn has been cooked and steeped in an alkaline solution (using water and *cal* or water and clean wood ash), which can be left whole for *pozole* (hominy), or ground into *masa*. Nixtamalization is the ancient process of adding an alkali solution (usually ash or lime, calcium hydroxide) to dried corn kernels, thus increasing bioavailability of vitamin B3 niacin which reduces the risk of pellagra disease, increasing calcium intake due to its absorption by the kernels during the steeping process.

*Kaqchiquel*   Mayan people of the midwestern highlands of Guatemala, closely related linguistically and culturally to the neighbouring K'iche' and Tz'utujil. The Kaqchiquel are agriculturalists, and their culture is syncretic, a fusion of Spanish and Mayan elements.

*kusha*       (also: *cusha*) a home-brewed spirit produced from corn
              since thousands of years. It was traditionally used in ancient
              rituals during which shamans would spit the drink over
              participants for its healing powers. As a moonshine, Kusha
              has no fixed recipe. This means some versions can be so
              strong as to cause blindness.

*lengua*      language; tongue.

*milpa*       a field in which farmers plant a dozen crops at once,
              including maize, avocados, multiple varieties of squash
              and bean, melon, tomatoes, chilis, sweet potato, and
              *jícama*. Milpa crops are nutritionally and environmentally
              complementary. The creation of *milpa* is a sacred act that
              binds together family, community, and the universe.
              It forms the core institution of Indigenous society in
              Mesoamerica.

*mozo*        worker; servant.

*octavo*      typical bottle of *agua ardiente* or *kusha*, moonshine; an
              eighth of a bottle.

*patrón*      boss; employer; master.

*petate*      grass mat; sleeping mat.

*quetzal*     unit of Guatemalan currency. The Quetzal is also the
              national bird of Guatemala, pictured on the country's flag
              and coat of arms. It is thought to be the spirit guide of a
              Mayan prince and hero, Tecún Umán, who fought against
              the Spanish conquest. In ancient Mayan culture the Quetzal
              bird's tail feathers were used as currency. The quetzal
              dollar is divided into 100 centavos, or len (plural lenes) in
              Guatemalan slang. The plural is quetzales.

*ranchera*    (also: canción ranchera) a genre of popular music in Mexico.
              In the post-1910 revolution period, when many rural
              Mexicans moved to the cities, rancheras were derived from
              folk and country songs. Ranchera songs are characterized
              by dramatic emotion; topics of love dominate their poetic
              lyrics.

*rebozo*      wrap; shawl.

*tiendita*    little store.

*traje*     traditional dress which has deep cultural significance to the Maya people. The tradition of weaving and use of symbolism has been passed from mothers to daughters for hundreds of years and supports the legacy of craftsmanship that defines the Guatemalan Maya culture. Most *traje* consists of four different articles: the *huipil* (blouse), the *faja* (belt/sash), the *corte* (skirt) and the *cinta* (headband). A man from the same area may wear a *chaqueta* or open jacket, a *faja* (belt), a *pantalón* (pants), a locally made straw hat and Western-style sweater.

**United States**

Bowman, Frank O. "Stories of Crimes, Trials and Appeals in Civil War Era Missouri." *Marquette Law Review* 93, Article 2, Symposium: Criminal Appeals: Past, Present, and Future.

Cobb, Jelani and David Remnick. *A Matter of Black Lives: Writings from the New Yorker.* Harper Collins, 2021.

*Whose Streets*, directed by Sabaah Folayan. https://www.whosestreetsfilm.com.

Garza, Alicia. *The Purpose of Power: From the Co-Founder of Black Lives Matter.* Penguin Random House, 2020.

Harriot, Michael. *Black AF History: The Un-Whitewashed Story of America.* Dey Street Books, 2023.

Hess, Monica. "A Young Mother Disappeared 13 Years Ago. What Did it Mean?" *Washington Post*, August 9, 2023.

Morrison, Toni and Ta-Nehisi Coates. Foreword to *The Origin of Others*, The Charles Eliot Norton Lectures. Harvard University Press, 2017.

Morrison, Toni. *The Source of Self-Regard: Selected Essays, Speeches, and Meditations.* Vintage. January 14, 2020.

Morrison, Toni. "Nobel Lecture." December 7, 1993, Stockholm, Sweden. https://www.nobelprize.org/prizes/literature/1993/morrison/lecture/

Trexler, Harrison Anthony. *Slavery in Missouri 1804–1865.* Johns Hopkins University Studies. The Johns Hopkins Press, 1914.

Wilkerson, Isabel. *Caste: The Origins of Our Discontents.* Random House, 2020

Wilkerson, Isabel. *The Warmth of Other Suns: The Epic Story of America's Great Migration.* Random House, 2020.

# Guatemala


Asturias, Miguel Angel. *El Señor Presidente.* Translated by David Unger. Penguin Group, 2022. Nobel Prize 1967.

Burrell, Jennifer L. *The Maya After the War: Conflict, Power, and Politics in Guatemala.* University of Texas Press, 2013.

Calel, Edgar. 2021. *"Not all things are for sale" artist Edgar Calel's family portrait.* Tate. https://youtu.ber/1kMIosGTGMk?si=UcDtfdlnuUxGFhXf

Chasteen, John Charles. *Born in Blood and Fire: A Concise History of Latin America.* Norton and Company, 2016.

Coe, Michael D., and Stephen Hanson. *The Maya.* Thomas and Hudson, 2022.

Del Castillo, Diaz Bernal. *The True History of the Conquest of New Spain.* Translated by Janet Burket and Ted Humphrey. Hackett Publishing, 2012.

De Las Casas, Bartolomé, ed. *A Short Account of the Destruction of the Indies.* Translated by Nigel Griffin. Penguin Classics, 1999.

Houston, Stephen and Takeshi Inomata. *The Classic Maya* (Cambridge World Archaeology). Cambridge University Press, 2009.

Menchú, Rigoberta and Elisabeth Burgos-Debray, ed. *I Rigoberta, Rigoberta Menchu: An Indian Woman in Guatemala.* Verso Books, 1984. Nobel Prize 1992.

Molesky-Poz, Jean. *Contemporary Mayan Spirituality: The Ancient Ways Are Not Lost.* EPUB9780292778627, 1995.

Schlesinger, Stephen, and Stephen Kinzer. *Bitter Fruit: The Story of the American Coup in Guatemala.* Rev. ed. Series on Latin American Studies. Harvard University, 2020.

National Geographic. "Modern Day Maya." https://education. nationalgeographic.org/resource/modern-day-maya

Warman, Arturo. *Corn and Capitalism: How a Botanical Bastard Grew to Global Dominance.* University of North Carolina Press, 2003.

# Haiti


Alexis, Jacques Stephen. *General Sun, My Brother.* University of Virginia Press, 1999.

Arthur, Charles and Michael Dash, eds. *Libète: A Haiti Anthology.* Markus Wiener Publishers, 2009.

Farmer, Paul. *The Uses of Haiti.* Common Courage Press, 2005.

Greene, Graham. *The Comedians.* Viking Press, 1965

James, C. L. R. *The Black Jacobins: Toussaint Louverture and the San Domingo Revolution.* Vintage Press, 2023.

Louverture, Toussaint. *The Haitian Revolution.* Verso Books, 2019.

Trouillot, Michel-Rolph. *Silencing the Past: Power and the Production of History.* Beacon Press, 2018.

Wilentz, Amy. *Farewell Fred Voodoo: A Letter from Haiti.* Simon and Schuster, 2013.

———. *The Rainy Season: Haiti—Then and Now.* Simon and Schuster, 2010.

### United States

African American Planning Commission (homelessness, domestic violence and more): **https://aapci.org**

AAS Resource Center, Department of Afro-American Studies, Howard University: **https://afroamericanstudies.howard.edu**

Library of Congress Research Guides: **loc.gov.african-americans**

### Guatemala

Aldea: Strengthening Mayan Communities since 1967 (founded by Dr. Bernhorst): **https://aldeaguatemala.org**

Guatemala Aid Fund: **https:// guatemalaaidfund.org**

Ixatan: **https://ixatan.org**

North American Congress on Latin America: **https://nacla.org**

### Haiti

Hôpital Albert Schweitzer: **https://hashaiti.org**

Fonkoze: **https://fonkoze.org**

Haitian Health Foundation: **https://www.haitianhealthfoundation.org**

Haitian American Community Organisation:
**https://www.hccinc.org**

Partners in Health: https://www.pih.org/country/haiti

## International

Human Rights Watch: **https://www.hrw.org**

Amnesty International, Women's Rights: **https://www.amnesty.org/
en/what-we-do/discrimination/womens-rights/**

Guatemalan Human Rights Commission:
**https://www.ghrc-usa.org/**

Association for Women's Rights in Development:
**https://www.awid.org**

Global Fund for Women:
**https://www.globalfundforwomen.org/**

MADRE: **https://www.madre.org**

# AUTHOR'S BIO

Clémence Overall, writer, poet, anthropologist and therapist, was born in Georgia, USA, and raised in Morocco, Puerto Rico and across Europe. For over 30 years, Overall worked as an advocate and therapist for undocumented immigrants and victims of war in the United States and Central America, and much of her writing has grown out of these experiences. She has published three bilingual graphic books for refugees and two books of poetry, as well as articles in numerous journals. Overall moved to Australia in 2015 to undertake a residency at the Dunmoochin Foundation, near Melbourne to devote her time to writing. Her stories have been shortlisted in local and international competitions and she was awarded the local poet prize in the Nillumbik Literary Competition in 2017. Her memoir *Down to the Bone* won the 2019 AWW unpublished manuscript award. She presently lives in Fernleigh, New South Wales, Australia.